The Gazer's Spirit

THE GAZER'S SPIRIT

Poems Speaking to Silent Works of Art

JOHN HOLLANDER

THE UNIVERSITY OF CHICAGO PRESS
Chicago and London

John Hollander is the A. Bartlett Giamatti Professor of English at
Yale University. Awarded the Bollingen Prize for poetry in 1983
and a MacArthur Fellowship in 1990, Hollander is the author of
more than a dozen books of poetry and several books of criticism,
among them *Melodious Guile: Fictive Patterns in Poetic Language.*

The University of Chicago Press, Chicago 60637
The University of Chicago Press, Ltd., London
© 1995 by The University of Chicago
All rights reserved. Published 1995
Printed in the United States of America
04 03 02 01 00 99 98 97 96 95   1 2 3 4 5

ISBN: 0-226-34949-7 (cloth)

Library of Congress Cataloging-in-Publication Data

Hollander, John.
        The gazer's spirit : poems speaking to silent works of art /
    John Hollander.
        p.   cm.
    Includes index.
    1. Art—Poetry. I. Title
    PS3515.03485G39   1995
    811'.54—dc20   94-25606
                                                  CIP

♾ The paper used in this publication meets the minimum require-
ments of the American National Standard for Information
Sciences—Permanence of Paper for Printed Library Materials,
ANSI Z39.48-1984.

For Andrew Forge

CONTENTS

ACKNOWLEDGMENTS

The Gazer's Spirit is not a theoretical study of ecphrasis. It is rather a book that takes the reader on walks through a notional gallery, hung both with images and with poems addressing those images. Whether, in each case, the poem should be thought of as hanging across from, below, alongside of, inscribed in, helping to frame, or even turning away from the picture or piece of sculpture in question, the reader will decide. The exhibits are chronologically arranged, and it will not be surprising to observe that it is primarily in the early nineteenth century that the poet's experience of encountering the work of art, often in its surroundings, gets to constitute more and more of what it is the poem confronts. The degree to which the poetry acknowledges and deals with the artistic medium itself—rather than the objects of representation—will also be seen to emerge after the eighteenth century. I have deemed it useful to start out with a somewhat long introductory discussion, establishing some discursive guidelines, and acknowledging a certain amount of territory not covered in the separate discussions. In particular, the role of notional ecphrasis as a necessary precursor of poetry confronting actual, identifiable images—and one that continues to haunt them—was central to analyses of the individual confrontations, and I have expounded this in some detail.

This book had its genesis in a course I taught in collaboration with a philosopher and critic of photography, Norton Batkin, some years ago; last year, with a different agenda, I collaborated on it again, this time with the painter and critic to whom this volume is dedicated. I learned so much from these two colleagues that I cannot imagine framing or completing this study without the benefit of working with them. I am perhaps most deeply indebted to Jean H. Hagstrum, whose wonderful *The Sister Arts* first opened up the depths and intricacies of this subject for me and whose meticulous reading of my manuscript was absolutely invaluable.

A great many friends, colleagues, students and others were extremely generous to me, and I should like to acknowledge the invaluable help, ranging from exploratory conversation, suggestions, advice, and answers to queries from out of the blue, of Leonard Barkan, Jonathan Brown, Hennig Cohen, Andrew Elfenbein, Alan Fern, David Freedberg, Paul Fry, Peter Galassi, Creighton Gilbert, Amy Golahny, Kenneth Gross, George Hersey, Robert L. Herbert, Elizabeth Hollander, Martha Hollander, Richard Howard, Linda Nochlin, J. D. McClatchy, Kevin Muller, Adrienne Munich, Lowry Nelson, Jr., Ronald Paulson, Jerome Pollitt, David Quint, Abigail Rischin, Leo Steinberg, Jennifer Wagner, and Bryan Wolf. I am in debt to all of them, and I hope that what appears in these pages will have merited their assistance. Alan Thomas of the University of Chicago Press waited patiently for this book to be finished, and helped me with support and encouragement throughout, and Randy Petilos was resourceful and attentive to a mass of essential details. Carol Saller edited my problematic manuscript with elegant care, for which I am most grateful. I should mention three fine books that appeared only after that manuscript was completed and from all of which it could have profited: James A. W. Heffernan's *Museum of Words*, Christopher Braider's *Refiguring the Real*, and W. J. T. Mitchell's *Picture Theory*. Finally, there is my immense gratitude, so graciously unsolicited as always, to the John D. and Catherine T. MacArthur Foundation for the fellowship that supported the completion of this book, and so much else.

Some of the material in the pages that follow appeared earlier in different form in the following places: "Words on Pictures," *Art and Antiques* 1.1 (1984): 80–91; "The Poetics of Ekphrasis," *Word & Image* 4.1 (1988): 209–19; "Introduction to Nadar," *Black and White* (1988), reprinted by permission of Charles Melcher; "The Gazer's Spirit: Romantic and Later Poetry on Painting and Sculpture," in *The Romantics and Us*, ed. Gene W. Ruoff (New Brunswick, 1990), 130–67; "Three Dazzlers," *Yale Review* 80.3 (1992): 101–26.

Translations of verse in this book, where not otherwise identified, are my own.

INTRODUCTION

$\mathcal{A}$ book about poems and works of art might well start out with a double caveat:

> You know, Phaedrus, that's the strange thing about writing, which makes it truly analogous to painting. The painter's products stand before us as though they were alive, but if you question them, they maintain a most majestic silence. It is the same with written words; they seem to talk to you as if they were intelligent, but if you ask them anything about what they say, from a desire to be instructed, they go on telling you just the same thing forever.
>
> —Plato, *Phaedrus* 275d, tr. R. Hackforth

Whoever writes about writing about artistic images will be a sort of triple fool. The Hellenistic epigram quoted below would appear at first to give the lie to what has been for nearly two decades of recent literary theory Plato's fashionable text. It questions a statue, and receives instructive answers, in what reads today like a short introductory course in iconography. The statue is a figure of *Kairos* (timeliness, due season, hence Opportunity or Occasion in the Renaissance) by Lysippus (ca. 270 B.C.), and the poem by his contemporary Posidippus (*Greek Anthology* 16.275) gives voice to the sculptor's bronze:

> *Where was your sculptor from?* Sicyon. *And his name?*
> Lysippus. *And you?* Kairos, who subdues
> All things. *Why on your toes?* I'm always running. *Why*
> *Wings on your feet?* I rush on with the wind.
> *Why hold a razor in your right hand?* To show men
> That I am keener than the sharpest edges.
> *Why does your hair hang down across your face?* Whoever
> I meet shall catch me by the forelock. *Why*
> *In God's name are you bald behind?* Because no one
> I have outrun can ever grab me now.
> *Why did the artist form you?* For your benefit,
> Stranger. He set me here to teach a lesson.

In the terms used in the following pages, we might call this a statue doing its own literal ecphrasis. But the modern academic theoretical joke here would be, of course, that Plato is only confirmed in this failed counterexample: it is only the fictive language of the epigram which makes a fictive version of a real statue speak. As will be seen, modern poems of this kind have enough to do to question, and try to answer, themselves. But this pair of texts—and the relation between them—will serve as an epigraph as well as any.

This book is concerned with some of the ways in which poetry has directly dealt with in the past, and continues to confront today, particular works of art. In its principal section, the reader will be presented with forty-eight instances of such confrontation. Throughout, these observations will be directed to instances of poetry in which (a) we know that a particular object is being confronted, (b) we know precisely what that object is, and (c) that actual object is available for our own consideration, paralleling that of the text in question. But before proceeding to these, the reader will be invited to consider some general questions of *ut pictura poesis* which underlie the whole question of poetic ecphrasis, embracing the many modes of rhetorical address to artist's images. And some exploratory investigation of situations in which (a) or (b) does not hold will help to provide a necessary background. The first of these situations occasions what I shall call "notional ecphrasis," the verbal representation of a purely fictional work of art. When (c) is indeed the case, we are dealing with "actual ecphrasis," the matter of this book.

One could call ecphrastic poems generally those which involve descriptions or other sorts of verbal representation of works of art.[1] Notional ecphrasis—or the description, often elaborately detailed, of purely fictional painting or sculpture that is indeed brought into being by the poetic language itself—abounds in antiquity and after. One thinks immediately of Homer's shield of Achilles, Hesiod's shield of Herakles, and dozens of epigrams in the *Greek Anthology*. Of particular interest to classicists and art historians are many passages from prose romance like *Daphnis and Chloe*, rhetorical displays like that of Lucian's description of a painting of Aetion, as well as in his dialogue called *Eikones* (for which the Loeb edition translator gives "Essays in Portraiture"), the celebrated *Eikones* of Philostratus, and the actual ecphrases of Callistratus. There are significant ecphrastic episodes in Virgil, in Dante, Ariosto, Tasso, and Spenser. Some of these will be considered below.

But actual ecphrastic poems entail engagements with particular and identifiable works of art, and they are obviously of great interest when the works so addressed are still extant. Particularly in the nineteenth and twentieth centuries there is a good deal of such poetry, addressing a wide range of good and bad, great and obscure, unglossed or overinterpreted works of art, and taking up a range of stances toward their objects. These include addressing the image, making it speak, speaking of it interpretively, meditating upon the moment of viewing it, and so forth. The interpretive agendas and programs of such poems—whether Hellenistic epigrams containing little more than a turn of wit or two, or complex romantic and modern poems concerned with the nature of a particular esthetic experience—range widely in complexity. As will be seen, they can take a graphic or sculptural representation as a mere particular instance of a conventional sign; on the other hand, they can be acutely responsive to the matter of the medium and its handling, which becomes increasingly important in the apprehension of works of art in the nineteenth and twentieth centuries. But they obviously share the common rhetorical predicament of representing in language what is itself representing visually yet something else. That something else may be material given *dal vero*, from direct observation; it may itself derive from a verbal fiction as well (and as for so many centuries it did). Yet in any case, the image in picture or piece of sculpture will necessarily allude to other images, just as the poem will allude to other poems.

"Ecphrasis" (frequently spelled in the directly transliterated form, *ekphrasis*) has been until the last decade or so a technical term used by classicists and historians of art to mean a verbal description of a work of art, of a scene as rendered in a work of art, or even of a fictional scene the description of which unacknowledgedly derives from descriptions of scenes. In recent literary theory, considerations of ecphrasis have concerned the ways in which space and time are involved in the various mutual figurations of actuality, text, and picture. Classicists are frequently concerned with the relation between the ecphrasis of a picture and the question of scenic description in fiction generally; of central interest there is the relation between the vividness or liveliness (in Greek, *enargeia*) of a painting, say, and the rhetorical vividness of the writing.[2] Historians of Renaissance art have been concerned to show how full or partial programs, or elements of iconographic detail, frequently derive from prose or even verse ecphrases from antiquity, usually Hellenistic or Roman; these could be actual—describing celebrated works of art since lost—or virtual. One of the most famous of these is Lucian's account of an allegory of Calumny by Apelles, retailed, along with Seneca's interpretation of the positions of the canonical dancing three Graces, by Leon Battista Alberti in his *Della Pittura* (1435–36).[3] In the Renaissance, a painting may find part of its program or iconography in such an actual or notional ecphrastic passage from antiquity, or from a moment in a poetic source. A poem directed to it may recover, or obfuscate, some textual background. Often, it may also follow upon another ecphrastic poem on the same piece. Notional ecphrases based on *Greek Anthology* poems to Myron's bull (there are several in the work of Giambattista Marino) are simply a matter of the neoclassical imitation so frequent in Renaissance and baroque poetry. On the other hand, consider Rubens's *Hero and Leander* (in the Yale Art Gallery): Marino has a little poem to it, which was later translated into Dutch by Vondel, which probably influenced a much longer one, more elaborate in its rhetoric and detailed in its ecphrasis, by Jan Vos.[4]

It is poetry which first likens itself to painting, and not the other way around. Horace's *Ars Poetica* propounds in passing the notion of *ut pictura poesis*—poems and pictures are briefly likened with respect to scale and detail, to modesty (whether of intention or accomplishment is not specified), and to interpretable substance:

> As painting, so is poesy. Some man's hand
> Will take you more, the nearer that you stand;
> As some the farther off: this loves the dark;
> This, fearing not the subtlest judge's mark,
> Will in the light be viewed: this, once the sight
> Doth please: this, ten times over will delight.
> —Ben Jonson's translation

> [Ut pictura poesis: erit quae, si proprius stes,
> te capiat magis, et quaedam, si longius abstes.

haec amat obscurum, volet haec sub luce videri,
iudicis, argutum quae non formidat acumen;
haec placuit semel, haec deciens repetita placebit.][5]

But Horace's phrase, *ut pictura poesis*, came to stand for an agenda of far more wide-ranging comparisons and contrasts. Modified by the famous apothegm, popularized (from Simonides of Ceos) by Plutarch, to the effect that painting is mute poetry and poetry speaking picture, it comes to be reinterpreted and refocused throughout postclassical history, colored by specific critical and analytic concerns. An energetic discussion of the unlikenesses occupies the first chapter of Leonardo da Vinci's treatise on painting known since the early nineteenth century as the *Paragone*—characteristically, he adapts the tag from Plutarch at one point as "Painting is mute poetry, and poetry is blind painting."[6] Leonardo is concerned with such issues as lack of immediacy of effect. He argues that a painter can get a viewer to fall in love with a picture, even if not of a living woman, and no poet can do that; poetry is condemned to proceed in time, part by part, whereas in a picture (and even, he implies, in musical polyphony) there is the power of simultaneity, and so forth. The question of how images take up space, while spoken or written language takes up time (to hear, to read) is central to Lessing's *Laocoön*, and a subsequent critical and theoretical tradition makes questions like this central ones for poetics once again. Whether constituting an ecphrastic moment in a narrative—by way of digression, pause, or deconstructed to a certain kind of forward movement after all—or a total "moment's monument" before a particular image in a poem, the study of either lyrical or narratological rhetoric of fiction has engaged ecphrasis more and more.

Of particular interest is the rhetoric of verbal representation: how does a passage of prose—let alone a poem, where there are potentially so many more devices for building metaphors of structural relations already apparent in what is being addressed or characterized—cope with an experience primarily spatial at first, and only afterward conceptual in other ways?[7] The question of what is most prominent in a constructed image may itself be so problematic, to begin with; but in any case, there is the rhetorical problem of how such prominence is to be represented in writing. Firstness? Centrality? The bottom line? What about rhetorical scale—how much prose goes for how much of the image? How does a prose passage have it that we read a painting: top to bottom? bottom to top? diagonally? crucial coded clue to obvious sign? picture-plane back into virtual space? And what are its own devices for so having it: does its own narrative guide you through, or across, or up or down or into-and-out-of the picture? How is the interesting problem of the relation, in prose or verse, between narrative and description hereby engaged? And, particularly, what are the resources of narrative and lyric poetry which can complicate and strengthen this mimesis of mimesis?[8]

The gap between word and image has been the subject of a good deal of contemporary theoretical exploration. It is indeed easy to consider how, for the talky poem, the mute image manifests its otherness, its figurative condition as object of desire, its vivid latency, given another sort of expressive power by having the breath of verbal life blown into it, and so forth.[9] The viewer's gaze which embraces a particular work can long for further consummation—to possess a represented object, whether person or thing, to enter into an interior scene or a landscape.[10] On the other hand, language can long for a further extension of its frail descriptive grasp of fully realized visual representation. In notional ecphrasis, some of these more urgent desires are not present.

In addition, a poem's detailed, or fragmentary, or even implicit account of what is in fact *there* or *going on in* a picture involves a strange sort of mirroring of a mirroring. In earlier iconographies, Truth's mirror is that of representation; Venus's mirror is the one in which she regards herself, and from whose image she perhaps derives power. A poem is both of these, but considers the visual image only as itself, Truth's looking-glass. Perhaps only a painter can know the ways in which a picture is indeed both of these—the mirror of representation and the mirror of empowering self-absorption—as much as the poem is. For the disapproving Socrates, a picture of a bed is unforgivably distant from true Bedness by three removes of mimesis: a mere bed is a mere instance—and hence a sort of trope—of Bedness; any view of an actual bed—plan, elevation, three-quarter, projected in whatever perspectival system—is one degree removed from the bed; any actual picture represents that view, and not the concrete bed itself: hence three removes.[11] An ecphrasis of the picture would be even more distant from reality. But the power of Art depends upon the power of those degrees of fictiveness: a thrice-removed painting can get at true Bedness better than a bed can and, Art would argue, better even than Plato's privileged mental faculty which alone can grasp the true form of Bedness. And ultimately, Poetry seems to imply, it can at very least help Art to make its point by showing how, in particular cases, Art is being made. In the presence of a work of Art, Poetry seldom makes the manifest claim that its own further removal gives it a greater authority, and its usual rhetorical stance is awed deference. But just such a claim is often latent.

Origins: Notional Ecphrasis

Given the aniconic disposition of the Hebrew Bible—in which accounts of the way things are made seem to substitute for forbidden descriptions of what they looked like[12]—the earliest ecphrases we have are the descriptions of the shields of Achilles and of Herakles by Homer and Hesiod respectively. The former is a digressive account, the latter preserved as an independent epical adventure. Homer's famous lines (in *Iliad* 18) map the description of the many scenes on the shield by recounting a putative sequence in which they were made. Indeed, the "description" of the shield privileges the narrative of creation and not an account of the appearance of the finished product: we learn what was done when, not what goes where, a point made very forcefully by Lessing in *Laocoön*. Hephaistos, as will be remembered, makes the shield and divides its surface up into five sections. Then he works upon it earth, sky, sea, sun, moon, and stars. Then he represents two human cities, the first, one of marriages, festivals, and judicial reconciliation of dispute, the second, one of war—both are described in detail. Then come scenes of daily life: plowing, reaping and harvesting of fields and vineyards, then the herding of sheep and of cattle—the latter attacked by lions—and, almost at the end

1. John Flaxman, *Shield of Achilles*

of the sequence, a long, energetic, and lyrical account of how Hephaistos made a dancing floor with young men and women in choral movement. There is something summary and perhaps teleologically conclusive about the affirmation of rotary motion and pattern in this last long account; it serves to initiate a return to an acknowledgment of the circularity and boundedness of the shield's surface.

But nowhere does the ecphrasis of the images indicate relative placement on the shield's disc. Only at the very end of the passage do narrational sequence in time and visual pattern come unambiguously together, when the account closes with how (and I quote Lattimore's version) "He made on it the great strength of the Ocean River / which ran around the uttermost rim of the shield's strong structure." Eighteenth-century and later scholars attempted to map the narration onto a circular area, some of them employing five concentric circles, some, five wedges cut out of some of the inner ones as well. John Flaxman actually cast a version of one of these (fig. 1). But they have no more or less authenticity than any interpretive illustration of any narrated, or described, or lyrically invoked object or scene.

Hesiod's description of Herakles' shield is about half again as long as Homer's.[13] It is described in a scene in which the hero is arming himself, and there is no recourse to a temporal sequence arising from an account of manufacture. Like Homer, Hesiod describes particular scenes in successive episodes, but proceeds quite clearly from a central image of a serpentine *Phobos* (Fear), through some similar scenes—the dance, for example, and the paired warring and peaceful cities (these come at the end in Hesiod)—moving outward. There is a lot more sound coming out of the images than there is in Homer; and even the similar, final vision of Ocean is, in Hesiod, marked by the presence of swans calling loudly. Here, too, the effects of the images on a viewer are implicitly rendered from time to time by the recorded perception of sounds (as when the Gorgons pursuing Perseus, in one of the scenes, cause the very shield itself to resound with a clear loud clanging). But in neither case does the narrative contain another agent's reading of the images, with an account of his or her interpretation of, and reactions to, them.[14]

Nor does this happen in the case, interesting for the subsequent history of the short poem, of the carved wooden cups offered as rewards for musico-poetic achievement in Greek and Roman pastoral poetry. In the first Idyll of Theocritus [ll. 29–56], the shepherd Thrysis is offered "an ivy-wood cup of some depth, which is coated with sweet wax / New-manufactured, two-handled, and redolent still of the chisel." The intense description of the carved or painted scene on the cup starts with allusion to a framing border of foliage, active, decorative, and profuse, and concludes with "Every which way on the goblet the fluid acanthus is rampant." What is framed is a little picture of a world rather like the one from which we view Theocritus's own little pictures of idealized pastoral life:

> Over the uppermost lip of the cup runs a border of ivy,
> Ivy encrusted with clusters of gold, and entwining about it
> Twists in a spiral a tendril adorned with its yellowy berries.
> Then, on the inside, a woman is fashioned, some masterpiece of the
> Gods' manufacture, outfitted with robe and with diadem. By her
> Side are two men with elaborate hair-do's, disputing in speech, one
> After another but none of their dialogue touches her deeply,
> Rather, she gazes on one of them one moment, absently smiling,
> Then in an instant she casts her attention again to the other.
> Next to this group is a fisherman in low relief and a scabrous
> Rock from whose top the old fellow is eagerly dragging a big net
> In for the cast, like a person who labors with might and with main. You'd
> Say he was "seining the speechless" with all of the strength of his limbs, the
> Sinews all over his neck are so terribly painful and swollen;
> Though he is grey-haired, surely his strength is the strength of a young man.[15]

—tr. Daryl Hine

In the various panels or regions of the picture we are seeing, as one critic has put it, "typical scenes of the non-pastoral world of competition and worry: the mistress with her unlucky suitors, the aged fisherman with his bulging muscles, the boy who is trying to trap a cricket while foxes raid his knapsack: cold love, hard work, plotting, deceitfulness."[16] The description ascribes movement, speech, and even motivation to the figures in the scene. Virgil, in his third eclogue, both amplifies and radically contracts the ecphrasis of Theocritus's cup. The shepherd Menalcas, rather than offer a cup in exchange for a display of singing, stakes a pair of carved beechwood cups on the outcome of a singing contest with Damoetas. The latter, in return, stakes a pair of cups of his own. They are made by the same craftsman, with twining acanthus leaves (as in Theocritus) among their handles, and in their midst Orpheus followed by the trees he has animated [et molli circum est ansas amplexus acantho, / Orpheaque in medio posuit silvasque sequentia]—the carved image is directly relevant to the matter of musico-poetic skill. But Menalcas's account of his cups is of surprisingly proleptic interest for modern actual ecphrastic poetry. He starts out with Theocritus's other framing vine, the ivy, "a pliant vine, overlaid with skillful chisel, drapes the clusters spread by the pale ivy" [lenta quibus torno facili superaddita vitis / diffusos hedera vestit pallent corymbos]. But then the account continues with an interesting interruption: "In the middle are two figures, Conon and—uh, who was the other one, who marked out for man the whole of the skies with his rod, the seasons of the reaper and the bending ploughman?" [in medio duo signa Conon et—quis fuit alter, / descripsit radio totum qui gentibus orbem, / tempora quae messor, quae curvus arator haberet?]. Menalcas forgets the name of the other astronomer (probably Eudoxus of Cnidus). While some commentators treat this merely as a deployment of naturalism in dialogue, it might be observed that it ruptures the fabric, as well as the certainty, of the ecphrastic reading, calling attention to the contingent and even fragile quality of the relation of a description to a depicted image.[17]

The framing of an ecphrasis, in a narrative that relates the effects of reading a notional image, will occur most significantly in the *Aeneid*. In a celebrated and influential scene in book 1, Aeneas confronts, on the walls of the temple Dido is building to Juno, a series of scenes of the fall of Troy, the sad story of which, he remarks, seems to have filled the world. Gazing at these—as Virgil says[18]—crying and sighing, Aeneas feasts his soul on the illusory picture [animum pictura pascit inani] of what he has already known directly. The narration recognizes—as Aeneas does—Achilles, Diomedes, Troilus, Hector, Priam, and, indeed, the hero himself. He can only weep and stand caught in one long gaze [dum stupet obtutuque haeret defixus in uno], unknowing yet of the future of a new Troy in his own subsequent founding of Rome. Most significantly, it is not so much the ecphrasis of a series of pictures that frames the matter of the images in this narrative situation, but rather a larger bracketing representation of a scene containing both pictures and a reader of them, reacting to what they mean for him.

The matter of narrated reactions to representations is so central in Dante that one would rightly expect that an encounter with depictions in cantos 10 and 11 of the *Purgatorio* would expand and complicate the Virgilian situation. On the first terrace, where pride is being purged in humility, Dante and Virgil move past a white marble bank adorned with carvings (*intaglie*—

this is usually construed to mean not literally intaglio carving but rather mid-relief). They are of such a quality that not only the famous Greek sculptor Polycletus, but Nature herself, would be shamed by them. Three scenes are depicted in adjacent sequential panels.[19] The first is the angel of the annunciation, so truly carved in a gentle attitude that it did not seem a silent image [*pareva sì verace / quivi intagliato in uno atto soave, che non sembiava imagine che tace*]:

> One would have sworn that he had uttered "Ave!";
> > For she was represented there, who turned
> > The key to open up the highest love,
> And in her very attitude these words—
> > "Ecce ancilla dei"—were imprinted
> > As clearly as a figure stamped in wax.

> [Giurato si sarìa ch'el dicesse "*Ave!*"
> > perchè in'era imaginata quella
> > ch'ad aprir l'alto amor vole la chiave;
> e avea in atto impressa esta favella
> > "*Ecce ancilla dei!*," proprïamente
> > come figura in cera si sugella.]

It is not yet that the *enargeia* of the art produces a seemed audition at this point, but that the language inheres in Mary's gesture. The pilgrim's gaze is fixed on this. But Virgil, who stands to his right (Dante is on *quella parte onde il cuore ha la gente*—that side of him where the human heart is placed), admonishes him not to keep his mind fixed on one place [*non tener pur ad un loco la mente*], and he moves on to the right, past Virgil to the next scene, that of the ark of the covenant before which David dances in his humility, "both more and less a king," while the reciprocal female figure, Michal, looks on *sì come donna dispettosa e trista*—like a woman scornful and sad. But here the question of the vividness of the scene engages the other senses, and *trompe-l'oeil* edges onto *trompe-l'oreille-et-le-nez*:

> In front there appeared people, and the whole
> > Group, partitioned into seven choirs
> > Made, of two of my senses, one says "No"
> The other, "Yes, they're singing"—as at the smoke
> > From the image of incense there the eyes and nose
> > Were made discordant with a *yes* and *no*.

> [Dinanzi parea gente; e tutta quanta
> > partita in sette cori, a' due mie' sense
> > faceva dir l'un "No," l'altro "Si, canta."
> Similemente al fummo degl' incensi
> > che v'era imaginato, li occhi e'l naso
> > a al sì e al no discordi fensi.]

Dante is himself led by its gleaming brightness to the next panel, showing Trajan in conversation with a widow in tears at the death of her son. The eagles on the standards above him seem to move in the wind, and the viewer seems to hear the discursive exchange between them. It is not, as in the first instance, the scriptural phrase of Mary's reply to the angel Gabriel, nor, as in the second, the music of choral song, but rather, an audible and comprehensible exchange of dialogue that causes the pilgrim to wonder at the skill of God that has created "visible speech" that is new to us because it is not found in our world [produsse esto visibile parlare / novello a noi perchè qui non se trova].

The sequence of designs on the pavement in canto 12 requires Dante, urged by Virgil to look at them to ease his passage, to bend his head in order to read them. They are like pavement tombs, representing a series of biblical and classical figures of fallen pride, starting with Satan and concluding with the destruction of Troy. Here, the ecphrastic pattern is subservient to a rhetorical scheme which engages visual prominence at another level, that of the inscribed word. In each of thirteen successive tercets (ll. 25–63), an act of reading and comprehension is recorded. Moreover, these are grouped by anaphora into three sequences of four tercets each. The first four all begin with *Vedea* [I saw], for example, "I saw Nimrod at the foot of his great work [the tower of Babel], as if bewildered" [Vedea Nembròt a piè del gran lavoro / quasi smarrito]. The next four are introduced with a responsive cry ("O ＿＿＿ ") from the viewer, an apostrophe to the specific condition of each of the figures: "O crazy Arachne, thus I saw you already half spider, wretched on the threads of the work you wrought to your own harm" [O folle Aragne, sì vedea io te / già mezza ragna, trista in su li stracci / dell'opera che mal per te si fè]. The last series is of those introduced by a more distanced "It [the pavement] showed" [mostrava]: "It showed how the Assyrians fled in rout after Holofernes was killed, and also the remains of that slaughter" [Mostrava come in rotto si fuggiro / li Assiri, poi che fu morto Oloferne, / e anche le reliquie del martiro].

A final tercet out of anaphoric series returns to the original "I saw," but with a finality that is more than merely lyrical rondure, for the Virgilian matter of the fall of Troy—the subject of the wall paintings encountered by Aeneas—completes the series of pictures by recalling an original scene of implicitly prophetic ecphrasis. The twelve anaphoric tercets have been celebrated for another reason: the initial letters of *Vedea, O,* and *Mostrava* form an acrostic (with *V* read as *U*) : the word *UOM* ["man"—whose pride is essential to his fallen nature]. But the sequence of moments of gaze—"I saw," "O!," "It showed"—is of additional interest here: the final, more objective and distanced report has been prepared for by two phases of personal and subjective testimony by the gazing witness, and the full strength of what it would mean to "show" something under such circumstances has already been established. Each of these might be considered a slightly different ecphrastic mode, and it will be seen how, in subsequent short poems, one or more of these, in various mixtures and at various interpretive levels, will be at work.

The influential Virgilian scene can be adapted to exigencies of medieval dream-vision, and thereafter, to Renaissance verse romance. In the case of Chaucer one might mention the mural paintings in the House of Fame, telling the story of the fall of Troy. But after introducing the

"I sawgh . . ." of the poem's ecphrastic convention for reading the images—as of Venus, "in portreyture, / I sawgh anoon-ryght her figure / Naked fletyng in a see"—the strictly ecphrastic account is interrupted:

> But as I romed up and doun
> I fond that on a wall ther was
> Thus writen on a table of bras:
> "I wol now singen, yif I kan,
> The armes, and also the man
> That first cam, thurgh his destinee
> Fugityf of Troy contree,
> In Itayle, with ful moche pyne
> Unto the strondes of Lavyne."

(In other words, the *Aeneid.*) All the narrator's subsequent "I sawgh's" are modulated by the implicit "I read, and I'm retelling how—"; and, indeed, he continues to narrate poetic history, rather than to read historical pictures, for the next three hundred lines or so. The paintings on the walls—not to speak of the described cultic images—in the temples of Venus and Mars in the "Knight's Tale" are more pictorially detailed (a statue of Venus, for example, likewise "Was naked, fletynge in the large see, / And fro the navele doun al covered was / With wawes grene, and brighte as any glas"). And in the case of Mars's temple, the scene includes an encapsulated image *en abîme*—a temple of Mars is therein depicted—and makes reference to what is audible in depiction—here, the sound of the storm in the boughs of the trees:

> First on the wal was painted a forest,
> In which ther dwelleth neither man ne best,
> With knotty, knarry, barren trees olde,
> Of stubbes sharpe and hideous to biholde.
> In which ther ran a rumbel in a swough
> As though a storm sholde bresten every bough.
> And dounward from an hille, under a bente,
> Ther stood the temple of Mars armypotente.

But generally in Chaucer, images are reported narratively, implying a sequential, thematic scanning, marked by the almost formulaic "I sawgh" (as opposed to a "methought I saw," which generally signals what is "seen" in a dream).

In the story of Arachne in book 6 of Ovid's *Metamorphoses*, we have a paradigmatic instance of how it is the narrative itself which calls for the ecphrastic set pieces. Moreover, the paired descriptions of Pallas's and Arachne's tapestries not only are offered with regard to the competition between the two, but themselves present competing ecphrastic modes. The very medium of weaving is first praised for its marvelous ability—like that of the rainbow—to modulate changes of color. Then the goddess depicts the hill of Mars in Athens and the dispute between herself and Neptune over the naming of the city. This was a dispute which she herself won, so that her offering is, as Ovid points out, a representation of her own victory in a prior competition. This first ecphrasis presents successively the "scene," the principals—Jove, Neptune, Minerva—and the narrative outcome. Then the verse scans the four corners of the picture, each with its inset ancillary story, each an admonitory Ovidian metamorphosis serving to give further warning to Arachne of the power of the gods. The description privileges structure and the constitution of authority—political and, at another level, technological— in judgment and in execution. It is worth considering here in a Renaissance translation because of its relevance to many texts that will be considered later on. This is from George Sandys's lively seventeenth-century version (but with modernized spelling):

> Pallas, in Athens, Mars's Rock doth frame:
> And that old strife about the city's name.
> Twice six Celestials sit enthroned on high,
> Replete with awe-infusing gravity:
> Jove in the midst. The suited figures took
> Their lively forms: Jove had a royal look.
> The Sea-god stood, and with his trident strake
> The cleaving rock, from whence a fountain brake,
> Whereon he grounds his claim. With spear and shield
> Herself she arms, her head a morion steeled.
> Her breast her aegis guards. Her lance the ground
> Appears to strike; and from that pregnant wound
> The hoary olive, charged with fruit, ascends.
> The gods admire: with victory she ends.

The conclusion of this first half of the description is rounded by a narrative and thematic conclusion. The second immediately follows:

> Yet she, to show the rival of her praise
> What hopes to cherish of her bold assays,
> Adds four contentions in the utmost bounds
> Of every angle, wrought in little rounds.
> One, Thracian Rhodope and Haemus shows,
> Now, mountains topped with never melting snows,
> Once human bodies, who durst emulate
> The blest Celestials both in style and state.
> The next contains the miserable doom
> Of that Pygmaean matron, overcome
> By Juno, made a crane, and forced to jar
> With her own nation in perpetual war.
> A third presents Antigone, who strove
> For unmatched beauty with the wife of Jove.
> Not Ilium, nor Laomedon her sire,

Prevailed with violent Saturnia's ire.
Turned to a stork, who, with white pinions raised,
Is ever by her creaking bill self-praised.
In the last circle, Cynara's was placed
Who, charged with grief, the temple's stairs embraced,
(Of late his daughters by their pride o'erthrown)
Appears to weep and grovel on the stone.
The web a wreath of peaceful olive bounds,
And her own tree her work both ends and crowns.

These last lines conclude many simultaneous accounts: a brief catalogue, a description involving both matter and format, a report of an image being assembled, and a tying-up of a creative act with a kind of flourish—indeed, Rolfe Humphries, in his fine translation of this passage, gives Ovid's lines here as "All this the goddess ended / With a border of peaceful olive-wreath around it, / Her very signature" [circuit extremas oleis pacalibus oras, / is modas est operisque sua facit arbore finem]. The olive is not only Minerva's own attribute, but an emblem of peace, of the resolution of strife that borders representations of it: Sandys himself footnotes this passage by observing of the olive and its signification that "Peace is the end for which war was made."[20] Certainly, this ecphrasis is bound up with a systematic kind of rhetorical and poetic closure.

Arachne's web, on the other hand, is rendered with less regard to the structure of the whole, and to representing rhetorically pictorial composition. It is also charged with much more *enargeia*—it is simply more vivid, and it calls attention to its own poetical character in characterizing the picture:

Arachne weaves Europa's rape by Jove:
The bull appears to live, the sea to move.
Back to the shore she casts a heavy eye,
To her distracted damsels seems to cry,
And from the sprinkling waves, that skip to meet
With such a burden, shrinks her trembling feet.
Asteria there a struggling eagle pressed,
A swan here spreads his wings o'er Leda's breast.
Jove, satyr-like, Antiope compels
Whose fruitful womb with double issue swells;
Amphytrio for Alcmena's love became;
A shower for Danae; for Aegina, flame;
For beautiful Mnemosyne he takes
A shepherd's form; for Deois, a snake's.
Thee also, Neptune, like a lustful steer,
She makes the fair Aeolian virgin bear,
And get th'Aloides in Enipe's shape;
Now turned t'a ram in sad Bisaltis' rape.

The passage continues with its rapid and lively series of glimpses, speeding up toward its conclusion, and finally ending in a border reciprocal to Minerva's (and, as Sandys observes of the emblematic plant in this case, "Well suiting with the wanton argument: Lasciviousness hieroglyphically represented by Ivy"): "About her web a curious trail [Arachne] designs, / Flowers intermixed with clasping ivy twines."

The representation of spatial as well as figural matters in Homeric, Virgilian, or Ovidian lines becomes, in the Renaissance, a question of framing phases, parts, regions, of a description in couplets, as here, or in stanzas, as in the host of notional ecphrases in Ariosto and Tasso, or in Spenser. Indeed, when the latter reworks this same Ovidian story in his *Muiopotmos*,[21] we may observe the way in which he uses a half of one of the poem's *ottava rima* stanzas for narrative framing of the elaborated description of Europa and the bull that occupies a whole subsequent stanza. The relation of narrative and description is central to the rhetoric of ecphrasis; in a narrative context, an image can be scanned by an agent in the fiction, or its assembly or composition can be reported (as of Achilles' shield by Hephaistos in Homer). These tend to be stories ("first he saw X and then he looked at the other side and saw Y"; or "first he put in an X with A and B; then, behind it, he made a broad Y," etc.); they can have the effect of providing an internal surrogate for the reader as viewer or scanner. The remarkable ecphrases of tapestries in book 3 of *The Faerie Queene* deploy an array of devices for controlling the moving and the stationary gaze. In Malecasta's House, Castle Joyeous, in canto 1,

> The wals were round about appareiled
> With costly cloths of Arras and of Tours,
> In which with cunning hand was pourtrahed
> The love of Venus and her paramoure,
> The fayre Adonis turned to a floure . . .

In four subsequent stanzas, the description of these starts out with conventional narrative-descriptive devices—"First did it shew . . . Then . . ."; "Now making girlondes of each flowre that grew . . . Now leading him . . . ," where the *now* is peculiarly both temporal and spatial, a gesture of *now . . . now* implying a descriptive *here . . . there* in the picture. But this soon dissolves into pretty straightforward Ovidian narrative. Only at the end of the last of these stanzas (38) does Spenser close out the sequence of stanzas, and the whole ecphrastic episode which has fallen into pure narrative, with a brilliant move:

> Lo! where beyond he lyeth languishing,
> Deadly engored of a great wilde bore,
> And by his side the goddesse groveling
> Makes for him endlesse mone, and evermore
> With her soft garment wipes away the gore,
> Which staynes his snowy skin with hatefull hew:

> But when she saw no helpe might him restore,
> Him to a dainty flowre she did transmew,
> Which in that cloth was wrought, as if it lively grew.

Adonis's metamorphoses are that of young man into flower, history into Ovid, Ovid into pictorial tapestry, tapestry into Spenser; only in the last line are we reminded of this sequence and, indeed, of the tapestry itself. That the final flower might also appear to grow "lively" in the cloth also suggests that, as a bit of *millefleurs*, it might be part of the pictorial ground itself as well as a figure on that ground. One is reminded of an analogous device of closure at the end of a *Saturday Evening Post* story by Scott Fitzgerald called "The Offshore Pirate" (1920), a tale whose artificial implausibility (at the level of nineteen-twenties musical theater plots) is confirmed and allowed for in the concluding clause: "and reaching up on her tiptoes she kissed him softly in the illustration."

The tapestries in "the utmost rowme" in Busyrane's House at the end of book 3 are presented in a more complex fashion. They are initially described not for their narrative, but for their medium, which is negatively allegorized:

> For round about, the walls yclothed were
> With goodly arras of great majesty,
> Woven with gold and silk so close and nere
> That the rich metal lurked privily
> As faining to be hidd from envious eye;
> Yet here and there and everywhere unwares
> It shewed it selfe and shone unwillingly;
> Like a discolourd snake, whose hidden snares
> Through the greene gras his long bright burnished back declares.

The gold thread in the tapestry "fains" (and feigns) not to be seen, yet its bad faith is deconstructed in its very manifestation: the gold in the thread is a snake-in-the-grass. No good can come from the figures wrought against such fallen ground. And indeed, from this extreme close-up the account moves to the whole series of Ovidian rapes represented in successive hangings. Some get most of a stanza, some a few lines, and the varying lengths of the passages—and the way they occupy various parts of the complex, interlocking stanza form—provide a narrative pace that is internal to the tour of the room, the cataloguing of the scenes. And although the usual suspects—Jove, Apollo, Neptune, et al.—are involved, and the description of the room groups the stories by perpetrator, the point of the ecphrastic tour is that these all represent the power of Cupid, who is himself not depicted, but rather presented in another medium (a gold cult statue at the end of the room).

On the other hand, when the pause for a description of an image creates a hiatus or digression in the narrative it can provide a set piece of ecphrasis, an image described for a reader. In that case, the narrative, if any, is of that interesting figurative sort which governs the unfolding, unrolling, or playing out of a descriptive passage. It is generated by a kind of narrativity of argument, of larger elements of syntax, and even of prose or verse structure in itself. It is this internalized storytelling—the narrative of scanning, as it were—which characterizes the ecphrastic set piece, and with which most of this book will be concerned. Extrapolated ecphrases, without any narrative context, become modern lyric poems addressing themselves to actual works of art; and as in modern lyric poetry generally, the lyric is an implicitly "dramatic" one, only covertly revealing the nature and fictional constitution of its speaking persona, its lyrical "I," so the "story" lying behind the mere overt occasion of the ecphrastic encounter will seem to surface only in the course of the poem itself.

The role of ecphrastic moments in narrative becomes, after the seventeenth century, a matter for the study of the novel, and I will not discuss it further here. But before I leave the subject, one of the most remarkable of notional ecphrases in our literature must be considered. It involves paired ecphrastic treatments by both a narrator and a character in the narrated fiction, of the same image. It is worth considering at some length. The picture is the "painted piece" in Shakespeare's *The Rape of Lucrece*.[22] The young poet's heroine, still grieving over her dishonor, "Pausing for means to mourn some newer way," remembers a "piece / Of skillful, painting, made for Priam's Troy,"

> Before the which is drawn the power of Greece,
> For Helen's rape the city to destroy,
> Threat'ning cloud-kissing Ilion with annoy;
>> Which the conceited painter drew so proud,
>> As heaven, it seem'd, to kiss the turrets bowed.

The paradoxes generated by questions of representation provide energy for the description itself, and for the ascription of energy to the painting:

> A thousand lamentable objects there,
> In scorn of nature, art gave lifeless life:
> Many a dry drop seem'd a weeping tear,
> Shed for the slaughter'd husband by the wife;
> The red blood reek'd to show the painter's strife,
>> And dying eyes gleam'd forth their ashy lights,
>> Like dying coals burnt out in tedious nights.

The represented eyes and acts of gaze continue significantly in the next stanza, and the doubling of the act of seeing the picture and the acts of seeing in it is almost manifest—given the grammatical ambiguity—in the couplet:

> There might you see the labouring pioner
> Begrim'd with sweat and smeared all with dust;
> And from the towers of Troy there would appear
> The very eyes of men through loop-holes thrust,
> Gazing upon the Greeks with little lust:
>> Such sweet observance in this work was had,
>> That one might see those far-off eyes look sad.

Traditional testimony to the *enargeia* or vividness of a work of art in ecphrastic writing can praise it for its likeness to the vividness of experience itself—for example, in one of the three brief notional ecphrases produced as part of the trick on Christopher Sly in act 1, scene 2 of *The Taming of the Shrew*, a painting is invoked "of Io as she was a maid, / And how she was beguiled and surpris'd / As lively painted as the deed was done."[23] But as we see here, it can extend to the brilliance or clarity with which expressive gesture demands inferences about the inner states—emotions, intentions, conditions of knowledge—of persons in a scene. The narrator continues in this vein, but with unusually close attention to details, their effects, and the artistic intention thereby manifested. Thus, around Nestor were:

> . . . . a press of gaping faces,
> Which seem'd to swallow up their sound advice,
> All jointly list'ning, but with several graces,
> As if some mermaid did their ears entice,—
> Some high, some low, the painter was so nice:
> The scalps of many almost hid behind,
> To jump up higher seem'd, to mock the mind.

The mind is "mocked" because the art of the piece is to make still things appear to move, but the mockery is twofold, that of imitation as well as of derision. The description continues:

> Here one man's hand lean'd on another's head,
> His nose being shadowed by his neighbour's ear;
> Here one being throng'd bears back, all boll'n and red [swollen];
> Another smother'd seems to pelt and swear:
> And in their rage such signs of rage they bear
> As but for loss of Nestor's golden words,
> It seem'd they would debate with angry swords.
>
> For much imaginary work was there,—
> Conceit deceitful, so compact, so kind,
> That for Achilles' image stood his spear
> Gripp'd in an armed hand; himself behind
> Was left unseen, save for eye of mind:
> A hand, a foot, a face, a leg, a head
> Stood for the whole to be imagined . . .

Here again, the "imaginary work" elicits another sort of imaginary work—pictorial and poetic inference—from the spectator. The highly wrought character of these stanzas (the doubling of "rage . . . rage," the play on "conceit deceitful," etc.) keeps calling attention to the fact that they are, as ecphrasis, generating a verbal *enargeia* reciprocal to the pictorial one they celebrate. But then the exigencies of the narrative complicate the picture, as it were, of the story of the picture.

"To this well-painted piece is Lucrece come," and there beholds Hecuba, "Staring on Priam's wounds with her old eyes"; Lucrece gazes "on this sad shadow"—both Hecuba as a "shadow" of her former glorious self, and, more prominently, in the usual earlier sense of "image, picture": what Lucrece sees is the shadow of a shadow. But the image is silent, the painter having been "no god to lend her" sound, the tones and words of complaint and grief.

> "Poor instrument," quoth she, "without a sound
> I'll tune my woes with my lamenting tongue,
> And drop sweet balm on Priam's painted wound,
> And rail on Pyrrhus that hath done him wrong,
> And with my tears quench Troy that burns so long.

Some theorists might suggest that this is an essential ecphrastic moment. Mute, painted Hecuba has no voice; given that she is painted, this is trivial; given that "In her the painter had anatomiz'd / Time's ruin" and in her image had shown "life imprison'd in a body dead," perhaps she is doubly silenced. But given further that in the story of her—and Troy's—ruin Lucrece perceives her own plight (the lust of Paris causing the downfall of the city as, indeed, Tarquin's lust will prove not only her undoing, but that of the house of Tarquin), the silence is not only tragic but painful. The remainder of Lucrece's own ecphrasis of the piece employs the familiar rhetoric of "See, here is X, and here Y" ("Lo here weeps Hecuba, here Priam dies, / Here manly Hector faints, here Troilus swounds"). But then the narrator's account resumes, and we are given distance from the process of reading the picture:

> Here feelingly she weeps Troy's painted woes,
> For sorrow, like a heavy hanging bell
> Once set on ringing, with his own weight goes;
> Then little strength rings out the dolefull knell,
> So Lucrece set a-work, sad tales to tell
>   To pencill'd pensiveness and colour'd sorrow;
>   She lends them words, and she their looks doth borrow.

The sorrow is not only painted, but generally considered here as troped, "colours" of rhetoric being tropes and schemes; and along with the quibble on "pencil" and "pensive," we are again reminded that the colors of the ecphrastic rhetoric are here painting the colors of the piece. We are then told how Lucrece "throws her eyes about the painting round" until she lights on the figure of the traitor Sinon, in whom "the painter labour'd with his skill / To hide deceit":

> The well-skill'd workman this mild image drew
> For perjur'd Sinon, whose enchanting story
> The credulous old Priam after slew;
> Whose words like wildfire burnt the shining glory
> Of rich-built Ilion, that the skies were sorry,
>   And little stars shot from their fixed places
>   When their glass fell, wherein they viewed their faces.

The narrator's own well-skill'd work is made evident here in the vivid but purely verbal hyperbole (it is not that this trope is naively diagrammed in the picture); but beyond that, the notion of mirroring is immediately brought back to Lucrece, for whom the painting is doing some subtle mirroring of another kind. The next two stanzas present the remarkable climax of an unfolding pattern of reading images in this scene. As Lucrece gazes at the figure of Sinon, the tongue with which she would give tongue to mute Hecuba is itself pushed into an overdetermined *lapsus linguae* by the pressure of her memory of Tarquin's deceit. And yet that very slip leads her to make manifest the comparison between her ruin and that of Troy:

> This picture she advisedly perus'd
> And chid the painter for his wondrous skill,
> Saying some shape in Sinon was abus'd:
> So fair a form lodg'd not a mind so ill.
> And still on him she gaz'd, and gazing still,
>> Such signs of truth in his plain face she spied,
>> That she concludes the picture was belied.
>
> "It cannot be," quoth she, "that so much guile,"—
> She would have said,—"can lurk in such a look."
> But Tarquin's shape came in her mind the while,
> And from her tongue "can lurk" from "cannot" took:
> "It cannot be" she in that sense forsook,
>> And turn'd it thus: "It cannot be, I find,
>> But such a face should bear a wicked mind."

The turning of the sense here is from one skeptical mode to another one. She starts with the "it cannot be" of disbelief in the ultimate power of the painter (who is too good, really) to render smiling villainy without overdoing it, without making it stagy enough to be seen through. And she shifts to the reading of experience: "anybody looking that good has to be bad." It is a remarkable moment, I think, in the series of representations of the picture we have been given: the narrator's; Lucrece's own, recited under the demands of sympathetic—rather than erotic—desire; the narrator resuming the description, and finally reporting the effects of memory, and of a kind of moral shuddering, on a gazer's interpretation.[24] Aeneas weeping at the painting of Troy is doubtless behind this; in front of it lies the subsequent history of the novel, and of the ways in which pictures and sculpture—notional and actual—will work in complex narratological situations.

In extended fictions, the contrast may be between described images that are imaginary or available to the memory of a reader. A powerful instance is that of Browning's "The Statue and the Bust." A notional portrait in relief by one or another della Robbia is commissioned to perpetuate the face of a fictional lady looking from her window to watch her lover ride by below:

> Robbia's cornice, fine,
> With flowers and fruits which leaves enlace,
> Was set where now is the empty shrine—
>
> (And, leaning out of a bright blue space,
> As a ghost might lean from a chink of sky,
> The passionate pale lady's face—
>
> Eyeing ever, with earnest eye
> And quick-turned neck at its breathless stretch,
> Some one who ever is passing by—)

But the lover in the fiction is the actual Ferdinand de' Medici, who reciprocally commissions his own, actual, equestrian statue by Giambologna still in the Piazza Annunziata in Florence:

> Set me on horseback, here aloft
> Alive, as the crafty sculptor can,
>
> In the very square I have crossed so oft:
> That men may admire, when future suns
> Shall touch the eyes to a purpose soft,
>
> While the mouth and the brow stay brave in bronze . . .

The actual statue and the poem's own supplement, the notional bust, watch each other eternally, but of course fictively.

This kind of confrontation can be deployed in even longer fictions. For example, there are elaborate descriptions of the actual Fontana di Trevi, and of Kenyon's fictional Cleopatra, in Hawthorne's *The Marble Faun*; or the juxtaposed ecphrases, in Melville's *Pierre*, of Guido Reni's portrait of Beatrice Cenci and the mysterious, notional *No. 99: A Stranger's Head, By an Unknown Hand*, which "exactly faced each other; so that in secret they seemed pantomimically talking over and across the heads of the living spectators below."[25] This is a fascinating matter, but not to be treated of in these pages. In short poems, as opposed to long narratives, the ecphrastic occasion is usually a given, and any narrative that develops tends to be read into the image itself, making what is represented by or in it—or even making the representation itself—an etiologic fable. In expository prose that is not dedicatedly ecphrastic, such descriptive moments often come up as examples or parables. Thus Emerson, in "Experience": the whole passage containing an actual ecphrasis should be read for the typical way in which the picture—like any interjected Emersonian "example"—is adduced as if by way of argument:

> In this our talking America we are ruined by our good nature and listening on
> all sides. This compliance takes away the power of being greatly useful. A man
> should not be able to look other than direct and forthright. A preoccupied atten-
> tion is the only answer to the importunate frivolity of other people: an attention,
> and to an aim which makes their want frivolous. This is a divine answer, and leaves

no appeal and no hard thoughts. In Flaxman's drawing of the Eumenides of Aeschylus, Orestes supplicates Apollo, whilst the Furies sleep on the threshold.

> The face of the god expresses a shade of regret and compassion, but is calm with the conviction of the irreconcilableness of the two spheres. He is born into other politics, into the eternal and beautiful. The man at his feet asks for his interest in the turmoils of the earth, into which his nature cannot enter. And the Eumenides there lying express pictorially this disparity. The god is surcharged with his divine destiny.[26]

The mode of pictorial "expression" whereby the Eumenides can signify the disparity is not even in the eye, but only the visionary mind, of the beholder (as is the invisible "surcharge" in the sentence which clearly shows where Nietzsche went to school). It is almost as if Flaxman had provided nothing but a narrative scene for him, and the unique linearity of the representation is unnoticed. And perhaps similarly in William Cowper's epigram of 1793, "On Flaxman's Penelope":

> The suitors sinn'd, but with a fair excuse,
> Whom all this elegance might well seduce;
> Nor can our censure on her husband fall,
> Who, for wife so lovely, slew them all.
> Strange art! which both obliterates the guilt
> And makes the offender's blood seem justly spilt.

But we may also fancy, in the final couplet, a suggestion of an art of obliteration, a purely linear and unsentimentalized representation, transcending the merely expressive.

Notional Ecphrasis: The Short Poem

One mode of notional ecphrasis is imperative or optative: rather than describing or characterizing an image, it urges a painter or sculptor to make one with properties which are then detailed. This may originate in three of the Hellenistic Anacreontea (3–5) as a refusal of epic treatment. By instructing Hephaistos to make an alternative to the epic shield of Achilles, another minor poetic mode is thus being instantiated. The imperative is ad hoc here to turning the convention around, but it survives, as we will see, in another tradition. The most significant of the three short "instructions to the artist" poems (beginning "Ton arguron toreuôn / Hêphaiste moi poiêson / panoplian men ouchi")[27] instructs Hephaistos to make for me [the speaker], no silver panoply—what do I care about war?—but a deep cup—and no constellations on it, please, no Orion, no Pleiades [like those Homer had you putting on Achilles' shield], but rather Bacchus, and grapevines, and so forth. In other words, the matter of the Anacreontic poems—drink, love, song—is hereby being proclaimed, even as the little poem preceding this puts it another way: "Give me Homer's lyre, but without the bloody string on it." So, too, Ovid starts out his *Amores* by declaring that he had intended to write of war and heroic matters (in hexameters, of course), when Cupid, that naughty boy, filched a foot from his second line (thereby producing an elegiac couplet) and redirected the poetry from the heroic to the erotic.

Two longer Anacreontic poems (16 and 17) instruct a notional painter to render a beloved person—one a girl, one a boy—taking various qualities and attributes from various immortals; this is a device for parading commonplaces, such as "paint her nose and cheeks by mixing roses and cream" or "paint his downy cheek like a rosy apple." Both of these invoke the silence of images, the first by wittily concluding that, having concluded his remarks, the speaker now sees her, and that the colors themselves will be speaking in a moment [apechei: blepô gar autên, / tacha, kêre, kai lalêseis]; the second, in its lines that J. M. Edmonds, Herrick-like, renders "But let the silent colours be / A speaking taciturnity." These poems of instruction to a painter were known and imitated in the Renaissance.[28] In seventeenth-century England, Ben Jonson used the device in two paired poems of his cycle to "Eupheme" (the late Lady Venetia Digby). The first of these, "The Picture of Her Body," implicitly rebukes painting for its "falsehood fair," its inability to deal with the true, the highest beauty:

> Sitting, and ready to be drawn,
> What makes these velvets, silks, and lawn,
> Embroideries, feathers, fringes, lace,
> Where every limb takes like a face? ["takes" = "looks"]
> Send these suspected helps, to aid
> Some form defective, or decayed;
> This beauty, without falsehood fair,
> Needs but to clothe it but the air.

Instead, the poet suggests that the painter give way to the poet, to paint metaphor and metonymy, as it were, rather than what are more literally images:

> Draw first a cloud: all save her neck;
> And, out of that, make day to break;
> Till, like her face it do appear,
> And men may think, all light rose there.

Having drawn, in successive stanzas, heaven and paradise, the painter is commanded to

> Last, draw the circles of this globe,
> And let there be a starry robe
> Of constellations 'bout her hurled;
> And thou hast painted beauty's world.

Aside from the fact that the lady is now dead, and presumably in heaven, her beauty is universal, a world of beauty itself, so that in order to get it on canvas, one must paint it *as* the universe. The second, long poem ("The Mind") rejects the very possibility of pictorial representation after its opening stanzas:

> Painter, you are come, but may be gone,
> Now I have better thought thereon,
> This work I can perform alone;
> And give you reasons more than one.
>
> Not, that your art I do refuse:
> But here, I may no colours use,
> Beside, your hand will never hit
> To draw a thing that cannot sit.
>
> You would make shift to paint and eye,
> An eagle towering in the sky,
> The sun, a sea, or soundless pit;
> But these are like a mind, not it.
>
> No, to express this mind to sense,
> Would ask a heaven's intelligence;
> Since nothing can report that flame
> But what's of kin to whence it came.

And so mind itself—working unacknowledgedly through the poet's language—must be enjoined to praise the instance of itself in Eupheme's mind, otherwise imageless. There is nothing directly satirical about this rhetorical strategy of instructing a painter, save that it undercuts and disavows some of the common grounds for praising Renaissance portraiture, namely that it can represent moral abstractions in and by means of representing a noble face. Robert Herrick's related, but simpler, little poem ("The Eye") simply instructs the painter to depict heaven, and lower sky, changeable through day and night, sunshine and cloud,

> And when, wise Artist, that thou hast,
> With all that can be, this heaven grac't;
> Ah! what is then this curious skie,
> But onely my Corinna's eye?

The punch-line returns us to the notion that all this is simply the expansion of a familiar conceit. It is an easy move from the fictional injunction to "paint (subject, or attribute) X *as* Y" to the baldly satiric use of this, "paint X as Y" (caricaturing X physically or, more usually, conceptually).

Another of Herrick's little poems, "To the Painter, to Draw Him a Picture" is an instance of this. But none is so elaborate or influential as Andrew Marvell's "Last Instructions to a Painter," which itself satirizes an earlier poem by Edmund Waller commemorating a naval victory over the Dutch in 1665, and beginning "First draw the sea, that portion which between / The greater world and this of ours is seen." Waller continues to introduce with such imperatives his subsequent verse paragraphs embodying narrative stages. But between lines 67 and 286 of his enthusiastic account, he moves totally away from the notional painting, remarking on this lapse with an easy apology:

> Painter! excuse me, if I have awhile
> Forgot thy art and used another style;
> For, though you draw armed heroes as they sit,
> The task in battle does the Muses fit.

Marvell's much longer (almost a thousand lines) and bitingly satirical poem professes initial distaste for what it considers an overworked device by invoking the three sittings that were usual for a portrait:

> After two sittings, now our Lady State
> To end her picture does the third time wait.
> But ere thou fall'st to work, first, painter, see
> It be'nt too slight grown or too hard for thee.
> Canst thou paint without colors? Then 'tis right:
> For so we too without a fleet can fight.

A variety of pictorial modes is appealed to, from an inn sign to a practice of hiding outlines or silhouettes of recognizable objects (in this case, phallic ones) in clouds or smoke:

> Or canst thou daub a signpost, and that ill?
> 'Twill suit our great debauch and little skill.
> Or hast thou marked how antique masters limn
> The alley-roof with snuff of candle dim,
> Sketching in shady smoke prodigious tools?
> 'Twill serve this race of drunkards, pimps and fools.

But, perhaps because of its deployment in political satire, the advice-to-a-painter convention quickly exhausted itself, as witnessed by a broadside of 1680, quoted by an editor of Waller's poetry.[29] The joke is falsely to literalize the poetic trope, for what the device really does is to imply that all the painter can ever do is to illustrate the poet's words:

> Each puny brother of the rhyming trade
> At every turn implores the Painter's aid,
> And fondly enamour'd of his own foul brat,
> Cries in an ecstasy, Paint this! Draw that!

In the Renaissance, detailed notional ecphrases in short poems are not common. One instance of an adaptation of the Anacreontic poem takes the form of a sonnet by Barnabe Barnes, from *Parthenophil and Parthenophe* (1593), "Madrigal 4." The previous linked poem had represented the lady asleep in a garden: "Once in an arbour was my mistress sleeping / With rose and woodbind [honey-suckle] woven." Then follows (my modernization of spelling):

> There had my Zeuxis place and time to draw
> My mistress' portrait, which on platane table

> With nature matching colours as he saw
> Her leaning on her elbow, though not able
>   He gan with vermil, gold, white and sable
> To shadow forth; and with a skillful knuckle
>   Lively set out my fortune's fable,
> On lips a rose, on hand an honey-suckle.
> For nature framed that arbour on such orders
>   That roses did with woodbines buckle,
> Whose shadow trembling on her lovely face
> He left unshadowed, there art lost his grace;
> And that white lily-leaf with fringèd borders
>   Of angels' gold veilèd the skies
> Of mine heaven's hierarchy which closed her eyes.

(A "platane table" is a panel of plane-tree wood; "which" in the last line designates the "leaf" = eyelid.) The play on "shadow" (the verb here means "to paint, to depict generally") depends upon the variety of sixteenth- and seventeenth-century uses of the term. But the scene of the garden in which the lady lies sleeping in the previous poem is here transformed into the metaphors that the poem adduces for the vividness of the picture, "matching colours" with nature even as the poetic language matches those hues with "colours" (tropes and schemes) or rhetoric. The matter of *ut pictura poesis* is nicely and delicately handled here. But it should be noted that the brief framing narrative is important.

On the other hand, by the middle of the nineteenth century, with much more of a history of actual ecphrastic poetry behind them, notional poems need no putative occasion, and can simply proclaim themselves to describe (or even, thereby, to *be*) pictures. For example, in two brief notional ecphrases by Walt Whitman the title is ambiguous in just this way. "A Farm Picture" (1871) clearly establishes a recessional picture space in a view out of an interior; line by line it carries the eye of the reader who is turned viewer perhaps by virtue of the missing, or at least understood, verb:

> Through the ample door of the peaceful country barn
> A sunlit pasture field with cattle and horses feeding,
> And haze and vista, and the far horizon fading away.

"A Paumanok Picture" is also like this, but with a touch of the movie-shot in the recorded activity of its first three lines.[30] The late epigram "A Prairie Sunset" has as its title that of a painting, and for its rhetoric that of ecphrastic description and moralization:

> Shot gold, maroon and violet, dazzling silver, emerald, fawn,
> The earth's whole amplitude and Nature's multiform power consign'd for once to colors;
> The light, the general air possess'd by them—colors until now unknown,
> No limit, confine—not the Western sky alone—the high meridian—North, South, all,
> Pure luminous colors fighting the silent shadows to the last.

The last line (which sounds like D. H. Lawrence in the mode of a poem like "Bavarian Gentians") reminds us of the conventional notion that sunsets are daylight's swan songs. One might imagine for oneself a notional canvas by any American painter from Bierstadt to Church here; but the poem itself is pure Turner, although that poor kind of Turner invoked by Oscar Wilde's Vivian in "The Decay of Lying." (When asked to view a "glorious sky," he remarked, "And what was it? It was simply a very second-rate Turner, a Turner of a bad period, with all the painter's worst faults exaggerated and overemphasized.")

The rhetorical strategies of notional ecphrasis continue to show up in poetry even when there is no putative fictional picture or piece being invoked. A strange instance of this is, I think, Herman Melville's remarkable short poem about John Brown, called "The Portent," from his *Battle-Pieces*. The opening lines might or might not be thought of as referring to an actual representation of the scene of Brown's hanging in 1859:

> Hanging from the beam,
>> Slowly swaying (such the law),
> Gaunt the shadow on your green,
>> Shenandoah!
> The cut is on the crown
> (Lo, John Brown),
> And the stabs shall heal no more.

The image of the swinging shadow of the hanged man on the living, moving surface of the river seemingly anticipates a film shot. But in the second stanza, the issue of what can be seen in the notional picture, and what must be inferred from its mute prophecy, becomes central. The figure's "streaming beard" is linked with what was formerly thought to be the ominous prophetic character of comets (= "bearded" stars) and meteors:

> Hidden in the cap
>> Is the anguish none can draw;
> So your future veils its face,
>> Shenandoah!
> But the streaming beard is shown
> (Weird John Brown),
> The meteor of the war.

The assertion that no drawing, not even this putative one, could show the anguish in the face even if it were unhooded is a turn on what will be seen as a convention of the praise of portraits in the Renaissance, which were said to render visible just such emotions and moral abstractions (rather than to render the visible expression of them by a person). But the otherwise strange, ineptly passive-voiced diction of "the streaming beard is shown" makes sense only as the language of practical ecphrasis—"You can't see X in the picture, but Y is shown." But the artist doing the showing, the drawing, is ultimately the poet himself, putatively acting as the power that makes manifest a prophetic, historical moment. And historical moments themselves are always—from the point of view of prophecy—somewhat shrouded. But, the "is shown," like the diction and tone of Yeats's lines from "Lapis Lazuli" about the Chinese carving—"A third, doubtless a serving-man / Carries a musical instrument" (the "doubtless" is *perfect*)—implies a moment of ecphrastic interpretation here.

Similarly—and for a final instance here—the opening stanza of Wallace Stevens's "Sunday Morning," when taken with its title, might very well read as an elaborated late-nineteenth-century catalogue of a narrative genre painting—perhaps called *Sunday Morning*—and pointing to the fundamental notion that the woman in the picture is not at church. Certainly the lack of identification of the "She"—the central figure of the poem—is rhetorically conventional in the language of catalogue-copy and of picture-caption:

> Complacencies of the pegnoir, and late
> Coffee and oranges in a sunny chair
> And the green freedom of a cockatoo
> Upon a rug mingle to dissipate
> The holy hush of ancient sacrifice.
> She dreams a little, and she sees the dark
> Encroachment of that old catastrophe
> As a calm darkens among water-lights.
> The pungent oranges and bright, green wings
> Seem things in some procession of the dead,
> Winding across wide water, without sound . . .

And yet, in one documented case of an actual, but distantly, ecphrastic poem of Stevens's, the well-known "Angel Surrounded by Paysans," it might indeed be possible to recover the still life by Tal Coat on which it meditates. That painting is variously described by Stevens himself in several letters: "The objects are a Venetian glass vase with a sprig of green in it and then, nearby, various bottles, a terrine of lettuce, I suppose, a napkin, a glass half full of red wine, etc."[31] On the other hand, he responds to its formal and structural being: "The strong blue lines and the high point of the black line in the central foreground collect the group. The wine in the glass at the righthand edge warms, without complicating, the many cool blues and greens."[32] A third mode of reading the painting points toward the poem then in process: "I have even given it a title of my own: *Angel Surrounded by Peasants*. The angel is the Venetian glass bowl on the left with the little spray of leaves in it. The peasants are the terrines, bottles and glasses that surround it." But in the poem, the picture vanishes, and the angel announces himself as "the angel of reality / Seen for a moment standing in the door" and as "the necessary angel of earth / Since, in my sight, you see the earth again." We should have to say that the ecphrastic poetry resided in the titling itself; the poem works on a trope extracted from the title.

The Notional Gallery

The Italian baroque poet Giambattista Marino composed a large collection of almost five hundred short poems that he called his "Gallery." The epigrams and occasional strophic poems of *La Galeria* are all directed to works of art, painting, print, and sculpture, carefully categorized with respect to subject matter (portraits, classical mythology, biblical scenes, and so forth). Many of the poems in it deal with actual works of art, although many are notional as well, being addressed to mythological figures, or to particular artists, living and dead. But not much later in the seventeenth century, the English poet Andrew Marvell writes in "The Gallery" of a purely notional collection which is itself the realization of a metaphor. In the gallery of his mind hang many paintings, but they are all of Clora, the fictional lady to whom the poem is addressed. Marvell figuratively works through the conventions of seventeenth-century portraiture in which a sitter may be costumed, or otherwise framed, mythologically—*Lady X as Diana*, etc.—to the witty trope of a conventionalized love-object projecting herself *as* various personages. Four notional ecphrases are given, paired as images of pleasers or tormentors. Thus, "Here, thou art painted in the dress / Of an inhuman murderess" the most tormenting of whose weapons of destruction "are / Black eyes, red lips, and curlèd hair." "On the other side" (whether the obverse of the picture, or on an opposite wall of the gallery, is not clear) Clora is "drawn / Like to Aurora in the dawn, / When in the east she slumb'ring lies, / And stretches out her milky thighs." Or, after being shown as an enchantress in a cave (we might envision here one of those in which Teniers placed his assembly-line Temptations of St. Anthony), "Vexing thy restless lover's ghost," in another painting, she sits

> afloat
> Like Venus in her pearly boat;
> The halcyon, calming all that's nigh,
> Betwixt the air and water fly;
> Or if some rolling wave appears,
> A mass of ambergris it bears,
> Nor blows more wind than what may well
> Convey the perfume to the smell.

The lady is not only seen in the paired roles that conventional erotic rhetoric has given her, but in a thousand more. The images she projects are finer than those in the famous collection of paintings that Charles I acquired from the Duke of Mantua:

> For thou alone, to people me,
> Art grown a num'rous colony,
> And a collection choicer far
> Than or Whitehall's or Mantua's were.

But the metaphorical gallery walk concludes where it began, with the poet's first, pastoral image of Clora (whose name suggests *Chloris* or "green" + *Flora*—perhaps her true nature does lie in the green, pastoral world). This is the one with which the whole series of erotic fictions originated in literary history, and the one to which the poem finally returns:

> But of these pictures, and the rest,
> That at the entrance likes me best,
> Where the same posture and the look
> Remains with which I first was took:
> A tender shepherdess, whose hair
> Hangs loosely playing in the air,
> Transplanting flow'rs from the green hill
> To crown her head and bosom fill.

It is only a short step to the way, in "To a Lady," in which Alexander Pope uses the same pictorial practice (he refers in a note to the "attitudes in which several ladies affected to be drawn, and sometimes one lady in them all") to elaborate on the general proposition—advanced by a lady, in fact—that "Most women have no characters at all." Again, it is as if each woman were both artist and model, rendering herself *as* one figure or another, in a bewildering and unpredictable succession of expressed personalities. Pope's notional gallery is implicit, consisting of a paragraph hung with instances, including a shepherdess, a celebrated Roman adulteress, Mary Magdalen, and so forth:

> How many pictures of one nymph we view,
> All how unlike each other, all how true!
> Arcadia's countess, here in ermined pride
> Is, there, Pastora by a fountain side.
> Here Fannia, leering on her own good man,
> And there, a naked Leda with a swan.
> Let then the fair one beautifully cry
> In Magdalen's loose hair and lifted eye,
> Or dressed in smile of sweet Cecilia shine,
> With simpering angels, palms, and harps divine;
> Whether the charmer sinner it, or saint it,
> If folly grow romantic, I must paint it.[33]

In a tradition of seventeenth-century English political verse satire mentioned earlier (the "Advice to a Painter" type), a putative painter is urged to represent some person *as* something else in trope for metamorphic satirical distortion: "paint" = "write satire" (as opposed to the formulaic "sing" = "write epic or lyric"). In Pope's lines, the poet emerges as the true painter, in the quite unpictorial vignettes which comprise most of the poem. In the closing lines of this introductory section he seems to us today to have implicitly—and with poetry's continu-ing unwitting technological prophecy—invented the need for a "snapshot" from a "candid camera" (in earlier twentieth-century terminology):

> Come, then, the colours and the ground prepare!
> Dip in the rainbow, trick her off in air,
> Choose a firm cloud, before it fall, and in it
> Catch, ere she change, the Cynthia of this minute.[34]

Actual Ecphrasis

But it is the short poem on a particular, identifiable work of art with which the remainder of this book will be concerned. The presence of a gazer, reporting what he or she sees, various-ly describing what is there to be seen, is framing a moment of experience. This becomes more and more a matter for the modern lyric. In narrative, as we have seen, there is always the issue of pausing to describe the pictorial or sculptural representation, and then getting on with it. In later lyric and meditative poems, there is no larger narrative purpose, and nothing else to get on with. A narrative moment may complete itself expositorially; a poem has to complete itself in other sorts of ways. This makes fruitfully problematic the implicit story of what the poem's speaker is doing there, in front of that image. Sometimes a literary convention will make the issue moot; more often, from the later eighteenth century on, the very ecphrastic occasion will be part of the poem's fiction. In any case, there are a variety of ways in and by which the poem will approach its object, which will sometimes account for interpretive uncer-tainty. This may be related to the frequency with which romantic and later poems fall into *poetic* (as distinguished from merely *rhetorical*) questioning, and to an occasional breaking off of the poem's ecphrastic capacity, becoming overwhelmed by its own inability—or that of lan-guage generally—to embrace the image.

At the same time, it must be remembered that such linguistic resources—concentrated in the rhetorical strategies of poetry—derive from those of purely notional ecphrasis. We shall see the various ways in which every actually ecphrastic poem confirms its descent from the notional, and how the object represented is always, at heart, a poetic fiction.

A confirming instance of Melville's phrase "[the streaming beard] is shown" as repre-senting ecphrastic rhetoric (see above) appears in another of his poems, again from *Battle-Pieces*, and, again, tendentiously construing an image as prophetic. An Elihu Vedder portrait of Jane Jackson was first shown at the National Academy of Design in 1865 (listed as "Jane Jackson, formerly a slave"). The sitter was an old woman who sold peanuts on Broadway and whom Vedder apparently often encountered. In his *Digressions* he observed that "Her meekly bowed head and a look of patient endurance touched my heart and we became friends. She had been a slave down South and had, at the time, a son, a fine tall fellow, she said, fighting in the Union Army." Melville's poem seems slight at first, but develops a complex and power-ful metaphor in the third and final stanza which, as will be heard, picks up the significance of the word "prophetic" in the second one (fig. 2).

2. ELIHU VEDDER, *Jane Jackson*

"Formerly a Slave"

(An idealized Portrait, by E. Vedder, in the Spring Exhibition of the National Academy, 1865)

The sufferance of her race is shown,
    And retrospect of life,
Which now too late deliverance dawns upon;
    Yet she is not at strife.

Her children's children they shall know
    The good withheld from her;
And so her reverie takes prophetic cheer—
    In spirit she sees the stir

Far down the depths of thousand years,
    And marks the revel shine;
Her dusky face is lit with sober light,
    Sybilline, yet benign.

The poem sees her as seeing "in spirit" the consequences of emancipation and the war—not so much Jane Jackson, plucked up from Broadway to pose in Vedder's studio, but the mythologized image the poem reads into the portrait who figuratively sees a redeemed future. Robert Penn Warren wrote pointedly of this stanza: "As the slave woman has been an outsider looking in at the 'revel' of the privileged whites, so now, as she looks into the future, she is still an outsider—though a benign one—to the imagined revel of her own descendants."[35] One may also notice the reinforcement of the two modes of "seeing"—literal and figurative—by the two senses of the phrase "lit with sober light." This light is both literally a description of the light falling on the face in the shadowy painting, and, figuratively, the soberly radiant light of her countenance, as it were.

The matter of the past, the "retrospect of life," is quickly passed over in these lines—the past "is shown" in (on? around?) her face. But the whole poem claims her as looking only into the future. This whole matter of prophecy in the poem, and the particular word "Sybilline," seem to have affected Vedder. Ten years after the publication of *Battle-Pieces*, Vedder did a painting called *The Cumaean Sybil* about which he remarked that a mood he fell into after doing the painting we have been considering "found its resting place in the picture of 'The Cumaean Sybil.' Thus this fly—or rather this bee from my bonnet—was finally preserved in amber-varnish and, thus, Jane Jackson became the Cumaean Sibyl." Vedder's own image has all the complexity of some lines of Browning, but he does not add that the maggot from which the fly was hatched was probably Melville's poem. Here is an intriguing case of a painting's producing a radically interpretive ecphrasis which then seems to feed into a subsequent painting, much as Hellenistic ecphrases of lost originals fed into pictures in the Renaissance.

Unassessable Actual Ecphrasis

And here we might consider for a moment how, while we can be certain that a poem invokes an actual work of art, present to the writer if only in retrospect, there are very many cases of that object being lost or untraceable. The result is that the poem *might as well be notional.* Many epigrams from the *Greek Anthology* are directed to specific works of art and architecture we no longer possess, even as many of them may be indeed notional, or merely exercises in a genre which had become conventional. Some of the epigrams addressing—and often putatively spoken by—Myron's celebrated statue of a heifer (moved from the Athenian Agora to the Temple of Peace in Rome) may be actual.[36] There are nearly forty of them by various hands in book 9, and they nearly all work some turn on the oldest anecdotes in praise of works of art—reducing them to the issue of *trompe-l'oeil*. It is as if—as in many of these Hellenistic ecphrastic poems—the "lively" of *enargeia* could only be "lifelike." When the statue speaks in these, it claims to have wandered away from the herd and gotten stuck on its base, for example, or it warns a calf to keep away from it because it can't give milk. It almost moos; a gadfly tries to sting it; Myron didn't really model it: it turned into bronze from old age, and so forth. One, by Julian, prefect of Egypt, moves the rhetorical strategy to a more sophisticated level, claiming that Art and Nature (*Techna* and *Phusis*) contended for this cow, and that Myron gave each of them a prize: "When you gaze at it, Art tears sovereignty away from Nature; / When you touch it, Nature is nature." In the seventeenth century, Marino imitated and expanded material from several of these in *La Galeria;* but while this collection contains so many examples of actual ecphrastic epigrams whose original objects have been lost, these verses on the Myron *Heifer* are, of course, purely notional, ecphrastically speaking—he had in fact never seen it, but only read poems about it.

Now, even if we knew precisely which of two or three archaic *kouroi* in the Louvre Rilke was addressing in his celebrated and influential "Archaic Torso of Apollo" (from the 1908 *Neue Gedichte*) it could not matter that much in dealing with the poem. The actual ecphrasis in it (the torso still glowing "like a candelabrum, / By which his gaze, turned down low, // Holds fast and gleams," etc.) could apply to any one of a number of such paradigmatic pieces. On the other hand, Dante Gabriel Rossetti's sonnet of 1847, "For an Annunciation," is directed at an unidentified early German painting he had seen, according to his brother W. M. Rossetti's note, in an auction room. (The chances of ever discovering what it was seem minimal.) Even a general acquaintance with northern art would allow a reader to visualize the objects of the opening description: "The lilies stand before her like a screen / Through which, upon the warm and solemn day, / God surely hears . . . " But the scene unfolded in the sestet of the sonnet, with its obliquely identified angel, remains mysterious. The last two lines, in particular, pose a problem which only knowledge of the actual object could resolve:

> So prays she, and the Dove flies in to her
> > And she has turned. At the low porch is one
> > Who looks as though deep awe made him to smile.
> Heavy with heat, the plants yield shadow there;
> > The loud flies cross each other in the sun;
> > And the aisled pillars meet the poplar-aisle.

We may wonder how a number of flies, whether forming a sign of the cross, or merely glossed as doing so, could in any case be legible at all? And what, if any, is the structural and perspectival pattern being invoked—and troped—in the graceful chiasm of the last line, in which "the aisled pillars meet the poplar-aisle" and, perhaps, the designs of text meet the textures of design? (Noticeable, too, is the phonological sequence *yield > flies > aisled.* Without the painting, it cannot be known at what stages of figuration the conceit resides.[37]

Or another instance among so many: the fine minor Victorian poet Lord de Tabley's "The Knight in the Wood" may or may not be an actual ecphrasis—certainly it could be a Browningesque fiction—but it would be useful to know, and to be able to assess the degree of coarseness and crudeness attributed in the opening line. But in any event, the breaking-off of the description in the final line moves toward a convention of self-confessed ecphrastic failure noted first in Virgil (see above) and which will be seen in poems on images by poets as different as Rossetti and Randall Jarrell:

> The thing itself was rough and crudely done,
> Cut in coarse stone, spitefully placed aside
> As merest lumber, where the light was worst
> On a back staircase, Overlooked it lay
> In a great Roman palace crammed with art.
> It had no number in the list of gems,
> Weeded away long since, pushed out and banished,
> Before insipid Guido's over-sweet
> And Dolce's rose sensationalities,
> And curly chirping angels spruce as birds.
> And yet the motive of this thing ill-hewn
> And hardly seen *did* touch me. O, indeed
> The skil-less hand that carved it had belonged
> To a most yearning and bewildered brain:
> There was such desolation in the work;
> And through its utter failure the thing spoke
> With more of human message, heart to heart,
> Than all those faultless, smirking, skin-deep saints,
> In artificial troubles picturesque,
> And martyred sweetly, not one curl awry—[38]

And, breaking off its own dismissive gallery tour, the poem turns its gaze on the negative power of a vision reminiscent of the world of "Childe Roland to the Dark Tower Came":

> Listen; a clumsy knight, who rode alone
> Upon a stumbling jade in a great wood
> Belated. The poor beast with head low-bowed
> Snuffing the treacherous ground. The rider leant
> Forward to sound the marish with his lance.
> You saw the place was deadly; that doomed pair,
> The wretched rider and the hide-bound steed,
> Feared to advance, feared to return—That's all!

In a way, too, the poem's refusal to moralize any further than remarking on "desolation" and "failure" as empowering the piece (which, if actual, might be from a sarcophagus)—as if unwilling to add more finish to the "all!"—was a figure for the coarseness of the piece that triumphs over the picturesque, and the "skin-deep." In addition, the object selected is exemplary as a *privately* experienced one. It stands at the other end of a scale of familiarity from a piece of sculpture whose public institutionalization had constructed it either as statuary—like the commanding effigy of a ruler, or other public memorial—or as an aesthetic or cultural monument.

Raphael, *Abraham and the Angels*

Leonardo da Vinci, *Virgin of the Rocks*

J. A. M. WHISTLER, *Symphony in White no. 2: The Little White Girl*

J. M. W. Turner, *The Fighting "Téméraire"*

GIOVANNI BELLINI, *St. Francis in Ecstasy*

Henri Matisse, *The Red Studio*

FRA ANGELICO, *Last Judgment*

PIERRE-AUGUSTE RENOIR, *Luncheon of the Boating Party*

Similarly, it is unlikely that one might be able to retrieve "On a Landscape of Gaspar Poussin" discoursed upon at length in a poem of Robert Southey's—it is significant in that the speaker notionally climbs into the painting and takes an extended walk through the scene, climbing a hill, surveying the prospect from there, and so forth. Still more unlikely would be the identification of the actual painting in Mrs. Felicia Hemans's "On a Picture of Christ Bearing the Cross," identified by her as "Painted by Velasquez" and, in a note, as being "in the possession of Viscount Harberton, Merton Square, Dublin," since Velázquez painted no such picture. Even a Murillo (easily misattributed in the early nineteenth century) of that subject, now in Philadelphia, does not quite fit, its gazing female figure's eyes being lowered toward the figure of Christ. We could thus not take Hemans's third stanza as reading that figure as a surrogate for the poet herself, gazing up at the painting:

> And upward, through transparent darkness gleaming,
>> Gazed, in mute reverence, woman's earnest eye,
> Lit, as a vase whence inward light is streaming,
>> With quenchless faith, and deep love's fervency;
> Gathering, like incense round some dim-veil'd shrine,
> About the Form, so mournfully divine![39]

Emblems

Before a number of actual ecphrastic situations are differentiated, one should point out a common but almost limiting case, that of the Alciatian emblem and its tradition in the sixteenth through the eighteenth centuries. Here an image is accompanied by a glossary text (originally in Latin, soon after translated into vernaculars), whose function is frequently to tie a motto or tag line or proverbial bit to the object. The first book of emblems was that made by a lawyer named Andrea Alciati (or Alciato) in 1531. Erwin Panofsky paraphrases Alciati's commentator Claudius Minos on how an emblem is like a symbol, but particular, rather than universal; like a puzzle or riddle, but not as hard to unravel; like an apothegm, but visual rather than verbal; like a proverb, but erudite, rather than commonplace.[40] A simple example— shown in figure 3 in an early version of Alciati's number 178 in English from Geoffrey Whitney's *A Choice of Emblems* (1586)—retains the Latin motto *Ex bello pax*, or peace emerging from war. Modern theories of representation, obsessed with gender distinctions, might call this the feminized version of the male trope of beating "swords into ploughshares" and "spears into pruning hooks" (Isaiah 2.4). The degree to which such visual devices resurface in purely poetic figuration, by the way, can easily be observed in this instance. A poem published in 1590 about an old soldier retiring, probably by Queen Elizabeth's courtier and master of armaments, Sir Henry Lee, which begins "His golden locks time hath to silver turned," opens its second stanza with "His helmet now shall make a hive for bees." It will be noticed that the verse below the image purports to read not a picture, but a symbolic object of limited semiotic range. However depicted, the interpretive text deals with the image as if it were a diagram, treating all details of the representation as if they were invisible.

138   *Ex Bello , pax.*
                To HVGHE CHOLMELEY *Efquier.*

T H E helmet ftronge, that did the head defende,
    Beholde, for hyue, the bees in quiet feru'd :
And when that warres, with bloodie bloes, had ende.
They, hony wroughte, where fouldiour was preferu'd:
    Which doth declare, the bleſſed fruites of peace,
    How fweete ſhee is, when mortall warres doe ceaſe.

De falce ex enſe,   *Pax me certa ducis placidos curuauit in vſus:*
Martialis.   *Agricolæ nunc ſum, militis ante fui.*

3. GEOFFREY WHITNEY, *A Choice of Emblems*

Again, in Alciati's tenth emblem there is a lute, interpreted as *Foedera,* or alliances. The notion that a lyre of several strings "means" a political leader who will bind together and unite his fellows (a lyre, it was pointed out, develops a unity of its sounds), goes back to the Hellenistic *Hieroglyphs of Horapollo.* Alciati's poem, in which the lute is presented to Maximilian, Duke of Milan, pursues this conceit. It depends, among other things, on punning overtones of *fides/fides* ("faith" and "string") and *chorda/corda/concors* ("string," "heart," and "harmony"). The lute is shown in the woodcuts and engravings lying table-up on a canopied bed; in later editions, an open book of tablature music is added in the foreground. These are both naturalizing details, claiming the presence of the diagrammatic figure for the realm of sixteenth-century domestic interior. And yet, for all the text is concerned, the lute might as well be hanging—as they were usually kept—from a peg on the wall. The bed, the elaborate draperies—in the design and execution of which subsequent printmakers continued to indulge themselves—do not exist. (The lute is shown as it is, probably, because, when on the wall it would have hung rounded shell outward, and thus emblematically crucial strings would not have been part of the image. One could imagine, in a subsequent phase of semiotic sophistication, the lute hanging on the wall being poetically rebuked as hiding its face in shame, not showing its strings: why? are they broken? what might you have *done?*, etc.)

The relation between a woodcut or engraving and an emblem verse was very fluid, versions and translations of the texts of Andrea Alciati's original being associated with newly drawn and printed images for over a hundred years. In addition, a writer of new verses might use older engravings, as in the case of George Wither's 1635 *A Collection of Emblems*, which uses engravings done by Crispin van de Passe for a Dutch emblem book first published in 1611. Wither's long-winded verses are pedagogic and homiletic, in the Dutch manner. A glance at his version of Alciati's emblem number 144 shows the familiar image of a dolphin wrapped around an anchor (fig. 4). (It goes back to Roman times: one can see it in mosaic on the floor of one of the buildings of the resort town the Romans built on Delphi.) It became associated with the emperor Augustus's quoted motto, *Festina lente*, as did Vespasian's analogous device of crab and butterfly. The picture does indeed present an interesting notion. It is not of an Aristotelian scalar mediation between extremes. but rather a kind of dialectical entwining— if not actually a struggle—between the anchor of staying power, and the dolphin of exuberant marine motion. It was adopted as a colophon device by the great Venetian printer, Aldus Manutius. Alciati gives the emblem another reading entirely, his legal and political concerns coming foremost: whenever the winds disturb the sea, his verses declare, an anchor cast overboard aids the poor sailors, and the dolphin, devoted to mankind (*pius . . . homines*), enwraps it to fix it more firmly on the bottom; and so kings must know that what an anchor is to the sailors, so are they to their people. Wither, on the other hand, recovers the older association and augments it with ancillary glossings of his own—the anchor as an independent sign for hope, for example. Similarly, van de Passe's own concerns, as a seventeenth-century Dutch artist, allow him to frame the serpent and anchor not in the implicit nautical context of the older emblem, but to place it, like all the others in this collection, foregrounded against a landscape.

An extreme instance of emblematic readings of images can be seen in the tradition of the shaped or figured poem, beginning with Hellenistic ones like Theocritus's syrinx-shaped verses, and Simmias of Rhodes's wings of Eros, and best represented in English poetry by George Herbert's altar-shaped poem, "Easter Wings" (fig. 5).[41] Here the poem gives a reading to the image whose silhouette is generated by its own typographic arrangement. In these, the visual image is grasped on first glance—the lines of type being for the moment linguistically transparent, and their semiotic function altered—and the significance unrolls in the reading of the text, like any ecphrasis or emblem. But in the course of that reading, elements of the graphic medium (line length, altered justification) are themselves newly experienced and discovered *simultaneously with the unfolding of the interpretation.*

In any event, it is the graphically reductive character of emblematic readings which distinguishes them from the larger realm of pictorial ecphrasis. This is not to say that any poem's reading on an image may not collapse into emblematic reduction; this happens frequently, particularly before the nineteenth century, when poetry begins to acknowledge the existence of

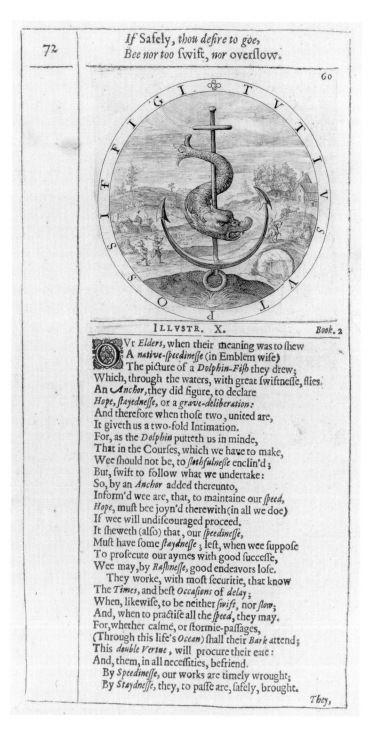

4. CRISPIN VAN DE PASSE, ". . . *Nor too* swift, *nor overslow*"

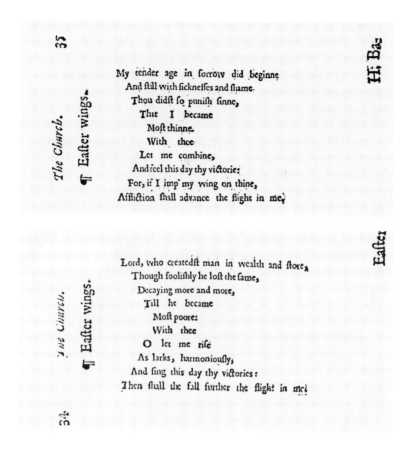

My tender age in sorrow did beginne
And still with sicknesses and shame.
Thou didst so punish sinne,
That I became
Most thinne.
With thee
Let me combine,
And feel this day thy victorie:
For, if I imp' my wing on thine,
Affliction shall advance the flight in me.

Lord, who createdst man in wealth and store,
Though foolishly he lost the same,
Decaying more and more,
Till he became
Most poore:
With thee
O let me rise
As larks, harmoniously,
And sing this day thy victories:
Then shall the fall further the flight in me.

5. GEORGE HERBERT, *"Easter Wings"*

various modes and levels of artistic medium as part of what is meant to be grasped. Poems on works of art might also be thought of as improvising their own ad hoc systems of emblematic reduction. For example, romantic poems may reduce what is being noticed about a work of art to an account of the circumstances in which it was being viewed. And it should be remembered that to assert in general that a picture, a piece of sculpture—indeed, a text—is "about" X rather than Y is to perform what is frequently a reductive interpretive act.

Actual Ecphrasis: Portraits

For Aristotle, portraiture is a mode of praise.[42] But portraiture involves other dimensions of representation. Classical fables of verisimilitude retold constantly in the Renaissance usually concern still life that appears to be quick, objects represented in natural size (rather than, say, most landscapes)—one thinks of those anecdotes in Pliny about Zeuxis and Parrhasius, grapes and birds and curtains. These become more complex when a person, rather than an object, known to the viewer is portrayed; a portrait may look like what its subject looks like, but it is frequently praised in the Renaissance, for example, as looking like—and thereby revealing—what a person really is (generating what the Book of Common Prayer calls a Sacrament, "an outward and visible sign of an inward and spiritual grace.") A fictional story about an occasion on which *trompe l'oeil* actually fools a viewer is one thing. Another matter is that of a poem that praises subject and painter together by showing how the artist gets to the character or essence of the subject by means of details—how the psychological or moral notion is revealed "in" a bit of facial feature, coexisting perhaps with the glossing of emblematic details surrounding the face. The pattern is so conventional that in act 1, scene 1 of *Timon of Athens,* in the typical *paragone,* or debate about the merits and functions of poetry and painting in the tradition of Leonardo da Vinci's observations, the Poet's ecphrasis of the painter's portrait of Timon is paradigmatic of actual sixteenth-century poetic practice:

> Admirable! How this grace
> Speaks his own standing[!] What a mental power
> This eye shoots forth! How big imagination
> Moves in this lip! To th' dumbness of the gesture
> One might interpret.

In the twentieth century, William Butler Yeats can read a baroque portrait ("of some Venetian gentleman") by Bernardo Strozzi in the Dublin National Gallery, interpreting most attentively "to the dumbness of the gesture":

> Whatever thought broods in the dark eyes of that Venetian gentleman has drawn its life from his whole body; it feeds upon it as the flame feeds upon the candle— and should that thought be changed, his pose would change, his very cloak would rustle, for his whole body thinks.[43]

On the other hand, he can wander, in the summer of 1937, through a room full of portraits of celebrated people he has known (in "The Municipal Gallery Revisited") and find portraiture wanting in the ability to represent character—perhaps because of his very knowledge of the subjects, perhaps because of the painter's want of genius. In any event, there is no longer here anything of the Renaissance rhetorical strategy, by which a poem purports modestly to defer to the painter's art, leaving unstated the fact that only in language could that deference be constructed:

> Mancini's portrait of Augusta Gregory,
> "Greatest since Rembrandt," according to John Synge;
> A great ebullient portrait, certainly;
> But where is the brush that could show anything
> Of all that pride and that humility . . .

Inevitably, the pen's superiority to the pencil here unequivocally emerges. We may be reminded of the intricacies of representation in which the pen elicits from the pencil's mute strokes what those strokes were in turn eliciting from the appearance of the person, which, in turn, the appearance was eliciting from spiritual depths or a transcendent invisible realm of moral qualities. And we may feel that, *pace* Plato, the more representational removes, the truer the final verbal "picture."

These questions also inhere in the case of the narrative or mythopoetic work of art. Earlier poetry, from the Renaissance through the eighteenth century, will often reduce, in an almost emblematic way, a representation of a classical or biblical figure to an occasion on which to address the matter of the figure itself, or, at most, the picture or piece's clarity of presentation, which makes the figure available for meditation, and perhaps enhances such meditation by the secondary wonder at the marvel of skill that has effected that very clarity. But more interestingly, a poem can address not only a figure, say, but a canonical interpretation of the figure; it can see that interpretation in a painting, or, on the contrary, declare the painting to present a revisionary one. Or it can, again, use the image as an occasion for presenting its own revision.

The Capriccio

Aside from the notional or actual gallery poem, there is another mode which is also to be distinguished from that of the actual ecphrastic encounter. Michael Baxandall in *Giotto and the Orators* quotes in prose translation several Latin poems to Pisanello by his contemporaries, including some lines by Tito Vespasiano Strozzi:

> How shall I tell of the living birds or gliding rivers, the seas with their shores? I seem to hear the roaring waves there, and the scaly tribe cleave the blue water. Prating frogs croak beneath the muddy runnel; you make boars lurk in the valley and bears on the mountain. . . . Yonder the swift hound is intent on the hare's destruction; here the rearing horse neighs and champs at its bit.[44]

He goes on to remark that this sort of thing is not, strictly speaking, actual ecphrasis, "since it describes not so much one particular work as the distinctive quality and range of the painter's general performance."[45] Such a poem is in a sense a notional ecphrasis, perhaps of what might be called an imaginary gallery with real paintings in it. But the poem is not so much a gallery tour as a constructed vision. A much-quoted stanza from canto 1 of James Thomson's *The Castle of Indolence* uses a notional ecphrasis to develop what the last two lines confirm as just such a capriccio, as it will be called. Here we have a conspectus of seventeenth-century landscape modes, and a momentary character of the work of three painters by a poet who had at least a bottom-line summary view of each of them:

> Sometimes the pencil, in cool airy halls
> Bade the gay bloom of vernal landscapes rise,
> Or Autumn's varied shades imbrown the walls:
> Now the black tempest strikes the astonished skies;
> Now down the steep the flashing torrent flies;

> The trembling sun now plays o'er ocean blue,
> And now rude mountains frown amid the skies;
> Whate'er Lorrain light-touched with softening hue,
> Or savage Rosa dashed, or learnèd Poussin drew.

The mode of ecphrastic capriccio is widely seen in modern poetry, where the oeuvre of a particular painter, summoned up by his or her name, gets to be a subject in itself. In D. H. Lawrence's "Corot," for example, it is those silver-stippled landscapes, often with birches in them—rather than, for example, some of the other work which we think of today as mediating between Poussin and Cézanne (and their luminosity, in particular)—which he seems to be confronting, as these stanzas from it suggest:

> The trees rise taller and taller, lifted
> On a subtle rush of cool grey flame
> That issuing out of the east has sifted
>   The spirit from each leaf's frame.
>
> For the trailing, leisurely rapture of life
> Drifts dimly forward, easily hidden
> By bright leaves uttered aloud; and strife
>   Of shapes by a hard wind ridden.
>
> The grey, plasm-limpid, pellucid advance
> Of the luminous purpose of Life shines out
> Where lofty trees athwart-stream chance
>   To shake flakes of its shadow about. . . .
>
> Ah listen, for silence is not lonely!
> Imitate the magnificent trees
> That speak no word of their rapture, but only
>   Breathe largely the luminous breeze.

The importance of "silence" in the last stanza, by the way, may be traced to an earlier draft of the poem, which opened with an avowal of the double silence of a (silent) painting of a silent scene—here presented in a paradoxical trope of music—and a characteristic confession of ecphrastic anxiety:

> The music of music is stillness, you birds,
> Cease a moment in reverence
> And listen, of Everything, listen, for words
> Foil the sense.

Capriccios of this sort can even occupy positions in gallery poems. A celebrated case is that of Baudelaire's "Les Phares" ("The Beacons"), with its successive stanzas each devoted to a summary conspectus of the work of Rubens, Leonardo da Vinci, Rembrandt, Michelangelo, the baroque sculptor Pierre-Paul Puget, Watteau, Goya, and Delacroix. Sometimes a direct reference may appear to present itself, as in this hint of the background landscape of the *Virgin of the Rocks* in the Leonardo quatrain:

> Leonardo da Vinci, deep mirror, and dark
> Where charming angels with mysterious
> Gentle smiles show up under the shade
> Of pines and glaciers which enclose their land.
>
> [Léonard da Vinci, miroir profond et sombre,
> Où des anges charmants, avec un doux souris
> Tout chargé de mystère, apparaissent à l'ombre
> Des glaciers et des pins qui ferment leur pays.]

And most remarkably, there is Herman Melville's "At the Hostelry," a poem of over six hundred lines containing anachronistic bits of imaginary conversations among Dutch, French, and Italian painters, in which the summary views are dramatically presented. For example, Watteau, addressing Veronese from his own historical moment, is also unwittingly characterizing his own work ("perchance, in way / To vindicate his own renown, / Modest and true in pictures done"):

> Ay, Signor; but—your leave—admit,
> Besides such scenes as well you've hit,
> Your *Pittoresco* too abounds
> In life of old patrician grounds
> For centuries kept for luxury mere:
> Ladies and lords in mimic dress
> Playing at shepherd and shepherdess
> By founts that sing *The sweet o' the year!*

Actual Ecphrastic Poems by the Artists Themselves

There is, of course, the particular case of artists who are, under whatever cultural circumstances, quite independently poets, and who write poems "for" or "to" or "after" works of their own.[46] One of the earliest and most celebrated pieces of ecphrastic verse by the artist himself is the quatrain by Michelangelo in which he gives voice to his own figure of *Night* from the Medici tomb in Florence (fig. 6). But the lines themselves exist only in answer to a previous quatrain addressed to the figure by Giovanni Strozzi—like its answer, preserved by Vasari in his life of Michelangelo:

> Night, which you see asleep in such a lovely
> Attitude was sculpted in this stone
> By an angel, and because she sleeps, has life:
> Wake her, if you don't believe it, and she'll speak.

6. MICHELANGELO, *Night*

[La Notte, che tu vedi in sì dolci atti
Dormire, fu da un angelo scolpita
In questo sasso: e perchè dorme, ha vita:
Destala, se no'l credi, e parleratti.]

The pun on Michelangelo's name is a frequent one, but the other one on *atti* ("acts" as well as "attitudes"), as one astute critic has observed,[47] is quite effective (*La Notte* acts by taking up motionless attitudes). Yet the artist's own riposte is both wittier and more profound. He *does* awaken Night and she does indeed speak, in that his trope of *La Notte* shifts its mode of representation. (Michelangelo did not, for example, cut a hole and let a speaking tube into, say, the pediment under the figure and in a Fellini-like manner whisper a rebuke to Strozzi through it.) Night talks through the sculptor-poet's voice:

> Caro m'è 'l sonno, e più esser di sasso,
> mentre che'l danno e la vergogna dura;
> non veder, non sentir m'è gran ventura;
> però non mi destar, deh, parla basso.

Wordsworth made two attempts at translating this, of which the second is far better:

> Grateful is Sleep, more grateful still to be
> Of marble; for while shameless wrong and woe
> Prevail 'tis best to neither hear nor see:
> Then wake me not, I pray you. Hush, speak low.[48]

In any event, Michelangelo's quatrain merely addresses the other poem, not his own particular representation; it might be any marble image of Night that is speaking. At another extreme of particularity, perhaps, would be the kind of versified catalogue copy that Turner, who wrote quite a bit of poetry, employed in exhibiting his paintings. He often appended quotations—as glossary epigraphs—from Milton, Thomson, and others, and in fact from his own long, unpublished poem, *The Fallacies of Hope*. The well-known lines attached to the very famous 1840 painting, *Slavers Throwing Overboard the Dead and Dying—Typhon Coming On*, for example, were by no means merely ecphrastic of this picture, but rather, as part of the long poem, come out of some of the same impulses as the painting:

> Aloft all hands, strike the top-masts and belay;
> Yon angry setting sun and fierce-edged clouds
>   Declare the Typhon's coming.
>   Before it sweeps your deck throw overboard
>   The dead and dying—ne'er heed their chains.
>   Hope, Hope, fallacious Hope!
>   Where is thy market now?[49]

But for a romantic poetic meditation on the painting, one would better look to Ruskin's extended discussion of it in *Modern Painters* (2.1846). On the other hand, Turner's couplets on his 1809 view of London from Greenwich are clearly ad hoc to the painting. They exhibit the same selective gaze that an independent poet might manifest, overlooking the prominent foreground view of Greenwich and the deer on its peaceable and presumably precapitalist hill, and reaching back and up, in its reading of the painting, to the fogged-in city in the distance. Ultimately, the painting (fig. 7) is reduced, in this little poem, almost to an emblem occupying about a quarter of its surface and, perhaps, deconstructing the prominence of the fore- and middle-ground prospect:

> Where burthen'd Thames reflects the crowded sail,
> Commercial care and busy toils prevail,
> Whose murky veil, aspiring to the skies,
> Obscures thy beauty, and thy form denies,

7. J. M. W. TURNER, *London*

Save where thy spires pierce the doubtful air,
As gleams of hope amidst a world of care.[50]

Most interesting in this mode are Dante Gabriel Rossetti's sonnets on his own pictures. These pose interesting textual-pictorial problems, such as those in the one on the unfinished "Found." (Narrative elements in the painting derive in part from Rossetti's own earlier poem, "Jenny," and William Bell Scott's "Rosabell," but the sonnet starts out with Keats's line "There is a budding morrow in midnight.") This poem has been much discussed. But perhaps more subtly significant here might be the sonnet called "Body's Beauty" when it was included as number 78 in *The House of Life*. Originally called "Lilith," it was written in 1867 for a painting, begun a few years earlier, of Fanny Cornforth, the poet-painter's model and mistress, represented as Lilith, the uncanonical first wife of Adam and heroine of so many antithetical mythologies (fig. 8).

Of Adam's first wife, Lilith, it is told
(The witch he loved before the gift of Eve,)
That, ere the snake's, her sweet tongue could deceive,
And her enchanted hair was the first gold.

8. D. G. ROSSETTI, *Lady Lilith*

And still she sits, young while the earth is old,
    And, subtly of herself contemplative,
    Draws men to watch the bright web she can weave,
Till heart and body and life are in its hold.

The rose and poppy are her flowers; for where
    Is she not found, O Lilith, whom shed scent
And soft-shed kisses and soft sleep shall snare?
    Lo! as that youth's eyes burned at thine, so went
    Thy spell through him, and left his straight neck bent
And round his heart one strangling golden hair.

Lilith's web is her hair, which she weaves as artist of attraction and as arachnoid killer. One thin strand of this deadly gossamer will do its work, as we see in the final line. The erotic rose and soporific poppy are emblematically glossed, but the poem does more with them than that: the lexical sequence—prominently marked by alliteration and assonance—"shed scent / And soft-shed kisses and soft sleep shall snare" figures a narrative one by associating "shed" with rose and "soft" with poppy. The narrative acquires "soft," then finally sheds "shed," emerging in a reversal of the initial consonantal patter of "soft-shed" in "shall snare." There is far more of the semiotics of structure in the poem than in the painting. That this poem mattered a great deal to Rossetti is additionally clear from his echoing of the "And subtly of herself contemplative" in his sonnet on the sonnet, which forms the (last written) epigraph to the whole assembled sequence of *The House of Life*. (He claims there that a sonnet, which is "a moment's monument," must be kept "Of its own arduous fulness reverent.") It also seems clear that Walter Pater perhaps unconsciously alludes to this sonnet in his celebrated paragraphs on Leonardo's *Mona Lisa* (see p. 237) as much as to Gautier's "Le Poème de la femme" from *Émaux et Camées*.

It is hard to resist quoting another relevant sonnet here, a notional ecphrasis by Swinburne from the brilliant set of parodies of fellow poets (including himself) he called his *Heptalogia*. Starting out with a cliche of Academy criticism, it moves in the first line directly to its hilariously accurate send-up of the diction of the poems in *The House of Life* (ranging from clotted contortion to almost Robert Frosty colloquial). In the process, it conjures up a ridiculous notional object. The reader may imagine a number of superimposed transparencies of Rossetti paintings of his various women in their mythological guises, and then read:

Sonnet for a Picture

That nose is out of drawing. With a gasp
    She pants upon the passionate lips that ache
    With the red drain of her own mouth, and make
A monochord of colour. Like an asp,
One lithe lock wriggles in his rutilant grasp.
    Her bosom is an oven of myrrh, to bake
    Love's white warm shewbread to a browner cake.
The legs are absolutely abominable.
    Ah! what keen overgust of wild-eyed woes
    Flags in that bosom, flushes in that nose?
Nay! Death sets riddles for desire to spell,
    Responsive. What red hem earth's passion sews,
But may be ravenously unripped in hell?

One sometimes wanders, in Rossetti's sonnets, in search of an antecedent to a pronoun; here, Swinburne plays with this habit to put the painter-poet into the picture as well.

Public Monuments

In the literary and artistic world of Victorian London, a Rossettian picture, with a poem of his on it, seems almost a public monument to be rhetorically defaced (or as some recent academic criticism has put it, dis-figured). But not *that* monumental: one might consider, for example, Lionel Johnson's verses "By the Statue of King Charles at Charing Cross" (1892). They are addressed to an image of the king who became after his death the subject of what Milton denounced as idolatry, but for an aesthetic, very recent Catholic convert like Johnson becomes a martyr of beauty as well as of faith ("His soul was of the saints; / And art to him was joy"). Yet Johnson also speaks specifically to the figurative significance of the appearance of Hubert Le Sueur's equestrian statue of 1630 in two contexts. One is the midnight urban setting as seen in the poem, empty of life and the commercial and political activity above which it stands. The other is the history of the statue itself, which was buried during the Commonwealth and re-erected in 1674. Indeed, Edmund Waller had addressed it, when in place in Charing Cross, as emblematic of the divinely ordained Restoration:

> That the First Charles does here in triumph ride,
> See his son reign where he a martyr died,
> And people pay that reverence as they pass,
> (Which then he wanted!) to the sacred brass,
> Is not the effect of gratitude alone,
> To which we owe the statue and the stone;
> But Heaven this lasting monument has wrought,
> That mortals may eternally be taught
> Rebellion, though successful, is but vain,
> And kings so killed rise conquerors again.
> This truth the royal image does proclaim,
> Loud as the trumpet of surviving Fame.[51]

For Johnson, the statue's problematic truth is not proclaimed so loudly, but rather obliquely and in the dark. Several stanzas present glimpses of just this matter of setting, oscillating back and forth in their designation of the dead king and the present effigy:

> Comely and calm, he rides
> Hard by his own Whitehall:
> Only the night wind glides:
> No crowds, nor yet rebels, brawl.
>
> Gone, too, his Court: and yet,
> The stars his courtiers are:
> Stars in their stations set;
> And every wandering star . . .

The stars and planets are only figuratively courtiers of the statue whose head, *only when seen at night from below,* they appear to surround. The soul of Charles is then ensconced among them only in heaven and in metaphor. Again:

> Alone he rides, alone,
> The fair and fatal king:
> Dark night is all his own,
> That strange and solemn thing.
>
> Which are more full of fate:
> The stars; or those sad eyes?
> Which are more still and great:
> Those brows; or the dark skies?
>
> .   .   .   .   .
>
> Armoured he rides, his head
> Bare to the stars of doom:
> He triumphs now, the dead,
> Beholding London's gloom.
>
> .   .   .   .   .
>
> And through the night I go,
> Loving thy mournful face.

It is the *poète maudit*—perhaps a figurative "wandering star" himself—in this poem "about London, about loneliness and martyrdom in London," as Johnson's best critic has put it; and "Charles as triumphant artefact becomes an emblem of what the speaker desires to be."[52]

From late antiquity on, poetry could consider such works of art which were objects of public, or private, wonder. In Johnson's poem, the confrontation is of a person with a statue, in a tradition which includes Pushkin's magnificent "Bronze Horseman" and its intricately structured representation of the relation between the poet and the statue of Peter the Great upon which Roman Jakobson wrote so remarkably (raising central questions about the whole issue—most important for modern art—of the difference between sculpture and statuary, which do not arise in this case).[53] But statuary—and sculptured art as statuary—invites praise or, more interestingly, derogation, in a public mode. In one sense, paintings, as well as sculpture, can become statuesque. The writer's experience of the image addressed can obviously itself be affected by the relative public or private status of the object presenting it. Whether a piece is a hitherto neglected or unknown *trouvaille*, or a familiar monument, overglazed or patinaed by anything from ideological viewing to simple gawking, can be significant as a kind of framing agenda for a poetic view of it. Different situations might produce confrontations with, variously, an idolized great masterpiece (the *Mona Lisa*, for example), a perfectly good piece of ancient sculpture politically ensconced (the *Venus de Milo*) and, finally, a piece of monumental statuary, politically conceived to begin with (Bartholdi's Statue of Liberty).

Michelangelo was, of course, not the only major sculptor whose pieces received versified address like Strozzi's.[54] Gian Lorenzo Bernini's seventeenth-century biographer, Filippo

Baldinucci, records a number of them. These include lines by Pier Filippo Bernini on the renowned figure of St. Teresa in ecstasy, in the Cornaro Chapel of Santa Maria della Vittoria:

> So lovely a faint
> Should be immortal;
> But since pain does not rise
> To the Divine Presence,
> Bernini eternalized it in this stone.
>
> [Un sì dolce languire
> Esser dovea immortale;
> Ma perché duol non sale
> A cospetto divino,
> In questo sasso lo eternò il Bernino.][55]

With regard to the matter of sculpture as public monument, it is interesting to consider how looted ancient Egyptian obelisks, set up in cultural triumph in European cities, have also been the focus of poetic address. Tennyson wrote some requested lines to be engraved on the base of Cleopatra's Needle when it was set up in London in 1878. They were never put there, perhaps for obvious reasons:

> Here, I stood in On beside the flow
> Of sacred Nile, three thousand years ago!—
> A Pharaoh, kingliest of his kingly race,
> First shaped, and carved, and set me in my place.
> A Caesar of a punier dynasty
> Thence haled me toward the Mediterranean sea,
> Whence your own citizens, for their own renown,
> Through strange seas drew me toward your monster town.
> I have seen the four great empires disappear.
> I was when London was not. I am here.

"On" is the Hebrew Bible's name for Heliopolis; the fate of the Assyrian, Persian, Greek, and Roman empires points too grimly toward the British one, perhaps. The obelisk is a brooding, silent witness to cycles of pride and downfall; until Tennyson gives it voice, its prophetic message is as indecipherable as its pre-Champollion hieroglyphs. On the other hand, the obelisks in Théophile Gautier's pair of poems, "Nostalgies d'obélisques," are lyric personages, each incapable of studying the nostalgias of the other. The obelisk exiled in Paris yearns for its native place:

> On this square I stand here, bored,
> Odd obelisk—one of a pair—
> Snow, frost, drizzle and rain
> Freeze my already rusted side

And my old needle, reddened in
The ovens of a fiery sky,
Takes on the pallors of nostalgia
In this air which is never blue.

[Sur cette place je m'ennuie
Obélisque dépareillé:
Neige, givre, bruine et pluie
Glacent mon flanc déjà rouilleé;

Et ma vielle anguille, rougie
Aux fournaises d'un ciel de feu,
Prend des pâleurs de nostalgie
Dans cet air qui n'est jamais bleu.]

And the local river now is hardly the Nile:

The Seine, black sewage of the streets
Filthy river of gutter-streams
Defiles my foot which in its floods
The Nile, father of waters, kissed . . .

[La Seine, noir égout des rues
Fleuve immonde fait le ruisseaux,
Salit mon pied, que dans ses crues
Baisait le Nil, père des eaux . . .]

And so forth. But its brother, alone now in Luxor, sees only death and desolation about him:

Sterile, silent, infinite,
The desert, under a dull sun
Toward a horizon limitless,
Unrolls its yellowed winding-sheet.

[A l'horizon que rien se borne
Stérile, muet, infini,
Le désert sous le soleil morne,
Déroule son linceul jauni.]

Likewise full of ennui, his complementary nostalgia is for a living land, to be transported to great Paris and stand by his brother's side in a public place there:

There yonder, he sees living men
Pausing to scan his images,
Hieratic writing whose
Meaning is spelled out in dream.

Fountains there on either side
Play across his granite's dust
Their iridescent spray; and he
Is reddened, and made young once more!

From red veins of Syenite
Like me he nonetheless emerged
But I stay in my ancient place.
He is alive and I am dead.

[Là-bas, il voit à ses sculptures
S'arrêter un peuple vivant,
Hiératiques écritures,
Que l'idée épelle en rêvant.

Les fontanes juxtaposées
Sur la poudre de son granit
Jettent leurs brumes irisés;
Il est vermeil! il rajeunit!

Des veine roses de Syène
Comme moi cependant il sort,
Mais je reste à ma place anciennne;
Il est vivant et je suis mort!]

In "The Great Pyramid," Melville's ecphrastic ventriloquism is not of such a literal sort as Gautier's or Tennyson's. Perhaps it is the matter of awful scale, of mass and geometric simplicity that leads him at first simply to ask "Your masonry—and is it man's? / More like some Cosmic artisan's." But toward the end of the poem, something approaching what Harold Bloom has called the theomorphic character of the object unfolds as the pyramid is identified with its utterance:

All elements unmoved you stem,
Foursquare you stand and suffer them:
Time's future infinite you dare,
While, for the past, 'tis you that wear
    Eld's diadem.

Slant from your inmost lead the caves
And labyrinths rumored. These who braves
And penetrates (old palmers said)
Comes out afar on deserts dead
    And, dying, raves.

Craftsmen, in dateless quarries dim,
Stones formless into form did trim,
Usurped on Nature's self with Art,
And bade this dumb I AM to start,
    Imposing him.[56]

Architectural Ecphrasis

But with the Pyramids the question of architectural ecphrasis arises. Architecture often seems to be perhaps the most totally "public," not to say "political" in many of the senses of that currently abused term. Poetry can be "about" architecture generally, particularly verse which can be said to be expository in any way—discursive poetry with putative subjects. For example, here is Pope, in his 1731 Epistle to Lord Burlington (*Moral Essays*, IV), warning that great impresario of Palladian architecture in eighteenth-century England of the horrors of fashionable imitativeness even as he praises him:

You show us, Rome was glorious, not profuse,
And pompous buildings once were things of Use.
Yet shall (my Lord), your just, your noble rules
Fill half the land with Imitating Fools;
Who random drawings from your sheets shall take,
And of one beauty many blunders make;
Load some vain Church with old Theatric state,
Turn Arcs of triumph to a Garden-gate;
Reverse your Ornaments, and hang them all
On some patch'd dog-hole eke'd with ends of wall,
Then clap four slices of Pilaster on't,
That, lac'd with bits of rustic, makes a Front.
Or call the winds thro' long Arcades to roar.
Proud to catch cold at a Venetian door;
Conscious they act a true Palladian part,
And, if they starve, they starve by rules of art.

Even more brilliant is the satiric description of the villa of the immensely rich vulgarian he calls Timon. Pope starts out with a simple association of huge scale with moral grossness; but it gets even better as it goes on:

Lo, what huge heaps of littleness abound!
The whole, a labour'd Quarry above ground.
Two Cupids squirt before: a Lake behind
Improves the keenness of the Northern wind.
His Gardens next your admiration call,

On ev'ry side you look, behold the Wall!
No pleasing Intricacies intervene,
No artful wildness to perplex the scene;
Grove nods at grove, each Alley has a brother,
And half the platform just reflects the other.
The suff'ring eye inverted Nature sees,
Trees cut to Statues, Statues thick as trees . . .

It is the witty poetry here, not the accurate eye of descriptive architectural prose, which makes two elements of a tediously oversymmetrical system bore each other, put one another—as a sharp trope of putting the spectator—to sleep.

Notional ecphrasis can thus describe both imaginary and paradigmatic structures, as in Pope's case or, even more interestingly, the *experience* of actual structures. Poems can contain ecphrastic descriptions of facades or views, which makes them more like those that confront painting, print, or relief sculpture—or, more interestingly, interior spaces.[57] The very fact that certain architectural monuments often present a number of canonical exterior views, depending upon distance, perspective, and scale, informs Melville's little sequence called "The Parthenon," which in the first section is

Seen Aloft from Afar

Estranged in site,
Aerial gleaming, warmly white,
You look a suncloud motionless
In noon of day divine;
Your beauty charmed enhancement takes
In Art's long after-shine.[58]

Subsequent sections ("Nearer Viewed," "The Frieze," and "The Last Tile") work sequentially in time to represent a sort of cinematic sequence which had not yet been invented.

In the matter of interiors and exteriors, one might consider some of Byron's stanzas, in book 4 of *Childe Harold's Pilgrimage* (1818), on Rome. In the case of the open ruin of the Coliseum, to be within it is still to be outdoors:

Arches on arches! as it were that Rome
Collecting the chief trophies of her line,
Would build up all her triumphs in one dome,
Her Coliseum stands; the moonbeams shine
As 'twere its natural torches, for divine
Should be the light which streams here to illume
This long explored but still exhaustless mine
Of contemplation . . .[59]

These lines generate a typical fiction of reading a structure: the tiered arches are read as if each were a triumphal, rather than a structural, arch, each one celebrating another victory for the forces of the empire. This is a typically brilliant ecphrastic conceit. (It is made all the more effective by its echo of Pope's famous lines, from *An Essay on Criticism*, about the daunting vistas that appear to the seeker of learning—how, after climbing a mountain of study, "Th'increasing Prospect tires our wandring Eyes, / Hills peep o'er Hills, and *Alps* on *Alps* arise!") But consider Byron's representation, in some previous stanzas, not of the dome of St. Peter's, but of what it is like to walk into the church—specifically, to encounter and cope conceptually with its scale (and from a very different point of view from Pope's):

> Enter: its grandeur overwhelms thee not;
> And why? it is not lessen'd; but thy mind,
> Expanded by the genius of the spot,
> Has grown colossal, and can only find
> A fit abode wherein appear enshrined
> Thy hopes of immortality . . .[60]

Byron's lines here remind us that the conventionalized trope of the *genius loci* (the "spirit of a place") peculiar to it and giving it its character can become even more present and palpable in architectural spaces than in natural ones, and that our experience of that space may be construed as that very spirit itself. But Byron continues with his putative spectator moving through St. Peter's:

> Thou movest—but increasing with the advance,
> Like climbing some great Alp, which still doth rise
> Deceived by its gigantic elegance;
> Vastness which grows, but grows to harmonise—
> All musical in its immensities;
> Rich marbles, richer painting, shrines where flame
> The lamps of gold, and haughty dome which vies
> In air with Earth's chief structures, though their frame
> Sits on the firm-set ground—and this the clouds must claim.

The next two stanzas extend this reading of the relation of scale to detail as a parable about our ability to comprehend vastness, not as an epistemological question, but as an aesthetic and moral one. The meditation is remarkable, and I quote it entire:

> Thou seest not all; but piecemeal thou must break
> To separate contemplation the great whole;
> And as the ocean many bays will make,
> That ask the eye—so here condense the soul
> To more immediate objects, and control
> Thy thoughts until thy mind hath got by heart
> Its eloquent proportions, and unroll

In mighty graduations, part by part,
The glory which at once upon thee did not dart,

Not by its fault—but thine. Our outward sense
Is but of gradual grasp: and as it is
That what we have of feeling most intense
Outstrips our faint expression; even so this
Outshining and o'erwhelming edifice
Fools our fond gaze, and greatest of the great
Defies at first our Nature's littleness,
Till, growing with its growth, we thus dilate
Our spirits to the size of that they contemplate.[61]

Byron implies here that our very capacity to *read* structures we confront and move through is capable of being expanded; it need not be a mere registrar of scale, and in this case, of our and its own puniness. Very different from this is the kind of moral distancing from a structure—corresponding in some way to a spatial one—represented by Herman Melville's reading of the tower of Pisa for the relation between mental and structural stresses, strains, and supports:

Pisa's Leaning Tower

The Tower in tiers of architraves,
Fair circle over cirque,
A trunk of rounded colonades,
The maker's master-work,
Impends with all its pillared tribes,
And, poising them, debates:
It thinks to plunge, then hesitates;
Shrinks back—yet fain would slide;
Withholds itself—itself would urge;
Hovering, shivering on the verge,
A would-be suicide![62]

Written in 1820, two years after the publication of Byron's stanzas quoted above, and notable for their account of the relation between sight and sound in an architectural space, are the first two of the three of Wordsworth's "Ecclesiastical Sonnets"[63] written as "Inside of King's College Chapel, Cambridge." At the end of the first of them, for example, the celebrated flamboyant fan vaulting is read as providing enclosures in which choired echoes lurk; the architect is seen as having

fashioned for the sense
These lofty pillars, spread that branching roof
Self-poised, and scooped into ten thousand cells,

> Where light and shade repose, where music dwells
> Lingering—and wandering on as loath to die . . .

Only in the next two, and final, lines of the poem does a simile return the poem to matters beyond "the sense" ("Like thoughts whose very sweetness yieldeth proof / That they were born for immortality"). Interpreting the light in church interiors gets to be almost conventional after this. George Santayana's "King's College Chapel" may or may not be reflecting Wordsworth's directly. After the opening quatrain—

> The buttress frowns, the gorgeous windows blaze,
>   The vault hangs wonderful with woven fans,
> The four stone sentinels to heaven raise
>   Their heads, in a more constant faith than man's.

—it moves quickly to consider darkness and music:

> Long rows of tapers light the people's places;
>   The little chorister may read, and mark
> The rhythmic fall; I see their wandering faces;
>   Only the altar—like the soul—is dark.

Sound and light again return in an analogous meditation of a contemporary English poet, Elizabeth Jennings, in "San Paolo Fuori le Mura, Rome." Yet, like so many later twentieth-century poems, it exhibits some knowledge of art-historical discourse, particularly that of the architectural guide-book, even as it reads the scene in a more subtle way:

> It is the stone makes stillness here. I think
> There could be not so much of silence if
> The columns were not set there rank on rank,
> For silence needs a shape in which to sink
> And stillness needs these shadows for its life.[64]

Whereas in Wordsworth's sonnets, the question of sound is derived from the meditation on light and shadow, this poet starts out in the knowledge of how this particular space and its liturgical function emphasize their reciprocities. (The first line is masterful, incidentally, in the way its sentence break and enjambed verb produce a pause, and a momentary sense of "and thus I think" before the return to the next line sorts the thinking out.) She continues:

> My darkness throws so little space before
> My body where it stands, and yet my mind
> Needs the large echoing churches and the roar
> Of streets outside its own calm place to find
> Where the soft doves of peace withdraw, withdraw.
> The alabaster windows here permit
> Only suggestions of the sun to slide
> Into the church and make a glow in it.

And yet, within the place of withdrawal and of a "past-dreamt-of peace," the aesthetic domain of the senses makes its final, almost moral claim on the meditation in the last stanza in an almost Paterian moment:

> For me the senses still have their full sway
> Even where prayer comes quicker than an act.
> I cannot quite forget the blazing day,
> The alabaster windows, or the way
> The light refuses to be called abstract.

Conversely, Rilke's meditation on another celebrated church interior is so silent as not to be broken even by the mention of silence itself. And in "San Marco" (from the 1908 *Neue Gedichte*) the matter of darkness and light—the light reflected from gold, in particular—is historical and institutional in its significance, and preserved, reflected light is a trope for a present both enriched by, and imprisoned in, a past:

> In this interior which, as if hollowed out,
> winds and vaults itself in the golden cobalt
> round-cornered, sleek, oiled with deliciousness
> this City's darkness was retained and piled
> up in secret, as a counterpoise
> to the light that so multiplied in all
> its objects that they nearly passed away.

> [In diesem innern, was die ausgehöhlt
> sich wölbt und wendet in den goldnen Smalten,
> rundkantig, glatt, mit Köstlichkeit geölt,
> ward dieses Staates Dunkelheit gehalten
> und heimlich aufgehäuft, als Gleichenwicht
> des Lichtes, das in allen diesen Dingen
> sich so vermehrte, das sie fast vergingen.]

The enthusiastic reading of structural detail as emblematic, but hardly in the reductive mode of the Renaissance emblem books, marks Hart Crane's great "Proem: To Brooklyn Bridge," with its ultimate complex prayer to its vaulting span to "descend / And of the curveship lend a myth to God." Such details can produce conceits from simple matters of engineering like stable equilibrium—

> And Thee, across the harbor, silver-paced,
> As though the sun took step of thee, yet left
> Some motion ever unspent in thy stride,—
> Implicitly thy freedom staying thee!

—and playing upon two senses of "staying": restraint and support. Or two separate readings of the formal structure—one focusing on the web of vertical cables, with a suggestion of a giant Aeolian harp, the other directed at the major contour—can be combined in acknowledgment that such a combination is effected by the energies of the ecphrastic imagination itself ("O harp and altar, of the fury fused, / (How could mere toil align thy choiring strings?"). Or the same structure when viewed at night—the darling of urban photography:

> Again the traffic lights that skim thy swift
> Unfractioned idiom, immaculate sigh of stars,
> Beading thy path—condense eternity:
> And we have seen night lifted in thine arms.

On the other hand, a bridge can be read ecphrastically as ancient and present monument. In a fine sonnet of 1874, Longfellow gives voice to the Florentine *Ponte Vecchio*, allowing the bridge itself to interpret emblematically the movement of water under it as a learned poet might:

The Old Bridge at Florence

> Taddeo Gaddi built me. I am old,
> >Five centuries old. I plant my foot of stone
> >Upon the Arno, as St. Michael's own
> >Was planted on the dragon. Fold by fold
> Beneath me as it struggles, I behold
> >Its glistening scales. Twice hath it overthrown
> >My kindred and companions. Me alone
> >It moveth not but is by me controlled.
> I can remember when the Medici
> >Were driven from Florence. Longer still ago
> >The final wars of Ghibelline and Guelph.
> Florence adorns me with her jewelry;
> >And when I think that Michael Angelo
> >Hath leaned on me, I glory in myself.

The conceit of a bridge or a river city holding subversive force in check may have come to Longfellow from Spenser (it figures in *The Faerie Queene*). The allusion to the jewelry sold in the shops along the bridge, and the quasi-typological connection between St. Michael and Michael Angelo, are both elegantly deployed to complement it. But Hart Crane's major trope of connection—of bridging as itself a metaphor for metaphor itself—is not in the least at issue here; the privileged architectural figure is of surmounting water, not linking populous regions.

It may be noticed that among architectural structures which elicit special modes of ecphrastic attention fountains are of some interest. Bernini's familiar fountain in Piazza di Spagna in Rome was done at the behest of Pope Urban VIII. As Baldinucci (see above) reports,

In the middle of the basin, almost as if it were rising and falling in the midst of the sea, he placed a fine and graceful ship. From several parts of the ship water gushed forth abundantly, as if from so many cannons. This concept seemed so beautiful to the Pope that he did not scorn to illustrate it with the following lines:

> The papal war machines dispersed not flames
> But sweet waters that kill the fires of war.

> [Bellica Pontificum non fundit machina flammas
> Sed dulcem, belli qui perit ignis, aquam.][65]

But (as Baldinucci cannot refrain, however crossly, from reporting) some anonymous wag attached to the fountain itself an answering couplet to the effect that the Urban Poet could make fountains of poems, but not poems of a fountain, and thus it was that poetry pleased itself. Speaking not as by, but for, the fountain, the poem itself condemns the laudatory good faith of such poetry. But the experience of fountains—what draws us near to them and prompts reverie in an antithetical analogue of what Gaston Bachelard characterized as the meditative attraction of fire—would await late romantic and modern poetic interpretation. In another instance, Baldassare Castiglione wrote the celebrated lines speaking for (and as) a statue of Cleopatra made into a fountain by Pope Leo X, which Pope paraphrased; the almost inevitable matter is of the queen now, as a fountain, being given leave, after centuries, to weep (and thereby being connected with Niobe, who "Still, tho a rock, can thus relive her woe, / And tears eternal from the marble flow.").[66] There are very few poems, however, which attain the vividness and energy of the wonderful description of the Trevi Fountain in Rome in chapter 30 of Hawthorne's *The Marble Faun.*

One or two instances of special situations involving the architectural framing of an image might be noticed here. A poem's putative observer may have to approach a wall to peer at, or into, an *intimiste* painting or tiny print in a gallery or room or, conversely, stand back and look up high at a mural or inset panel (as in the case of Washington Allston's poem, below). The bulk of George Santayana's verses on King's Chapel, mentioned earlier, catalogues the biblical scenes in the stained-glass windows that he, rather than the iconographically innocent choir-boys, is mandated to read, and to meditate upon in the fading light of historical faith:

> The twilight deepens, and the blood-dyed glories
> Of all these fiery blazonings are dim.
> Oh, they are jumbled, sad, forgotten stories!
> Why should ye read them, children? Chant your hymn.

> But I must con them while the rays of even
> Kindle aloft some fading jewel-gleam
> And the vast windows glow a peopled heaven,
> Rich with the gathering pageant of my dream.

Eden I see, where from this leafy cover
    The green-eyed snake begins to uncoil his length
And whispers to the woman and her lover,
    As they lie musing, large, in peaceful strength . . .

On the other hand, for Thomas Warton, in the later eighteenth century, the occasion of a painted glass window—almost a modern color transparency—by Sir Joshua Reynolds in the Gothic wall of an Oxford college poses no specific narrative or iconographic questions. (The window, executed by Thomas Jervais, presents a large elevated central panel of an Adoration of the Shepherds, with separate figures, ranged each in a separate light below this, of Temperance, Fortitude, Faith, Charity, Hope, Justice, and Prudence.) Instead, style is at issue, and the question of neoclassic modernity, and the realm of the painterly, superseding Gothicity. And yet Warton allows the Gothic—and primarily the architecture and the romantic darkness it generates—to take its best shot.[67] The whole first part of his poem is spoken by an antithetical poet, who protests—with an almost Blakean self-deconstructing stance,

Ah, cease to spread the bright transparent mass,
With Titian's pencil, o'er the speaking glass!
Nor steal, by strokes of art with truth combin'd
The fond illusion of my wayward mind!

Having been a lover of Gothic, he confesses,

    enraptured have I lov'd to roam
A lingering votary, the vaulted dome,
Where the tall shafts, that mount in massy pride,
Their mingling branches shoot from side to side.

This is the place

Where SUPERSTITION, with capricious hand
In many a maze the wreathed window plann'd,
With hues romantic ting'd the gorgeous pane,
To fill with holy light the wondrous fane . . .
To suit the genius of the mystic pile
Whilst as around the far-retiring ile,
And fretted shrines with hoary trophies hung,
Her dark illumination wide she flung,
With new solemnity, the rooks profound,
The caves of death, and the dim arches frown'd . . .

Given the Miltonic hell evoked by the quoted "caves of death," this is a realm of "darkness visible." But a second poetic persona takes over, one who praises Reynolds for banishing such darkness, however "romantic," and who, eschewing the old rigidity of mullioned fragments, makes a newer technology come to the aid of the genius of painting, and who

> calls the lineaments of life compleat
> From general alchymy's creative heat;
> Obedient forms to the bright fusion gives,
> While in the warm enamel Nature lives.

Indeed,

> Reynolds, tis thine, from the broad window's height
> To add new lustre to religious light:
> Nor of its pomp to strip this ancient shrine,
> But bid that pomp in proper radiance shine:
> With arts unknown before, to reconcile
> The willing Graces to the Gothic pile.

There are political issues lurking behind the matter of a stained-glass window for an English poet. Puritan iconoclasm had taken its toll of so many of these in English churches in the seventeenth century that, for an Anglican bishop like Richard Corbett (in a volume published in 1648), the iconography of the windows is again not the question; the remarkable fact of their having uniquely survived destruction becomes what the poet sees. "Upon Fairford Windows" meditates upon the twenty-eight stained-glass windows of biblical scenes in the church of St. Mary the Virgin in Fairford, Gloucestershire. Corbett's lines address the Puritans as "anti-saints," mocking their own use of the term "saint" for the elect, denouncing their rhetoric and doctrine, and alluding to their destruction of memorial brasses and windows, and to the fact that Blackfriars Church, the neighborhood of a glass factory, was a Puritan stronghold.

> Tell me, you anti-saints, why glass
> With you is longer-lived than brass?
> And why the saints have 'scaped their falls
> Better from windows, than from walls?
> Is it because the Brethren's fires
> Maintain a glass-house at Blackfriars?
> Next which the church stands north and south,
> And east and west the preacher's mouth?
> Or is't because such painted ware
> Resembles something that you are,
> So pied, so seeming, so unsound
> In manners, and in doctrine found
> That, out of emblematic wit,
> You spare yourselves, in sparing it?
> If it be so, then, Fairford boast
> Thy church hath kept what all have lost,
> And is preserved from the bane

> Of either war, or Puritan,
> Whose life is colored in thy paint:
> The inside, dross, the outside, saint.

The wit here is fierce: all of the properties of the windows which might easily be praised are here taken negatively, and shown to figure their putative destroyers' faults. On the other hand, Corbett's contemporary, William Strode, in these lines from "On Fairford Windows," reads the same glass for its mute homiletic truth. He starts out with a characteristic demurrer about the power of language to do justice to visual art, which is nonetheless undercut by the two senses of "coloured"—literal (as applied to art), and figurative (as applied to language, where it means, in fact, rhetorical colors or figures):

> I know no paint of poetry
> Can mend such coloured imagery
> In sullen inke: yet, Fairford, I
> May relish thy fayre memory.
>   Such is the Echo's fainter sound,
> Such is the light when sun is drowned;
> So did the fancy look upon
> The work before it was begun:
> Yet when those shows are out of sight
> My weaker colours may delight.
>   Those Images so faithfully
> Report true feature to the eye
> As you may think each picture was
> Some visage in a looking-glass . . .
> Each pane instructs the Laity
> With silent eloquence: for here
> Devotion leads the eye, not ear,
> To note the catechizing paint,
> Whose easy phrase doth so acquaint
> Our sense with Gospel that the Creed
> In such a hand the weak may read
> Such types even yet of virtue be,
> And Christ, as in a glass we see.[68]

The particular *virtus vitri* is highlighted here by the sense, previously introduced, of "glass" as "mirror"—and hence, conventionally, as meaning a true representation—in the last line.

The conventional tetrameter couplet of the seventeenth century serves for these observations, just as the public mode of the essayistic heroic couplet frames Warton's address. Only in a later age would a poem—in this case, a pair of sonnets—addressing a stained-glass window seek to form a kind of diptych itself. Rilke's "Adam" and "Eve" in the 1908 *Neue Gedichte* commences with parallel and reciprocal openings. By this means they themselves refigure an earlier visual convention in which spatial location may figure typological relation. For Adam's "Dazed, he stands at the cathedral's steep rise, near the rose-window, as if affrighted by the apotheosis" [Staunend steht er an der Kathedrale / steilem Aufstieg, nah der Fensterrose, / wie ershcreckt von der Apotheose], there is Eve's "Simply, she stands at the cathedral's great rise, near the rose-window, holding the apple in the 'apple pose'" [Einfach steht sie an der Kathedrale / grossem Aufstieg, nah der Fensterrose, / mit dem Apfel in der Apfelpose].

Photographs

Poetic readings of photographs raise other questions. While one seldom sees them before the later nineteenth century (Herman Melville's, in *Battle-Pieces*, may be a very early instance) the particular aura of the daguerreotype—with its highly reflective surface and somewhat fleeting image—is a special instance. Poems on daguerreotype portraits (where the pictures themselves are almost always lost), such as Rilke's "Portrait of My Father as a Young Man" ("Jugend-Bildnis meines Vaters") must be carefully considered in this regard. Its talk is of erasures and cloudings and indiscernibilities ("obliterated as if we did not understand / and dulled deep in its own depths" [ausgelöscht als ob wirs nicht verständen / und tief aus seiner eignen Tiefe trüb]. In the penultimate line, "Du schnell vergehendes Daguerreotyp" should not be rendered as "quickly fading photograph": the conditions of evanescence would be misplaced.[69]

Recent poetry has been concerned with photographs as invented pictures in themselves—given the history in the twentieth century of various notions and counternotions of "art" photography—as well as with their documentary status. But the fact remains that most poems on photographs are still directed to portraits and that, indeed, photography is the most authentic contemporary form of portraiture. The documented trace of a past personal presence is always compelling. Then, too, the photographic portrait has captured an actual moment of the sitter's experience. A painted portrait is generated in a complex set of imaginative revisions, associations, and transformations of an encounter, *dal vero*, between sitter and painter; what it produces is a kind of essence. But post-Paterian modernist sensibility sanctifies the momentary, and whatever essentiality is thereby revealed. A successful portrait climaxes a problematic quest; a successful photographic one is the result of a kill.

A few unusually powerful poems anticipate or recapitulate some of the theoretical writing about the epistemological and moral status of photography which has become a fashionable intellectual question. An example of this is one of a group of six poems by David Ferry on photographs by Thomas Eakins. Again, the contemplation of a portrait, it raises—among others—the question of the impersonality of the camera—the fact that it, unlike the maker of other sorts of print (let alone the painter), has no memory, and that its associative imagination is limited to its reduction of presence to trace, to projected shadow. In the poem, the camera's unknowing is implicitly seen as reflecting a lack of self-knowledge in the sitter (fig. 9):

9. THOMAS EAKINS, *Cowboy in Dakota Territory*

*Plate 134. By Eakins. "A cowboy in the West.
An unidentified man at the Badger Company Ranch."*

His hat, his gun, his gloves, his chair, his place
In the sun. He sits with his feet in a dried-up pool
Of sunlight. His face is the face of a hero
Who has read nothing at all, about heroes.
He is without splendor, utterly without
The amazement of self that glorifies Achilles
The sunlike, the killer. He is without mercy
As he is without the imagination that he is
Without mercy. There is nothing to the East of him
Except the camera, which is almost entirely without
Understanding of what it sees in him.
His hat, his gun, his gloves, his homely and
Heartbreaking canteen, empty on the ground.[70]

This sonnet-like poem is full of deliberate patternings, phonological ("Achilles / The sunlike, the killer") and syntactic ("He is without mercy / As he is without imagination that he is / Without mercy"). They seem to be reaching out to the reductions of the photograph, acknowledging visual pattern but refusing to ascribe any more reflectiveness to the picture as to the sitter. Its near-rhyming final couplet completes the sequence of patternings by revising the repetition of the inventory taken in the third line and amplifying the enjambment there ("his place / In the sun," with its discovery of an augmented meaning of "place"): coming down strongly on "and" as if it were a substantive, and an item in the list, the "homely and / Heartbreaking" concludes the reading of the photograph with an appeal to feelings that works like a conceptual moralization in older poetic and pictorial traditions.

Prints Generally

Some other photographic ecphrases will be considered below, but in general, the subgenre itself is of very recent lineage. It might be remembered that photographs (unlike daguerreotypes, which are in fact a sort of monotype), are prints; and that engravings, etchings, lithographs, vignettes, become increasingly important for modern ecphrastic poetry. They are frequently encountered in books—amidst, or otherwise accompanying, printed text—and can appear to leap out at the reader—who has suddenly become a gazer—with a kind of suddenness that approaching a painting or piece of sculpture in a gallery or church seldom provides. It is significant that so many of Baudelaire's poems allusive of works of art will invoke prints[71]—by Goya, Callot (see below), Goltzius, Vesalius, John Mortimer, et al.)—whereas the other great ecphrastic poet of the mid–nineteenth century, Dante Gabriel Rossetti—will almost invariably address paintings. It should also be remembered that paintings from the fifteenth through the early nineteenth centuries were frequently engraved or etched with accompanying verses, almost as if to turn the image into an emblem. For example, Watteau's little painting (in the Kimbell Art Museum in Fort Worth) of children playing gets its title, *L'Heureux âge d'or,* from some verses attached to an engraving of it, which radically misread the image. The print is read through a moralizing agenda.[72]

Varieties of Ecphrastic Agenda

An exemplary case—unusually well documented—of a poem reading a picture not only in a moralizing way, but through a prior mental image, is that of an obscure text by Wordsworth. The rather bad poem known as "The Gleaner" originally appeared under another title, "The Country Girl," in *The Keepsake* (1829), to accompany an engraving after a rather bad painting by James Holmes (1777–1860) (fig. 10). In a letter to his wife and sister in March 1828, the poet reported that he had "written one little piece, 34 lines, on the Picture of a beautiful Peasant Girl bearing a Sheaf of Corn. The Person I had in mind lives near the Blue Bell, Fillingham—a sweet Creature, we saw her going to Hereford." The lines start out with what seems to be more of an evocation of the "Person . . . in mind" than the conventionally Greuze-like sim-

10. J. HOLMES, engraving after *The Country Girl*

pering figure in the engraving (whose locks, if from summer skies, could only be from those of a summer night):[73]

> That happy gleam of vernal eyes,
> Those locks from Summer's golden skies,
>   That o'er thy brow are shed;
> That cheek—a kindling of the morn,
> That lip—a rose-bud from the thorn,
>   I saw; and Fancy sped
> To scenes Arcadian, whispering, through soft air,
> Of bliss that grows without a care;
> Of happiness that never flies—
> (How can it where love never dies?)
> Of promise whispering, where no blight
> Can reach the innocent delight;
> Where Pity to the mind convey'd
> In pleasure is the darkest shade,
> That time, unwrinkled grandsire, flings
> From his smoothly-gliding wings.

The poem's account of the girl the poet sees dissolves as Fancy (here perhaps hand in hand with sentimental pictorial conventionality) takes over, and the poem's rhyme scheme becomes one of tetrameter couplets. There is nothing of the picture here; the poem takes actual notice of it only in the last two sections, and even there (Wordsworth may have seen the painting itself), it is ultimately the sheaf of grain that marks the subject for him:

> What mortal form, what earthly face,
> Inspired the pencil, lines to trace,
> And mingled colours that could breed
> Such rapture, nor want power to feed?
> For, had thy charge been idle flowers,
> Fair damsel, o'er my captive mind,
> To truth and sober reason blind,
> 'Mid that soft air, those long-lost bowers,
> The sweet illusion might have hung, for hours!
>
> Thanks to this tell-tale sheaf of corn,
> That touchingly bespeaks thee born,
> Life's daily tasks with them to share,
> Who, whether from their lowly bed
> They rise, or rest the weary head,
> Do weight the blessing they entreat
> From heaven, and *feel* what they repeat,
> While they give utterance to the prayer
> That asks for daily bread.

Whether Wordsworth had seen the painting—and thus could literally invoke "mingled colours"—or only the engraving, the opening lines of the second stanza are eighteenth-century cliche; it is perhaps appropriate that they still belong to the illusory realm of the earlier part of the poem, the realm that is denied in the egregious pentameter line ending the section. The last—and best—stanza reads the sheaf of wheat narratively, rather than emblematically. As a detail, it is "tell-tale," and forces the poet into a new identification of the subject, even as an iconographic sign or attribute in an earlier picture would identify a figure as mythological, or biblical.

The poem, interestingly enough, implicitly becomes a Wordsworthian anecdote of an act of noticing, as well as making its point that those who deal with wheat can more meaningfully utter the Lord's Prayer. The girl in the picture is identified as a working, authentically praying sort of farm girl, resting a "weary head," and associated with the actual "sweet creature" he had "in mind," not the kind of pictorial creature looking out coquettishly—at any viewer of the engraving—from under her bonnet. The poem finally turns to the picture in affirmation of a reality principle, but at the price of art-critical reality. The final line returns to the trimeter and the rhyme of the third and sixth ones at the very opening, even as another sort of moralizing Fancy—briefly telling the tale of the "sheaf of corn"—concludes in its own whispering.

But it should be added that Wordsworth is capable of several modes of ecphrastic reading. There is the sonnet "To Lucca Giordano," written in 1846, on a painting of Cynthia and Endymion (probably a copy of the one in Verona) brought back to England by Wordsworth's son John. Of interest are the fifth through the eighth lines, with their psychologizing narrative reading, and its concluding personal recollection (fig. 11).

> Giordano, verily thy Pencil's skill
> Hath here portrayed with Nature's happiest grace
> The fair Endymion couched on Latmos-hill;
> And Dian gazing on the Shepherd's face
> In rapture,—yet suspending her embrace,
> As not unconscious with what power the thrill
> Of her most timid touch his sleep would chase,
> And, with his sleep, that beauty calm and still.
> O may this work have found its last retreat
> Here in a Mountain-bard's secure abode,
> One to whom, yet a School-boy, Cynthia showed
> A face of love which he in love would greet,
> Fixed, by her smile, upon some rocky seat;
> Or lured along where green-wood paths he trod.

Sometimes a poem will address the known or imagined circumstances of the composition of the work of art itself. While this might tend to become merely anecdotal, it is often more than that. Ezra Pound's extremely Browningesque little reading of a reclining Venus, then still ascribed to Jacopo del Sellaio, in the National Gallery ("The Picture," 1912) neatly finesses the mythological subject, and just as characteristically ignores the iconographic *elements* (the putti, for example). It seemingly speaks only of the living studio model, now long dead: "The eyes of this dead lady speak to me / For here was love, was not to be drowned out. / And here desire, not to be kissed away." Surely Venus is not the dead lady; and yet "here was love . . . and desire," which are just that immortal goddess's domain. In a subsequent epigram "Of Jacopo del Sellaio," Pound turns from the subject to the painter, and perhaps plays with the *Greek Anthology topos*, mentioned earlier,[74] a joke about Praxiteles' Cnidian Aphrodite who asks, "When did he see me naked?": "This man knew the secret ways of love" (and here, Pound echoes Swinburne's description in "A Ballad of Death," where Venus's garments are painted with "all the secret ways of love"). Pound continues,

> No man could paint such things who did not know.
> And now she's gone who was his Cyprian,
> And you are here, who are "The Isles" to me.

Which is, after all, to imply that Jacopo painted his model as Venus; that the model died; that

11. LUCA GIORDANO, *Cupid and Psyche*

Venus, immortal, survives; that the ambiguous "you"—whether the Poundian poet's supposed lady, or the residual surviving image on the canvas (whose survival is our best trope of Venus's immortality)—mirror the mimetic process by being Venus-as-you.

A particularly deft witty turn is given to some ecphrastic lines on an Italian evening landscape of Corot (fig. 12); they form part of a generally expository and ecphrastic verse essay on the Salon of 1839, "A Trois Paysagistes" (Bertin, Aligny, and Corot) by Théophile Gautier. Gautier has just finished describing a sunlit scene by Aligny on the Roman *campagna*, "embrasé et feconde," with a group of laborers resting "classically posed" [dans des poses antiques]— "A simple group, calm in its easy grace, / Which Poussin might have limned, and Virgil loved." (This and the following lines are in Richard Howard's lovely translation.) Immediately thereafter there follows a consciously Virgilian pastoral transition:

> But now the evening creeps down from the hills,
> The shadows deepen and their kingdom's come:
> The green sky glistens with lemon and with orange—
> The sunset frays, and shortens its bright fringe.
> The cricket leaves off—nothing can be heard

12. COROT, *Italian scene*

But the murmuring stream that spins itself away . . .
High above the world, the silent hours
Twist their long, brown, nocturnal tear-stained braids
And barely enough light is left to see,
Corot, your modest name in the black corner.

[Mais voici que le soir du haut des monts descend:
L'ombre devient plus grise et vas s'enlargissant;
Le ciel vert a des tons de citron et d'orange.
Le couchant s'amincit et va plier sa frange;
La cigale se tait, et l'on n'entend de bruit
Que le soupir de l'eau qui se divise et fuit
Sur le monde assoupi les heures taciturnes
Tordent leurs cheveux bruns mouillés des pleurs nocturne.
A peine reste-t-il assez de jour pour voir,
Corot, ton nom modeste écrit dans un coin noir.]⁷⁵

Long before cubist painting would incorporate printed letters and words with a new sort of
formal and semiotic simultaneity, Gautier here claims the artist's signature (indiscernible at
the lower left in almost any reproduction) for a bit of implicit allegorizing: the "modesty" of

the signature is associated with the dimming of egotism, like the surface of the stream stretching away into darkness, whose *soupirs* are audible in, and by means of, the ecphrastic transcription itself.

Gautier's final lines take him and the reader away from all this with a wrench; we are immersed in fog and rain, "Sur un pavé de boue et sous un ciel de suie" [Over a muddy pavement, under a sooty sky] and ejected into the streets of cold, wet, northern Paris. His whole poem starts out with the urbanely casual discourse of a journalistic critic, and moves more and more, in its readings of a sequence of scenes and images, toward a guarded sublimity. It also belongs to the class of "gallery poems," composed before the nineteenth century, mostly of the purely notional, and frequently satiric, ecphrases mentioned earlier. In these, a walk through a sequence of pictures itself occasions a quasi-narrative expository structure; when, in the nineteenth and twentieth centuries, the private gallery becomes a public museum, there arise the complex social and institutional distinctions between a palace of art and the city around it that begin to be touched on here. Yeats's "The Municipal Gallery Revisited" also engages this genre.

Consciousness of the institutional history of art involves knowledge of invisible penumbras of information framing an object. One remarkable instance of the matter of provenance drifting in like a ghost to haunt a poetic ecphrasis is that of Herman Melville's poem, called "The Coming Storm," from his *Battle-Pieces* of 1866. Its title is from the painting it addresses, one of a number of Adirondack landscapes by Sanford R. Gifford. Melville had seen this one, shortly after Lincoln's death, at an annual exhibition of the National Academy of Design in New York. Melville's subtitle identifies the painting—it shows a lake in the foreground and high, storm-clouded mountains behind—and adds that it was "owned by E. B." Only the first three lines of the second quatrain read anything in the painting directly, and the poem moves quickly to the matter of the presence, almost *in* the painting for him, of "E. B." Edwin Booth was playing Hamlet in Boston when he learned that his brother, John Wilkes Booth, had assassinated Lincoln (and thereby killed his own country's father). From the opening lines—with their obsessive repetition of the word "feel"—and thereafter, the poet is feeling for, and with, the former owner of the painting. He senses the dramatic ironies of foreknowledge, of what can, even casually, be said to "antedate":

> All feeling hearts must feel for him
> 　　　Who felt this picture. Presage dim—
> Dim inklings from the shadowy sphere
> 　　　Fixed him and fascinated here.
>
> A demon-cloud like the mountain one
> 　　　Burst on a spirit as mild
> As this urned lake, the home of shades.
> 　　　But Shakespeare's pensive child

> Never the lines had lightly scanned,
>   Steeped in fable, steeped in fate;
> The Hamlet in his heart was 'ware,
>   Such hearts can antedate.
>
> No utter surprise can come to him
>   Who reaches Shakespeare's core;
> That which we seek and shun is there—
>   Man's final lore.

As Robert Penn Warren remarked so cogently, "Melville concludes that such horrors are no surprise to those who, like Edwin Booth, have reached the core of Shakespeare's tragic vision."[76]

A final, pathological instance—of an actual iconic poem which is nonetheless notional—is one by Filippo Baldinucci, Bernini's biographer (quoted above). It is addressed to "a large and beautiful piece of marble" out of which Bernini had prepared to carve a figure of Time (as unveiler of Truth, to match his carving of Truth as Unveiled by Time). But he never got to do it; and Baldinucci confesses that he eventually wrote the following lines, as if spoken by the marble block:

> From my ancient rock,
> To give me breath, and voice—
> Yet not voice only, and breath, but motion and flight—
> An artist, unique in the world,
> Dragged me out one day, and his hand
> Wanted, with busy chisel
> And careful hammer
> Pounding vital blows down on me,
> To make a stupendous image of Time.
> When contented and satisfied
> To have conceived such a notion,
> He spoke aside to himself thus:
> "Can, then, your hands, accustomed
> Only to eternalize heroes
> Make manifest amongst us
> Glories readied for a cruel tyrant
> Who seeks to destroy
> Whatever beauty art and nature have made?
> Your loveliest works
> Perhaps fear the severity
> Of his ravenous bite
> And to beg for peace

Do you feel you need so to honor him?
No: because true virtue
Despite our Age remains forever whole."
Therefore his hand and his gaze
Turned to another object
And broke off, thinking of me no more.
With him fled my hope
Of having any life, alas:
And I remained, as ever, a stone.

[Dall'antica mia rupe,
Per darmi spirto, e voce;
Man non pur voce, e spirto; e moto e volo
Fabro, che al mondo è solo
Trassemi un giorno e già volea la mano
Coll'industre scalpello,
E'l discreto martello
Piombar sopra di me colpi vitali,
Per far del Tempo una stupenda imago;
Quando contento e pago
Di aver con mente un tal pensiero espresso
In tal guisa parlò volto a se stesso:
Dunque tue man potranno,
Avezze solo ad eternare eroi,
Far veder qui fra noi
Glorie apprestarsi ad un crudel tiranno,
Che distrugger procura
Quanto feron di bello arte, e natura?
L'opere tue più belle
Temon forse rigore
Di suo dente vorace,
E per chiedergli pace,
Ti fie d'uopo di fargli un tale onore?
No: perchè virtù vera
Malgrado dell'Età fia sempre intera,
Quindi la mano e'l guardo
Ad altro oggetto ei volse,
E senza più pensar da me si tolse.
Con lui fuggi mia speme
D'aver più vita, ahi lasso,
Ed io qual sempre fui restai di sasso.][77]

The wit here is more pointed than it seems: if Bernini had indeed honored Time—the destroyer of artists and of their stone images—by carving the figure, then the piece of stone would not have remained so relatively lifeless. But now, its potentiality vitiated for a more precarious life (if for John Donne, Death must die, then even more literally will "Time" [= Bernini's carved figure] be ruined by—and in—Time), it remains dead rock, less liable to be broken. Yet poetic language has given it more than enough *voce, e spirto* to be able to testify to the inner monologue of the sculptor who refused to give it another life. The poem addresses not a Michelangelesque stone image hidden in the rock, but one hidden in the thought of the sculptor who will, for vengeful reasons, never give it expression. (Or, at least, not in that form: Time, a bronze skeleton with an hourglass, unveils Truth on Bernini's famous Tomb of Alexander VI.)

Like notional ecphrases in romance narrative, extended readings of pictures can unfold a sequence of details—whether seen or inferred—throughout a stanzaic structure. We might look at part of Giambattista Marino's longish poem, from *La Galeria*, on Titian's painting of a repentant Magdalen (ca. 1535) now in the Pitti Palace in Florence (fig. 13). In fourteen stanzas of *ottava rima* it constructs its own blazon—or catalogue (usually erotic)—of features (refraining from remarking on the iconographically standard ointment pot, for example). The second stanza does indeed address the crucial narrative matter of the weeping and, in Titian's figure, of the hair:

> See how she makes her plaint to him, and how
> She waters the pale April of her face
> And, former burdens laid down from her heart,
> She moans now with a languid look, and modest;
> And falling, her wild tresses make a golden
> Necklace here for her naked alabasters;
> Those tresses once bound others, now herself,
> Bound her to earth, now heaven; she weeps and prays.

> [Ecco come con lui si lagna e come
> Del volto irriga il palidetto aprile,
> E, deposte del cor l'antiche some,
> Geme in sembiante languido ed umile;
> E fanno inculte le cadenti chiome
> Agl'ignudi albastri aureo monile;
> Le chiome, ond'altrui già, se stessa or lega,
> Già col mondo, or coil cielo; e piagne e prega.]

Successive stanzas consider, with appropriately baroque and detailed figurative elaboration: her eyes, tears, tresses, mouth, and hand (presumably the right one, at once expressive and semiotic in its pointing heavenward. Of the tears, for example, Marino declares that "Not the sea with pearls adorned, nor with stars / The sky, as you adorn her lovely face" [Non così

13. TITIAN, *Maddalena*

'l mar di perle, il ciel di stelle, / S'orna come di voi s'orna il bel viso]. And he continues in the next stanza not to look at the painting at all, but rather into his own trove of *meraviglia*, of wit. The "you" here are probably the tears:

> They were living mirrors, your pure and mournful crystals,
> In which the soul discerned itself; the soul
> Saw, when it had aspersed itself in you
> The paths, oblique, of its long wandering,
> There where she submerged as in the ocean
> Sins too grave and far too shameful, when
> To bathe those holy feet, she loosened you
> Her hair being the veil in which she wrapped them.

[Fûr viv specchi, in cui l'alma si scerse,
I vostri puri e flebili cristalli;
E vide, allor che 'n voi se stessa asperse,
De'suoi sì lunghi error gli obliqui calli;
Là dove quasi in pelago sommerse
I gravi troppo e vergognosi falli,
Quando a lavar que santi piè vi sciolse
E fûr le chiome il velo onde gli avolse.]

The elaborate pictorial matter of Titian's handling of the figure's hair—its activity and mass, the light, the formal and painterly rhythms in its disposition—might perhaps be thought of as present before the next stanza:

Tresses which, loosed in a precious downpour,
Wove over roses, over frozen dew,
O blessed are you, for in an older fashion
Loose and careless, let down and dispersed,
You near the heights which even Berenice's
Fabulous lock can never quite attain!
Amber defers to you, and gold, who only
Touched that foot to which the sun is subject.

[Chiome, che, sciolte in preziosa pioggia,
Su le rose odeggiate e su le brine,
Beate o voi, che 'n disusata foggia,
Incomposte e neglette e sparse e chine,
Quell'altezza appressaste ove non poggia
Di Berenice il favoloso crine
Ceda a voi l'ambla e l'or, poscia che sole
Quel piè toccaste e cui soggiace il sole.]

The hand, two stanzas later, in particular, "looks" more like the rhetorical pattern of "erotic then—divine now" than it responds to the painted one: "Pure hand, who were once the impure mistress / Of filthy arts and lewd accomplishments . . . Ah, with what a sweet and loving care, / Generous minister of merciful deeds / —As, recently, of pain and woe to swains / You were the snare and chain of the human god" [Candida man, che già maestra impura / Fosti d'immondi studi e d'artifici . . . Ahi! con che dolce affetüosa cura, / Larga ministra di pietosi uffici, Come dianzi de'vaghi affano e pena, / Fosti de l'uman Dio laccio e catena]. The catalogue concludes with this hand, at the bottom of the painting: the gaze of wonder has read down to it, starting with the eyes. Ultimately, what all these delights add up to for Marino is that both nature and truth yield to imagination: the painted image is so beautiful and alive because the "learned artificer," Titian [dotto artefice] had her so "in his soul and his mind."[78]

Nearly all the other poems in Marino's *La Galeria* are quite short. There are, in particular, many sonnets scattered among the more frequent *madrigali*, or shorter epigrams. When Wordsworth, revising Milton, reconstructed the English sonnet into the epitome of the short meditative lyric, it seemed to provide an almost inevitable form for poems addressed to works of art. This may be partially due not only to the scale, but to the possibilities, in a sonnet's interior structure, of developing rhetorical figurations of a whole range of visual elements in the object of the poem's attention. The very visual format of a printed sonnet, picture-like rather than song-like or even page-like, may be of relevance here; and even in the case of Rossetti's unvarying convention—influenced by the Italian—of carefully separating, in a stanza-like way, octave and sestet, the pattern is put to mimetic use: background/foreground, and image/interpretation are some of the oppositions paired across the divisions of the versification. From Washington Allston's few fine sonnets on paintings, through Wordsworth's and Rossetti's, we can see the development of a sort of subgenre. The fin-de-siècle American Trumbull Stickney, for example, allows it to shape his mythopoetic reconstruction from a piece by Rodin, *L'Illusion, fille d'Icare* (fig. 14). His title (rather touchingly, for a reader who knows of a vague strain of incestuous longing in many of his poems) misremembers Rodin's. The brief memorial is of a myth even more belated than Keats's Psyche:

On Rodin's "L'illusion, Soeur d'Icare"

She started up from where the lizard lies
Among the grasses' dewy hair, and flew
Thro' leagues of lower air until the blue
Was thin and pale and fair as Echo is.
Crying she made her upward flight. Her cries
Were naught, and naught made answer to her view.
The air lay in the light and slowly grew
A marvel of white void in her eyes.
She cried: her throat was dead. Deliriously
She looked, and lo! the Sun in master mirth
Glowed sharp, huge, cruel. Then brake her noble eye.
She fell, her white wings rocking down th'abyss,
A ghost of ecstasy, backward to earth,
And shattered all her beauty in a kiss.[79]

The unrolling of the little narrative is continuous here throughout the sonnet. On the other hand, Yeats, in his famous "Leda and the Swan," revises the Rossettian pattern by confining his (half-notional) ecphrasis to the octave, retreating into an interpretive distance in the first half of the sestet, and, finally, distancing himself so totally that the verb tense changes to the preterite in the last three lines. A contemporary American like Robert Mezey also finds the sonnet a perfect space in which to confront a wonderful etching of Edward Hopper's in his "Evening Wind."

14. RODIN, *l'Illusion, fille d'Icare*

The length, and even the typographic scale, of a poem may or may not reflect the scale of a work of art it engages. In Douglas Crase's meditation on Jackson Pollock's *Blue Poles*, for example, the poet does not shrink from confronting the immediate matter of scale—the vastness of the painting (about 7 feet by 16) is indeed most initially prominent. The poem "enters" the painting so totally (in conception rather than narratively, as one might discursively enter a landscape scene)—even in the opening act of seeming to have left it behind—that its reading of where the present place of description in fact *is* remains totally figurative. Crase's opening "topic" of scale might be likened to the matter of whiteness as deployed by A. C. Swinburne in his poem on a painting of Whistler's (see p. 191). But the poem moves directly into its central and thereafter unrelenting trope of mapped landscape and represented experience:

> What we bring back is the sense of the size of it,
> Potential as something permanent is, the way a road map
> Of even the oldest state suggests in its tangled details
> The extent of a country in which topography and settlement
> Interrupt only at random into a personal view . . .[80]

On the other hand, Donald Davie's charming little "Cherry Ripe" playfully picks up what the knowledge and sensibility behind it understand as a problematic emphasis on "subject-matter" in the title of Juan Gris's extremely flat 1915 painting, *The Cherries*, with a typically geometric structure in which some cherries on a tablecloth generate the only curved—but otherwise none too prominent—forms. Very prominent in and for the poem is Thomas Campion's early seventeenth-century song (beginning "There is a garden in her face") with its famous refrain about the lady's lips, "There cherries grow which none do buy / Till 'cherry-ripe' themselves do cry." This is itself doubly resonant, in quoting from the canonical street-cry of the London cherry-vendors—"cherry ripe, ripe ripe"—and even echoing its melody in the musical setting of the phrase. Davie's meditation starts out with observing that when cherries ripen, their shape does not swell or change the way other fruits' may, and which would "spoil the ripening that is art's alone":

> This can be done with cherries. Other fruit
> Have too much bloom of import, like the grape,
> Whose opulence comes welling from a root
> Struck far too deep to yield so pure a shape.
>
> And Cherry ripe, indeed, ripe, ripe I cry;
> Let orchards flourish in the poet's soul
> And bear their feelings that are mastered by
> Maturing rhythms, to compose a whole . . .[81]

Davie quotes Campion's refrain—with his interpolated "indeed" as an acknowledgment of his figurative revision of it—in his own metamorphosis of the erotic conceit into a matter of cubist painting, of music into another mode of rhythm, composing, and feeling. But it is not just "a picture of cherries" (even, indeed, some Chardin cherries, say) which has raised for him the matter of what might be called *encampioned cherry-ripeness*—it was specifically these particular few Juan Gris cherries, in this painting, which is itself framed in its own art-historical presence.

Trumbull Stickney's sonnet supplied a mythopoetic narrative for Rodin's figure without any other prior one to tell his tale against. When, in modernity, longer narrative poems take off from pictures, they can, like Stickney, supply a story when none seems in any way given; this is a little like taking an image, assuming it illustrated a moment in some narrative, and reframing the image as illustration by writing the narrative. (Most notional ecphrasis, as has been noted, occupies moments of pause in an unfolding narrative, whether in verse or prose.) There is a series of fragmentary actual ecphrases—some perhaps identifiable as spotlighting details in paintings by Poussin, Claude, and Titian, among others—at the end of Keats's "Sleep and Poetry." But they inventory the pictures in the room of Leigh Hunt's house in Hampstead in which Keats goes to sleep at the end of a day whose recounting has been touched with several unacknowledged ecphrastic glimpses, so that the acknowledged pictures form a kind of recapitulation. On the other hand, when the picture in question is just that sort of narrative painting anyway, there is little injustice done to the image, and little to be gained by the poem in a struggle against that image's own powerful story. Browning's "In a Gondola" is such a case. Daniel Maclise's narrative painting *The Serenade* was exhibited in 1843 with some lines of Browning as a catalogue entry; they are those putatively spoken by the man in the gondola, singing to the woman looking down at him; they were written from a prose ecphrasis of the painting, and only after he had seen it did Browning include the more specifically ecphrastic material in the last four lines quoted here:

> I send my heart up to thee, all my heart
> On this my singing.
> For the stars help me, and the sea bears part;
> The very night is clinging
> Closer to Venice's streets to leave one space
> Above me, whence thy face
> May light my joyous heart to thee its dwelling-place.

But Browning went on to compose an elaborate narrative, in a sort of sung dialogue between the man and the woman, of over 230 lines, ending in betrayal and violence of a sort that the sentimental shadowing on the night scene in the painting is implicitly shown to have repressed.

Richard Howard's wonderful, willful misreading of Caspar David Friedrich's *The Chalk Cliffs of Rügen* is still somewhat Browningesque in its use of dramatic monologue for narrative innuendo. Writing considerably before Friedrich's current vogue, Howard knowingly substitutes for the established identities of the three figures in the painting (the artist, his wife, and brother) a fictional trio of "Franz," "Ottilie," and "Walther." The poem's rambling dramatic monologue reconstructs the moment of the painting, what the three figures looking across the water at the dramatic white cliffs have recently been doing, and are now doing, through a series of remarks on art and life mixed with personal gossip during a sort of high-minded picnic. Then, after 115 lines, the poem concludes with an actual ecphrasis of the landscape (and thereby of part of the painting) by one of the characters in it, and the narrator finally confronts the problem of self-identity:

> There are two boats
> on the Hiddensee. The sun,
> hewing the cliffs, is mighty now. Perhaps
> we have discovered what their shape, sharp
> against the water beyond,
> reminds us of: it is a womb, a birth,
> a spanning of the earth no longer
> just a grave, delivering
> Ottilie splayed against her alder-stump,
> and Walther sprawled at the verge, and Franz
> under his birch. So we are
> born, each alone, in chaos while that waiting
> silence glows.
> And you will never know
> which of us has told you this.[82]

We are reminded by the stunning coup of closure, and in the same instant, that we have suspended the question of which of these three figures in the painting is indeed speaking out of it, of which one is indeed the narrator and that we are never to find out. At the same time, the poem ends up by leading us back into the major problem posed for us by all those Friedrich *Rückenfiguren,* or figures seen from behind facing a landscape perhaps as a surrogate for the viewers of the painting. Their faces—and, in a novelistic context, their identities—are always averted from our knowledge and our gaze.

Less well known is the momentary pause, at the beginning of Robert Duncan's beautiful "Poem Beginning with a Line by Pindar," for an ecphrasis of a rather obscure Goya painting of *Cupid and Psyche* in Barcelona (fig. 15). The second strophe plunges right into a longish reading of the painting that moves into mythography and, as in the last two lines quoted here, into a blending of the consciousness of the gazing viewer with those of the figures viewed:

> In Goya's canvas Cupid and Psyche
> have a hurt voluptuous grace
> bruised by redemption. The copper light
> falling upon the brown boy's slight body
> is carnal fate that sends the soul wailing
> up from blind innocence, ensnared
>   by dimness
> into the deprivations of despairing sight.
>
> But the eyes in Goya's painting are soft,
> diffuse with rapture absorb the flame.
> Their bodies yield out of strength.
>   Waves of visual pleasure
> Wrap them in a sorrow previous to their impatience . . .[83]

Perhaps the limiting case for a contemporary poem on a painting is John Ashbery's long and complex "Self-Portrait in a Convex Mirror."[84] There is insufficient room to discuss it in detail here. But it may be observed that Francesco Parmigianino's celebrated anamorphic self-portrait (fig. 16) becomes, as the object of elaborately digressive meditation, a skewed representation of a skewed representation. This itself comprises, in its intense mimetic function, another sort of figurative mirror in which the self-portrait of the artist generates an image of the poet at work, and thereby of anyone at the rest of life. It starts out with a casual ecphrasis (the opening sentence seems syntactically to start with the poem's—and the picture's—title), but concentrates on the hand in the foreground.

> As Parmigianino did it, the right hand
> Bigger than the head, thrust at the viewer
> And swerving easily away, as though to protect
> What it advertises. A few leaded panes, old beams,
> Fur, pleated muslin, a coral ring run together

15. GOYA, *Cupid and Psyche*

> In a movement supporting the face, which swims
> Toward and away like the hand
> Except that it is in repose. It is what is
> Sequestered . . .

This sequestering, this sense of "life englobed," is a major trope of the first part of the meditation, worked through in momentary allegorizations such as

> The surface
> Of the mirror being convex, the distance increases
> Significantly; that is, enough to make the point
> That the soul is a captive, treated humanely, kept
> In suspension, unable to advance much farther
> Than your look as it intercepts the picture.

16. Francesco Parmigianino, *Self-Portrait in a Convex Mirror*

The ever-problematic gaze of the subject in self-portraiture is compounded here by the matter of the distortion, and by that of the mirroring of viewer's gaze as well. The poem moves remarkably in and out of attention to the painting, anecdotes about its composition, citations of commentaries on it (e.g., Vasari, and the contemporary art-historian Sidney Freedberg), and multifaceted reflections (in the meditative sense of the word) on art's own reflectiveness of itself and what is around it, on time and chance and intention. The inaccessibility of the image in, *on*, the curvature points toward

> the strict
> Otherness of the painter in his
> Other room. We have surprised him
> At work, but no, he has surprised us
> As he works . . .

The poem not only reads the painting, but reads the readings that it itself gives to it, and develops a remarkable extended fiction which encloses, and comes to terms with, "This otherness, this / 'Not-being-us'" which seems, at bottom, "all there is to look at / In the mirror." The poem makes its own title mirror, anamorphically in a world of trope, Parmigianino's—indeed, a good part of the poem might be said to concern the ulterior agenda of what could be meant by the identity of the titles. The painting invites us to read, and the refusal to yield up, except in a warping of the warpings of perspective, its depths. This is what we have seen at the heart of most such encounters, and the deeper the poem is empowered to reach, the more the heart of the painting recedes into its own fictive space.

Conclusion

These observations may well conclude with a look at a notional ecphrastic text, interestingly problematic in its form as well as in the theoretical questions it raises. A serious and amusing undoing of the merely picturesque, it nonetheless avoids any brush with the lofty or profound sublime. The text is from a series of prose poems by Leigh Hunt called "Dreams on the Borders of the Land of Poetry." The seventh one, "An Evening Landscape," opens with a question suggesting that what follows will be a sort of shaped poem, whether emblematic in the seventeenth-century way, or in the modern mode of Guillaume Apollinaire or e. e. cummings, but in any case one whose text itself—as we have seen—supplies its own image, and whose emblem provides its own motto. But Hunt's fancy raises more interesting questions for ecphrastic poetry. Here it is entire:

> Did any body ever think of painting a picture in writing? I mean
> literally so, marking the localities as in a map.
>
> The other evening I sat in a landscape that would have enchanted Cuyp.
>
> Scene—a broken heath, with hills in the distance. The immediate picture
> stood thus, the top and bottom of it being nearly on a level in the perspective:

Trees in a sunset, at no great distance from the foreground
A group of cattle under them, party-coloured
principally red, standing on a small landing place;
the Sun coming upon them through the trees.
A rising ground   A rising ground
Broken ground.
with trees.   with trees.
Another landing place, nearly on a level
with the cows, the spectator sitting and looking at them.

> The Sun came warm and serious on the glowing red of the cattle, as if
> recognising their evening hues; and everything appeared full of that quiet spirit of
> consciousness, with which Nature seems rewarded at the close of its day labours.[85]

This "picture painted in writing" frames a good, deep joke about ecphrasis to which we shall return in a moment. But first, it may be observed that the larger issue of art inventing nature is proleptic here of Wilde: we may remember that Vivian, in "The Decay of Lying," remarks that a particular sunset he was asked to admire was "simply a very second-rate Turner," and that "Nature gives us, on one day a doubtful Cuyp, and on another a more than questionable Rousseau." I seem to remember that Whistler, when someone remarked that an evening walk along the Embankment had revealed a prospect just like one of his Thames *Nocturnes,* replied, "Ah yes, Madam, Nature is creeping up." In the case of Hunt's little text, that Nature had crept up to Cuyp—probably by the mid–eighteenth century in England—is figuratively confirmed by the sun's coming "warm and serious on the glowing red of the cattle, as if recognising their evening hues." (And as if recognizing their kinship in pigment.)

The little lesson about ecphrasis, on the other hand, is less outrageous but more original. The typographic "scene" is not, indeed, a *calligramme* of the notional painting itself. Cuyp would have had a lot of sky; and to correct for this, a more literally mimetic text would have had to double the height of the ruled borders to create a squarer rectangle, and fill the top with something like

---

A Dutch Sky with

Bunched and

L a y e r e d

C l o u d s

Instead, we have what is unambiguously *text.* The largest objectified visual masses—the trees—come first in an order of cataloguing that extends, verse-like, down the page. Then, too, word order and line order can only momentarily serve as troped figures for the visual images their words designate. Trees, cattle, and "landing place," in the first three "lines," are all named in lines of type correspondingly layered, and the phrase "under them" is self-descriptive. But in line four, the sun is no longer "under," and the two extensions of "rising ground / with trees" on either side require at least the resources of Miltonic verse—something like "And with other trees / A rising ground" might map them more appropriately. It would be irrelevant, however, to demand that Hunt anticipate Apollinaire or e. e. cummings, and have the type set up as "Bro^{k}en gr$_o$u$_n$d" or the like. There is a nonfunctional, counterproductive "enjambment" of "nearly on a level / with the cows," probably so arranged for the trivial symmetry of a traditional inscription-pattern.[86] But it would have been far more effective in a pseudo-pictorial way had the line broken at "nearly on a / level with the cows," thus "nearly" placing the cows on—in—the same line of type that frames the spectator's viewpoint.

We may also observe that the ruled box includes said spectator, as if C. D. Friedrich-like, from behind, as a Dutch landscape would not. The presence, simultaneously in and outside the scene, of the spectator of the painter-poet is finally connected with "that quiet spirit of consciousness with which nature seems rewarded at the close of its day labours"—the consciousness itself ambiguously bestowed upon the scene—and thus to inhere in it, until darkness falls. And what can so reward nature but poetry itself, pretending to do the more obviously, but less eternally rewarding, work of painting?

In their various modes, ecphrastic poems purport to speak up for the silent picture, to make it speak out in some way. But poems are writing, and what "speaks" in iconic poems is their use of a complex set of generic, schematic, formal, and other rhetorical conventions. These can range from the elemental way in which lines of verse follow one another by being vertically stacked, and having to be read downward in sequence, to the intricate sort of allegorizing of sonnet structure as foreground/background, event followed by interpretation, letter leading to anagoge, which will be seen below (p. 151) in the parable of octave-sestet in a great sonnet by Rossetti on a painting by Leonardo da Vinci. All ecphrastic writing, whether in verse or prose, must exploit deeper rhetorical design as well as respond to a number of more obvious considerations. These would include, for example, the matter of scale: the scale of writing and of parts of the written text as well as of reading the image. Then, too, there is the identification—and thereby, often, the construction—of parts or elements of the image being addressed: selection among these, and ascriptions of relative primacy or ancillary quality, of relative prominence and importance. There is the emergence of some explanatory or interpretive agenda, perhaps only after an initial or conventional one has been worked through. In every case there may be—at some level—possible mimesis of elements in the image, be they purely narrative, iconographic, formal, or, in pictorial and poetic modernity, formally and structurally semiotic.

Critical or analytic expository ecphrasis in prose may start out with what would be, interpretively speaking, "the bottom line," or else gradually argue toward it. But the structure and form of poetic "argument" are another matter. For there the text's own schemes and tropes—patterns and fictions—elicit or insinuate meanings from or in the image. The moment of gazing at, and being somehow gazed at, by any work of art becomes an authentic poetic occasion, as enabling for poetry from Wordsworth and Coleridge to our own time as any epiphanic flash of transcendence—any revelation of what Gerard Manley Hopkins called "inscape"—from the surface of the ordinary, focused and empowered in the depths of the poetic consciousness. An ecphrastic poem is not occasional in the way a hireling laureate's birthday ode might be, but rather, for a true poet, the scene of the occurrence of some internal occasion. Even satirical literary verse, perhaps wanting in high seriousness, according to some critical perspectives, takes up the challenge of some falsity or bad faith—often in an image propounded as a public monument—with the force of imaginative revelation.

The silence of images may itself constitute anything from a Gorgon's deadly stare to the wondrous labyrinth of a Gordian knot; from an erotic object to be possessed by language, to the trace of an absence; from a virginal object untouched yet by interpretation, to a noble but fallen captive, ill-used by false expositors. In any case, the poem engaged in an encounter with the presence of such otherness, such an absence of and from the body of discourse, will often be led to an awareness of the problematic nature of its own mode of existence, of its own consciousness.

Coleridge appended to a scene of his play *Remorse* some lines in praise of Titian:

> Who, like a second and more lovely Nature
> By the sweet mystery of lines and colours
> Changed the blank canvas to a magic mirror,
> That made the absent present; and to shadows
> Gave light, depth, substance, bloom, yea, thought and motion.[87]

In short, he *animated*—both as we use the word today to mean drawn images in motion pictures, and in the sense of a sort of ensoulment—those representations. Giving them "thought" is still close to the old ecphrastic ideal of giving them voice. Giving them motion, anticipating a kind of visionary cinema with which poems engage static pictures, notional or actual, is the province of major poetry from Milton on. And thus at one further remove, these verses apply as well to the figurative painting of verse, turning the blank page, the silent gaze, into a speaking mirror of the nature of art.

PREFACE TO THE GALLERY

In the section that follows, images in the plates are paired with the texts of poems. Occasionally, several poems will address the same painting, print, or piece of sculpture, and sometimes the discussion will wander into an adjoining pairing. The reader may want to read some of these poems while looking at the picture, and in some instances to cover the picture or only return to it after. Each of the poem-image encounters is different, and it is a function of these differences which will determine how the reader will ultimately want to deal with the pairing. The format used here is the one of optimum flexibility. I have added some rather informal footnotes of acknowledgment and identification; they are not numbered, but keyed to the principal poem-picture pairing in each case.

This could be thought of as a sort of overcatalogued gallery, save that the texts of the poems are part of the exhibition. The pairings are arranged chronologically, according to the date of publication of the primary poem; in some instances, like the opening portrait and poem, additionally adduced poems and images may span a considerable period of time. Throughout, however, the reader may perceive a periodic evolution of ecphrastic agendas: Renaissance and baroque praise for the mimetic powers of the painter and *enargeia* of the piece, or an emblematic perception, however reductive, yields—unsurprisingly—to a romantic conflation of the reading of a work with a celebration of the experience of encountering it. It is, finally, only in modernity that some acknowledgment of the medium will be noticed. It will also be observed that a considerable number of these poems address sculpture, although, characteristically, less and less in the modern period.

A quirky prolegomenon to all poetry about pictures is Richard Lovelace's brilliant but neglected little epigram, from his *Lucasta* (1648), "Upon the Curtain of Lucasta's Picture, It Was Thus Wrought":

> O stay that covetous hand—first turn all eye,
> All depth and mind, then mystically spy
> Her soul's fair picture, her fair soul's, in all
> So truly copied from th'original
> That you will swear her body by this law
> Is but its shadow, as this, its—now draw.

The hand that desires to unclothe the painting—as it might desire to unclothe a living person, or even a painted one—is enjoined to pause, and momentarily refigure touch as sight, to become "all eye, / All depth and mind." With a lurking pun on "turn," it is subsequently urged to avert its gaze as well as its touch, and "turn all eye" away from the palpably visible, to some unpainted image of Lucasta's soul. It is perhaps implied that, for a moment, vision turns all platonic *nous* to comprehend an idea, to "mystically spy" it. The elegant syntactic chiasmus of "her soul's fair picture, her fair soul's" here suggests a mirroring and, by extension, that the fairness of the image will appropriately represent the fairness of the soul it figures. And so appropriately, in fact, that it momentarily convinces even the lusting eye and hand that her body is only the "shadow" or picture of her soul (or even of her soul's picture—invisible, but open to meditation). It is only now that the addressee may have access to the painter's "shadow" of the embodied Lucasta. It is only at the end of this cycle of figurations—of bridgings of Plato's "three removes" that separate the painting of the couch from its ideal form—that the material painting of Lucasta's clothed body, still hidden by its conventional curtain, may be seen, thanks to the now licensed services of the hand. The final punning overtone of "draw" perhaps implies that by drawing aside the curtain, the addressee—now at the end confirmed as the *reader* of a notional text notionally wrought on a notional curtain hiding a notional picture of a notional poetic mistress—will be thereby "drawing" or painting that image, realizing it by interpreting the poem. In any event, issues invoked here—of desire, and troped desire, for persons and images; of hand and eye and mind; of curtains of intervening text—have been seen as central to contemporary considerations of what happens when poetic language touches on visual image. The reader has been implicitly invited to consider the first section of this book as a curtain pulled across the exhibits in this textual gallery.

—Now draw.

THE GALLERY

Anon., *Laocoön*

The Poem of Jacobus Sadoletus on the Statue of Laocoon

From heaped-up mound of earth and from the heart
Of mighty ruins, lo! long time once more
Has brought Laocoon home, who stood of old
In princely palaces and graced thy halls,
Imperial Titus. Wrought by skill divine
(Even learned ancients saw no nobler work),
The statue now from darkness saved returns
To see the stronghold of Rome's second life.
What shall begin and what shall end my lay?
The hapless father and his children twain?
The snakes of aspect dire in winding coils?
The serpents' ire, their knotted tails, their bites?
The anguish, real, though but marble, dies?
The mind recoils and pity's self appalled,
Gazing on voiceless statues beats her breast.
Two serpents flushed with rage gather in coils
To one loose ring, and glide in winding orbs,
And wrap three bodies in their twisted chain.
Scarce can the eyes endure to look upon
The dreadful death, the cruel tragedy.
One serpent darting at Laocoon's self,
Enwraps him all, above, below; then strikes
With poisonous bite his side; the body shrinks
From such embrace. Behold the writhing limbs,
The side that starts recoiling from the wound.
By keen pain goaded and the serpent's bite,
Laocoon groans, and struggling from his side
To pluck the cruel teeth, in agony
His left hand grapples with the serpent's neck.
The sinews tighten, and the gathered strength
Of all his body strains his arm in vain;
Poison overcomes him; wounded sore he groans.
The other serpent now with sudden glide
Returned, darts under him its shiny length,
Entwines his knees below and binds him fast.

The knees press outward, and the leg compressed
By tightening windings swells; the blood confined
Chokes up the vitals and swells black the veins.
His sons no less the same wild strength attacks,
And strangles them with swift embrace and tears
Their little limbs; even now the gory breast
Of one whose dying voice his father calls
Has been its pasture; round him wrap its coils
And crush him in the mighty winding folds.
The other boy, unhurt, unbitten yet,
Uplifts his foot to unloose the serpent's tail;
His father's anguish seen he stands aghast,
Transfixed with horror—his loud wailings stay,
His falling teardrops stay—in double dread.

Then ye, the makers of so great a work,
Great workmen, still in lasting fame renowned
(although by better deeds a deathless name
Is sought, although to some it was given to leave
A higher talent far to coming glory).
It is noble still to seize what chance is given
For praise, and strive the highest peak to gain.
It is yours with living shapes to quicken stone,
To give hard marble feeling till it breathes.
We gaze upon the passion, anger, pain,
We all but hear the groans, so great your skill,
You famous Rhodes of old extolled. Long time
The graces of your art lay low; again
Rome sees them in a new day's kindly light,
She honors them with many a looker on,
And on the ancient work new charms are shed.
Then better far by talent or by toil
To increase the span of fate, than still increase
Or pride or wealth or empty luxury.

(Translated by H. S. Wilkinson)

One of the most famous examples of ancient sculpture became the object of a celebrat-
ed occasion for theorizing. The *Laocoön* group, probably of the second century B.C., was already
celebrated by Pliny, who ascribed it to the sculptors Hagesander, Polydorus, and Athenodorus
of Rhodes and acclaimed it as superior to any other work of painting or sculpture. It was
rediscovered in 1506 in a vineyard on the Esquiline Hill in Rome, quickly identified as the

group mentioned by Pliny, particularly admired by Michelangelo, copied, drawn, and reconstructed often in the sixteenth century and celebrated in a number of Renaissance Latin poems. The group depicts a terrifying moment in the story of Troy which befell the noble and wise Trojan Laocoön (he had been skeptical enough to throw a spear into the side of the Trojan horse to agitate—and prove to the other Trojans the existence of—the Greeks hidden therein). As Virgil tells it, having been chosen Neptune's priest by lot, Laocoön

> Was on the point of putting to the knife
> A massive bull before the appointed altar,
> When ah—look there!
> From Tenedos, on the calm sea, twin snakes—
> I shiver to recall it—endlessly
> Coiling, uncoiling swam abreast for shore,
> Their underbellies showing as their crests
> Reared red as blood above the swell; behind
> They glided with great undulating backs.
> Now came the sound of thrashed seawater foaming;
> Now they were on dry land, and we could see
> Their burning eyes, fiery and suffused with blood,
> Their tongues a-flicker out of hissing maws.
> We scattered, pale with fright. But straight ahead
> They slid until they reached Laocoön.
> Each snake enveloped one of his two boys,
> Twining about and feeding on the body.
> Next they ensnared the man as he ran up
> With weapons: coils like cables looped and bound him
> Twice round the middle; twice about his throat
> They whipped their back-scales, and their heads towered,
> While with both hands he fought to break the knots,
> Drenched in slime, his head-bands black with venom,
> Sending to heaven his appalling cries
> Like a slashed bull escaping from an altar,
> The fumbled ax shrugged off. . . .
> Laocoön had paid, and rightfully,
> For profanation of the sacred hulk
> With his offending spear hurled at its flank.

—Aeneid 2.203–31, tr. Robert Fitzgerald

(It might be added that the effect of these sufferings is to bring upon the Trojans even greater ones: impressed with the vividness of the punishment, the Trojans let the horse in. The terror breeds what will turn out to be folly among those upon whom it registers, a point not lost on later commentators like Lessing.)

The sculpture, probably designed at least a century and a half before Virgil wrote, depicts this moment in the story, although differing considerably in detail. When uncovered in the sixteenth century, Laocoön's right hand (as well as that of his elder son, reaching up below it, and some other pieces) were missing; the arm we now have was restored, at one time by a diagonally outstretched one, but later by the familiar one grasping the snake high above the figure's head.

One sixteenth-century Latin poem claims that the missing arm was appropriate retribution for Laocoön's having thrown his spear at the horse's wooden side ("Quanta est iam numinis ira, / dextera, quae laesa est machina, trunca perit"). But by all accounts the finest poetic tribute paid to the piece in the sixteenth century was by Jacopo Sadoleto (1477–1547). Sadoleto's poem remained extremely influential as a reading of the group up through the eighteenth century. It is given above in the canonical translation by H. S. Wilkinson.

Commencing with the wonder of the uncovering of the piece—and perhaps a gesture toward Pliny's praise of it—the poem proclaims the marble's rebirth in a reborn Rome. The formulaic sort of rhetorical question of classicizing poetry ("What shall begin and what shall end my lay?") is interestingly revivified here: the old matter of "How can I ever describe what it was like when? . . . Where shall I start?" doubles with an ecphrastic question: "Where shall I start out in my description of this complex, active, mute, but agitated image?" The implicit catalogue of the opening questions reads Father, Sons, Snakes, Anguish. But the detailed ecphrasis of the piece with which the poem starts answering its own questions follows the sinuous lines of the snakes in its present-tense narrative. It is narrative not of what happened (as, e.g., Virgil recounted it), but of what *is happening* in—which is to say, as one gazes at—the marble group. It is as if the active sinuosity of the snakes provided a cue in scanning the piece; in any event, they are the active agents, creating the grouping in the first place by their attack on all three, creating an ad hoc sort of family group of their own. Sadoleto repeatedly remarks on Laocoön's inaudible groaning; at the end of the first "section" (marked only in the translation: in the Latin it ends in midline, and there are no breaks) the son's suppressed cries (as expressed in his face) seem implicitly to invoke the total silence of the whole scene, of the group, of sculpture generally. (The Latin is most expressive here: "Et iam iam ingentes fletus, lachrymasque cadentes / Anceps in dubio retinet timor.")

The poem's concluding section returns to the piece as monument, as well as to an old issue in the poetic praise of visual image. It is commended as work of a skill so great as, indeed, to have given life to inert matter,

> . . . to quicken stone,
> To give hard marble feeling till it breathes.
> We gaze upon the anger, passion, pain,
> We all but hear the groans, so great your skill
>
> [Vos rigidum lapidem vivis animare figuris
> Eximii, et vivos spiranti in marmore sensus
> Iserere, auspicimus motumque iramque doloremque,
> Et pene audimus gemitus]

The traditional ecphrastic matter of giving voice to silence is implicitly—and likewise traditionally—handled in the praise of the workmanship for creating figures whose voices one can almost hear. Sadoleto concludes—again, in a way which is subtly paradigmatic for later poems addressing works of art—with an implicit acknowledgment of the reciprocal virtues of his own age (and perhaps, its spirit speaking in his poem): "Rome sees them in a new day's kindly light" [quos rursum in luce secunda / Roma videt].

This poem was itself celebrated and well known. J. J. Winckelmann pointedly refers to it in the passage on the Laocoön group from his 1755 *On the Imitation of the Painting and Sculpture of the Greeks*, which, eleven years later, occasioned Lessing's "Essay on the Limits of Painting and Poetry" called *Laocoön*. This is Henry Fuseli's rather ecstatic translation of 1765:

> It is in the face of Laocoon this soul shines with full lustre, not confined however to the face, amidst most violent sufferings. Pangs piercing every muscle, every labouring nerve; pangs which we almost feel ourselves, while we consider—not the face, nor the most expressive parts—only the belly contracted by excruciating pains: these however, I say, exert not themselves with violence, either in the face or gesture. He pierces not heaven, like the Laocoon of Virgil; his mouth is rather opened to discharge an anxious overloaded groan, as Sadoleto says; the struggling body and the supporting mind exert themselves with equal strength, nay balance all the frame.

The matter of the groan is totally absent from the excellent, compact reading of the group given by that celebrated (particularly in Germany) poetic pictorialist of the eighteenth century, James Thomson. In book 4 of his long poem, *Liberty* (1736), in which he also gives ecphrases of the *Apollo Belvedere* and the Hercules Torso, her "marble race," Sculpture at last finds "her utmost masterpiece":

> That Maro fired—the miserable sire,
> Wrapt with his sons in fate's severest grasp.
> The serpents, twisting round, their stringent folds
> Inextricable tie. Such passion here,
> Such agonies, such bitterness of pain
> Seem so to tremble through the tortured stone
> That the touched heart engrosses all the view.
> Almost unmarked the best proportions pass
> That ever Greece beheld; and, seen alone,
> On the rapt eye the imperious passions seize—
> The father's double pangs, both for himself
> And sons convulsed; to heaven his rueful look,
> Imploring aid, and half accusing, cast;
> His fell despair with indignation mixed,
> As the strong curling monsters from his side
> His full extended fury cannot tear.

More tender touched, with varied art, his sons
All the soft rage of younger passions show.
In a boy's helpless fate one sinks oppressed;
While, yet unpierced, the frighted other tries
His foot to steal out of the horrid twine.

—*Liberty* 4.185–207

Given that even Lessing was unsure about the date of the group, and about whether or not Virgil's lines were known to the Rhodian sculptors, the line "That Maro fired—the miserable sire" (it tends to imply a relation somewhere between "That Maro sired" and "That Maro inspired"; neither, of course, was the case) was not egregious in the eighteenth century. These are lines which, to some degree, Milton fired: the inverted syntax is put to expressive pictorial use throughout (e.g., the last two lines, in which the perfectly plausible metrical and syntactic option "tries / To steal his foot," and so forth, yield to the inversion which, for the reader, momentarily tangles the foot just a bit in the twines of the syntax). Somewhat Miltonic, too, is the momentary allegorizing of the snakes ("in fate's severest grasp"). But more significant is that the outcry, or moan, or shriek, is not considered, and that something approaching Winckelmann's concerns—the classical triumph of heroic serenity even amidst *agon*—begins to surface in the lines about how the pain that seems to "tremble through the tortured stone" occludes for the viewing eye "the best proportions . . . that ever Greece beheld."

Lessing, in his great declaration of the respective independences of the arts of poetry and visual image, evinces no love for the kind of literary pictorialism so well known in Thomson's *The Seasons.* His great essay on the Laocoön group and what had been said about it makes the crucial points that whereas poetry can range over time in its representation of the course of an action, visual expression must represent a moment in that course, and that the particular resources of each art must generate paradoxes in attempts of each to represent elements of the other. The piece itself; the moment it occupies in the story of the fall of Troy, whether Virgilian or not; issues of expressed pain and anguish, on the one hand, and represented heroic dignity, on the other, and the way the relation between them might constitute a mode of beauty—all these constitute the text upon which *Laocoön* is a far-ranging and profound commentary, after which the concept of *ut pictura poesis* would never be the same.

Byron's Childe Harold in Rome pauses for a stanza over the Laocoön group; and although his lines amount to little more than a dutiful caption, they nonetheless pay their rhetorical homage with good grace. The last six lines, with their Miltonically entwined syntax, the phonological patterning of "the long envenom'd chain / Rivets the living links" and the "pang on pang . . . gasp on gasp" construction which he had used in an earlier stanza on the Coliseum ("arch on arch") all work up a bit of rhetorical pictorialism of their own.

> Or, turning to the Vatican, go see
> Laocoön's torture dignifying pain—
> A father's love and mortal's agony
> With an immortal's patience blending. Vain
> The struggle; vain, against the coiling strain
> And gripe and deepening of the dragon's grasp,
> The old man's clench; the long envenom'd chain
> Rivets the living links, the enormous asp
> Enforces pang on pang, and stifles gasp on gasp.
>
> —*Childe Harold's Pilgrimage* (1818), 4.160

But unlike the stanzas on the *Apollo Belvedere* which immediately follow (see p. 137), there is no touch of allegorization here, and the matter of the "torture dignifying pain" acknowledges much traditional commentary on the piece.

On the other hand, William Blake's engraving of the Laocoön group (done around 1820) is by way of being a satiric cartoon and, as always with Blake, of the highest seriousness. The whole is labeled "*Yah* [in Hebrew, for English 'Jehovah'] & his two Sons Satan & Adam as they were copied from the Cherubim of Solomons Temple by three Rhodians & applied to Natural Fact. or History of Ilium." The whole field of the engraved plate is filled with aphorisms about Art, Religion, and Money; but it is clear that the agony of the sculptured group is being taken for that of a kind of cosmic double bind, the Angel of the Divine Presence and his creatures being caught together in the twistings of remorse and of the consequences of a Creation which was itself a Fall. The minor nineteenth-century American poet and novelist Josiah Gilbert Holland (1819–81) was undoubtedly innocent of Blake's stipulative reading of the group. But he was probably well acquainted with the Protestant revisionism by which, for example, imperial Rome (as allegorized by Babylon in Revelation) is made to figure papal Rome for the Reformation. In a somewhat Browningesque poem of over 370 lines called "The Marble Prophecy," *Laocoön* is celebrated as a kind of prophetic text of its own. Meditating upon the piece, alone in the Vatican with an antipapal agenda, the speaker first addresses its uniqueness:

> There lives none though in marble like to thee!
> Thou hast no kindred in the Vatican,
> But standest separate among the dreams
> Of old mythologies—alone—alone!
> The beautiful Apollo at thy side
> Is but a marble dream, and dreams are all
> The gods and goddesses and fauns and fates
> That populate these wondrous halls; but thou,
> Standing among them, liftest up thyself
> In majesty of meaning . . .

This greater significance soon reveals itself, as the speaker addresses the central figure of the group:

> Ay, Adam and his offspring, in the toils
> Of the twin serpents, Sin and Suffering,
> Thou dost impersonate; and as I gaze
> Upon the twining monsters that enfold
> In unrelaxing, unrelenting coils,
> Thy awful energies, and plant their fangs
> Deep in thy quivering flesh, while still thy might
> In fierce convulsion foils the fateful wrench
> That would destroy thee, I am overwhelmed
> With a strange sympathy of kindred pain . . .

This leads to an extremely nineteenth-century parable of the transcendence of art, and of the ironies of historical consciousness:

> Those Rhodian sculptors were gigantic men,
> Whose inspirations came from other source
> Than their religion, though they chose to speak
> Through its familiar language,—men who saw
> And, seeing quite divinely, felt how weak
> To cure the world's great woe were all the powers
> Whose reign their age acknowledged. So they sat—
> The immortal three—and pondered long and well
> What one great work should speak the truth for them,—
> What one great work should rise and testify
> That they had found the topmost fact of life,
> Above the reach of all, philosophies
> And all religions—every scheme of man
> To placate or dethrone. That fact, they found,
> And moulded into form. The silly priest
> Whose desecrations of the altar stirred
> The vengeance of his God, and summoned forth
> The wreathed gorgons of the slimy deep
> To crush him and his children, was the word
> By which they spoke to their own age and race,
> That listened and applauded, knowing not
> That high above the small significance
> They apprehended, rose the grand intent
> That mourned their doom and breathed a world's despair!

Then, after imperial Rome "fell prone at length / Among the trophies of her crimes and slept," the new Christian order arises which, in the speaker's account, yields creative and imaginative power to the rebirth, in the *quattrocento*, of the old gods (as mythopoetic bearers of signification, animated by the energies of art):

> And when the gods were on their feet again,
> It was thy time to rise, Laocoön!
> Those Rhodian sculptors had foreseen it all.
> Their word was true: thou hadst the right to live . . .

And again today, religion is of no help:

> . . . Rome has failed:
> Humanity is writhing in the toils
> Of the old monsters as it writhed of old,
> And there is neither help nor hope in her.
> Her priests, her shrines, her rites, her mummeries,
> Her pictures and her pageants, are as weak
> To break the hold of Sin and Suffering
> As those her reign displaced. Her iron hand
> Shrivels the manhood it presumes to bless . . .

And so he concludes with a reaffirmation of the central figure's agonistic prophetic truth, calling out

> . . . Ay Laocoön!
> Thy word is true, for Christian Rome has failed,
> And I behold humanity in thee
> As those who shaped thee saw it, when old Rome
> In that far pagan evening fell asleep.

And these observations on some of the *Laocoön*'s interpretive consequences will conclude with a brilliant and brief demonic parable, on the group and its fame and its significance, from Ambrose Bierce's *The Devil's Dictionary* (1911):

> LAOCOON, *n.* A famous piece of antique sculpture representing a priest of that name and his two sons in the folds of two enormous serpents. The skill and diligence with which the old man and lads support the serpents and keep them up to their work has been justly regarded as one of the noblest artistic illustrations of the mastery of human intelligence over brute inertia.

The wit here centers on how the material, structural *support* given the serpents by the arms of the figure might be construed as *encouragement*, in an agonistic self-destruction, by some late romantic poem: one can imagine a Browning monologist playing with the idea. But here it is a deflating joke that depends upon the dumb materiality of stone and what can be done with it. And it is this joke that, at the end of the passage, literally has the splendid last word.

TITIAN, *Portrait of Francesco Maria della Rovere, Duke of Urbino*

If famous Apelles with his hand of art
        portrayed the face and bosom of Alexander
        he did not represent the elusive subject,
        the lofty vigor that his soul possessed.

But Titian, with a greater share from Heaven,
        shows outwardly all invisible ideas
        since the great Duke in his painted aspect
        reveals the victories within his heart.

Between his two brows there is awesomeness,
        his spirit in his eyes, nobility
        on his face, seat of honor and good counsel.

In his breastplate, and in his readied arms,
        burns the courage, which protects from perils
        Italy, sacred to his accounted virtues.

[Se 'l chiaro Apelle, con la man de l'arte
        rassemplò d'Alessandro il volto e 'l petto,
        non finse già di pellegrin subietto
        l'alto vigor, che l'anima comparte.

Ma Tizian, che dal cielo ha maggior parte,
        fuor mostra ogni invisibile concetto;
        però 'l gran duca nel dipinto aspetto
        scopre le palme entro al suo cuor sparte.

Egli ha il terror fra l'uno e l'altro ciglio,
        l'animo in gli occhi, e l'alterezza in fronte,
        nel cui spazio l'onor, siede e 'l consiglio.

Nel busto armato e ne le braccia pronte
        arde il valor, che guarda dal periglio
        Italia sacra a sue virtuti conte.]

WILLIAM LESCAZE, *Portrait of Hart Crane*

ALLEN TATE

Sonnet
To a Portrait of Hart Crane

Unweathered stone beneath a rigid mane
Flashes insurgent dusk to ancient eyes
Dreaming above a lonely mouth, that lies
Unbeaten into laughter out of pain:
What is the margin of the lovely stain
Where joy shrinks into stilled miseries?
From what remembrance of satyrs' tippled cries
Have you informed that dark ecstatic brain?

I have not grasped the living hand of you,
Nor waited for a music of your speech:
From a dead time I wander—and pursue
The quickened year when you will come to teach
My eyes to hold the blinding vision where
A bitter rose falls on a marble stair.

ADRIEN TOURNACHON, *Portrait of Nadar*

RICHARD HOWARD

Nadar

for Rosalind Krauss

You will be obscured by a cloud of postures
    and a roster of great names,
but here, in your high thirties, you can hardly

    be more distinct, distinguished
by hair, hope and the heroic resolution
    to present life with an image

unretouched—had it not been the fallacy
    of centuries to *correct?*
Edited, glossed, conflated, expurgated—

    what was left to believe in?
All men are mad when they are alone, almost
    all women: that was your text

and your testimony, the acknowledgment
    of a balloonist whose pride
it was to announce that countless things have been

    seen and remain to be seen,
and for whom humility was equivalent
    to seeing things as they are,

opacity being a great discoverer.
    Why else is it your portraits
loom likelier for us now than all preening

    identifications since?
Because you made your Act between consenting
    adults a Sacred Game

wherein the dead god is recognized, the change
    being from darkness to light
and revelation—the god reborn. You were

our demiurge: from a world
where chaos and cosmos are superimposed,
     from a world where anything

can happen but nothing happens twice, you spoke
     your *fiat lux* or *fiat*
nox to bring forth the creation of nature

     against nature within nature.
Now you have sixty years in which to retrieve
     the visionary from the visual,

then fade into the once and future classics,
     leaving us to enlarge on
what cannot be divided, individuals.

The two earliest sonnets on portraits we have might as well be notional: the portrait of
Laura by Simone Martini addressed by Petrarch (*Rime Sparsi*, 77–78) is now lost, but in no case
could we recognize it from the poems, whose attention is directed beyond mere visual detail.
In the first one, the painter is acknowledged to have been in Heaven, where he must have
encountered his subject:

Sure, my Simone was in Paradise
(whence has come this most noble lady)
he saw her there, and rendered her on paper
here below to bear witness to her face.

[Ma certo il mio Simon fu in Paradiso
(onde questa gentil donna si parte)
ivi la vide, et la ritrasse in carte
per far fede qua giù del suo bel viso.]

The second is notable for bemoaning the absence of voice, as well as of presence, in the paint-
ed image, and ends with an almost inevitable expression of desire:

Pygmalion, how delighted you must be
with your image, having got a thousand times
what I desire to have if only once.

[Pygmalion, quanto lodar ti dei
de l'imagine tua, se mille volte
n'avesti quel ch'i' sol una vorrei.]

But in subsequent post-Petrarchan Renaissance poetry, individual, nonsequential sonnets
on pictures, full of the notion that portraiture is itself a mode of praise, seek to bear explic-

it witness to the qualities which the painted image can only imply, or "express." The poem praises the painting, in effect, for allowing its silent message access to the oral performance of poetic text. Some of this can be seen in Pietro Aretino's sonnet on Titian's portrait of the Duke of Urbino. It employs, like so many other poems on portraits of the sixteenth and seventeenth centuries, what had become almost natural Petrarchan rhetorical strategies. Outward appearance is taken as the mere residence or locus of some transcendent virtue, or other abstract quality (e.g., "In her X dwells A"). But in such poems, it becomes the encomiastic tactic to praise both sitter and painter, the first for possessing the virtue, the second for being able to reveal it. This ability to represent the invisible A in the almost palpable X comes to replace the classical cliche of eikastic perfection as praised in the poems about visual images in, say, the Greek anthology. (Frequently, there, the subject—Aphrodite, for example—needs no encomium, and all the praise goes to the sculptor for being up to her, as it were.) The poem makes linguistically available this substance of Renaissance portraiture that John Pope-Hennessy, following Leonardo, called the portraying of the "motions of the mind."

Aretino elevates Titian above Apelles, who portrayed merely Alexander but not "the rare subject, / the noble vigor his soul possessed" [pellegrin subietto, / l'alto vigor, che l'anima comparte]. Titian, conversely, paints the awesome power lurking between the Duke's eyebrows, the honor and good counsel residing in his face, and so forth. It is only the last tercet which is actually ecphrastic, reading Titian's painting rather than cataloguing a set of paradigmatic conventions: "In his breastplate and in his readied arms / burns courage" [Nel busto armato e ne la braccia pronte / arde il valor]. The painterly light reflected in the breastplate is momentarily allegorized (through the word *arde*) as "valor," even as the gesture of the ducal hands on sword and, elegantly foreshortened, on mace are literally read.

Interesting in this connection, too, is the companion sonnet to a companion portrait, that of the Duchess of Urbino, Eleonora Gonzaga. It is of particular iconographic concern because of the clock placed between the sleeping dog and the open window in the left-hand portion of the painting; Erwin Panofsky, pointing out that rather newly developed table clocks were rare and expensive, showed that it could be taken as "a kind of status symbol" in this and other Titian portraits containing one. Additionally, it could indicate a well-regulated temperance and, ultimately, a version of Time's, and thereby Death's, hourglass. Panofsky concludes that it "would seem to serve the double purpose of an *insigne virtutis* and a *memento mori . . .* the double connotation of temperance and transience." But nothing could be further from the eye and mind of Aretino's sonnet here, and all that his lines see in the painting are the virtues that lurk in her, and surround her: "Unassumingness sits with her, humble in deed, / Honesty inhabits her attire, / Modesty veils and honors her breast and hair," and so on [Seco siede modestia in atto umile, / Onestà nel suo abito dimora, / Vergogna il petto e il crin le vela e onora]. The poetic blazon, or catalogue, of virtues, and the iconographic reading of the elements of an emblem, have not yet come together in poems written to portraits.

An interesting modern case of ecphrasis of portraiture occurs when the poet knows the subject only through correspondence, but has never seen him or her. In such a case, it is almost inevitable that a subtle kind of epistemological problem arise for the poem, involving two kinds of mental picture. A familiar matter of "Here you are, just/not/almost (save for . . .) as I remember you" becomes something like "Here you are, I guess, just/not/almost (save for . . .) as I'd imagined you." A young painter from Geneva who was to become a famous American architect, William Lescaze drew a portrait of his friend Hart Crane in Cleveland, Ohio, in the fall of 1921. The pencil drawing is hardly masterful, but it shows considerable awareness of European modernism in its geometric reductions and its ellipses, in the rhyming linear *m*-form in the hairline, the brows, and the upper lip, and in its negatively curved counterpart in the lower lip and chin. Certainly the eyes are central (the mouth less so, but more recognizable as Crane's in a trivial mode of likeness). Crane himself, writing to another friend that he had been "futuristically sketched," added that he liked it but that "most of my friends insist on saying that I never look quite so insane as the picture suggests"—in many ways a rather typical, trivial reaction to modernist images of face or figure. Allen Tate, whose close and eventually problematic friendship with Crane had commenced in correspondence in 1922, wrote a sonnet to this drawing—although the two had not yet met—that was published in a periodical called *The Double-Dealer* in the spring of 1923. He did not appear in the least to think that the drawing makes Crane look crazy.

Certainly his sonnet suggests not madness, but rather a trace of the demonic. It addresses itself to the sitter, in re his face in the drawing, immediately followed by a pair of somewhat Rossettian ecphrastic questions. The opening lines speak to the postcubist, geometric quality of the drawing: the hair and forehead—"unweathered stone beneath a rigid mane"—and the mouth "that lies / Unbeaten into laughter out of pain"—the hint of hammer, anvil, and forging may speak to a reading of the still somewhat geometric mouth as seeming metallic. "The margin of the lovely stain / Where joy shrinks into stilled miseries" refers both to the shading around the mouth (and not the smudges visible at the corners which, a former owner has said, "are traces of the glue Hart used to mount it") and to a moral abstraction; paired with the second question, it invokes Dionysian sources of energy in both bed and bottle.

The sestet moves totally away from the drawn image. Quite specifically, it comments on the purely textual nature of the two poets' acquaintance, again with an almost Rossettian "Now is still the winter of our not having met; some spring will bring us together" (the sonnet may in fact have been written in February). "I have not grasped the living hand of you" partakes of the diction and syntax that mark Crane's work more than Tate's, but Tate exhibits them in his poetry of the 1920s. The final image would be quite enigmatic but for its allusion. It clearly echoes the end of Edwin Arlington Robinson's poem (published in book form in 1916) about a mother's deluded sense of her son's virtues and talents (she "transmutes him with her faith and praise / And has him shining where she will"). "The Gift of God" concludes:

> His fame, though vague, shall not be small
> As upward through her dream he fares,
> Half clouded with a crimson fall
> Of roses thrown on marble stairs.

Robinson was admired by both poets, but more by Tate than by Crane; in a letter to Tate written before the poem appeared, Crane refers to "the merely personal sketches and digs that Robinson has been getting you into." Certainly the questions of talent, fame, promise, were loaded and unvoiced in their correspondence. Manifestly, the figure designates the vision of Crane's poetry, a (for Tate) bitter romanticism (with regard to which they would eventually fall out). Latently, the source in Robinson suggests an unconscious prescience. The sonnet predicts a meeting; its undersong seems to prefigure a climate of parting.

Photographic portraits pose special problems, as do photographic images generally, for poetic ecphrasis. So far, there have not been that many interesting examples of such poems by important modern poets, in the work of Whitman and Melville, for example. There is always a tendency to documentary reduction—as with emblem verse attached to symbolic images in the Renaissance, which ignores the medium totally—and to focus the attention on the recorded event, as if the camera's eye were totally objective, transparent, and unselective, as if it only provided some sort of record. Because this last is indeed true to a degree (some subject person, place, or arrangement of things was indeed recorded at a particular time), the imaginative or visionary gaze of the poetic text is frequently occluded by such a matter of factuality.

Richard Howard's two series of poems on photographic portraits of French writers and artists by Nadar (Gaspard Felix Tournachon, 1820–1910) are particularly interesting in view of his considerable number of previous poems on painting and sculpture (see p. 000). In the Nadar poems Howard acknowledges both the documentary and graphically creative dimensions of photographic portraiture and uses them in a variety of ways. His poems speak sometimes only to the subject of the picture, at first as if only a mental image of the person were being addressed, or even that of a specter conjured up only from intimate knowledge of the person's works, then only to be reminded—and to remind us—that there the he or she was, sitting in *that* studio for *that* picture at *that* moment of time in his or her life, and in the life of modern history. Sometimes a detail from the photograph will be picked up and worked on by the poem's inquiring mind. Howard's great gift for dramatic monologue—he is Browning's major follower in this mode—gets significantly displaced in these poems. What he might have written earlier in his work as an actual monologue by one of Nadar's subjects in this series— Sarah Bernhardt, Baudelaire, Rossini or Offenbach, Hugo or Gustave Doré—becomes transmuted into an address, not to some historical absolute, but to another sort of being: that person *as photographed by Nadar*. Like Renaissance poems on portraits such as the Aretino on the Titian (which are flatly explicit in this regard), Howard's implicitly address the photographer who has created this image—this version, this glimpse—of the personal subject.

In the concluding poem of his first sequence, he addresses Nadar himself through what is all but a self-portrait (a photograph taken by his brother Adrien, called "Nadar Jeune"). This is not remotely even sonnet-like but is composed in tercets made of alternating long (eleven-syllabled) and short (mostly seven-syllabled) lines. The periodic syntax weaves through these, and the conceptual thread they carry gathers up, in a sense, the pieces of him that had been hidden in the "cloud of postures" and the "roster of great names" that had constituted his work. But one may notice how, right at the outset, the poet seizes on three different orders of entity. First there is the phenomenon of the patently gestural hair of the subject. Then, the inferred attributes of the subject, "recovered" or revealed by the image: manifested hope—always the artist's hope, generally, but particularly here, the early photographer's hope for what will come out: the image in a painting or print can be moved about during its making, but a plate has to be retaken. And, finally, and most audaciously, there is the "resolution," triumphing in the cause of that hope, but, in an elegant pun on the technical term for a matter of optics—of a quality of lenses and of what they project—designating as well part of the manner, the means, of effecting that very triumph.

Noticeable, too, is that turn of wit by which the photographer becomes a kind of original Creator. His *fiat lux* ("Let there be light" in the Vulgate) is necessarily coupled with a complementary but not really antithetical *fiat nox* ("Let there be night," which rhymes in English but only half-rhymes in Latin): the photographer's creations are always matters of shadow, of the joint efforts of *lux* and *nox.* Ultimately, the poem can even celebrate the achievements of poetic language itself which, at one remove from the way in which even Nadar's images are held to do this, "retrieve / the visionary from the visual."

It might be added that daguerreotype portraits constitute a different case. They were not prints, but monotypes; they faded quickly, and their image was otherwise evanescent because of their mirror-like surfaces, which imprisoned not only slightly unstable images (depending upon how the light fell on them), but which could reflect the viewer of them. Rilke's celebrated pair of sonnets (from the 1907 *Neue Gedichte*) present an actual ecphrasis, of a (now lost) portrait and a purely notional one. The first (see above, p. 67), shows an image of his father as a young man, revealed only in the final lines as a fragile monument: "You quickly vanishing daguerreotype / in my slowly vanishing hands" [Du schnell vergehendes Daguerrotyp / in meinen lansamer vergehenden Händen]. The second reads a fictional photograph—the "Self-Portrait" of the title is nonliteral—but starts out by seeing in the lineaments of the poet's face when young a trace of resistance to time; it perceives "The old long noble race's / durability in the structure of the eyebrow" [Des alten lange adeligen Geschlechtes / Feststehendes in Augenbogen-bau]. Implicit in the pairing there is perhaps a trace of the Renaissance commonplace about how poetry outlives brass monuments (from Horace's *monumentum aere perennius*): the notional image of the poet's own youth—the poet being still alive—as opposed to the vivid (it was a colored daguerreotype) actual image of a young man now dead.

BEN JONSON

The Mind of the Frontispiece to a Book

From Death and dark Oblivion, ne'er the same
    The Mistress of Man's life, grave History
Raising the World to Good or Evil Fame
    Doth vindicate it to eternity.
Wise Providence would so: that nor the good
    Might be defrauded, nor the great secured,
But both might know their ways were understood
    When Vice alike in time with Virtue dured.
Which makes that (lighted by the beamy hand
    Of Truth that searcheth the most hidden springs
And guided by Experience, whose straight wand
    Doth mete, whose line doth sound, the depth of things),
She cheerfully supporteth what she rears
    Assisted by no strengths but are her own,
Some note of which each varied pillar bears,
    By which, as proper titles, she is known:
Time's witness, Herald of Antiquity,
    The Light of Truth, and Life of Memory.

Ben Jonson's poem accompanying the engraved title page of Sir Walter Ralegh's *History of the World* (1614) provides an interesting variation on the more traditional emblem verse. Its very title is a little problematic. "Mind" seems to designate "meaning" or "significance" (almost as if it were the German, *Sinn*), and "frontispiece" refers to the title page itself, rather than an illustration facing it. (We tend to think of the word as if it were compounded as *frontis* + *piece*; its actual derivation is from Latin *frontispicium*, "front-view," facade, or, by extension, elevation of a building.) An allegorical frontispiece like the one in question, typical of the seventeenth century, would represent the subject or matter of a speculative book by mapping it onto a neoclassical or baroque facade. This would often contain symbolic personages in niches; as Walter J. Ong put it, "signifying no architectural or other mode of interaction between the individual items," it would organize "pleasingly and geometrically the neutral space in which the individual items would otherwise float." On the other hand, the basic architectural metaphors of supporting members, higher and lower levels, steps as stages in a development, and so forth, would be equally often in active operation in composing "the mind of the frontispiece," as in this instance.

Renold Elstrack, *Engraved Title Page of
Sir Walter Ralegh's* History of the World

Ralegh's picture of history, engraved by Renold Elstrack, shows her bare-breasted, sun-crowned, and holding aloft the globe (which is itself surmounted directly only by the Eye of Providence). She is labeled in Latin "mistress of life" and is shown trampling beneath her feet Death and Oblivion. Her attendants, framed by their own ancillary pillars, are Experience—between what Jonson translates as "Time's Witness" (the column decorated with books) and "Herald of Antiquity" (the one covered in hieroglyphs)—and Truth, naked, as always, between the "Light of Truth" (covered with flames) and the "Life of Memory" (covered with laurel garlands). Jonson's reading of the image is teacherly, not only in expounding the didactic content of the symbolism, but in pointing out the significance of details in a homiletic aside. Thus, in the very first line, he reminds the reader that Death and Oblivion are not the same. But he glosses over the fact that history's triumph over the first of these is figurative (the world would "die" if not recorded), and over the other, literal (the world would be forgotten if not remembered.) He also makes a claim that the engraving does not, namely that the four columns, with clear structural firmness of their own, are merely the semaphores of the names of History's own "strengths," rather than parallel or analogous ones. The picture itself offers a view of three levels: (1) Death and Oblivion at the bottom; (2) History and her ancillae, with (3) the World borne up to the roof of the structure, the domain of Good and Evil Fame; but Jonson's account cares as little for this as for the axial symmetries around the central vertical sequence of circular forms. Nor does it attempt systematically to unroll, in its own pattern of enjambed quatrains run together into what look like classical elegiac couplets on the page, some representation of this spatial structure (e.g., by starting at the top or bottom, and reading up or down). Instead, he concentrates on iconographic detail (Experience's measuring instruments, etc.).

In this regard, it might be noted that the figure of History in this picture does not coincide with the more familiar one from Cesare Ripa's centrally important *Iconologia* of 1593, a source for so much traditional iconography of personification in the following centuries. There, she is shown and described as a winged figure, looking backward (for history is a record of the past), writing in a book, with her foot on a square block of stone (for history must have a firm foundation in truth). The book is resting on Time's back. Although the "strengths" inscribed on the bases of the columns appear in Ripa's account as History's epithets, the picture's sense of the role of Time is more complex than Ripa's. Similarly, the latter's picture of Experience differs from the present one, save for her being an old woman and in her characteristic bare-bellied dress; in Ripa she carries a staff with a banderole labeled *Magistra rerum*, "Mistress of Things," and the idea that her staff is a measuring rod is probably Jonson's addition.

In a reversal of another traditional seventeenth-century mode, the poem written for a portrait, Jonson acknowledges the virtues of the likeness but maintains that the artist could *not* represent the salient feature of the sitter's inner nature. In his lines accompanying Martin Droeshout's engraving of Shakespeare in the first folio edition of Shakespeare's *Works*, the poem exhibits a not uncommon total blindness to the picture—the conception, design, and execution of the particular image:

This figure, that thou seest here put,
      It was for gentle Shakespeare cut;
Wherein that Graver had a strife
      With Nature, to out-doo the life:
O, could he have but drawne his wit
      As well in brasse, as he hath hit
His face; the Print would then surpasse
      All that was ever writ in brasse.
But, since he cannot, Reader, look
      Not on his Picture, but his Booke.

"Wit" here means poetic imagination; and since the claim is that the portrait's image can not draw what it is that produces such wonderful writing, the use of "writ in brasse" for "engraved" is more pointed than merely rhetorically conventional.

To My Worthy Friend Mr. Peter Lilly: on that Excellent Picture of His Majesty, and the Duke of York, drawne by him at Hampton-Court

See! what a *clouded Majesty!* and eyes
Whose glory through their mist doth brighter rise!
See! what an humble bravery doth shine,
And griefe triumphant breaking through each line;
How it commands the face! so sweet a scorne
Never did happy misery adorn!
So sacred a contempt! that others show
To this, (oth' height of all the wheele) below;
That mightiest Monarchs by this shaded booke
May coppy out their proudest, richest looke.

Whilst the true *Eaglet* this quick luster spies,
And by his *Sun's* enlightens his owne eyes;
He cares his cares, his burthen feeles, then streight
Joyes that so lightly he can beare such weight;
Whilst either eithers passion doth borrow,
And both doe grieve the same victorious sorrow.

These my best *Lilly* with so bold a spirit
And soft a grace, as if thou didst inherit
For that time all their greatnesse, and didst draw
With those brave eyes your *Royall Sitters* saw.

Not as of old, when a rough hand did speake
A strong Aspect, and a faire face, a weake;
When only a black beard cried Villaine, and
By *Hieroglyphicks* we could understand;
When Chrystall typified in a white spot,
And the bright Ruby was but one red blot:
Thou dost the things Orientally the same,
Not only paintst its colour, but its *Flame:*
Thou sorrow canst designe without a teare,
And with the Man and his very *Hope* and *Feare:*
So that th'amazed world shall henceforth finde
None but my *Lilly* ever drew a *Minde.*

Sir Peter Lely, *Charles I and the Duke of York*

Sir Peter Lely's portrait of King Charles I and his second son, James, Duke of York, was painted in 1647 when the already partially eclipsed king was being held by the army at Hampton Court. They appear in a pictorial format made popular by Vandyck: the background divided, with drapery and, frequently, a column on one side; on the other, an open landscape. The cavalier poet Richard Lovelace, a friend of Lely (and a knowledgeable lover of painting who had probably read both Vasari and Carel van Mander) wrote these lines addressed *to* his friend, *on* the matter of the royal portrait. The poem reads the portrait in a powerful way— or rather, misreads it, by taking the matter of the clouds visible behind the head of James (and possibly moving toward the king himself) as if it were an allegorical detail in the painting— which it certainly was not—however naturalistically domesticated. Since Lovelace's concern as a poet is with the sorts of verbal paradox that characterize for him, a lyrical royalist, a particular moment in the decline of the king's fortunes, he starts out in the first line with what will be one of the poem's two governing images:

> See! what a *clouded Majesty*! and eyes
> Whose glory through their mist doth brighter rise!

The oxymoron of "clouded Majesty" connects the painted sky behind James with the monarch's own occluded reign. In addition, it engages the question of gaze and eyes, which will re-emerge in importance after the next lines of reiterated paradox ("humble bravery"— where "bravery" still has its older meaning of "splendidly showy"—and "happy misery"). The "lines" or lineaments of the painted face, and those lines of verse of the poem addressing it, are delicately associated here, as later the eyes of the king are more forcefully connected with those of the painter himself. But the comparison which immediately follows turns its attention to the eyes of the young prince, more prominently directed than those of the king, in a strange trope which makes the son a young eagle and his father the shining sun, an English *roi soleil*. Son and sun are punningly intertwined, and the antecedents of "he" and "his" remain curiously ambiguous, and intertwined as well.

This has, so far, exhibited a significant problematic feature of poetic ecphrasis: its strangeness lies as much in what the poem does not notice as what it singles out as prominent points for interpretation. Another viewer might ask, for example, What is the boy handing his father? What is the paper the king is holding? On the other hand, Lovelace's poem broods upon cloudedness, and upon eyes. Its attention next shifts to the painter Lely himself, and praises him, in essence, for having painted what was only in Lovelace's poem:

> These my best *Lilly* with so bold a spirit
> And soft a grace, as if thou didst inherit
> For that time all their greatnesse and didst draw
> With those brave eyes your *Royal Sitters* saw.

"Those brave eyes"—the painter's eyes, not so much courageous as themselves resplendent—are now seen to be focused upon as an object of the royal gaze, perhaps in the intervals of posing; the poem puts us momentarily in the room at Hampton Court where the painting is being done. There is a touch in these lines, though not at all in the painting, of some of the recently propounded epistemological puzzles of Velasquez's *Las Meniñas*.

The rest of the poem abandons ecphrasis for a more conventional seventeenth-century kind of encomium of Lely, in this case, for painting feelings and virtues directly, without being reductively and perhaps fussily iconographic, depending upon semiotic cliches (in Lovelace's term, understanding "by Hieroglyphickes"). It ends with a revisionary allusion to an epigram of the late Latin poet Ausonius, well known in the seventeenth century, that Lovelace had himself earlier translated. It challenges a painter, who would depict the nymph Echo as a personification, with a more figurative agenda: "If you'll paint me like," says Echo, "paint a sound" (the nymph, in Ovid's story of Echo and Narcissus, having pined away bodily and become nothing but a voice). The analogy is extended to the modern portraitist's obligation, to paint not only the "colour" of a thought or emotion, but "its flame" (not only, in another sense of the word, a rhetorical figure, but a passion of the soul) "So that th'amazed world shall henceforth finde / None but my *Lilly* ever drew a *Minde*."

This famous poem is, as was observed previously, problematically selective in its reading of detail, and calls attention to itself. It feigns that the Vandyckian convention of framing a portrait half in landscape is the painting's own vision; and it energetically deploys poetry's figurative resources to represent what it feels to be those of painting. Save for the imperative "See!" used twice, the poem eschews the rhetorical formulas of much earlier notional ecphrastic writing (e.g., the Horatian "Here an X, and there a Y . . . behold an A appear, and then a B") so common in seventeenth-century verse. If the poem is emblematically reductive, after all, it is in a radically original reading (*See this picture? It means—it should be* called—*something like* "Clouded Majesty") that concludes by praising the painter for not being merely an emblematic designer.

Some of the devices Lovelace uses here are typical of seventeenth-century English poetry in this mode. Thus, his contemporary Edmund Waller addresses a great painter in "To Vandyck" ("Rare artisan, whose pencil moves / Not our delights alone, but loves!"—and we must remember that, up through the nineteenth century, "pencil" means "paintbrush"). Praising him primarily here for his portraits of beautiful women, Waller similarly invokes the trope of getting below the color to the emotional energy beneath:

> Strange, that thy hand should not inspire
> The beauty only, but the fire;
> Not the form alone, and grace,
> But act and power of a face.

This performs a dainty turn on the Renaissance commonplace that praises an artist for representing in a portrait what the present face of the actual sitter might not necessarily reveal. (See my comments on Aretino's poem on a Titian portrait of the Duke of Urbino, above.) Waller speaks, in another poem, to one particular Vandyck portrait, of Lady Dorothy Sidney; but in that case, his whole concern is to praise her great-uncle, the poet Sir Philip Sidney. He sees the lady—as painted by Vandyck—as the summation of all the beauties in her illustrious ancestor's great prose romance: "All the rich flowers through his Arcadia found / Amazed we see in this one garland bound." But the delicately tactful end of the poem brings it back from the praise of poetry to the matter of bodily presence, claiming that reality turned the great poet and courtier into an even better ancestral "author" than an imaginative one. And the matter of Vandyck's paint and Waller's ink, and of the ability of pen, pencil, and even progenitive penis all to leave beautiful traces, is kept with equal tact just beneath the surface:

> Just nature, first instructed by his thought,
> In his own house thus practised what he taught;
> This glorious piece transcends what he could think,
> So much his blood is nobler than his ink.

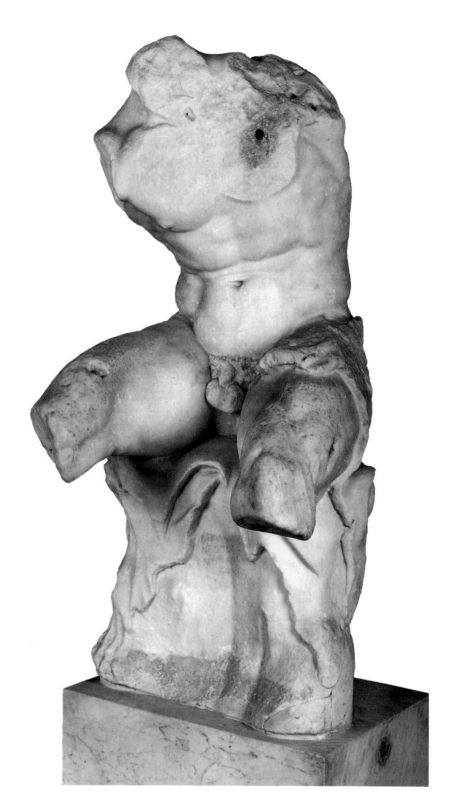

ANON., *Torso Belvedere*

To the Fragment of a Statue of Hercules, Commonly Called the Torso

And dost thou still, thou mass of breathing stone,
(Thy giant limbs to night and chaos hurled)
Still sit as on the fragment of a world;
Surviving all, majestic and alone?
What tho' the Spirits of the North, that swept
Rome from the earth when in her pomp she slept,
Smote thee with fury, and thy headless trunk
Deep in the dust mid tower and temple sunk;
Soon to subdue mankind 'twas thine to rise,
Still, still unquelled thy glorious energies!
Aspiring minds, with thee conversing, caught
Bright revelations of the Good they sought;
By thee that long-lost spell its secret given,
To draw down Gods, and lift the soul to Heaven!

The famous Torso Belvedere was interpreted in the Renaissance as representing Hercules (and probably wrongly—it may have been a Philoctetes, or a Marsyas, for example). In J. J. Winckelmann's *History of Ancient Art* (1764) he writes of having seen in the torso

> a shape at the full development of manhood, such as it might be as if exalted to the degree of divine sufficiency. He appears here purified from the dross of humanity, and after having attained immortality and a seat among the gods; for he is represented without need of human nourishment, or further use of its powers. No veins are visible, and the belly is made only to enjoy, not to receive, and to be full without being filled . . . In that powerfully developed chest we behold in imagination the breast against which the giant Geryon was squeezed, and in the length and strength of the thighs we recognize the unwearied hero who pursued and overtook the brazen-footed stag, and travelled through countless lands even to the very confines of the world.

Samuel Rogers's sonnet, most likely written in 1802, is still of the eighteenth century, and has none of the structural power of the romantic sonnet from Wordsworth on: after the first quatrain, it degenerates into a string of couplets. It opens with a characteristic query addressed to the piece and its fragmentary character; but it is a rather empty one—a question rhetorical, with too easy an answer, rather than, despite the echoes of Milton, poetic: "And dost thou still . . . alone?" —*Well, yes*, we want to say. Only the old issue of fragmentation and ruin has been addressed. We are closer to the prose of Gibbon than to the notional ecphrasis and the matter of fragmentation's hearsay in Shelley's "Ozymandias."

But in the remainder of the poem, the death of antiquity is followed nonetheless by the resurrections of art, and it is no mere sentimental meditation on yet another antique fragment that we are left with. For Rogers, the marble arises in the Renaissance, and has as its consequences the art of the *cinquecento*. The "aspiring minds, with thee conversing" are Neoplatonic artists like Michelangelo (who praised the piece and drew from it for the Medici tombs), Raphael, and others. The direct poetic echo here is of Eve addressing Adam (in *Paradise Lost* 4.368): "With thee conversing, I forget all time"; with the almost spousal address of the great artists to the fragment, all time is forgotten and new art is born. After this one poetic moment, though, the poem concludes with an epigrammatic cliche about drawing heavenly beings down to earth—a piece of rhetorical filigree from baroque poetry mass-produced in a later century. We are reminded that the form of this poem is in no way engaged itself in an act of sympathetic representation. And we end up with a somewhat reductive reading of the object, considered as a fragment of what once was Hercules, as signifying not ruin, but recreation.

WILLIAM WORDSWORTH

Elegiac Stanzas
Suggested by a Picture of Peele Castle, in a Storm,
Painted by Sir George Beaumont

I was thy neighbor once, thou rugged Pile!
Four summer weeks I dwelt in sight of thee:
I saw thee every day: and all the while
Thy Form was sleeping on a glassy sea.

So pure the sky, so quiet was the air!
So like, so very like, was day to day!
Whene'er I looked, thy Image still was there;
It trembled, but it never passed away.

How perfect was the calm! it seemed no sleep;
No mood, which season takes away, or brings:
I could have fancied that the mighty Deep
Was even the gentlest of all gentle Things.

Ah! THEN, if mine had been the Painter's hand,
To express what then I saw; and add the gleam,
The light that never was, on sea or land,
The consecration, and the Poet's dream;

I would have planted thee, thou hoary Pile
Amid a world how different from this!
Beside a sea that could not cease to smile;
On tranquil land, beneath a sky of bliss.

Thou shouldst have seemed a treasure-house divine
Of peaceful years; a chronicle of heaven; —
Of all the sunbeams that did ever shine
The very sweetest had to thee been given.

A Picture had it been of lasting ease,
Elysian quiet, without toil or strife;
No motion but the moving tide, a breeze,
Or merely silent Nature's breathing life.

SIR GEORGE BEAUMONT, *Piel Castle in a Storm*

Such, in the fond illusion of my heart,
Such Picture would I at the time have made:
And seen the soul of truth in every part,
A stedfast peace that might not be betrayed.

So once it would have been, — 'tis so no more;
I have submitted to a new control:
A power is gone, which nothing can restore;
A deep distress hath humanised my Soul.

Not for a moment could I now behold
A smiling sea, and be what I have been:
The feeling of my loss will ne'er be old;
This, which I know, I speak with mind serene.

Then, Beaumont, Friend! who would have been the Friend,
If he had lived, of Him whom I deplore,
This work of thine I blame not, but commend;
This sea in anger, and that dismal shore.

O 'tis a passionate work! — yet wise and well,
Well chosen is the spirit that is here;
That Hulk which labours in the deadly swell,
This rueful sky, this pageantry of fear!

And this huge Castle, standing here sublime,
I love to see the look with which it braves,
Cased in the unfeeling armour of old time,
The lightning, the fierce wind, and trampling waves.

Farewell, farewell the heart that lives alone,
Housed in a dream, at distance from the Kind!
Such happiness, wherever it be known,
Is to be pitied; for 'tis surely blind.

But welcome fortitude, and patient cheer,
And frequent sights of what is to be borne!
Such sights, or worse, as are before me here.—
Not without hope we suffer and we mourn.

In the spring of 1806 Wordsworth visited in London with Sir George Beaumont, a connoisseur and patron of the arts, and a devoted amateur painter. It was then that the poet saw Beaumont's painting of a marine storm raging around the ruins of Peele (or Piel) Castle on a promontory off the coast of North Lancashire. Wordsworth's brother, John, had been lost at sea early in 1805, and it is this death by drowning that constitutes the "deep distress" mentioned at the end of the ninth stanza. Wordsworth's meditation starts from the image of the tower and immediately moves back to another, remembered image of it, undarkened by Beaumont's paint and his own current sense of loss, from twelve years before. The rhetorical movement suggests at once the opening of his own earlier Tintern Abbey poem. There, something very like a transparency of remembered image gets overlaid upon an otherwise immediate prospect, in what seems almost a matter of confronting a portrait of oneself when young ("I looked like you, once, thou—"). The castle is being treated as a subject which has, like the reader-rememberer, aged and darkened and been stormed over; the present painting starts out by dissolving into what Wordsworth in "Tintern Abbey" had called, with resonant ambiguity, "the picture of the mind."

But that remembered, virtual picture itself contains a depiction. In a "glassy" (i.e., "mirror-like") sea is reflected the "Form" of the castle in a time of unchanging perfection, and we are reminded that a relatively unruffled mirroring on the surface of water implicitly signals atmospheric—and, allegorically, spiritual—calm. And in an almost outrageous gesture, far beyond ecphrastic corrective reading or misreading, the poet devotes five stanzas to the picture he would have painted then, had he been able to paint. The light on it—in it—was (as an emended version of these lines added by Wordsworth in 1820, and subsequently deleted, ran) of "a gleam / Of lustre, known to neither sea nor land, / But borrowed from the youthful Poet's dream." In the original—and ultimate—lines, "the light that never was" (as opposed to "that never was on sea or land," unseparated by commas) is a stronger formulation of the illusoriness of that light of false vision. But in Beaumont's painting, the dark air and stormy sea do not allow the ruined tower to coexist with its bright image, and we understand that "Poet's dream" as delusion, not as aspiration, or positive prophetic vision. Indeed, it was horribly unprophetic, for the sea was not like that, but rather like what Beaumont painted, the locus of violent storm and death by drowning.

And yet, the poet has "submitted to a new control"—whether of moral law, or of some sort of reality principle which must do the work, now, that illusion once did—and the distress has "humanised" his soul. It is significant that he returns to an ecphrastic reading of the castle in Beaumont's painting. It is the picture of a survivor, not only of marine violence, but, as the sublime, of false memories of the beautiful or the picturesque:

> And this huge Castle, standing here sublime,
> I love to see the look with which it braves,
> Cased in the unfeeling armor of old time,
> The lightning, the fierce wind, and trampling waves.

It is almost a picture of his own, strangely "humanised" moral survival; and although "the unfeeling armor of old time" cannot help but suggest one kind of isolation that comes from protection, it is the earlier image, "Housed in a dream," walled in by illusion, which he thinks of as being distant from the kindred of other persons. Unlike this image of a battered pile, it enjoys a happiness pitiful and blind. And, as Geoffrey Hartman observed, "the last line . . . in its brevity and isolation is like the inscription on a tomb," and seals up the modulating series of representations.

WASHINGTON ALLSTON

On the Group of the Three Angels
Before the Tent of Abraham,
by Rafaelle, in the Vatican

Oh, now I feel as though another sense
From Heaven descending had informed my soul!
I feel the pleasurable, full control
Of Grace, harmonious, boundless, and intense.
In thee, celestial Group, embodied lives
The subtle mystery; that speaking gives
Itself resolv'd: the essence combin'd
Of Motion ceaseless, Unity complete.
Borne like a leaf by some soft eddying wind,
Mine eyes, impell'd as by enchantment sweet,
From part to part with circling motion rove,
Yet seem unconscious of the power to move;
From line to line through endless changes run,
O'er countless shapes yet seem to gaze on One.

This unfamiliar but important poem presents an unusual instance of a harmonization of elements that involves the inclusion of the picture-reading subject in the ecphrastic object. It is all the more interesting for being by a painter. The American artist Washington Allston lived for a while in England, where he was in close contact with Coleridge and Wordsworth. Some time before 1811 he had written a sonnet on one of the frescoes of a series of biblical scenes high on the walls of the *loggie* in the Vatican. Known as "Raphael's Bible," they were designed but not executed by him (the one in question here is thought to have been painted by Penni). The scene represented is one of the angels (or so they have been officially construed by later Judaic and Christian interpreters—in the biblical Hebrew they are simply called "men") before the tent of Abraham at Mamre (Genesis 18). In the King James Version, the text is as follows:

> 1 And the Lord appeared unto him in the plains of Mamre: and he sat in the tent door in the heat of the day;
> 2 And he lifted up his eyes and looked, and, lo, three men stood by him; and when he saw them, he ran to meet them from the tent door, and bowed himself toward the ground . . .

RAPHAEL, *Abraham and the Angels*

Sarah, his wife, lurking at the tent door at this point, will, we remember, overhear the three saying to Abraham that they, "old and well stricken in age," would have a son, and then "laughed within herself, saying, After I am waxed old shall I have pleasure, my lord being old also?" At which point she is strongly rebuked for her laughter, but the memory of it inheres in the name she gives the son born to them, Isaac (in Hebrew, "laughter").

Raphael's design represents the moment of verse 2 quoted above. Allston's sonnet contemplates not only the frescoed scene, but the consequences of its placement in the room. It incorporates the matter of two related acts. The first is that of gazing—and then of scanning—from below, and of the physical, mental, and spiritual condition in which this puts one. The second is that of construing a picture structurally—formally—and hermeneutically, for the "subtle mystery" of "Unity complete." The descent from heaven in the opening lines is not that of an angelic messenger. Rather, it is, for the viewer who stands under a heavenly work of art, the gift of a new power of visual understanding. The painter-poet's eye reads as much for graphic structure as for scriptural interpretation here (for example, trying to discern the presence of God—who finally breaks forth into anger at Sarah's laughter—among the three "men").

A formal "Unity complete" concludes the octave of Allston's sonnet, itself unifying at a higher level the combined essences, first, of the restless motion of the scanning eye, and the pattern that scanning reveals; second, of the matter of motion and perceived structure or "unity" in the very design itself. (The syntax of "that speaking . . . resolved" is itself something of a mystery. It may be construed as "mystery that, speaking, gives . . . " or alternatively, with the "that" as demonstrative.) To whatever degree the poem sees the embodied "mystery" as a possible type of a theologically Trinitarian one, the esthetic matter overwhelms it. And this is followed by a strangely analogous passage in the sestet. It constitutes a scanning of the very act of scanning a pictorial structure, particularly as a painter might scan form, medium, composition, and effect. The Wordsworthian opening of the poem speaks to the condition of looking upward in general, while the last six lines are more epistemological in their concerns. The "One" at the end (like the "Unity") is a concept both esthetic and divine—a final putting together of those elements of the reading of the painting, and the aforementioned problematic presence of the Lord textually and pictorially hidden among the three. Allston, who had been exposed to ad hoc Unitarian scriptural reading at Harvard, was both cognizant of—and personally distanced from—the matter of a Trinitarian pattern.

The structure of versification of Allston's sonnet itself, also very Wordsworthian in mode, breaks the usual formal orders of octave-sestet organization in its original and ad hoc rhyme scheme—*abbaccde / deffgg*. This has the effect of concluding the octave on a suspended or contingent—because quite unrhyming—"complete" (in this it has affinities with Keats's wonderful sonnet "If by dull rhymes our English must be chained"), and of connecting octave and sestet by the cross-rhymed quatrain that they share. And to a limited but pointed degree, the pattern implies a reciprocal activity in the eyes of the reader of the poem, looking down at it on the page, themselves roving "from line to line" if only to construe the relation of rhymed groups of lines to causes and to stages in the argument. This poem seems to have impressed Coleridge; in his essays *On the Principles of Genial Criticism Concerning the Fine Arts* (1814) he discusses Allston and Raphael together under the rubric of beauty defined as "Multeity in Unity." He also appears to echo, in his own ecphrastic prose passages (of, among other pictures, a painting of Allston's), the latter's invocation of the process of reading a painting—rather than merely decode the sign of, say, an emblem—eyes moving "from part to part with circling motion," yet seeming "unconscious of the power to move."

Allston wrote some other sonnets on paintings, including "On a Falling Group in the Last Judgment of *Michael Angelo* in the Capella Sistina" addressing the "weight" of "the thought / Of space interminable" and praising the giant hand of the painter who could hurl "human forms, with all their mortal weight / Down the dread void": "Already now they seem from world to world / For ages thrown." Another is more abstractly directed to a Rembrandt of Jacob's dream, a third to an *Aeolus* by P. Tebaldi in Bologna, and there is a longish poem on a Horatio Greenough sculptured group. Most interesting is a sonnet "On the Luxembourg Gallery"; it engages the ambivalence that many "struggling gazers" at many times have felt for Rubens at his grandest scale:

> There is a Charm no vulgar mind can reach,
> No critick thwart, no mighty master teach;
> A Charm how mingled of the good and ill!
> Yet still so mingled that the mystick whole
> Shall captive hold the struggling Gazer's will,
> Till vanquish'd reason owns its full control.
> And such, oh Rubens, thy mysterious art,
> The charm that vexes, yet enslaves the heart!
> Thy lawless style, from timid systems free,
> Impetuous rolling like a troubled sea,
> High o'er the rocks of reason's lofty verge
> Impending hangs; yet, ere the foaming surge
> Breaks o'er the bound, the refluent ebb of taste
> Back from the shore impels the wat'ry waste.

But only the Raphael poem partakes so strongly of the impulses of English and American romantic poetry to engage subject and object at once and, especially in this case, to evoke the figure of the descent of a "new sense." It frames a more general parable: truly seeing every true painting reveals that it needs some equivalent or analogous conferring of a new sense particular to it—whether by "descent"—or leaping out, or drawing in, or whatever.

GEORGE GORDON, LORD BYRON

From Childe Harold's Pilgrimage, *canto 4*

Or view the Lord of the unerring bow,
The God of life and poesy and light,—
The Sun in human limbs array'd, and brow
All radiant from his triumph in the fight;
The shaft hath just been shot—the arrow bright
With an immortal's vengeance; in his eye
And nostril beautiful disdain and might
And majesty flash their full lightnings by,
Developing in that one glance the Deity.

But in his delicate form—a dream of Love,
Shaped by some solitary nymph, whose breast
Long'd for a deathless lover from above
And madden'd in that vision—are exprest
All that ideal beauty ever bless'd
The mind with in its most unearthly mood,
When each conception was a heavenly guest—
A ray of immortality—and stood,
Starlike, around, until they gather'd to a god!

And if it be Prometheus stole from Heaven
The fire which we endure, it was repaid
By him to whom the energy was given
Which this poetic marble hath array'd
With an eternal glory—which, if not made
By human hands, is not of human thought;
And Time itself hath hallow'd it, nor laid
One ringlet in the dust; nor hath it caught
A tinge of years, but breathes the flame with which 't was wrought.

ANON., *Apollo Belvedere*

The *Apollo Belvedere* is one of the most celebrated pieces of Greek sculpture. Discovered in the fifteenth century, it was moved by Pope Julius II to the Cortile del Belvedere in the Vatican after 1503, and ever since has entailed the necessary pilgrimage by artist and tourist. It was usually—and without iconographic grounds—interpreted as an image of Apollo with drawn bow about to kill the Python. That there was scorn and anger to be read in the figure's eyes seems to have been agreed upon early on; in the seventeenth century Giambattista Marino's epigram on it in his *Gallery* reads the figure for its eyes, and then goes on to engage the conventional Petrarchan conceit of glances—usually those of a lady's anger or rebuke—being shot from the eyes, or even from under the curved bows of eyebrows:

> How beautifully graceful
> Is this marbled Archer, God
> Of Delos and proud disdain
> Whose menacing bolts are shot
> From the angry vengeance of beautiful eyes
> More than arrows from the hand.
> And if Pontifical and pious zeal
> Had not released and disarmed
> Him of arrow and of bow,
> Niobe, though having wept herself to stone,
> Would yet fear that she'd have a stony heart.

> [Quant'è bello e vezzoso
> questo marmoreo Arcier, Nume di Delo
> tanto fiero e sdegnoso
> par che minacci e scocchi
> assai più da' begli occhi ire e vendette,
> che de man saette.
> E se Pontifical pietoso zelo
> già disarmato non l'avesse, e scarco
> e di quadrella e d'arco,
> Niobe se ben di senso ha il petto casso,
> fatta ancor sasso, il temeria di sasso.]

Niobe, who boasted of herself and her children, so offended Apollo's (and Artemis's) mother that the two gods killed her children and turned them to stone; Niobe wept copiously at this, until she became stone herself—hence her relevance to the matter of a stone Apollo. Marino alludes to the source and provenance of the piece as well as to the Ovidian story in the mythological background of the god represented.

In the later eighteenth century, J. J. Winckelmann had praised the piece as an instance, lying before our eyes, of the best of what "Natur, Geist und Kunst"—Nature, Mind, and Art—are capable. And he speaks of the figure's lofty look, filled with a consciousness of power, [which] seems to rise far above his victory, and to gaze into infinity. Scorn sits upon his lips, and his nostrils are swelling with suppressed anger, which mounts even to the proud forehead; but the blissful calm remains undisturbed, and his eye is full of sweetness as when the Muses gathered around him seeking to embrace him.

The serene regard and calm forehead produced for Winckelmann a presiding composure which prevented the other two represented sensations from compromising the beauty of the figure. (It should be observed that Henry Fuseli had translated Winckelmann's essay on the *Apollo Belvedere* in 1768.)

James Thomson in the fourth part of *Liberty* (1736) had previously invoked the *Apollo Belvedere* as evidence of the rebirth of culture from medieval barbarism ("Amid the hoary ruins, / Sculpture first, / Deep digging from the cavern dark and damp, / Their grave for ages, bade her marble race / Spring to new light"). Here is the Apollo:

> All conquest-flushed from prostrate Python came
> The quivered God. In graceful act he stands,
> His arm extended with the slackened bow:
> Light flows his easy robe, and fair displays
> A manly-softened form. The bloom of gods
> Seems youthful o'er the beardless cheek to wave:
> His features yet heroic ardour warms;
> And sweet subsiding to a native smile,
> Mixed with the joy elating conquest gives,
> A scattered frown exalts his matchless air.

("Scattered" is used here to mean "dropped negligently" [OED sense 3b].) Aside from the Virgilian change of tense in the first two lines, this reading might be one of the Hellenistic ones. Like Winckelmann, Thomson perceives a mixture of feelings suffusing the face, but here they are heroic ardour, whatever it is that produces a "native smile," and the joy of conquest. This might itself be an epic description, a piece of notional ecphrasis embedded in a heroic fable. There is nothing revisionary about it, no ad hoc mythmaking occurs (for example, a moralizing of Apollo as Renaissance culture and the Python as the last resentful residuum of barbarism), and the consciousness of the gazer does not inhere in the object in any way.

But not so in Byron's lines from what might be called the visionary travelogue of canto 4 of *Childe Harold's Pilgrimage*, in a section that also addresses the Laocoön, the Gladiator, and the architectural monuments of the Coliseum and St. Peter's. The first of his stanzas goes into the nature of what Thomson had called "the quivered God" and similarly reads back into the piece the bow, not slackened, but rather as having just loosed an avenging arrow (but at what or whom? the Python? and what would *that* mean?). Thomson's "scattered frown" is replaced by the rhythmic energy with which the "beautiful disdain and might / And majesty flash their full lightnings by." Byron adds, in a moment of an almost Hegelian history of mythmaking, that—through such lightnings—disdain, might, and majesty are "Developing in that glance the Deity." It is as if he had interestingly reworked Winckelmann's triad of serenity rising above (in eyes and brow) indignation and contempt into a yet higher order of transformation.

In Byron's second stanza, the mythmaking is quite explicit, and the relations among bodily beauty, desire, and an ideal of *to kalon*, the Beautiful, are revealed in their complexity. This is no Ovidian story of one of Apollo's attempted rapes, but more of the post-Spenserian sort of fable one might encounter in Shelley. And there is a theogony parallel to—but revisionary of—the one in the previous stanza. Here it is not universals ("beautiful disdain," "majesty," etc.) but the conceptions of desire—themselves emanations of immortality—that coalesce into deity. Here, too, a *furor poeticus* is invoked, and a vision of those conceptions standing "starlike, around"—almost as if they were themselves gazers, like Childe Harold, starstruck at the image of godhead as "life and poesy and light." And the poesy is what it comes down to. In the last of these stanzas, the refigured light, glancing off and modeling the carved marble as if in an immortal animation, becomes further refigured in the fire of art and imagination.

It is amusing to observe that when the young Benjamin West first arrived in Rome in 1760 he was shown the Vatican marbles by Cardinal Albani (whose librarian was Winckelmann) and a company of *cognoscenti*, with the notion of seeing how this virtual savage might react to great works of art. As Van Wyck Brooks recounted it, they

> set out to see the Apollo Belvedere, as this was regarded as the most perfect of the ornaments of Rome and therefore most likely to produce an effect. West was placed before the cabinet in which the Apollo stood . . . and it was then that he spoke the words, "How like a Mohawk warrior!"—a natural phrase to be uttered by a man from the forest.

But it is more than possible that West, an ambitious young portrait-painter from Pennsylvania, had himself already internalized the form of the figure's famous *contrapposto* which was so paradigmatic for full-length portraits in the eighteenth century.

ANON., *The Head of Medusa*

On the Medusa of Leonardo da Vinci in the Florentine Gallery

I

It lieth, gazing on the midnight sky,
　　Upon the cloudy mountain-peak supine;
Below, far lands are seen tremblingly;
　　Its horror and its beauty are divine.
Upon its lips and eyelids seems to lie
　　Loveliness like a shadow, from which shine,
Fiery and lurid, struggling underneath,
The agonies of anguish and of death.

II

Yet it is less the horror than the grace
　　Which turns the gazer's spirit into stone,
Whereon the lineaments of that dead face
　　Are graven, till the characters be grown
Into itself, and thought no more can trace;
　　'Tis the melodious hue of beauty thrown
Athwart the darkness and the glare of pain,
Which humanize and harmonize the strain.

III

And from its head as from one body grow,
　　As [river-] grass out of a watery rock,
Hairs which are vipers, and they curl and flow
　　And their long tangles in each other lock,
And with unending involutions show
　　Their mailèd radiance, as it were to mock
The torture and the death within, and saw
The solid air with many a raggèd jaw.

IV

And, from a stone beside, a poisonous eft
     Peeps idly into those Gorgonian eyes;
Whilst in the air a ghastly bat, bereft
     Of sense, has flitted with a mad surprise
Out of the cave this hideous light had cleft,
     And he comes hastening like a moth that hies
After a taper; and the midnight sky
Flares, a light more dread than obscurity.

V

'Tis the tempestuous loveliness of terror;
     For from the serpents gleams a brazen glare
Kindled by that inextricable error,
     Which makes a thrilling vapour of the air
Become a [dim] and ever-shifting mirror
     Of all the beauty and the terror there —
A woman's countenance, with serpent-locks,
Gazing in death on Heaven from those wet rocks.

The painting in the Uffizi in Florence that is in question here is seventeenth century, probably Flemish, and possibly done after a lost original by Leonardo, or at least after Vasari's description of it. To romantic eyes, this somewhat Caravaggesque image represented the problematic and murderous beauty after she had been killed by Perseus. For Walter Pater, this seemed to be the canonical view of the Gorgon, and he remarked of this painting that "The subject has been treated in various ways; Leonardo alone cuts to its centre; he alone realises it as the head of a corpse, exercising its power through all the circumstances of death." The remainder of this passage from *The Renaissance* is itself remarkable:

> What may be called the fascination of corruption penetrates in every touch of its exquisitely finished beauty. About the dainty lines of the cheek the bats flit unheeded. The delicate snakes seem literally strangling each other in terrified struggle to escape the Medusa brain. The hue which violent death always brings with it is in the features; features singularly massive and grand, as we catch them inverted, in a dexterous foreshortening, crown foremost, like a great calm stone against which a wave of serpents breaks.

The poem ascribed to Shelley "On the Medusa of Leonardo da Vinci in the Florentine Gallery" (and Mary Shelley may indeed have collaborated with him on it) typifies the kinds of displacement which can occur in modern as well as romantic poems on paintings. Its five stanzas start out with literal description—"It lieth, gazing on the midnight sky / Upon the cloudy mountain-peak supine"—although the mountain-peak in question here is not in the picture, but somewhere in Shelley's memory of the myth. By the second stanza, the gazer has become Medusa's victim: "Yet it is less the horror than the grace / Which turns the gazer's spirit into stone," and the terror has become that of a petrifying loveliness. Finally, there is an additional gazer, the reader who looks through the text of the poem at the invoked image. It is significant that from the sixteenth through the early nineteenth centuries, the noun "gaze," in OED sense 1, designated the *object* of a concentrated stare, and not the stare itself. (Analogously, today, something is said to have a "look" if arranged to appear to a fashionably conscious—and thereby aesthetically and epistemologically beclouded—act of looking, or "look.")

Subsequent stanzas are intent upon the snakes, the attendant lizards, and so forth. The matter of the harmonization of horror and beauty pervades the rest of the poem's *ascriptive description* (for so one might term all poetic ecphrasis). Finally, at the end, the gaze is turned upon the victor-victim herself. Perseus's mirroring shield protected him from the Gorgon's literally petrifying stare; but, in Shelley's last stanza, the mirroring is revised. The concluding lines are themselves entranced by the skyward gaze of the dead Medusa's head. The very air becomes a mirror of beauty and terror, and the sublimity leaps out of the conceptual scheme of the image and the myth. And even as, in the second stanza, the viewer of the painting becomes its victim, here that same viewer seems momentarily safe from the monster's gaze which, however, has turned the very air into a mirror.

An additional stanza—which might or might not be an authentic final one—was first published by Neville Rogers in 1959: it might well seem better placed between the first and second stanzas, and its concluding oxymoron seems insufficiently strong or resonant to conclude the poem. I give it here without further comment:

> It is a woman's countenance divine
> > With everlasting beauty breathing there
> Which from a stormy mountain's peak, supine
> > Gazes into the [mid-?] night's trembling air.
> It is a trunkless head, and on its feature
> > Death has met life, but there is life in death,
> The blood is frozen—but unconquered Nature
> > Seems struggling to be the last—without a breath
> The fragment of an uncreated creature.

It may be instructive to compare Shelley's Medusa poem with a much earlier one, of the older sort that shows no traces of self-scrutiny, and only the most oblique hints of self-reference. Such poems from the sixteenth and seventeenth centuries are both more epigrammatic—in their tendency to reduce the painted image to a paradigm—and more likely to regard the specific interpretation of the avowed "subject" by the artist, as well as the matter of execution, as a mere occasion for encomium. Giambattista Marino's little poem, from the prodigious collection of ecphrastic verses in *La Galeria* confronts a head of Medusa by Caravaggio, also in the Uffizi. It speaks only to the fact that the head is on a shield, and that the shield belongs to the Duke of Tuscany. Otherwise, the poem might be "on" any Gorgon's head on a shield and, indeed, seems to evade the fact that Medusa's head traditionally occupies the boss of the shield of Athena herself.

The Head of Medusa on a Rotella of Michelangelo da Caravaggio, in the Gallery of the Grand Duke of Tuscany

> What foes are there who could not suddenly
> Turn, cold, into marble
> On looking at that Gorgon in your shield,
> Proud, Signor, and cruel,
> For whose locks bundled vipers horribly
> Frame a dreary ornament, and frightful?
> But Oh! the fearsome monster
> Would be of little help to you in war,
> The real Medusa being your own valor.

> [Or quai nemici fian, che freddi marmi
> non divengan repente
> in mirando, Signor, nel vostro scudo
> quel fier Gorgone, e crudo,
> cui fanno orribilmente
> volumi viperini
> squallida pompa e spaventosa ai crini?
> Ma che! Poco fra l'armi
> a voi fia d'uopo il formadibil mostro:
> chè la vera Medusa è il valor vostro.]

Here the Duke's own *valor* surpasses the image's own *spavento*, or horror, which is about all Marino credits it with, as he directs his observation not to the shield but to its owner, asking what foes there could possibly be who would not turn to stone on seeing it. But this is a far cry from "the beauty and the terror" of Shelley's conception of the head in the later painting.

One other earlier epigram on Medusa by William Drummond of Hawthornden (1585–1649) is very much like Marino's in form and versification (it was indeed probably suggested by a Latin epigram of the fifteenth-century Antonio Tebaldeo). Since it is specifically on a notional stone statue of Medusa, an easy paradox of self-petrification is available to reinforce the older cliche of wondering praise for the artist's skill ("This isn't an image of X. Why, it is X herself!" etc.). In the third line, by the way, the archaic "None" is modern "no."

CARAVAGGIO, *The Head of Medusa*

The Statue of MEDUSA

Of that MEDUSA strange
Who those that did her see in Rockes did change,
None image carv'd is this;
MEDUSAS selfe it is,
For whilst at Heat of Day,
To quench her Thirst Shee by this Spring did stay,
Her curling Snakes beholding in this Glasse,
Life did her leave, and thus transform'd Shee was.

JOHN TRUMBULL, *The Declaration of Independence*

The National Painting

Awake, ye forms of verse divine!
    Painting! descend on canvas wing, —
And hover o'er my head, Design!
    Your son, your glorious son, I sing;
At T[rumbull]'s name I break my sloth,
    To load him with poetic riches:
The Titian of a table-cloth!
    The Guido of a pair of breeches!

Come, star-eyed maid, Equality!
    In thine adorer's praise I revel;
Who brings, so fierce his love to thee,
    All forms and faces to a level:
Old, young, great, small, the grave, the gay,
    Each man might swear the next his brother,
And there they stand in dread array,
    To fire their votes at one another.

How bright their buttons shine! how straight
    Their coat-flaps fall in plaited grace!
How smooth the hair on every pate!
    How vacant each immortal face!
And then the tints, the shade, the flush,
    (I wrong them with a strain too humble),
Not mighty S[herred]'s strength of brush
    Can match thy glowing hues, my T[rumbul].

Go on, great painter! dare be dull —
    No longer after Nature dangle;
Call rectilinear beautiful;
    Find grace and freedom in an angle;
Pour on the red, the green, the yellow,
    Paint till a horse may mire upon it,
And, while I've strength to write or bellow,
    I'll sound your praises in a sonnet.

John Trumbull began work in 1784 on a series of paintings celebrating the triumph of the American Revolution. Eight of them were completed, and planned for engraving; eventually, huge versions of them ended up around the rotunda of the Capitol in Washington. One of the best known of these is *The Declaration of Independence*, representing not the historical moment of the signing of the instantiating document, but rather of its presentation, by Thomas Jefferson, to John Hancock. It contained at least thirty-seven historical portraits done from life, and represented the interior space—based on Jefferson's recollections, and sketches—of the plan of the ground floor of the old State House in Philadelphia. The treatment of the particular moment represents an enactment of a secular version of the Old Testament Covenant, the occasion of setting up a political order based on free choice, assumed obligation, and the sovereignty of popular will. As one perceptive critic has explained, "This is the theme Trumbull tries to suggest, at least partly by the presence of banners and battle trophies on the back wall that seem to hover over the heads of the central group like an image of the Holy Spirit." Completed in 1786, it hangs in the Yale Art Gallery, along with the other paintings of the series.

A huge (122 x 18 feet) replica of the painting, identical save for one missing figure (that of Thomas Nelson, Jr.), was completed in 1818 and exhibited in the autumn of that year in New York. It was seen there by, among others, the promising, witty, early nineteenth-century man of letters Joseph Rodman Drake (he died in 1820, at the age of 25) who, early in the next year, and under the pseudonym of "Croaker" that he usually appended to his comic and satiric work, published his neoclassical spoof of a neoclassical narrative painting. The verses send up not only the antipainterly deadliness of Trumbull's scene ("The Titian of a tablecloth! / The Guido [Reni] of a pair of breeches!"), but the analogous diction and conceptual personifications ("Painting" and "Design") with which academy pictures had been praised in the preceding century. Jacob Sherred, invoked in the fourth stanza, was a prosperous painter and glazier in New York City at the time. The whole thrust of the wit in these verses is a familiar one, ridiculing any attempt to render near-contemporary events in heroic terms (as if heroes had to be draped, or stage-costumed, while whoever wears breeches is just one of us). Drake's success is sealed by the compact scale of his ridicule, as opposed to the pious grandeur of the painting.

DANTE GABRIEL ROSSETTI

For
"Our Lady of the Rocks"
By Leonardo da Vinci

Mother, is this the darkness of the end,
    The Shadow of Death? and is that outer sea
    Infinite imminent Eternity?
And does the death-pang by man's seed sustain'd
In Time's each instant cause thy face to bend
    Its silent prayer upon the Son, while he
    Blesses the dead with his hand silently
To his long day which hours no more offend?

Mother of grace, the pass is difficult,
    Keen as these rocks, and the bewildered souls
        Throng it like echoes, blindly shuddering through.
    Thy name, O Lord, each spirit's voice extols,
        Whose peace abides in the dark avenue
Amid the bitterness of things occult.

Dante Gabriel Rossetti's sonnets on pictures are so central to the modern tradition of ecphrastic poetry that one could devote many pages to these alone. That Rossetti used the sonnet form as a strong and flexible framework for his verbal representations of picturing emerges clearly from a study of any one of them. Probably the greatest of these is the one for Leonardo's Madonna in the National Gallery in London, written, purportedly, "in front of the picture." Leonardo's famous image (Rossetti calls it "Our Lady of the Rocks") is of the Madonna and child with the young John the Baptist and the angel Gabriel, right, witnessing the fact that Jesus is blessing his older precursor. (In the version of this celebrated painting in the Louvre, the angel literally points this out.) The celebrated background has to this day not been given an authoritative iconographic interpretation. One scholar suggested a somewhat reductive construction of its rocks as illustrating a medieval reading of a verse in the Song of Songs (2.14—"my dove that art in the clefts of the rock, in crannies in the wall" referring to the Virgin Mary, and the rocky places and caves as Christ). A. Richard Turner adumbrates on this:

LEONARDO DA VINCI, *Virgin of the Rocks*

More generally, Leonardo seems to suggest that the coming of grace is the culminating event in a world very old, a world where growth and decay of both the organic and the inorganic co-exist in an eternal rhythm. A spiritual mystery is conceived as inseparable from the process of time itself.

It is just with the looming, dark enigma of the landscape, the complex background with its structures of rock, water, and occluded access to distances, that this poem is most concerned. It starts out with the kind of poetic question common to many poems about visual images, including some more of Rossetti's own. (Three of his many poems on paintings—two on Memling, one on his own *Astarte Syriaca*—begin with a grammatical absolute, the self-propounding word "Mystery"; and his "Pandora" and "A Sea-Spell" are both all interrogative.) But here, the inquiry is directed neither at the painting nor at the painter, but instead at the figure of the Virgin herself, and is absorbed in wonder at the meaning of the darkness, the shadows, and the distant, gleaming ocean. The octave of this sonnet is all questions; the sestet comprises two dark assertions, as if—but only darkly and metaphorically—in answer. The first is addressed to the "Mother" (which word opens both octave and sestet), the other to the child. The poem asks *Is this a picture of Death, rather than of the childhood of Eternal Life?* The very phrase "The Shadow of Death," ultimately from the English translation of Psalm 23, is a complex one, grammatically and tropologically, given the dense semantic history of the term "shadow" in the Renaissance and after (it can mean shade, cast shadow attached or unattached, image or picture of any kind, verbal trope, antitype of an interpretative figural relation, version or altered form, etc.). "The Shadow of Death" can be a literal darkness cast by an occluding presence (a personification of death, say), the shadow or image of something else that such a personification itself constitutes, a shaded region in which death lurks, the frightening but ultimately fictive stuff—given the ransom paid by the Christian sacrifice—of which our sense of death is made, and so forth.

The mother in the painting seems, like the other figures in it, to be unaware of the landscape, even to the degree to which Mona Lisa might be said to smile faintly and knowingly in some kind of enigmatic knowledge of the scene opening out behind her. But the poet reads a consciousness of the landscape's meaning here into Mary's gesture and, more outrageously, adduces the matter of death in regard to the Son's blessing. This, enacted by his gesture, transcends his mother's knowledge of mortality—even as a probable pun on "ours / hours" frees "his long day" from the tincture of fleeting human instants. "The darkness of the end" in the opening line, and "that outer sea," both guide the scanning eye rapidly into the pictorial space toward the ultimate clefts in the rocks through which far distant light thrusts itself.

Whether it has heard answers to these questions—whether it has propounded its own, or even deemed them to be answerable as put, the sestet moves deep into the background of the painting. In cadences that sound like lines from T. S. Eliot's "Ash-Wednesday" written eighty years later ("Mother of grace, the pass is difficult, / Keen as these rocks . . ."), the sestet calls attention to its own passages: to the poem's "pass" from octave to sestet, from interrogative to declarative sentences, from foreground figure to background place, and to rhymes not on "He" and "outer sea" and "Eternity," but on the bracketing of "difficult" and ultimately "occult." The ways through the rocks are of life's entrances and exits—the pass of the birth canal or, conversely, the narrow room of dying. These lead to or from the maternal, oceanic spaces through which "the death-pang by man's need sustained" causes us all to move and move again, "blindly shuddering through" (the crowds of "bewildered souls" come, it has been suggested, from Leonardo's *Adoration* in the Uffizi in Florence, whose remembered presences themselves "echo" in the words on this other painting). The opening to the sea on the left is balanced by the cleft on the right, filled with a towering phallic rock. The ambiguous syntax (*whose* peace is it that "abides in the dark avenue"? the Lord's? that of "each spirit"?) makes for no dark puzzle. But the poem's one remarkable omission is another matter.

The angel Gabriel gazes at the infant John, while the younger Son seems to follow the indication with his gaze and benedictional hand. But Gabriel looks out at the viewer, for whom the act of pointing-at is more generally one of pointing-out (i.e., that "such-and-such is the case"). Gabriel serves as what art-historians call a *Sprecher*—a figure in a narrative scene who looks out of it, figuratively speaking to a viewer—for the picture's meaning. George Hersey, in a fascinating unpublished commentary on this poem, suggested a decade ago that it is the Dante Gabriel (indeed, Rossetti was called "Gabriel" by family and friends) who replaces the Angel Gabriel as speaker. The whole sonnet, with its recasting of foreground events in the dark light of the background, its radical poetic mistaking of the matter of shadow (for Leonardo, shadow was not a matter of death, but of giving life to form), its obscure lesson about deaths and entrances, and its insistence on nature rather than grace, after all, is a triumphantly audacious replacement for the direct, at most twofold, act of ostension by the undiscursive Gabriel in the painting.

But Gabriel emerges as a central figure in Charles Lamb's scarcely known poem on the same painting, in which the landscape is never mentioned. His "Lines: On the Celebrated Picture by Leonardo da Vinci, called the Virgin of the Rocks" starts out with the question of Mary's engagement in—and lack of knowledge of the consequences of—the domestic scene around her:

> While young John runs to greet
> The greater infant's feet,
> The Mother standing by, with trembling passion
> Of devout admiration,
> Beholds the engaging mystic play, and petty adoration;
> Nor knows as yet the full event
> Of those so low beginnings,
> From whence we date our winnings,
> But wonders at the intent
> Of those new rites, and what that strange child-worship meant . . .

The metrical scheme seems deliberately allusive of Italian poetry—and the wit of the rhyme on "winnings" / "beginnings" is pointedly baroque—but the question of Mary's consciousness is close to the one Yeats's speaker raises about Leda ("Did she put on his knowledge with his power? . . . ") and feels like a precursor text of both Rossetti's and Yeats's sonnets. But the remainder of the poem centers on Gabriel, the *Sprecher* and the knower.

> But at her side
> An angel doth abide,
> With such a perfect joy
> As no dim doubts alloy,
> An intuition,
> A glory, an amenity,
> Passing the dark condition
> Of blind humanity,
> As if he surely knew
> All the blest wonder should ensue,
> Or he had lately left the upper sphere,
> And had read all the sovran schemes and divine riddles there.

"The dark condition / Of blind humanity" perhaps hints of the dark rocks through which Rossetti's souls come "blindly shuddering through." But the poem concludes in acknowledgment of enigma, with perhaps an overtone of reference to ecphrastic puzzlement as well, the "sovran schemes" of artists yielding up what are nonetheless "divine riddles."

Ecphrasis then, its own sort of a dangerous supplement, has in Rossetti's great sonnet stood in for—represented—the image of a figure. Starting with a question, it ends in a hermeneutic realm of difficulty, darkness, occulted light, and knowledge. As such, it is paradigmatic of the modern iconic or pictorial poem in at least three ways: first, the allegorical use of its own formal scheme and rhetorical structure in the representation of something spatial and structural it sees in the picture; second, the way it looks to other texts and even other pictures—here, the Psalm—as a filter through which the light of the painting is read; and finally, the way the poem regards its own breaking of silence, its own usurpation of the realm of image, speaking for it because it will not speak for itself.

TITIAN, *Concert Champêtre*

For
A Venetian Pastoral
By Giorgone
(In the Louvre)

Water, for anguish of the solstice: —nay,
　　　But dip the vessel slowly, —nay, but lean
　　　And hark how at its verge the wave sighs in
Reluctant. Hush! Beyond all depth away
The heat lies silent at the brink of day:
　　　Now the hand trails upon the viol-string
　　　That sobs, and the brown faces cease to sing,
Sad with the whole of pleasure. Whither stray
Her eyes now, from whose mouth the slim pipes creep
　　　And leave it pouting, while the shadowed grass
　　　　　Is cool against her naked side? Let be: —
Say nothing now unto her lest she weep,
　　　Nor name this ever. Be it as it was, —
　　　　　Life touching lips with Immortality.

A painting in the Louvre, once ascribed to Giorgione and now thought to be by Titian, occasioned another of Rossetti's remarkable ecphrastic sonnets. Walter Pater, quite aware of this "delightful sonnet," wrote in *The Renaissance* of this and other Venetian landscapes (of "The School of Giorgione") that its favorite incidents were "music or musical intervals in our existence." (He meant not "interval" in our technical sense of an octave or a third, but rather a silence or space or gap of time in our experience, here made "musical" only in a figurative sense):

> Life is conceived as a sort of listening, listening to music . . . to the sound of water, to time as it flies . . . in the school of Giorgione, the presence of water—the well, or marble-rimmed pool, the drawing or pouring of water, as the woman pours it from a pitcher with her jewelled hand in the *Fête Champêtre*, listening, perhaps, to the cool sound as it falls, blent with the music of the pipes—is as characteristic, and almost as suggestive, as music itself.

Pater—in the course of expounding his dictum that "all art constantly aspires towards the condition of music"—is himself poetically associating maritime Venice with music and water in the visions of its art. But the pitcher in the well, with which Rossetti's poem commences (and drawing, not pouring), is clearly audible in the background of Pater's thought.

Rossetti sees invisible elements of the painting—the way well water will slowly move into the narrow lip of the pitcher, and the averted mouth ("pouting"—because still forming its wind-playing embouchure) of the seated woman. He asks a question which he decides to leave unanswered. But it is not one of the more obvious ones, such as "Are these mortals or gods?" or "What are the men saying to one another?" or "How are the men and women to be paired?" or "What makes that distant house deserve to be the apex of just that important triangle in the formal structure of the painting?" Instead, he asks, "What is she looking at?" It is this question, perhaps, which lurks behind Richard Wollheim's suggestion—occupied as it is with the matter of *le regard* which often concerns him—that "we even become sensitized to the gaze of the seated woman who has her broad back turned to us." And although there is no structural parallel between foreground/background in the painting and octave/sestet in the sonnet—as in the case of Rossetti's poem on the Leonardo Madonna—the viewer-reader is still led through the painting as the sonnet unfolds. From the nude woman with the water, we move deep into—even beyond—the background ("beyond all depth, / The heat lies silent at the bank of day"). Then we are brought forward again to the men and the music, and, finally, to the woman on the right.

An earlier version of this sonnet was published in *The Germ* in 1850. It is instructive to compare the two. The first one is accompanied by a minimal prose ecphrasis of the painting: "In this picture, two cavaliers and an undraped woman are seated in the grass, with musical instruments, while another woman dips a vase into a well head, for water." And it is almost as if to gloss this last word that the sonnet—in both versions—opens. But consider the unrevised one:

> Water, for anguish of the solstice, —yea
> Over the vessel's mouth still widening
> Listless dipt to let the water in
> With slow vague gurgle. Blue, and deep away,
> The heat lies silent at the brink of day.
> Now the hand trails upon the viol-string
> That sobs; and the brown faces cease to sing,
> Mournful with complete pleasure. Her eyes stray
> In distance; through her lips the pipe doth creep
> And leaves them pouting; the green shadowed grass
> Is cool against her naked flesh. Let be:
> Do not now speak unto her lest she weep, —
> Nor name this ever. Be it as it was: —
> Silence of heat, and solemn poetry.

The "nay" for the earlier "yea" is not as significant as the loss of the designated colors, blue and green (only "brown faces" remain in the later poem), or as the question about what the recorder-playing lady is looking at which replaces the descriptive observation that her eyes "stray / In distance." The description of the water in this version is interesting for the poetic *enargeia*, the vividness, of its phonology and syntax in telling of the water "still widening" over the mouth of the vessel that is "listlessly dipt to let the water in / With slow vague gurgle." The listlessness, perhaps of pastoral *otium*, gives way to an injunction to dip the vessel—and perhaps to disturb thereby the water's reflective surface—slowly. Rossetti himself remarked of the final line in this version that it "seems to me quite bad. 'Solemn poetry' belongs to the class of phrase absolutely forbidden, I think, in poetry. It is intellectually incestuous—poetry seeking to beget its emotional offspring on its own identity." Of the equivalent line in the final version, he added, "It gives only the momentary contact with the immortal which results from sensuous culmination, and is always a half-conscious element of it."

A far more radically "poetic" reading of the relation of the women to the men in the painting was advanced over thirty years ago by a professionally unpoetic art-historian. He argued that the female figures are not ladies of the Veneto, but rather nymphs, and therefore live and move and have their being, as it were, in a different realm from the men who, as a consequence of this, cannot see them. One could indeed imagine a Rossettian sort of sonnet which might, in its octave, embrace the epistemology of the painting (the women, as women, are *there*) and then, in the sestet beginning with a "But no, for, . . . " advancing the contrary view. But despite some literal "mistakes" in reading the objects in the painting (the musical instruments here are a lute, not a viol, and a recorder or flute, not "pipes") Rossetti moves to a romantic poetic conception of the heart of the pictorial matter by pointing to the momentary suspension—Pater's "musical interval"—of the sound of water and of wind-music in the recorder. That moment of pause even in the women's music is the relation between Wordsworthian spots of time and the clear expanse of eternity designated in the final version of the poem's last line, which, as W. M. Rossetti suggested, was to substitute ("Nor name this [picture] ever") for a museum curator's title.

Hiram Powers, *The Greek Slave*

Hiram Powers' Greek Slave

They say Ideal beauty cannot enter
The house of anguish. On the threshold stands
An alien Image with enshackled hands,
Called the Greek Slave! as if the artist meant her
(That passionless perfection which he lent her,
Shadowed not darkened where the sill expands)
To so confront man's crimes in different lands
With man's ideal sense. Pierce to the centre,
Art's fiery finger! and break up ere long
The serfdom of this world! appeal, fair stone,
From God's pure heights of beauty against man's wrong!
Catch up in thy divine face, not alone
East griefs but west, and strike and shame the strong,
By thunders of white silence, overthrown.

The Greek Slave by the American sculptor Hiram Powers was a sensational piece in its day. Conceived and modeled in 1842, the first of five surviving full-size versions of the figure was completed in 1844 and shipped to London, where it was exhibited at Graves's Rooms in Pall Mall the following year, and six years later in the Crystal Palace; it was the second version, finished in 1847, that caused the work to be so widely known in the United States. The "world renowned statue over which Poets have grown sublime, and Orators eloquent" (as one hand-bill put it) was taken on tour through the East Coast and parts of the Midwest (the same handbill announced that—presumably because of the nudity of the piece—"None but ladies and families will be admitted during the afternoon of each day"). Sometimes attacked for its nudity, it was often praised for its purity: "The Greek slave is clothed all over with sentiment, sheltered, protected by it from every profane eye." A journal in New York in 1847 puts it even more splendidly:

> Loud talking men are hushed into a silence which they themselves wonder; those who came to speak silently and utter ecstasies of dilettantism sink into corners where alone they may silently gaze in pleasing penance for their audacity, and groups of women hover together as if to seek protection from the power of their own sex's beauty.

—or, in other words, feelings of boisterous lust, coarse connoisseurship, and modest blushes are alike transfigured by the sacred loftiness of the white marble, the posture taken from the *Venus pudica* tradition of the Cnidian Aphrodite—passed through the easy neoclassical generalizing of the work of Thorvaldsen (who praised it) and Canova—and, of course, the averted gaze. Even more significant is the fact that, replacing the usual classical drapery, here was a piece of fringed fabric easily identified with modern, rather than with ancient, Hellas.

Elizabeth Barrett Browning's sonnet has more on its mind than had the drivel of approbation in both prose and verse that flowed from American pens ("Naked yet clothed with chastity, She stands / And as a shield throws back the sun's hot rays, / Her modest mien repels each vulgar gaze," etc.). In the first place, the issue of Greek independence—so dear to Byron and other English romantic poets—was still a recent one: Powers had conceived of a Greek girl being taken by Ottoman Turks to be sold in Constantinople, "too deeply concerned to be aware of her nakedness." Browning's poem is also acutely aware of the shadow cast on both the white marble and the matter of Greek independence by the unended horror of Negro slavery in America, and assimilates, although with considerable rhetorical awkwardness ("not alone / East griefs but west") their claims on the conscience. The figure of "Ideal beauty" standing on the threshold of "the house of anguish" is, of course, a white and silent one, but her association with the "thunders" that ended at Appomattox remains a little hard to construe.

The very whiteness of Powers's marble and its constant flash of highlights is recalled, incidentally, in a sonnet on his *Ideal Head of* [Samuel] *Rogers' Genevra* by the American Southern poet Richard Henry Wilde, which concludes in a familiar but neatly arranged sequence of tropes of expressive radiance. Samuel Rogers's textual heroine, figured in the sculptor's white marble, finally gleams textually again in Wilde's verses:

> And poor Genevra's innocence which gleams
> In Rogers' verse even through her fearful bier
> In Power's [*sic*] marble now immortal beams.

Mrs. Browning had also written an ecphrastic sonnet on Benjamin R. Haydon's portrait of Wordsworth on Mount Helvellyn, which starts out by urging the landscape, behind the famous image of the poet with crossed arms and lowered head, to get its mimetic act together: "Let the cloud / Ebb audibly along the mountain-wind / Then break against the rock, and show behind / The lowland valleys floating up to crowd / The sense with beauty." But it ends, rather creakingly, with an Academic air in its tired cliche about portraiture: "Nor portrait this, with Academic air! / This is the poet and his poetry." The more Shelleyan conclusion of the Hiram Powers sonnet is more satisfying.

R O B E R T   B R O W N I N G

The "Moses" of Michael Angelo

And who is He that, sculptured in huge stone,
      Sitteth a giant, where no works arrive
      Of straining Art, and hath so prompt and live
The lips, I listen to their very tone?
Moses is He — Ay, that, makes clearly known
      The chin's thick boast, and brow's prerogative
      Of double ray: so did the mountain give
Back to the world that visage, God was grown
Great part of! Such was he when he suspended
      Round him the sounding and vast waters; such
          When he shut sea on sea o'er Mizraïm.
And ye, his hordes, a vile calf raised, and bended
      The knee? This Image had ye raised, not much
      Had been your error in adoring him.

Michelangelo's great *Moses* (finished in 1516) was originally planned as part of a massive tomb for Pope Julius II. Now in the church of San Pietro in Vincoli in Rome, it is a fabled icon, if only for its scale, its attractively enigmatic seated position, the extremely problematic activity of the hands, and, most obviously, the horns emerging from the head of Moses. These are the result of a literal visual representation of the text of the Vulgate, which translates the Hebrew of Exodus 34.29, telling of how Moses came down from Sinai bearing the tables of the law—"Moses wist not that the skin of his face shone" (King James Version). The original uses the Hebrew verb *karan* ("to be radiant") as if it were the noun *keren* ("horn"), and the Latin takes the latter meaning for its *quod cornuta esset facies sua* ("and his face was horned"). Both the horns and the tablets indicate a narrative moment after the decent from Sinai, but not while he was wearing—as according to the end of Exodus 34—a veil on his face. Yet what Moses is actually doing, and what he is thinking and feeling, have remained in continual dispute. Vasari's praise of the piece builds in wonder to a final complimentary conceit of the kind one finds in contemporary and later poetic epigrams, but it begs all the questions of narrative:

> Seated in a serious attitude, he rests with one arm on the tables, and with the other holds his long glossy beard, the hairs, so difficult to render in sculpture, being so soft and downy that it seems as if the iron chisel must have become a brush. The

MICHELANGELO, *Moses*

beautiful face, like that of a saint and mighty prince, seems as one regards it to need the veil to cover it, so splendid and shining does it appear, and so well has the artist presented in the marble the divinity with which God endowed that holy countenance. The draperies fall in graceful folds, the muscles of the arms and bones of the hands are of such beauty and perfection, as are the legs and knees, the feet being adorned with excellent shoes, that Moses may now be called the friend of God more than ever, since God has permitted his body to be prepared for the resurrection before the others by the hand of Michelagnolo.

Vasari adds that "The Jews still go every Saturday in troops to visit and adore it as a divine, not a human thing."

Robert Browning's sonnet translates quite faithfully one by Giambattista Felics Zappi (1667–1719). (The syntax of the Italian original may inhere in the somewhat Miltonic cast of Browning's own lines here.) Either Browning or Zappi, or both, may very well have been thinking of Vasari's last sentence in the somewhat outrageous conceit at the end of the sonnet. But it was surely Browning—with his own anti-iconic Nonconformist background and his acutely dialectical sense of images and representations—for whom the irony here was sharpest: an image of the Giver of the Law stating that *There Shall Be No Images* is less sinfully to be adored than the most famous one he himself had broken. The trope of the mountain giving "Back to the world that visage, God was grown / Great part of" reflects a memory of the biblical text, as does Browning's use of the Hebrew "Mizraïm" for "Egypt" (the "vile calf" is the golden calf of Exodus 32.4), and the "double ray" translates directly Zappi's *doppio raggio in fronte*—the horns are not an issue.

Tied to its Italian original as it may be, Browning's sonnet may be instructively compared with one of the epigrams from Giambattista Marino's *La Galeria* on "The Moses of Michelangelo Buonarotti." Marino plays upon Michelangelo's name (he is the "ANGEL terreno" corresponding to the heavenly Angel of Death), and upon the tradition (Deuteronomy 34.6) that nobody can know where Moses was buried. The syntax of the Italian is characteristically contorted, so that the complex crisscross of relations in the last two lines—like the way in which the "white stone" somehow redeems the "dark rock"—underscores the poem's insistent confusions of life and art:

> It was an ANGEL from heaven
> Who shut away in death and in dark rock
> On the great mountain the good Hebrew Leader.
> An ANGEL of earth is this
> Who now returns alive to the great Temple
> This noble image in sculpture of white stone.
> Judge now, Nature, which ANGEL
> Is owed more—the giver of the tomb
> By the body elsewhere, or
> By the one that's carved here, the giver of life.

[ANGEL fu de' celesti
quel che'l buon Duca Hebreo da morte oppresso
chiuse già su'l gran monte in pietra oscura.
ANGEL terreno è questi,
ch'or vivo il rende entro il gran Tempio espresso
di bianco sasso in nobile scultura.
Giudice or sia Natura
a qual ANGEL piu deggia
l'imago, o in carne altrove, o qui scolpita
ad dator de la tomba, o de la vita.]

Sigmund Freud wrote at length about the *Moses* in a paper in 1914 in which he was primarily concerned to locate the exact moment of experience being frozen in the piece. There he raised and addressed many of the traditional interpretive questions about it: Is Moses about to jump up in rage at the worship of the golden calf and break the tablets before burning the idol? Is he inwardly agitated while displaying nothing but outward calm? Freud separates these two emotional states sequentially, feeling that the piece ambiguously traces "the passage of a violent gust of passion in the signs left by it on the ensuing calm." He fastens on the hands holding the tables and touching the beard, and reconstructs a series of comic-strip-like frames of their positions in order to demonstrate his view that this Moses is subversively uncanonical. Freud claims that he is being shown at a moment of having recovered a grip on the tablets after they had begun to slip from his hand—agitated about the idolatry, he reaches across with his right hand "to the left and upwards into his beard, as though to turn his vehemence against his own body." Then, noticing that the tablets are about to break, he is brought back to his gentler senses: "This brought him to himself. He remembered his mission and renounced for its sake an indulgence of his feelings." And thus Freud reads the figure ("viewed from above downwards") as exhibiting

> three distinct emotional strata. The lines of the face reflect the feelings which have become predominant: the middle of the figure shows suppressed movement; and the foot still retains the attitude of the projected action. It is as though the controlling influence had proceeded downward from above . . . The [left] hand is laid in his lap in a mild gesture and holds as though in a caress the end of the flowing beard. It seems as if it is meant to counteract the violence with which the other hand had misused the beard a few moments ago.

The wondering gaze of the Renaissance continues to end up in modernity's pondering.

FORD MADOX BROWN

The Last of England

"... The last of England! O'er the sea, my dear,
Our homes to seek amid Australian fields.
Us, not our million-acred island yields
The space to dwell in. Thrust out. Forced to hear
Low ribaldry from sots, and share rough cheer
From rudely nurtured men. The hope youth builds
Of fair renown, bartered for that which shields
Only the back, and half-formed lands that rear
The dust-storm blistering up the grasses wild.
There learning skills not, nor the poets dream,
Nor aught so loved as children we shall see."
She grips his listless hand and clasps her child;
Through rainbow tears she sees a sunnier gleam.
She cannot see a void, where he will be.

Ford Madox Brown, although never formally a member of the Pre-Raphaelite Brotherhood, remained in close association with the group. It was in connection with the departure of one of them, sculptor Thomas Woolner (1825–92), for Australia and the gold-diggings there in 1852, that he painted one of his most famous pictures. (Indeed, it might be thought of as playing an analogous role, as a widely known image, to Alfred Stieglitz's celebrated photograph *The Steerage*, in the United States seventy years or so later.) Brown himself, under straitened circumstances in 1854–55, was considering emigrating to India, and the doubling of subjects here—Brown used himself and his wife as models—gave the painting of it, over three years from 1852 to 1855, some added urgency. It shows what is clearly a middle-class couple (her gloved hand appearing in his, her hairstyle, his appropriate traveling hat, attached to a button so that it can't blow away in a wind, all attest to this), she with their baby, whose hand she grasps in her other, bare one, under her cloak. The *tondo* in which the scene is framed helps organize the partial figures visible on the left behind the man—and perhaps it is the child whose self-absorbed gaze focuses what the artist called "the pathos of the subject"—as a representative sample of emigrating humanity.

Brown wrote of this picture in considerable detail in the catalogue on an 1865 exhibition. He said that he was thinking historically "of the great Emigration Movement which attained its culminating point in 1852 . . . [these are] a couple from the middle-classes, high enough

Ford Madox Brown, *The Last of England*

through education and refinement to appreciate all that they are now giving up . . . The hus-band broods bitterly over blighted hopes and severances from all that he has been striving for. The young wife's grief is of a less cantankerous sort, probably confined to the sorrow of part-ing with a few friends of early years." (One wonders if it is partly in allusion to the *tondo* for-mat of the painting that he adds, "The circle of her love moves with her.") Then follows Brown's inventory of narrative details:

> The husband is shielding his wife from the sea spray with an umbrella. Next them, in the background, an honest family of the greengrocer kind, father (mother lost), eldest daughter and younger children, make the best of things with tobacco-pipe and apples, &c., &c. Still further back, a reprobate shakes his fist with curses at the land of his birth, as though that were answerable for *his* want of success; his old mother reproves him for his foul-mouthed profanity, while a boon companion, with flushed countenance, and got up in nautical togs for the voyage, signifies drunken approbation. The cabbages slung around the stern of the vessel indicate, to the practised eye, a lengthy voyage; but for this their introduction would be objectless. A cabin-boy, too used to 'laving his native land' to see occasion for much sentiment in it, is selecting vegetables for the dinner out of a boatful.

He goes on to say that "To insure the particular look of *light all around* which objects have on a dull day at sea, it was painted for the most part in the open air on dull days, and, when the flesh was being painted, on cold days . . . The minuteness of detail which would be visible under such conditions of broad daylight I have thought necessary to imitate as bringing the pathos of the subject home to the beholder." But the pathos of many subjects of Victorian narrative painting was frequently brought "home to the beholder" by means of just those acutely placed details—of the sort Brown has previously listed—which furnished clues to the story of what was happening.

Aside from this canonical ecphrasis (of the narrative, at least), Brown also wrote a son-net for this painting, as he did for his larger, more ambitious masterpiece, *Work*. The poem causes his own painting to speak out, quite literally: the man utters the first twelve lines, which comprise his interior monologue. And although there is no specific gender-determining clue to which of them it is, the matter of the man's gaze is clearly what is being spoken for. Eyes both strangely raised and lowered at once (looking out from under the protective hat) they are staring spatially, but looking—and seeing—temporally, ahead. All the viewer of the painting can see of what he *sees* is perhaps a hint of the "low ribaldry from sots" in the "reprobate" and his "boon companion"; all the rest is the content of the man's gaze itself. The poem's clos-ing lines return to the gaze of the woman, focused elsewhere. There is more than a hint here of Eve's lines to Adam, on their leaving Eden at the end of book 12 of *Paradise Lost*:

> In me is no delay; with thee to go
> Is to stay here; without thee here to stay
> Is to go hence unwilling; thou to me
> Art all things under heaven, all places thou.

For a painter, the rainbow's biblical promise may not have been vitiated—as it had for poetry from the eighteenth century on—by Newton's optical science. And unusually fragile as the rainbows in spray on shipboard are, and short as the woman's thoughts here, and simpering as her look, the balance of a possible new hope is not totally overwhelmed by what has preceded it.

More than a century later, Peter Porter (1929–), a poet of Australian birth who emigrated to England in 1951, wrote an avowedly pendant poem to Brown's poem and painting pair. Its major ironies are twofold: the details not of a painting, but of a condition of a realm, are listed; and the Australian-English migration pattern is seen reversed in such matters as the mid-twentieth-century importation, with disastrous consequences, of the myxomatosis which spread out of control among the rabbit population. This is all underlined by the punning temporality of the title that suggests the inescapability—even by any internal emigration—of England's terminal condition:

The Last of England

It's quiet here among the haunted tenses:
Dread Swiss germs pass the rabbit's throat,
Chemical rain in its brave green hat
Drinks at a South Coast Bar, the hedgehog
Preens on nylon, we dance in Tyrolean
Drag whose mothers were McGregors,
Exiled seas fill every cubit of the bay.
Sailing away from ourselves, we feel
The gentle tug of water at the quay—
Language of the liberal dead speaks
From the soil of Highgate, tears
Show a great water table is intact.
You cannot leave England, it turns
A planet majestically in the mind.

A contracted sort of unrhymed and unmeasured sonnet, the poem introduces a world in which "is" and "will be" are haunted by "was," and chronicles its sad grotesques and ludicrousness.

The second seven lines reverse the harshness at another level of hope—almost as if, recalling Brown's couple and his sonnet as well, the second half of the poem spoke for a milder companion presence.

C.-R. M. Leconte de Lisle

Venus de Milo

Sacred marble, clothed in spirit and strength,
Resistless Goddess with victorious air
As pure as lightning and as harmony,
Venus! Beauty, white mother of the Gods!

You are not Aphrodite cradled in waves
Your snowy foot poised on your azure shell,
While all about you, vision pink and blonde,
Fly golden putti and Cupids in a swarm.

You are not Cytherea, supply posed,
Scented with kisses of the blithe Adonis,
Your only witness on the unending boughs
Amorous pigeons, alabaster doves.

Nor indeed are you the Muse, with eloquent lips,
Venus pudica, nor the soft Astarte
Who, forehead by roses and acanthus crowned,
Swoons with pleasure on a lotus bed.

No! Cupids and the Graces interlaced,
Blushing with love, form not your retinue,
Your cortege is composed of rhythmed stars,
The choiring spheres attendant on your steps.

Adored symbol of impassive bliss,
Calm as the sea in her serenity,
No sob can shatter your unyielding breast,
Your beauty never dimmed by human tears.

Hail! At the sight of you the heart leaps up,
Marmoreal waves are washing your white feet;
You go forth, proud and nude, and the world throbs,
And the world, wide-hipped Goddess, is all yours.

Isles, abode of the Gods! Greece, sacred mother!
Would that I had been born in the holy Aegean,

Anon., *Venus de Milo*

In glorious centuries when the Earth, inspired,
Saw the heavens descend at her first call.

And though my cradle was never caressed, afloat
On ancient Thetis, by her warming crystal;
Nor prayed beneath an Attic pediment,
Triumphant Beauty, at your native altar;

Even so, ignite the sublime spark in my breast,
Seal not my fame in any frowning tomb,
And let my thoughts cascade in golden tides
Like divine metal in a harmonious mold.

[Marbre sacré, vêtu de force et de génie,
Déesse irrésistible au port victorieux,
Pure comme un éclair et comme une harmonie,
O Vénus! ô beauté, blanche mère des Dieux!

Tu n'es pas Aphrodite, au bercement de l'onde,
Sur ta conque d'azur posant un pied neigeux,
Tandis qu'autor de toi, vision rose et blonde,
Volent les Rires d'or avec l'essaim des Jeux.

Tu n'es pas Kythérée, en ta pose assouplie,
Parfumant de baisers l'Adônis bienheureux,
Et n'ayant pour témoins sur le rameau qui plie
Que colombes d'albâtre et ramiers amoureux.

Et tu n'es pas la Muse aux lèvres éloquentes,
La pudique Vénus, ni la molle Astarté
Qui, le front couronné de roses et d'acanthes,
Sur un lit de lotos se meurt de volupté.

Non! les Rires, les Jeux, les Grâces enlacées,
Rougissantes d'amour, ne t'accompagnent pas.
Ton cortège est formé d'étoiles cadencées,
Et les globes en chœur s'enchaînent sur tes pas.

Du bonheur impassible ô symbole adorable,
Calme comme la mer en sa sérénité,
Nul sanglot n'a brisé ton sein inaltérable,
Jamais les pleurs humains n'ont terni to beauté.

Salut! A ton aspect le cœur se précipite.
Un flot marmoréen inonde tes pieds blancs;
Tu marches, fière et nue, et le monde palpite,
Et le monde est à toi, Déesse aux large flancs!

Iles, séjour des Dieux! Hellas, mère sacrée!
Oh! que ne suis-je né dans le saint Archipel
Aux siècles glorieux où la Terre inspirée
Voyait le Ciel descendre à son premier appel!

Si mon berceau, flottant sur la Thétis antique,
Ne fut point caressé de son tiède cristal;
Si je n'ai point prié sous le fronton attique,
Beauté victorieuse, à ton autel natal;

Allume dans mon sein la sublime étincelle,
N'enferme point ma gloire au tombeau soucieux;
Et fais que ma pensée en rythmes d'or ruisselle,
Comme un divin métal au moule harmonieux.]

The fame of the so-called Venus de Milo—as one art historian has put it—"Started by propaganda, has become perpetuated by habit." Just as millions of people knowing nothing of art know that Mona Lisa smiles, so those knowing nothing of antiquity and its frequently fragmented relics know that the Venus de Milo has no arms. (And what the missing arms were doing—holding Paris's golden apple as Venus Victrix, for example—can only be surmised.) The piece, Hellenistic, perhaps middle second century B.C., was found on Melos in 1820 and brought to the Louvre, where it was installed in the following year. The highly celebrated Venus de' Medici, found in Rome in the sixteenth century, brought to Florence in 1680, looted by Napoleon, and carried off to Paris, had only been returned to Italy in 1815, and the newly acquired Venus was immediately presented as being of greater beauty, significance, and value than the forcibly deaccessioned one.

James Thomson, in the same passage in his *Liberty* in which he addressed the *Apollo Belvedere*, invoked the Medici Venus, who bends in the paradigmatic pose of the *Venus pudica*, in a shrewd perception of the erotics of coyness, and ending in an almost coyly Browningesque concluding figure:

The queen of love arose, as from the deep
She sprung in all the melting pomp of charms.
Bashful she bends, her well-taught look aside
Turns in enchanting guise, where dubious mix
Vain conscious beauty, a dissembled sense
Of modest shame, and slippery looks of love.

> The gazer grown enamoured, and the stone,
> As if exulting in its conquest, smiles.

But the city of Paris, which had carried off one Venus, extended the golden apple of its self-regard to her replacement, the armless figure from Melos. The combination of archaistic elements in its head, allusive of fourth- and fifth-century sculpture, and the characteristic "baroque" torsion of the body, would figure prominently for a learned gaze, but not for a popular one. An icon of purported French cultural supremacy in the modern world, the image could become variously emblematic under different modes of poetic scrutiny.

The Parnassian poet Leconte de Lisle, whose aesthetic stance was one of antiromantic distance, carefully wrought rhetoric, and poised objectivity, enlisted the national treasure in the cause of his own group's aesthetic program. The figure becomes an avowed emblem of the *impassibilité* traditionally associated with the Parnassians ("Du bonheur impassible ô symbole adorable"). It opens with an invocation to the power both of the goddess and the famous image. The second, third, and fourth stanzas of the poem reject the possible significance for the white marble object of their gaze of various other versions or aspects of Aphrodite, whether mythological (Astarte; the Aphrodite Anadyomenê, rising from the waves) or icono-graphical (the form of the *Venus pudica*, covering her breasts and pubis, embodied in the loot-ed Medici Venus now lost to the Louvre). She emerges in the poem as the icon of an indus-triously preromantic conception of Beauty, a Beauty purged even of the residual sublimity that might have found some redeeming terror in her aspect or the consequences of her power. Despite the fourth stanza's disclaimer, she seems indeed to become the personal muse of the author's own kind of poetry.

But for romantic Hellenism she represented a different goddess. Published the same year (1852) as Leconte de Lisle's poem, the postscript to Heinrich Heine's last great collection, *Romancero*, composed on—and with reference to—his long, terminal sickbed (the "mattress-grave," he called it) records, in Heine's characteristic mode of sentiment undercut by irony, his last encounter with the image:

> I have forsworn nothing, not even my old pagan gods: to be sure, I have turned away from them, but we parted with love and friendship. It was in May 1848, on the day I went out for the last time, that I said goodbye to the gracious idols I worshiped in more fortunate times. I dragged myself to the Louvre only with great effort, and I almost broke down altogether when I entered the lofty hall where the blessèd goddess of beauty, Our Lady of Milo, stands on the pedestal. I lay at her feet for a long time, and I wept so hard that I must have moved a stone to pity. The goddess also gazed down on me with compassion, but at the same time so discon-solately as if to say: Don't you see that I have no arms and so cannot help?
>
> —tr. Hal Draper

The punch line here is more than a mere joking acknowledgment of the most ignorantly and popularly perceived feature of the figure, or a debunking—beyond even the ironic "Our Lady of Milo"—of the prior imploration. The returned gaze of the goddess mirrors the poet's own knowing look. It acknowledges implicitly that no image of beauty, no residue or monument of antiquity, indeed, no god or goddess, has any arms—of the kind that could ever "help"—in any case. This final avowal, of a far from personal sort, is reached through more immediate layers of low joke and shadowy poignancy.

A sonnet by the American poet Emma Lazarus pointedly addresses the Venus de Milo in its specific Parisian context—the title and the first line make it clear that the piece is being viewed in a culturally and historically particularized time and space. Even more pointed is the presence of Heine (as in the passage just quoted), as a sort of Virgil to her Dante, the great German having functioned as a powerful precursor figure for the American Jewish writer. In addition, she was viewing the figure, in the late 1880s, from her own incipient "mattress-grave," at the time of the onset of her final illness. The sestet of her sonnet is all Heine, the earlier poet—for Lazarus, at any rate—eternally shadowing the celebrated marble:

Venus of the Louvre

Down the long hall she glistens like a star,
The foam-born mother of Love, transfixed to stone,
Yet none the less immortal, breathing on.
Time's brutal hand hath maimed but could not mar.
When first the enthralled enchantress from afar
Dazzled mine eyes, I saw her not alone,
Serenely poised on her world-worshipped throne,
As when she guided once her dove-drawn car,—
But at her feet a pale, death-stricken Jew,
Her life-adorer, sobbed farewell to love.
Here *Heine* wept! Here still he weeps anew,
Nor ever shall his shadow lift or move,
While mourns one ardent heart, one poet-brain,
For vanished Hellas and Hebraic pain.

Implicitly acknowledging even the matter of the Venus de Milo as "Venus of the Louvre," as an icon of French culture, Lazarus's poem moves it into a successive realm, the scene of ironic cultural encounter. The figure has been "transfixed to stone"—a myth entombed—perhaps by the Gorgon-like pressure of the world's worshiping gaze, a stone Heine's tears moved to a most contingent pity. There is a trace of doubling here, of Venus-into-sculptured-stone with Greek-sculpture-into-public-icon. The viewer's "dazzled" eyes invoke the celebrated line from John Webster's *The Duchess of Malfi*—"Cover her face. Mine eyes dazzle. She died young"—as if "vanished Hellas" (rather than a particular idea of Beauty, or a particular cultic myth) had also "died young."

Again from the 1880s, a bit of verse by the American bellettrist Richard Watson Gilder sentimentally and rather trivially juxtaposes the famous image with another celebrated one. The presumed greater "humanity" of the second carved figure gets the last word, and without a trace of truly Browningesque dialectic with regard to the relations of the "two worlds" (how they coexist, how the image of beauty is that of a slave-owning culture, etc.) and which a strong poem might use for all sorts of imaginative purposes.

Two Worlds

I—The Venus of Milo

Grace, Majesty, and the calm bliss of life;
No conscious war 'twixt human will and duty;
Here breathes, forever free from pain and strife,
The old, untroubled pagan world of beauty.

II—Michael Angelo's Slave

Of life, of death the mystery and woe,
Witness in this mute carven stone the whole.
That suffering smile were never fashioned so
Before the world had wakened to a soul.

Heine's sense of the piece as a personal muse of sentiment sharpened by a fracturing irony gives way in a glimpse, from early modernity, of another sort of inspiring power nonetheless lodged in the very incompleteness of the female figure, in her "impossible embrace." The great Nicaraguan-born poet, Rubén Darío, begins a sonnet of 1901:

I follow a form my style does not meet up with
a bud of thought that seeks to be a rose,
it is heralded by a kiss placed on my lips
by the Venus de Milo's impossible embrace.

Green palms are adorning the white peristile;
the stars have foretold my vision of the Goddess . . .

[Yo persigo una forma que no encuentra mi estilo,
botón de pensiamento que busca ser la rosa;
se anuncia con un beso que en mis labios se posa
al abrazo imposible de la Venus de Milo.

Adornan verdes palmas el blanco peristilo;
los astros me han predicho la visión de la Diosa . . .]

But the image of Venus at the start of the poem itself then *se anuncia* a subsequent chain of romantic fictions (the Sleeping Beauty, a great white swan, etc.) of dormant, potential imaginative energy. In the case of another celebrated fragmentary image of antiquity, incidentally, Darío also uses the absence of the vanished elements, such as *la cabeza abolida*, the lost head, as a space for poetic language to fill, and [*hacer*] *vibrar toda lira*—to set the strings of the lyre, the lines of poetry, into trembling eloquence (1914):

The Victory of Samothrace

The missing head tells yet of the sacred day
on which, in winds of triumph, multitudes
paraded, inflamed, before the simulacrum
that sent Greeks seething in the Athenian streets.
This eminent image has no eyes, and sees,
no mouth, and calls out the supremest cry,
no arms, and sets the whole lyre in vibration;
the marble wings embrace the infinite.

[La Victoria de Samotracia

La cabeza abolida aún dice el dâ sacro
en que, al viento del triunfor, las multitudas plenas
desfilaron ardientes delante el simulacro,
que hizo hervir a los griegos en las calles de Atenas.
Esta egregia figura no tiene ojos y mira;
no tiene boca y lanza el más supremo grito;
no tiene brazos y hace vibrar toda la lira,
y alas pentélicas abarcan lo infinito.]

In fascinating contrast with Darío's treatment of the Venus de Milo's missing arms is César Vallejo's tortured hymn to asymmetry (poem 36 of his *Trilce* of 1922). The Venus—"whose clipped, increate / arm turns over and tries to breed an elbow" [cuyo cercenado, increado / brazo revuélvese ye trata de ecodarse]—is invoked as "Lassoer of imminences, lassoer / of the parenthesis" [Laceadora de inminencias, laceadora / del parentesis]. And in what is almost her own version of the injunctions to the viewer of Keats's urn and Rilke's Apollo torso, she is made by the poet's voice to urge: "Refuse—and all of you—to place the soles of your feet / in the twofold safety of Harmony! / Refuse symmetry, certainly" [Rehusad, y vosotros, a posar las plantas / en la seguridad dupla de la Armonía! / Rehusad la simetría a buen seguro]. Vallejo's privileging of "perennial imperfection" [perenne imperfección] is very much in line with a general modernist tendency to represent the fragment (rather than the romantic ruin) as more aesthetically and morally authentic than the finished work.

CHARLES BAUDELAIRE

Gypsies on the Move

The prophet tribe with burning eyes set forth
Yesterday on the road, bearing their young
On their backs or offering their proud hungers
Ever-ready treasures of their full breasts.

Under their gleaming weapons, all the men
Walk alongside the carts in which their people
Huddle, their eyes running about the sky,
Heavy with dull regret for absent visions.

The cricket, from within his sandy covert,
Observing them go by, redoubles his song;
Cybele, who loves them, amasses her greenery,

Makes the rocks run with water, the desert bloom
Before these wanderers for whom unrolls
The familiar empire of oncoming shades.

[Bohémiens en Voyage

La tribu prophétique aux prunelles ardentes
Hier s'est mise en route, emportant ses petits
Sur son dos, ou livrant à leurs fiers appétits
Le trésor toujours prêt des mamelles pendantes.

Les hommes vont à pied sous leurs armes luisantes
Le long des chariots où les leurs sont blottis,
Promenant sur le ciel des yeux appesantis
Par le morne regret des chimères absentes.

Du fond de son réduit sablonneux, le grillon,
Les regardant passer, redouble san chanson;
Cybèle, qui les aime, augmente ses verdures,

Fait couler le rocher et leuris le désert
Devant ces voyageurs, pour lesquels est ouvert
L'empire familier des ténèbres futures.]

Ces pauures gueux pleins de bonadueture
Ne portent rien que des Choses futures.

JACQUES CALLOT, *Les Bohémiens*

Baudelaire's poems associated with pictures cover—as has been noted—a wide array of images and of rhetorical approaches to the image: Goya ("Duellum" and "La lune offensé," relating to two of the *Caprichos* etchings), Delacroix ("Sur le Tasse in prison de Eugène Delacroix"), a woodcut of a skeleton by Vesalius (plate 21 of *De humani corporis fabrica*, in "Le Squelette laboureur"), an engraving by Hendrick Goltzius of an infant seated on a skull blowing bubbles (*Quis evadet?*, treated in "L'Amour et le crâne"), a sculpture by Ernest Christophe ("Le Masque"). One of the best known of these is his sonnet of 1852 (published in *Les Fleurs du mal*, 1857), "Bohémiens en Voyage." It takes as its title that of a series of four etchings by Jacques Callot in 1621 called *Les Bohémiens,* and specifically addresses the first of that group. It has been argued that these are indeed not gypsies, but probably mercenary marauders and camp followers of the Thirty Years' War. Its *légende,* or inscription (apparently not written by Callot), itself an interpretive ecphrasis, is also part of the pictorial matter for the poem: "These poor vagabonds, full of good fortunes [i.e., in their fortune-telling for others], / Bear with them only things to come" [Ces pauvres gueux pleins des bonadventures / Ne portent rien que des Choses futures], and the free end of the cracking whip of the driver in the center of the image almost seems to underline the matter of futurity. It is this matter of prophecy—of contracted versions of what Shelley called "the gigantic shadows which futurity casts along the present"—and of the problematic futures with which Baudelaire begins, and it obviously comes from the rubric.

But as the sonnet then turns toward the image, it does so by rejecting the figurative language of carrying ("Ne portent rien que des Choses futures") for the literal burdens borne by the people as they move—children, objects, weapons, a rooster—almost as if to say "Carrying nothing but futurities? *Look* at them! And by *Choses futures* you can't mean only their children's future lives." The prominence of the nursing mother above the cart wheel is acknowledged in the ecphrasis, and the way in which the line of the wheel leads down to the pregnant woman with two children, walking alongside just ahead, probably surfaces again in the sestet of the sonnet, in the appearance of Cybele, the "great mother," goddess of fecund nature.

Indeed, the sestet, unlike the octave, is occupied with its own *chimères absentes*—absent, in any event, from Callot's etching: Cybele, and the cricket who may act as a surrogate for the viewer's own angle of vision, from out of the covert, or behind the redoubt, of the picture plane, and who, at the passing of the group of wanderers, increases his lyrical eloquence. The relation of fecundity to futurity, so prominent in the pregnant walking woman, extends into the last tercet and is confirmed by the return, in the poem's final line, to the matter of the second line of the *légende.*

But the *ténèbres* come from the etched image: the deep, darkening shadows cast by the procession of figures suggest that the time is late afternoon, and the oncoming shades those of night, literally, and of indeterminacy, figuratively. The *Choses futures* borne by the vagabonds in the caption are replaced by the *ténèbres futures* opening out before them at the terminus of the text. It is almost as if the cast shadows in the etching had been reread as prophetic traces of the approaching darkness which will indeed erase them. But the element of heroic and mysterious questing that makes the caravan into a sort of allegorical chariot of spiritual journeying seems already there in the structures of line and shadow in Callot's etching, pointing so strongly out of the picture into a future which itself is like a homely goal.

Like Rossetti's sonnets on pictures, this poem of Baudelaire's uses the canonical Petrarchan octave-sestet structure not only as a rhetorical format, but in a metaphoric way ad hoc to the particular occasion of interpreting a particular image. The treatment of the procession itself, in the octave, yields to—or, in the ambiance of Cybele, yields *up*—the paired responses of figurations of the natural scene through which they move: the metonymic observer (the cricket), and the personification, in Cybele, of a central natural process. The octave/sestet distinction—analogous to, but unlike, the foreground figure/background scene separation in Rossetti's sonnet on the Leonardo *Virgin of the Rocks* (see p. 151)—also invokes a relation between presented image and eloquent response, perhaps even interpretation. And yet the return to the question of the rubric in the last line not only propounds a refrain-like rhetorical recursion, but implicitly sets up a complex alternative to that rubric's little couplet: "The prophet tribe with burning eyes set forth [toward] the familiar empire of oncoming shades," bracketing the internal structure and development of the intervening lines. A slightly different pattern holds, as David Scott has suggested, in Baudelaire's "Duellum" (based on one of Goya's *Caprichos* ("Quien lo creyera"); there, the first quatrain and first tercet describe the combat, and the immediately adjacent second ones invoke an application to the poet-speaker and his mistress, locked in analogous combat.

EMMA LAZARUS

The New Colossus

Not like the brazen giant of Greek fame,
With conquering limbs astride from land to land;
Here at our sea-washed, sunset gates shall stand
A mighty woman with a torch, whose flame
Is the imprisoned lightning, and her name
Mother of Exiles. From her beacon-hand
Glows world-wide welcome; her mild eyes command
The air-bridged harbor that twin cities frame.
"Keep, ancient lands, your storied pomp!" cries she
With silent lips. "Give me your tired, your poor,
Your huddled masses yearning to breathe free,
The wretched refuse of your teeming shore.
Send these, the homeless, the tempest-tost to me,
I lift my lamp beside the golden door!"

Liberté Éclairant le Monde ("Liberty Enlightening the World"—not just "lighting up": the
allegory has torch as light source and invokes the eighteenth century) by Frédéric Auguste
Bartholdi is better known as the Statue of Liberty. It was cast in sections and sent to New
York as a gift from the French people—of the Second Empire, no less—to the people of the
United States in 1863. The statue, whose internal iron structure was designed by the great
Gustave Eiffel, had at her feet a broken shackle, bore aloft a torch, and held in the other hand
the Tablet of the Law, inscribed, in fact, JULY IV, MDCCLXXVI. (The model for it has been var-
iously said to be either Bartholdi's mother, or Jeanne-Emilie Baheaux de Puysieux, for whom
the sculptor conceived a passion and eventually married.) Congress agreed to allocate suffi-
cient money to erect the statue, but not to provide a pedestal for it. A Bartholdi Statue
Pedestal Campaign was started by private citizens to raise funds, and in connection with it,
prominent authors were asked to write something occasional and donate the manuscripts
thereof for auction. Emma Lazarus was approached, among others, and although apparently
unwilling at first to write anything on commission, she eventually produced her now-famous
lines in a sonnet written in 1863, which were recited at the ceremonies dedicating the statue on
October 28, 1866, and eventually engraved on a plaque at its base. In France, Charles Gounod
composed a cantata for the statue, which invoked "mon corps de bronze et mon âme de
feu"—the words were by one Emile Guiard. On the other hand, while it has become a senti-

Frédéric Auguste Bartholdi, *Liberté éclairant le monde*

mental patriotic chestnut, Lazarus's poem is a far better one than might be supposed, and draws true poetic strength from its antithetical revision of older images.

"The New Colossus" immediately confronts a central question—the gigantic scale of the figure of Liberty—and acknowledges the arrogance and brutality inherent not only in great size generally, but specifically in the original Colossus of Rhodes, one of the Seven Wonders of the World in Hellenistic times. (Bartholdi himself has been quoted as often affirming that "the size of the statue must be in keeping with the magnitude of the idea.") It was a figure of the sun-god Helios (the popular fiction that it stood astride the harbor and that ships sailed between its legs dates only from the sixteenth century). The American replacement for the ancient figure is a female one, whose height and capaciousness signify a milder mode of conquering. (The senses of "brazen" in Lazarus's first line are twofold.) She also implicitly cancels and replaces the figure of a guardian angel with "a flaming sword which turned every way" [Genesis 3.23] assigned to seal up the eastern gate of lost, emptied Eden. In the opening paragraph of Franz Kafka's *Amerika,* the protagonist Karl Rossmann stands on the deck of a liner entering New York harbor, and

> a sudden burst of sunshine seemed to illumine the Statue of Liberty, so that he saw it in a new light, although he had sighted it long before. The arm with the sword rose up as if newly stretched aloft, and round the figure blew the free winds of heaven.

Kafka had, of course, never seen the statue, but whether the "new light" in which it is revealed to his protagonist (a poor boy of sixteen packed off to America by his parents because he had been seduced by a subsequently pregnant servant girl) is that of overdetermined solecism—poetically rather than politically licensed—is hard to know. It could just as well have been Kafka's own ironic trope of the guardian angel, in which case the "new light" is revisionary, and the arm with the sword is indeed "newly stretched aloft."

Lazarus's thoughts on this matter come up in a sonnet entitled "1492" (the year of the expulsion of the Jews from Spain as well as of Columbus's voyage), written earlier in 1863, and which seems to contain some first thoughts for "The New Colossus." The covering cherub's flaming sword is there, as yet untransformed; but the personified year turns, in the sestet of the sonnet, its more providential, Columbian, face, even as it reverses a faint echo of Dante's "lasciate ogni speranza, voi ch'entrate" [abandon all hope, you who enter here] at the gate of his inferno:

> Thou two-faced year, Mother of Change and Fate,
> Didst weep when Spain cast forth with flaming sword,
> The children of the prophets of the Lord,
> Prince, priest, and people, spurned by zealot hate.
> Hounded from sea to sea, from state to state,
> The West refused them, and the East abhorred.
> No anchorage the known world could afford,
> Close-locked was every port, barred every gate.

Then smiling, thou unveil'dst, O two-faced year,
A virgin world where doors of sunset part,
Saying, "Ho, all who weary, enter here!
There falls each ancient barrier that the art
Of race or creed or rank devised, to rear
Grim bulwarked hatred between heart and heart."

Lazarus's decision to broaden the matter of the Diaspora for the Bartholdi statue was a good one. In any case, both poems show some consciousness of Shelley's "Ozymandias" and his "England in 1819." Her Mother of Exiles bears aloft a torch aflame "with the imprisoned lightning" of war and violence, forced into its own sublimation as continuing, glowing, welcoming radiance. The imagined straddling of the Rhodian Colossus is replaced by a more sublime vision as seen by Liberty's "mild eyes": the twin cities of New York and Brooklyn framing an "air-bridged harbor" (it was not yet Roebling-bridged—work on the Brooklyn Bridge would commence four years after the sonnet was written). The overall structure of her poem—an octave of ecphrastic description, followed by a sestet of speaking for the statue's "silent lips"—embraces two major conventions of addressing an image.

John Greenleaf Whittier addressed these lines to the question of Franco-American liberty over twenty years later (1886):

The Bartholdi Statue

The land that, from the rule of kings,
    In freeing us, itself made free,
Our Old World Sister to us brings
    Her sculptured Dream of Liberty:

Unlike the shapes on Egypt's sands,
    Uplifted by the toil-worn slave,
On Freedom's soil with freemen's hands
    We rear the symbol free hands gave.

O France, the beautiful! to thee
    Once more a debt of love we owe:
In peace beneath thy Colors Three,
    We hail a later Rochambeau!

Rise, stately Symbol! holding forth
    Thy light and hope to all who sit
In chains and darkness! Belt the earth
    With watch-fires from thy torch uplit!

Reveal the primal mandate still
    Which Chaos heard and ceased to be,
Trace on mid-air th'Eternal Will
    In signs of fire: "Let man be free!"

Shine far, shine free, a guiding-light
    To Reason's ways and Virtue's aim,
A lightning-flash the wretch to smite
    Who shield his license with thy name!

The last lines avow that, by this time, Liberty was beginning to displace patriotism as the last refuge of a scoundrel. The later poet performs his own revisions of the creating Word in Genesis, and posits the statue's huge scale as a correction of the towering massiveness of slave-built Egyptian monuments, but it is a largely oratorical performance. It is Bartholdi himself who seems to be Whittier's later version of the Comte de Rochambeau, who led French forces against the British during the American revolution: in no way could Napoleon III be invoked.

In 1894, the brilliant journalist and satirist Ambrose Bierce addressed his own lines "To the Bartholdi Statue," lines that frame a bitterly Tory construction of the matter of Liberty's role in European history, and its possible legacy:

O Liberty, God-gifted—
    Young and immortal maid—
In your high hand uplifted,
    The torch declares your trade.

Its crimson menace, flaming
    Upon the sea and shore,
Is, trumpet-like, proclaiming
    That Law shall be no more.

Austere incendiary,
    We're blinking in the light;
Where is your customary
    Grenade of dynamite?

Where are your staves and switches
    For men of gentle birth?
Your mask and dirk for riches?
    Your chains for wit and worth?

Perhaps, you've brought the halters
    You used in the old days,

> When round religion's altars
> > You stabled Cromwell's bays?
>
> Behind you, unsuspected,
> > Have you the axe, fair wench,
> Wherewith you once collected
> > A poll-tax from the French?
>
> America salutes you—
> > Preparing to "disgorge."
> Take everything that suits you,
> > And marry Henry George.

The word "disgorge" in quotation marks is a scornful use of the term commonly employed in populist rhetoric and cartoon captions of the time, urging that "bloated plutocrats" be made to "disgorge" their ill-gotten gains, and so forth. For the conservative wit of this poem that sees Liberty (or, rather, *Liberté*) hiding behind her back the guillotine that collected a literal "poll-tax" by decapitation, the rhyme of "disgorge" and the name of the radical social theorist Henry George is nastily appropriate.

It may be noted that Robert Lowell hailed the "stately Symbol" in one of the characteristically fragmentary, unrhymed-sonnet entries in his late *Notebook*. Lowell's "Statue of Liberty" is interesting primarily for the inchoate display of mixed feelings about Liberty, the statue, any monument, any affirmation, and America generally. One feels acutely that the writer is invoking some strange, inner image in "the treasonable bulge behind your iron toga, / the thrilling, chilling silver of your laugh" of the "Amazon, gazing on me, pop-eyed, cool."

None of these poems seems concerned to notice the statue's spiked crown, or the tablet of the law that she carries. It bears nothing inscribed on it but the date of the birth of the American nation: does this imply a clean slate on which Liberty will write—with the help of Montesquieu, Rousseau, Locke, or, as John G. Whittier implies, a popular version of scripture—her own law? Perhaps it is because the colossal size of the statue, and the unbending structure of its personification, claim the attention both of ordinary sightseers' gawking and—pregnant with sermon—poetic gazing. It is only in the opening quatrain of Hart Crane's great "To Brooklyn Bridge" that the "liberty" personified in the statue is freed from the statue's rigidity. The device is a powerful one by which a piece of rhetorical public statuary is undermined by a living presence, whether the toppled statues in Eisenstein's *Ten Days That Shook the World*, or more poetically revised as in the opening of Chaplin's *City Lights*. Here it is the flight of a seagull, "Shedding white rings of tumult, building high / Over the chained bay waters Liberty" who constructs a new trope of freedom, outsoaring the height of a monument to the old one. The ambiguous syntax reads both "building Liberty (an abstraction, not a statue) high over . . . waters," and with "building" intransitive, "chained bay waters" as a paradoxical epithet for the statue itself, those very words redolent both of Blake's "charter'd Thames" and, perhaps, Lazarus's "air-bridged" (now, most emphatically for Crane, "Brooklyn-bridged") harbor.

A final look at *torch-bearing* Liberté sees her not as an easily glossed emblem—for in May Swenson's poem she could be a Statue of Anything—but as an Object of Sightseeing. "To the Statue" echoes in its title that of Virginia Woolf's *To the Lighthouse*, but in this case the cynosure is continually and overwhelmingly being reached by large numbers of people who have contemplated it from a distance. It is these which, from its own distance, the poem contemplates in turn:

> The square-heeled boat sets off for the Statue.
> People are stuck up tight as asparagus stalks
> Inside the red rails (ribbons tying the bunch).
>
> The tips, their rigid heads against the fog,
> all yearn toward the Statue; dents of waves
> all minimize and multiply to where
>
> she, fifteen minutes afar (a cooky-tin-shaped
> mother-doll) stands without a feature
> except her little club of flame.

These aggressively domestic images undercut the statue's official significations, even as the poem's attention is directed toward the little voyage to Bedloe's Island (as it was then still known) presided over by the police helicopter:

> Other boats pass the promenade. It's exciting
> to watch the water heave up, clop the pier,
> and even off: a large unsteady belly,
>
> oil-scaled, gasping, then breathing normally.
> On the curved horizon, faded shapes of ships
> with thready regalia, cobweb a thick sky.
>
> Nearer, a spluttering bubble over the water
> (a mosquito's skeletal hindpart, wings detached
> and fused to whip on top like a child's whirltoy)
>
> holds two policemen. They're seated in the air,
> serge, brass-buttoned paunches behind glass,
> serene, on rubber runners, sledding fog.
>
> Coming back, framed by swollen pilings,
> the boat is only inches wide, and flat . . .

—and only now, with the returning boat having deposited its passengers at—and eventually into—the statue, does Swenson reassume the poem's gaze, but, again, with a return to the precise, low-comic image of bunched, wrapped asparagus:

Stalk by stalk, they've climbed into her head

(its bronze is green out there, and hugely spiked)
and down her winding spine into their package,
that now bobs forward on the water's mat.

Soon three-dimensional, colored like a drum,
red-starved, flying a dotted flag,
its rusty iron toe divides the harbor;

sparkling shavings curl out from the bow.
Their heads have faces now. They've been to the Statue.
She has no face from here, but just a fist.
(I think of the flame carved like an asparagus tip.)

The internal rhyming (bow/now) here introduces the insinuation of cause ("Their heads have faces now[:] *or* [that's because] They've been to the Statue." And the final line, added to this last tercet to make it a quatrain (and, in fact, to set up an assonant, almost-rhyming, final couplet) ultimately and wryly avows, as an attached afterthought, the matter of statuesque and humanly scaled heads and faces. Earlier in the poem, there had been a faintly aristocratic perception that the consequences of immigration presided over by the statue are now the internal immigrations of tourists, crossing the bay rather than the sea to get not "Here," but to It. Perhaps, too, there had been a memory of William Carlos Williams's "The Yachts" in its waves-as-populations that "minimize and multiply," as well as in its tercet form. In any case, the idea had become not merely monumentalized, but mundanely institutionalized. And mainly, the Statue of Liberty has lost all its original meaning and instead become, like the Colossus of Rhodes in Hellenistic times, merely one of the Wonders of the World.

Before the Mirror
(Verses written under a Picture)
Inscribed to J. A. Whistler

I

White rose in red rose-garden
    Is not so white;
Snowdrops that plead for pardon
    And pine for fright
Because the hard East blows
Over their maiden rows
    Grow not as this face grows from pale to bright.

Behind the veil, forbidden,
    Shut up from sight,
Love, is there sorrow hidden,
    Is there delight?
Is Joy thy dower or grief,
White rose of weary leaf,
    Late rose whose life is brief, whose loves are light?

Soft snows that hard winds harden
    Till each flake bite
Fill all the flowerless garden
    Whose flowers took flight
Long since when summer ceased,
And men rose up from feast,
    And warm west wind grew east, and warm day night.

II

"Come snow, come wind and thunder
    High up in air,
I watch my face, and wonder
    At my bright hair;
Nought else exalts or grieves
The rose at heart, that heaves
    With love of her own leaves and lips that pair.

J. A. M. WHISTLER, *Symphony in White no. 2: The Little White Girl*

"She knows not loves that kissed her
      She knows not where.
Art thou the ghost, my sister,
      White sister there,
Am I the ghost, who knows?
My hand, a fallen rose,
      Lies snow-white on white snows, and takes no care.

"I cannot see what pleasures
      Or what pains were;
What pale new loves and treasures
      New years will bear;
What beam will fall, what shower,
What grief or joy for dower;
      But one thing knows the flower, the flower is fair."

III

Glad, but not flushed with gladness,
      Since joys go by;
Sad, but not bent with sadness,
      Since sorrows die;
Deep in the gleaming glass
She sees all past things pass,
      And all sweet life that was lie down and lie.

There glowing ghosts of flowers
      Draw down, draw nigh;
And wings of swift spent hours
      Take flight and fly;
She sees by formless gleams,
She hears across cold streams,
      Dead mouths of many dreams that sing and sigh.

Face fallen and white throat lifted,
      With sleepless eye
She sees old loves that drifted,
      She knew not why,
Old loves and faded fears
Float down a stream that hears
      The flowing of all men's tears beneath the sky.

An interpretive poem can often affirm the complexity of an image's significance by making it even more problematic, and by forthrightly eliciting latent material as if it were manifest, rather than by asking it to reveal itself. Whistler's *Symphony in White no. 2: The Little White Girl* is a portrait of Jo Heffernan, the artist's model and mistress, done in 1864. The picture was marked by its affinities with French painting in the formal structure of its design, in its loose treatment of surface, and in its allusion to Japanese art in the fan, the porcelain, and the placement of the flowers. (Its title and that of its 1861 precursor perhaps derive from Théophile Gautier's "Symphonie en blanc majeur.") Algernon Charles Swinburne's "Before the Mirror" was written for the painting and so pleased the artist that he had these lines printed on gold paper and pasted to the frame, using two stanzas as well in the exhibition catalogue. Perhaps as a result of this, the poem was published in book form with the otherwise puzzling subtitle "Verses Written under a Picture" (composed there? inscribed there?). Swinburne's poem deploys, in its three sections of three stanzas each, three different modes of confronting an image.

He starts out by addressing the theme of whiteness that had been privileged in Whistler's typical, polemically abstract title—the matter of *blanc majeur*—and allows the anecdotal and pictorial only a secondary role. White roses and white snowflakes, related to sorrow or delight, are both hidden in the unreadability of the girl's meditative mask ("What is she thinking about?"). But the second section of the poem gives voice to the girl herself, speaks for her and out of—and thereby for—the picture. Or perhaps—and here the problem is part of the meaning of the poem—the lines speak for the mirrored image. They answer, obliquely and subtly, the questions in part 1 about joy or grief by transcending those two alternatives, and allowing the meditation to sink into a contemplation of its own beauty. The white rose, the "she" of the second stanza, is associated with the girl and her image by both metaphoric identity and partial synecdoche (the white hand fallen on the white mantelpiece like a white rose petal).

Swinburne had written to Whistler about the poem in 1865 that "the idea . . . was entirely and only suggested to me by the picture, where I found the metaphor of the rose, and the notion of sad and glad mystery in the face languidly contemplative of its own phantom and all other things seen by their phantoms." That "notion of sad and glad mystery" finally surfaces in the third section. This focuses, ultimately, on the mirror itself, rather than on the girl's relation to her own image—her other self—revealed in it. The poem now moves inside the girl's reveries to the traces of the past that must inevitably emerge from its depths, even as—in Swinburne's verse throughout this poem—the internal rhymes emerge in the ultimate line of each strophe. The poet's characteristic extravagant phonological patterning is never more effective—

> Old loves and faded fears
> Float down a stream that hears
>   The flowing of all men's tears beneath the sky.

—and his equally well-known semantic pairings and oppositions resonate delicately in this context of reciprocity and mirrored replication. The last resonance of the poem's title—

"Before the Mirror"—is that the text itself, ending in a purely fictive sound, itself holds up a mirror to the nature of picturing. From being the engine of narcissistic contemplation, the mirror has become that of the seer of truths beyond the gazer's own beauty, like the mirror of the Lady of Shalott, like the glass of art itself.

J. M. W. TURNER, *The Fighting "Téméraire"*

The Temeraire

(Supposed to Have Been Suggested to an Englishman of the Old Order
by the Fight of the Monitor and Merrimac)

The gloomy hulls, in armor grim,
    Like clouds o'er moors have met,
And prove that oak, and iron, and man
    Are tough in fibre yet.

But Splendors wane. The sea-fight yields
    No front of old display;
The garniture, emblazonment,
    And heraldry all decay.

Towering afar in parting light,
    The fleets like Albion's forelands shine—
The full-sailed fleets, the shrouded show
    Of Ships-of-the-Line.

The fighting Temeraire,
    Built of a thousand trees,
Lunging out of her lightnings,
    And beetling o'er the seas—
O Ship, how brave and rare,
    That fought so oft and well,
On open decks you manned the gun
    Armorial.
What cheerings did you share,
    Impulsive in the van,
When down upon leagued France and Spain
    We English ran—
The freshet at your bowsprit
    Like the foam upon the can.
Bickering, your colors
    Licked up the Spanish air,
You flapped with flames of battle-flags—
    Your challenge, Temeraire!

The rear ones of our fleet
      They yearned to share your place,
Still vying with the Victory
      Throughout that earnest race—
The Victory, whose Admiral,
      With orders nobly won,
Shone in the globe of battle glow—
      The angel in that sun.
Parallel in story,
      Lo, the stately pair,
As late in grapple raging,
      The foe between them there—
When four great hulls lay tiered,
And the fiery tempest cleared,
And your prizes twain appeared, Temeraire!

But Trafalgar is over now,
      The quarter-deck undone;
The carved and castled navies fire
      Their evening-gun.
O, Titan Temeraire,
      Your stern-lights fade away;
Your bulwarks to the years must yield,
      And heart-of-oak decay.
A pigmy steam-tug tows you,
      Gigantic, to the shore—
Dismantled of your guns and spars,
      And sweeping wings of war.
The rivets clinch the iron-clads,
      Men learn a deadlier lore;
      Your ghost it sails before:
O, the navies old and oaken,
      O, the Temeraire no more!

The celebrated *Téméraire* was a French ship-of-the-line of ninety-eight guns, captured by Nelson in 1798 at the Battle of the Nile. At Trafalgar seven years later, it was placed next to Nelson's flagship, *Victory*. In 1839 it was broken up, and in Turner's painting of the following year we see it being towed away in a blazing sunset by a steam tug. The light of the sky is reflected more redly in the water. The rising moon, high in the sky on the left over the pale and ghostly hulk, signals in its relation to the sinking sun—and the sun is often a very complex emblem for Turner—a nodal point, a moment of change of historical phase. The black funnel and side wheel of the tugboat are balanced by the golden light on its prow and, particularly, by the way the fire from its funnel—before it turns into a white, cloudy plume of smoke—matches that of the sky to the right. The painting is full of ambivalences about old glories and new energies, and is far from sentimental about the latter.

Melville's poem is part of his great American Civil War sequence called *Battle-Pieces and Aspects of the War*. It relates there to the battle between the newly built *Monitor* and the newly ironclad screw frigate *Merrimack*—rechristened *Virginia* by the Confederate navy—an indecisive stand-off of a particularly grim and unpicturesque sort (*Monitor* was referred to by its foe as a "Yankee cheese-box on a raft") that proved nonetheless prophetic for the future of armored warships. Melville's own note to his poem suggests a reason for its framing *persona* of "an Englishman of the old order":

> The *Temeraire*, that storied ship of the old English fleet, and subject of the well-known painting by Turner, commends itself to the mind seeking for one craft to stand for the poetic ideal of those great historic wooden warships, whose gradual displacement is lamented by none more than by regularly educated navy officers, and of all nations.

Melville, in the 1860s (perhaps cued somewhat by the fact that *Merrimack* was originally a mixed sail-steam ship, abandoned by the Union navy and burned, then raised and rebuilt by the Confederacy), remembers the central image of outmoded sail being drawn away by steam in Turner's painting. He correspondingly makes his putative aged Englishman remember the Battle of Trafalgar, and the incident in which *Téméraire* took two prize ships while sailing just behind *Victory*. The remarkable quality of the sunset is merely emblematic for this poem of the twilight of an era ("The carved and castled navies fire / Their evening-gun"), of a sort of nautical *Götterdämmerung*. Of the "gun / Armorial" Melville notes that "some of the cannon of old times, especially the brass ones, unlike the more effective ordnance of the present day, were cast in shapes which Cellini might have designed, were gracefully enchased." But for the poem, the matter of the smoke of the tug blackening the reddened sky and mixing with higher cloud, if present at all, has been completely absorbed into the point about the end of the traditionally pictorial naval battle. The poem ends with what feels like the opening of an "old ballad," or even a refrain.

In a subsequent poem, Melville's characteristically dialectical turn of thought led him to posit another, more skeptical, American speaker. In "A Utilitarian's View of the Monitor's Fight" the speaker seems to be deriding the rhetoric as well as the sentiments of the previous verses, as well as the very state of mind that would call up the Turner painting to begin with. Indeed, he seems implicitly almost to take the side of the tug towing *Téméraire* out of the picture:

> Plain be the phrase, yet apt the verse,
>   More ponderous than nimble;
> For since grimed War here laid aside
> His Orient pomp, 'twould ill befit
>   Overmuch to ply
> The rhyme's barbaric cymbal.

Hail to victory without the gaud
    Of glory; zeal that needs no fans
Of banners; plain mechanic power
Plied cogently in War now placed—
    Where War belongs—
Among the trades and artisans. . . .

(The verse in this poem, with its recurring disyllabic rhymes like nimble/cymbal, is indeed far more nimble than that of the previous one; but that is one more irony.) It concludes

War shall yet be, and to the end;
    But war-paint shows the streak of weather;
War shall yet be, but warriors
Are now but operatives; War's made
    Less grand than Peace,
And a singe runs through lace and feather.

An unsurprisingly more rhetorically flamboyant poem by James Russell Lowell allegorically interprets the image in Turner's painting as a type of the church being superseded in an undogmatically Protestant American vision. "Turner's Old Téméraire: Under a Figure Symbolizing the Church" begins with four stanzas of invocation to the ship/church:

Thou wast the fairest of all man-made things;
The breath of heaven bore up thy cloudy wings,
And, patient in their triple rank,
The thunders crouched about thy flank,
Their black lips silent with the doom of kings.

The storm-wind loved to rock him in thy pines,
And swell thy vans with breath of great designs;
Long-wildered pilgrims of the main
By thee relaid their course again,
Whose prow was guided by celestial signs.

How didst thou trample on tumultuous seas,
Or, like some basking sea-beast stretched at ease,
Let the bull-fronted surges glide
Caressingly along thy side,
Like glad hounds leaping by the huntsman's knees!

Heroic feet, with fire of genius shod,
In battle's ecstasy thy deck have trod,
While from their touch a fulgor ran
Through plank and spar, from man to man,
Welding thee to a thunderbolt of God. . . .

The old metaphor of the Ship of State here becomes the Warship of the Church Militant, of Institutionalized Faith; the images adduced apparently in mere decoration—calling other ships "pilgrims of the main," for example—become reliteralized in the allegory (e.g., the "pilgrims" being, in fact, pilgrims). There may be a touch, too, of Leviathan in the "basking sea-beast."

The ecphrasis of Turner's painting starts in the next stanza, but with the allegory unabated:

> Now a black demon, belching fire and steam,
> Drags thee away, a pale, dismantled dream,
> And all, thy desecrated bulk
> Must landlocked lie, a helpless hulk,
> To gather weeds in the regardless stream.
>
> Woe's me, from Ocean's sky-horizoned air
> To this! Better, the flame-cross still aflare,
> Shot-shattered to have met thy doom
> Where thy last lightnings cheered the gloom,
> Than here be safe in dangerous despair.
>
> Thy drooping symbol to the flagstaff clings,
> Thy rudder soothes the tide to lazy rings,
> Thy thunders now but birthdays greet,
> Thy planks forget the martyrs' feet,
> Thy masts what challenges the sea-wind brings.
>
> Thou a mere hospital, where human wrecks,
> Like winter-flies, crawl those renownëd decks,
> Ne'er trodden save by captive foes,
> And wonted sternly to impose
> God's will and thine on bowed imperial necks.
>
> Shall nevermore, engendered of thy fame,
> A new sea-eagle heir thy conqueror name,
> And with commissioned talons wrench
> From thy supplanter's grimy clench
> His sheath of steel, his wings of smoke and flame?
>
> This shall the pleased eyes of our children see,
> For this the stars of God long even as we;
> Earth listens for his wings; the Fates
> Expectant lean; Faith cross-propt waits,
> And the tired waves of Thought's insurgent sea.

Lowell's ambivalence about the nature and function of the church, past and present, reflects that in the painting itself. Yet neither Lowell nor Melville seems much interested in

Turner's own visual poetry, and neither poem reads the painting with any attention. None of its significant patterns and structures—faint diagonal rays from the sun as opposed to a vertical track in the water, the moon's more palpable reflected light, the role of the dark buoy in the right foreground—comes up for consideration. The painting seems always to have been taken emblematically, even if wrongly: one review in 1839 declared that "a gorgeous horizon poetically intimates that the sun of the Temeraire is setting in glory." But is this red glory or merely gory? John Ruskin associated the red in Turner's paintings with the matter of death, and in this one as well. Given the detailed observations he made about the *Téméraire* canvas at various times, one may observe with interest how his most elaborate vision of it (in his notes on the Turner Bequest) is like that of Melville's old Englishman, in that it uses the picture's light of embattled sunset as a medium for conjuring up the light of past embattled glory, reading through the pale ghost to the living ship. The conclusion of it is worth quoting entire; starting out with a figure of the ship as a human life, it moves through the carefully built periods of the last sentence of the first paragraph, to a quiet vision of peace as recycled war, and of lives returning, if not as leaves of grass, than as spreading moss:

> [O]f all pictures of subjects not visibly involving human pain, this is, I believe, the most pathetic that was ever painted. The utmost pensiveness which can ordinarily be given to a landscape depends on aspects of ruin: but no ruin was ever so affecting as this gliding of the vessel to her grave. A ruin cannot be, for whatever memories may be connected with it, and whatever witness it may have borne to the courage or glory of men, it never seems to have offered itself to their danger, and associated itself with their acts, as a ship of battle can. The mere facts of motion, and obedience to human guidance, double the interest of the vessel: nor less her organized perfectness, giving her the look, and partly the character of a living creature, that may indeed be maimed in limb, or decrepit in frame, but must either live or die, and cannot be added to nor diminished from—heaped up and dragged down—as a building can. And this particular ship, crowned in the Trafalgar hour of trial with chief victory—prevailing over the fatal vessel that had given Nelson death—surely, if ever anything without a soul deserved honour or affection, we owed them here. Those sails that strained so full bent into the battle—that broad bow that struck the surf aside, enlarging silently in steadfast haste, full front to the shot—resistless and without reply—those triple ports whose choirs of flame rang forth in their courses, into the fierce revenging monotone, which, when it died away, left no answering voice to rise any more upon the strength of England— those sides that were wet with the long runlets of English life-blood, like press-planks at vintage, gleaming goodly crimson down to the cast and clash of the washing foam—those pale masts that stayed themselves up against the war-ruin, shaking out their ensigns through the thunder, till sail and ensign drooped—steep in the death-stilled pause of Andalusian air, burning with its witness-cloud of human souls at rest,—surely for these some sacred care might have been left in our thoughts—some quiet space amidst the lapse of English waters?

Nay, not so. We have stern keepers to trust her glory to—the fire and the worm. Never more shall sunset lay golden robe on her, nor starlight tremble the waves that part at her gliding. Perhaps, where the low gate opens to some cottage-garden, the tired traveller may ask, idly, why the moss grows so green on its rugged wood; and even the sailor's child may not answer, nor know, that the night-dew lies deep in the war-rents of the wood of the old *Téméraire*.

THOMAS CRAWFORD, *Columbia, Goddess of Liberty*

JOHN JAMES PIATT

To the Statue on the Capitol:
Looking Eastward at Dawn

What sunken splendor in the Eastern skies
      Seest thou, O watcher, from thy lifted place?—
Thine old Atlantic dream is in thine eyes,
      But the new Western morning on thy face.

Beholdest thou, in reäpparent light,
      Thy lost Republics? They were visions, fled.
Their ghosts in ruin'd cities walk by night—
      It is no resurrection of their dead.

But look, behind thee, where in sunshine lie
      Thy boundless fields of harvest in the West,
Whose savage garments from thy shoulders fly,
      Whose eagle clings in sunrise to thy crest!

The statue of ever-armed and vigilant Liberty atop the dome of the national Capitol in Washington, variously called in the past *Columbia, The Goddess of Liberty, The Goddess of Freedom,* and *The Indian Goddess,* was put in its present position in 1863, during the Civil War. Standing 19.5 feet high, the figure rests her right hand on the hilt of a sheathed sword, while, resting on a shield, her left one holds an olive branch. The drapery at her waist is gathered under a brooch with "U.S." on it. She wears a helmet surmounted by eagles' plumes in an arrangement—according to the sculptor, Thomas Crawford—"suggested by the costume of our Indian tribes."

Originally, Crawford had wanted her to hold a *fasces* and wear "a cap of Liberty" encrusted with a circlet of stars. He had been extremely attentive to the ways in which an allegorical personification, made hugely public by monumental statuary, is often conceptually defined by its emblems. He wrote, in 1855, of an earlier model of his piece:

> I have said that the statue represents "armed Liberty." She rests upon the shield of
> our country, the triumph of which is made apparent by the wreath held in the same
> hand which grasps the shield; in her right hand she holds the sheathed sword, to
> show the fight is over for the present, but ready for use whenever required. The
> stars upon her brow indicate her heavenly origin; her position upon the globe rep-

resents her protection of the *American* world—the justice of whose cause is made apparent by the emblems supporting it.

Equally attentive, particularly to possible contemporary significations of the *fasces* of the Roman republic and the liberty cap worn by freedmen therein, was the then secretary of state, who wrote in 1856 to the army officer in charge of the Capitol Extension suggesting that Liberty wear a helmet instead:

> The language of art, like all living tongues, is subject to change; thus the bundle of rods, if no longer employed to suggest the functions of the Roman Lictor, may lose the symbolic character derived therefrom, and be confined to the single signification drawn from its other source—the fable teaching that in union there is strength. But the liberty cap has an established origin in the use as the badge of a freed slave; and though it should have another emblematic meaning today, a recurrence to that origin may give it in the future that same popular acceptation which it had in the past.

The signatory of this letter was Jefferson Davis, and if at the moment the emblem of union was not as politically distasteful to him as the badge of a freed slave, it might soon have become one. In any event, a helmet it was.

Very little of all this symbolic imagery can be visible to the viewer at ground level. John James Piatt, a poet, journalist, and diplomat, lived for a number of years in Washington, where he was librarian of the House of Representatives. His poem to the statue regards not its emblems, but rather the way it engages the particular American mythology of easterly-westerly direction, of eastern past and western future, mapped out on the continent by the then still viable concept of the moving frontier. "Westward the course of empire takes its way" wrote Bishop Berkeley in the early eighteenth century in "Planting Arts and Learning in America," and ever since we have faced the complex prospect of having the sun set into our future, and rise out of our past. And so, for Piatt, the direction of the statue's gaze becomes crucial. "Thine old Atlantic dream is in thine eyes, / But the new Western morning in thy face" plays nicely with this paradox: as a representation, the human image *faces* and looks eastward; but as a piece of reflective surface, that bronze face, shining with morning light, is a fragment of westward panorama. For America, the West is the *Morgenland,* not the scene of the dying of the old day. And given the matter of westering, the eagle feathers and Indian allusions take on a new, hopeful meaning as well, albeit for the conquerors, not the Native American tribes.

As has been seen, poetic responses to large, public images will be oblique at best. Walt Whitman expressed in 1885 his displeasure at the Washington Monument. He did not, like the sculptor Horace Greenough, object to the scale and the inappropriateness of such an obelisk for such a memorial, but rather to the cliche of a localized shaft of marble:

> Ah, not this marble, dead and cold:
> Far from its base and shaft expanding—the round zones circling, comprehending,

> Thou, Washington, art all the world's, the continents' entire—
>   not yours alone, America,
> Europe's as well, in every part, castle of lord or laborer's cot . . .

and he concludes with an old Renaissance commonplace about the contingency of stone (Shakespeare's "Not marble, nor the gilded monuments / Of princes can outlive this powerful rhyme") blended with what would thereafter become an American one—

> Wherever sails a ship, or house is built on land, or day or night,
> Through teeming cities' streets, indoors or out, factories or farms,
> Now, or to come, or past—where patriot wills existed or exist,
> Wherever Freedom, pois'd by Toleration, sway'd by Law,
> Stands or is rising thy true monument.

The poetic stance is not merely one against personification—for indeed, notice how Whitman himself uses a pure eighteenth-century mode of invocation of what might be a carved image of Freedom—but of limitation, of a metaphorical monument which is rendered inadequate by the mere fact of localization itself, and not because of an old-fashioned specificity of imagery. The previous year, Whitman, presumably on request, had written an "Impromptu on Buffalo City's monument to, and reburial of "Red Jacket" (1750–1830), in which he reads the figure of the old Iroquois warrior himself, "Upon this scene, this show, / Yielded today by fashion, learning, wealth," as looking down, "a half-ironical smile curving its phantom lips, / Like one of Ossian's ghosts," in scorn at the event, and perhaps even at its own statuary mode of existence. Like it, Whitman's Washington Monument poem implicitly affirms an earlier American ideal of putting imaginative energy—like capital itself—to work, instead of burying one's talent in the ground, or one's hopeful rhetoric in marble.

Albrecht Dürer, *Melencolia*

JAMES THOMSON ("B. V.")

From The City of Dreadful Night

Anear the centre of that northern crest
      Stands out a level upland bleak and bare,
From which the city east and south and west
      Sinks gently in long waves; and thronèd there
An Image sits, stupendous, superhuman,
The bronze colossus of a wingèd Woman,
      Upon a graded granite base foursquare.

Low-seated she leans forward massively,
      With cheek on clenched left hand, the forearm's might
Erect, its elbow on her rounded knee;
      Across a clasped book in her lap the right
Upholds a pair of compasses; she gazes
With full set eyes, but wandering in thick mazes
      Of sombre thought beholds no outward sight.

Words cannot picture her; but all men know
      That solemn sketch the pure sad artist wrought
Three centuries and threescore years ago,
      With phantasies of his peculiar thought:
The instruments of carpentry and science
Scattered about her feet, in strange alliance
      With the keen wolf-hound sleeping undistraught;

Scales, hour-glass, bell, and magic square above;
      The grave and solid infant perched beside,
With open winglets that might bear a dove,
      Intent upon its tablets, heavy-eyed;
Her folded wings as of a mighty eagle,
But all too impotent to lift the regal
      Robustness of her earth-born strength and pride;

And with those wings, and that light wreath which seems
      To mock her grand head and the knotted frown
Of forehead charged with baleful thoughts and dreams,
      The household bunch of keys, the housewife's gown
Voluminous, indented, and yet rigid
As if a shell of burnished metal frigid,
      The feet thick shod to tread all weakness down;

The comet hanging o'er the waste dark seas,
      The massy rainbow curved in front of it,
Beyond the village with the masts and trees;
      The snaky imp, dog-headed, from the Pit,
Bearing upon its batlike leathern pinions
Her name unfolded in the sun's dominions
      The "Melencolia" that transcends all wit.

Thus has the artist copied her, and thus
      Surrounded to expound her form sublime,
Her fate heroic and calamitous;
      Fronting the dreadful mysteries of Time,
Unvanquished in defeat and desolation,
Undaunted in the hopeless conflagration
      Of the day setting on her baffled prime.

Baffled and beaten back she works on still,
      Weary and sick of soul she works the more,
Sustained by her indomitable will:
      The hands shall fashion and the brain shall pore
And all her sorrow shall be turned to labour,
Till death the friend-foe piercing with his sabre
      That mighty heart of hearts ends bitter war.

But as if blacker night could dawn on night,
      With tenfold gloom on moonless night unstarred,
A sense more tragic than defeat and blight,
      More desperate than strife with hope debarred,
More fatal than the adamantine Never
Encompassing her passionate endeavour,
      Dawns glooming in her tenebrous regard:

The sense that every struggle brings defeat
      Because Fate holds no prize to crown success;
That all the oracles are dumb or cheat

Because they have no secret to express;
That none can pierce the vast black veil uncertain
Because there is no light beyond the curtain;
        That all is vanity and nothingness.

Titanic from her high throne in the north,
        That City's sombre Patroness and Queen,
In bronze sublimity she gazes forth
        Over her Capital of teen and threne,
Over the river with its isles and bridges,
The marsh and moorland, to the stern rock-ridges,
        Confronting them with a coëval mien.

The moving moon and stars from east to west
        Circle before her in the sea of air;
Shadows and gleams glide round her solemn rest.
        Her subjects often gaze up to her there:
The strong to drink new strength of iron endurance,
The weak new terrors; all, renewed assurance
        And confirmation of the old despair.

James Thomson (1834–82), who published poetry under the initials "B. V." (for "Bysshe Vanolis," invoking Shelley and, in anagram, Novalis), lived and died in alcoholic depression and despair, having written a considerable body of poetry (much destroyed by fire). The best of it is a long, tortured, atheistic visionary poem called "The City of Dreadful Night," first published in 1874. In some ways—given the fictional city's nightmarish associations with London—it looks forward to Eliot's "The Waste Land"—it is a place in which Hope, Faith, and Love have all died, and its condition of night seems something beyond even despair. The poem concludes, in its twenty-first and final section, with a description of a horrific presiding statue, a "bronze colossus" generated from—but outrageously claiming to be a prototype of—Albrecht Dürer's celebrated dark angel of Melancholy. Yet by the third stanza, Thomson is describing Dürer's engraving of 1513 and his personal vision. His account reads, rather than neglects, the complex iconography about which Erwin Panofsky wrote so enlighteningly and compellingly, but reads it for the poem's own gloomy ends. Thomson's poem reconstructs the image into the "sombre Patroness and Queen" of his city of life-in-death, "Unvanquished . . . Undaunted . . . Baffled and beaten back . . . Weary and sick of soul," without hope of anything lying beyond perished faith.

But it is a powerful reading. He sees "The instruments of carpentry and science / Scattered about her feet, in strange alliance / With the keen wolf-hound sleeping undistraught," and that "strange alliance" is a formal and an allegorical one: the hound, jammed angularly in between the polyhedron, the figure, and the geometric instruments, folded up in sleep, partakes of their abandonment both subjectively and objectively, an image of his great mistress and yet one of the instruments of knowledge she has allowed to lie idle. Thomson sees her keys—an emblem for Dürer of power, as her purse, also disused, is for wealth—as those of a chatelaine. But the poem does not acknowledge the existence of the strange little figure of the *putto*, the child doodling on its slate. "The comet hanging o'er the waste dark seas, / The massy rainbow curved in front of it" is what the French poet Gérard de Nerval refigured—in an emblem on the lute of his melancholic troubadour, *El Deschidado*—as "Melancholia's black sun," "le soleil noir de la Mélancolie." It becomes a portent for Thomson, even as the relative solidity of the form generated by the engraved arc of the rainbow makes it "massy" and oppressive, an element of heavy sadness rather than the biblical one of hope. Or of a promise of "confirmation of the old despair."

Dürer's image of inward-looking meditation, of the melancholy of the artist, has always been a compelling one, and the modern reader tends to see its traces even in descriptions which might very well be alluding only to an emblem-book's paradigm, or a conventional pattern from seventeenth-century poetry. Thus Alexander Pope's totally outdoor image—"But o'er the twilight groves, and dusky caves, / Long-sounding isles and intermingled graves, / Black Melancholy sits, and round her throws / A death-like silence and a dread repose," and so forth ("Eloisa to Abelard," 163–66)—has led some writers to invoke *Melencolia I* (but unconvincingly: perhaps Milton's "Il Penseroso," or one of the images on the engraved title page of Burton's *Anatomy of Melancholy*, might have been more apposite). An amusing inability to cope with exactly what kind of dense iconographic poem the great engraver had devised can be seen in the remarks by John Landseer, father of the famous Victorian painter, in his *Lectures on the Art of Engraving*. He sounds almost petulant about the symbolic objects with which the figure is surrounded:

> The expression of his figure of Melancholy, which would else have approached Sublimity, is considerably injured by the introduction of a multitude of objects, most of which the mind does not readily assimilate with the subject of Melancholy: It must first be perceived, or discovered, that these objects are allusions to Astrology, Alchemy and the occult Sciences, as they were called:—The performance addresses itself therefore to the curious part of mankind, and not to Man: and as neither the eye nor the mind can at once dilate with greatness and descend to littleness, it is evident that the research it requires must be the destruction of Sublimity.

This is no longer evident to us, who can be led to the sublime through puzzled wonder, or by the hand of the learned researches of others. Erwin Panofsky wrote profoundly and in great detail of all of the elements in this engraving, tracing traditional emblems of melancholy, like the dog and the bat (who "emerges at dusk and lives in lonely, dark and decaying places"), the geometric objects and scientific instruments put aside, the signs of Saturn and the realm of the cold, dry earth, and the "morose little *putto* who, perched on a disused grindstone, scribbles something on a slate," active but unknowing even as the great, brooding winged figure is full of thought and knowledge but cannot act. "Hers," says Panofsky "is the inertia of a being which renounces what it could reach because it cannot reach for what it longs."

John Ruskin, who often wrote admiringly of this engraving, expressed himself "in some doubt respecting its special symbolism." This freed him to propound his personal parable in describing the figure as a design "in praise of Labor," and the thrust of its moralizing is characteristic:

> The labor indicated is the daily work of men. Not the inspired or gifted labor of the few (it is labor connected with the sciences, not with the arts), shown in its four chief functions: thoughtful, faithful, calculating and executing. Thoughtful, first; all true power coming of that resolved, resistless calm of melancholy thought. This is the first and last message of the whole design. Faithful, the right arm of the spirit resting on the book. Calculating (chiefly in the sense of self-command), the compasses in her right hand. Executive—roughest instruments of labor are at her feet: a crucible, and geometric solids, indicating her work in the sciences. Over her head the hour-glass and the bell, for their continual words, "Whatsoever thy hand findeth to do." Beside her, childish labor (lesson-learning?) sitting on an old millstone with a tablet on its knees . . . In the distance, a comet (the disorder and threatening of the universe) setting, the rainbow dominant over it.

Théophile Gautier's long "Melancholie," after an opening disquisition in praise of the qualities of northern painting, presents a more thorough ecphrasis of Dürer's print than is found in any other poem. It reads it as romantic self-portraiture, as an image of the artist's own *daemon*:

> The soul of bitterness, filled with disgust,
> You've painted, Dürer, in your *Melancholy*,
> And taking pity on you, your spirit in tears
> Has thus personified you in its creation.
> I don't know what is finer in the world,
> More filled with revery and deepest pain
> Than this great seated angel, wing folded back
> In stillness of the most complete repose.
> His garment, in an austere manner hung,
> Extends mysteriously down to his foot;
> His forehead crowned with nenuphar and parsley,
> Blood does not animate his pallid face;
> No muscles move, and one would say that life
> Lived in the world is ravaged from this frame,
> And yet one sees that this is not a corpse.
> His eyebrow, black, writhes like a wounded snake,
> The gaze of his eye glitters like a lamp,
> His hand presses his temple fitfully.

A thousand things are strewn around him there,
Attributes of the arts and sciences:
The ruler, hammer, emblematic circle,
The hour-glass and the bell, the magic square—
Objects unnamable in Faust's study crammed.
But still, this is an angel, not a demon,
The huge bunch of keys that dangles from his belt
Is used by him to get at Nature's secrets.
He has touched bottom of all human learning
But finding at the end of every road
Always those same eyes blazing out of the shadow
He is sorrowful, having gone up the ladder
Of rungs without number, and his wearied hound
Sleeps alongside him, old and totally broken.
At the foot of the picture, along a boundless horizon,
Old Father Ocean lifts his dreary face,
And the blue crystal of his deepest mirror
Reflects a great and utterly black sun's beams.
A bat escaping from a turret bears
A banderole inscribed on his open wing:
Melancholy. On a mill-stone below
Sits a child, eyes beneath long lashes veiled
The viewer left doubting whether he's awake.
Or if, rocked in a dream, himself asleep.
Behold how Dürer, the great German master,
Symbolically and scientifically
Has represented in his weird design
His heart's dream for us in an angel's form.

But then, Gautier shifts abruptly to Parisian modernity, and a notional ecphrasis of a contemporary image that begins

Our Melancholy's not at all like that:
Our painters do her differently, like this:
Here's a young girl and frail, and sickly, too,
Her fair blue eyes turned down by the river-bank
Like a forget-me-not bent in the wind,
Her hair undone, her comb having fallen down,
Blonde scattered locks across her shoulders curled . . .

But at the end of his poem, James Thomson returns to his first image of the statue cast from Dürer's engraving, gazed up at by her subjects in her City of Dreadful Night, "The strong to drink new strength of iron endurance, / The weak new terrors." And the dark angel in the print herself remains a puzzling figure of the viewer's puzzlement, sitting, in Panofsky's words, "neither a miser nor a mental case, but a thinking being in perplexity. She does not hold on to an object which does not exist, but to a problem which cannot be solved."

SANDRO BOTTICELLI, *Primavera*

For
Spring
By Sandro Botticelli
(In the Accademia of Florence)

What masque of what old wind-withered New-Year
    Honours this Lady? Flora, wanton-eyed
    For birth, and with all flowrets prankt and pied:
Aurora, Zephyrus, with mutual cheer
Of clasp and kiss: the Graces circling near,
    'Neath bower-linked arch of white arms glorified:
    And with those feathered feet which hovering glide
O'er Spring's brief bloom, Hermes the harbinger.

Birth-bare, not death-bare yet, the young stems stand
    This Lady's temple-columns: o'er her head
    Love wings his shaft. What mystery here is read
Of homage or of hope? But how command
    Dead Springs to answer? And how question here
    These mummers of that wind-withered New-Year?

Even more celebrated, and much more complex and mysterious in its own poetic program,
is Botticelli's great picture of Spring—"Primavera," as it was first called by Vasari. Its struc-
ture and fiction are far from simple, and a viewer's first expectations of seeing, in one of the
figures, a single personification of the season are immediately defeated. In the center, embow-
ered both naturally and architectonically in her Hesperidean garden—where, according to old
mythographers, all is perpetual spring—stands Venus. As the goddess of love and marriage
gestures toward the dancing figures of the three Graces on her right and overhead, her son
Cupid, blindfolded according to a Renaissance tradition (for "Love is blind"), aims an arrow
at the Grace facing in on the left. Behind her, Mercury—as son of Maia, whose name became
that of May—stands dissolving storm clouds that might otherwise threaten the scene. To the
right of Venus is another group of figures: the Roman goddess Flora (*mater florum*, Ovid calls
her), strewing flowers from her bounteous store; and the pair of the nymph Chloris, pursued
by Zephyr (*Favonius* in Latin), the west wind whose trumpeting prophecy is of spring.

What we confront may be thought of as a painted poem full of allusions to printed ones. A prodigious array of classical, medieval, and *quattrocento* texts seems to modern scholars to explain the collocation of figures in the painting, and sometimes their precise relationships. Consider the three Graces, for example, known from later antiquity on as Thaleia (flowerer), Aglaia (shining), and Euphrosyne (delight). The full import of their moralized meaning ranges across "graciousness," "gracefulness," "gratefulness" (as well as some aspects of "charity"—the Graces were also called *charites*), and, particularly, the interrelations of what is separately implied by those English words. Their representation as a group of three intertwined nude figures, the two on the sides facing forward, the central one with her back to the viewer, was canonical in Roman times, and known to *quattrocento* Italy. The accompanying allegorization of the figures is also traditional: so Seneca "[some have it that] there is one for bestowing a benefit, another for receiving it and a third for returning it . . . The sisters are dancing in a ring because a benefit passing from hand to hand nevertheless returns to the giver; the beauty of it all is destroyed if the transmission is anywhere broken" (*De beneficiis* 1.iii.2–7). And so Alberti in *Della Pittura* in the 1430s: "I would like to see those three sisters to whom Hesiod gave the names of Aglaia, Euphrosyne and Thalia, who were painted laughing and taking each other by the hand, with their clothes girdled and very clean. This symbolizes liberality, since one of these sisters gives, the other receives, the third returns the benefit; these degrees ought to be in all perfect liberality." (As if this were a kind of chain letter.) The nudity of Botticelli's Graces is contingent, in that it is half concealed, half disclosed by diaphanous drapery, almost as if depicting thereby how classical fable becomes refigured in Renaissance poetic fiction. Most important, one of the Graces is about to be hit by Cupid's arrow, and we are made aware of a phase of transition in her status: she will be initiated into the erotic and married realm presided over by Cupid's mother.

This change of status is also reflected in the group on the right. Ovid in his *Fasti* has the goddess herself speak of her nature and origins saying, "I who am now Flora used to be Chloris: a Greek letter in my name is corrupted in Latin" [Chloris eram, quae Flora vocor: corrupta Latino / nominis est nostri littera Graeca sono]; she goes on to tell of how, as a nymph, she was wandering in the springtime when she caught the eye of Zephyrus, who pursued and raped, but thereafter married, her. Since then,

> I enjoy spring always; always lovely is the whole year,
> The tree with leaves always, the ground with grasses;
> In the fields that were my dowry, I have a full garden
> Fanned by breezes, watered by a running spring.
> My husband filled this place with noble flowers
> And said, "Be queen, Goddess, of flowers."
> Often I wanted to count the array of colors
> But couldn't—they were innumerable . . .
> Now the Graces approach and intertwine
> Wreaths and crowns to bind their heavenly hair . . .

The contiguity of Chloris and Flora in Botticelli's painting is not so much a picture of a metamorphic moment (which, even in Ovid, does not occur), but rather of a mythographic transition—perhaps a hint of something like the initial Greek letter *chi* becoming a Latin *f.* Certainly the two are independent figures, and their relation is a temporally causative one, reading back, as it were, from present Flora to a previous Chloris (beginning to become floral in the flowers coming from her mouth, which in fact this Flora might have flung).

The association of Mercury, Graces, Venus, Flora, not to speak of particular iconographic details (such as the dragons on Mercury's caduceus) has been adduced from an array of sources, such as Lucretius (book 5 of *De rerum natura*, for Venus, Cupid, Zephyr, and Flora), Horace (*Odes* 1.4, for Venus and Graces in springtime, and Favonian winds; 1.30, for Venus, Cupid, Graces, and Mercury), and poems by Poliziano and Lorenzo de' Medici. Commissioned by Lorenzo di Pierfrancesco de' Medici, a second cousin of Lorenzo the Magnificent with interests in and knowledge of Platonic philosophy, the *Primavera* may—as has been argued—have been done for his wedding in 1482, in which case the moment of initiation of eros and of flowering as fruition has another allusive dimension. A number of topically political and Neoplatonic readings of the painting's allegory (so that, in the second instance, Mercury might be seen as stirring up gathering clouds, rather than clearing them away, in the interests of that Hermetic sort of half concealment which attests authenticity) have also been adduced.

But nineteenth-century poets, addressing the painting before much modern scholarship on it, would have considerable room for their own readings. Rossetti's sonnet commences with an almost canonical ecphrastic question, and indeed, if the remainder of the octave is considered part of the first question, glossing "What masque?" then the poem is almost all questions. (Rossetti's sonnet on the Leonardo *Virgin of the Rocks* starts out with a query, as does his poem on his own painting, *Pandora: A Sea-Spell*.) "What's going on here?" the poem asks, but what it sees is quite particular. For the "here" is an "old wind-withered New Year," not a present vernal processional. Venus is never properly identified, but referred to as "this Lady" (glossed by Rossetti in a strange note: "The same lady, here surrounded by the masque of Spring, is evidently the subject of a portrait by Botticelli formerly in the Pourtales collection in Paris. This portrait is inscribed 'Smeralda Bandinelli'"—Rossetti has turned Venus into one of his own figures). Flora is "wanton-eyed / For birth"; Aurora, save that she is mythologically the mother of Zephyrus, is not in the picture, nor is the transience of "Spring's brief bloom," for the image of Venus's spring bower is one of eternal blooming and self-renewal. The Graces' "bower-linked arch of white arms glorified" connects them with the bower-arch of the trees behind Venus, whose trunks stand as "temple-columns."

In the sestet of the sonnet, the glossing ecphrasis continues, but the interpretive agenda remains somewhat darkened: "Birth-bare, not death-bare yet." Yet the attempt to pluck the heart out of a silent mystery (and, indeed, three of Rossetti's other poems on paintings open with the propounding word "Mystery:" in a grammatical absolute) again must fail. "What mystery . . . ?" must go unanswered, canceled by the next, purely rhetorical question: dead Springs cannot talk, and the presences in old great paintings may themselves be dead. To this degree, they are revived and made to speak only by art-historical scholarship; and yet, alive, they are different beings. This is, again, the sort of confession of interpretive failure first noted in Virgil's third eclogue; Rossetti is clearly uneasy both in his questioning and in the way he avows his inability to answer.

An untitled sonnet (but referred to as "On Sandro's Flora") by the remarkable American Trumbull Stickney, written in 1897 in Paris when he was twenty-three, is half-conscious of Rossetti, but primarily interested in one figure in the painting, and in her half-smiling look, complicated by her palpably unspeaking closed mouth. What he sees in her face is his own doubt:

> She is not happy as the Poets say,
> And passing thro' her garden paradise
> She scatters the divine wet flower that dies
> For so much gathered in the luscious day.
> Behind, the rioting Satyr has his play,
> A wind lays near the Graces' draperies,
> And the sweet Earth with inattentive eyes
> Mildly remembers toward the growing day.
> Her lips would sing but, fearing hazard, press
> The music inward where her breath is caught.
> She dances to an under-melting stream.
> But dubious of this utter happiness
> She dulls her simple ecstasy with thought,
> And lacking Summer doubts herself a Dream.

Whether, in the ambiguous syntax of the first line, Flora is not *as* happy—or, indeed, happy at all—as mythological tradition (and Stickney was a learned classicist) has it, her mood is a meditative one. She stands almost as a surrogate for the interpretive voice from outside the painting which might fracture the composure and composition of the whole scene that—in this poem—contains her. The "hazard" would be the effects of such an intrusion, like the vanishing of the vision of the Three Graces and the dancing ring of a hundred naked girls in book 6 of *The Faerie Queene*, or the smashing of the grove in Wordsworth's "Nutting." The partial ecphrasis here is clearly from somewhat faulty memory, for Stickney adds a nonexistent satyr (perhaps imported from Botticelli's *Mars and Venus* painting, perhaps a metamorphosed version of Zephyr in this one). The poem's power to grasp Flora's inner state is modulated generally by unusual bits of diction—the earth remembering "toward the growing day," the flower dying "For so much gathered in the luscious day," the "under-melting stream" (her unexpressed music—she is dancing not to her own singing, but to her own internal, unvoiced song). And Flora herself cannot even remain untroubled in her garden paradise. Like Rossetti, Stickney knows the whole vision to be transitory, and whether his lady—and here again, the syntax goes both ways—"doubts herself" into a dream (of, say, absent Summer), or whether she doubts that she is herself a dream, a visionary form informing her *locus amoenus*, her proper bower, she is silent in thought. And finally, she is at one with her speaking interpreter, who just avoids the Rossettian mode of final questioning ("Is she worried that she's dreaming? Is she worried that she's *not* dreaming? And how can we know?").

GEORGE INNESS, *The Valley of the Shadow of Death*

WALT WHITMAN

Death's Valley

To accompany a picture; by request. "The Valley of the Shadow of Death,"
from the painting by George Inness

Nay, do not dream, designer dark,
Thou hast portray'd or hit thy theme entire;
I, hoverer of late by this dark valley, by its confines, having glimpses of it,
Here enter lists with thee, claiming my right to make a symbol too.
For I have seen many wounded soldiers die,
After dread suffering—have seen their lives pass off with smiles;
And I have watch'd the death-hours of the old; and seen the infant die;
The rich, with all his nurses and his doctors:
And then the poor, in meagerness and poverty;
And I myself for long, O Death, have breath'd my every breath
Amid the nearness and the silent thought of thee.

And out of these and thee,
I make a scene, a song (not fear of thee,
Nor gloom's ravines, nor bleak, nor dark—for I do not fear thee,
Nor celebrate the struggle, or contortion, or hard-tied knot),
Of the broad blessed light and perfect air, with meadows, rippling tides, and trees and
    flowers and grass,
And the low hum of living breeze—and in the midst God's beautiful eternal right hand,
Thee, holiest minister of Heaven—thee, envoy, usherer, guide at last of all,
Rich, florid, loosener of the stricture-knot call'd life,
Sweet, peaceful, welcome Death.

On the Same Picture

Intended for first stanza of "Death's Valley"

Aye, well I know 'tis ghastly to descend that valley:
Preachers, musicians, poets, painters, always render it,
Philosophers exploit—the battlefield, the ship at sea, the myriad beds, all lands,
All, all the past have enter'd, the ancientest humanity we know,

Syria's, India's, Egypt's, Greece's, Rome's:
Till now for us under our very eyes spreading the same to-day,
Grim, ready, the same to-day, for entrance, yours and mine,
Here, here 'tis limn'd.

George Inness's visionary landscape of 1867 is titled after one of the most famous and resonant lines in the English Bible, from the Twenty-third Psalm—"Yea, though I walk through the valley of the shadow of death, I will fear no evil." Whitman wrote this poem "by request" some time after 1889; it appeared, facing a reproduction of the painting, in *Harper's Magazine* a month after his own death in 1892. (The additional lines, given their present title by Whitman's friend Horace Traubel, may well have been intended at one point for—or as part of—an opening stanza of the poem. But a bit more on these shortly.) Inness's painting "illustrates" the scriptural line in the King James Version of the Old Testament, which is itself a Christian allegorical reading of the Hebrew Bible. The light of hope in the painting emanates from the region of the sky around the cross, which could only have been present in the mind of the psalmist in the typological interpretation of Christianity.

But Whitman was no Christian, and it is significant that his phrase "this dark valley" touches on a well-known textual, and perhaps even hermeneutic, problem in the original Hebrew of the famous phrase. What gets into English as "valley of the shadow" is something like "deep-shadowed valley" and means only a dark valley perhaps menacing to a traveler; the matter of death comes about only in a familiar sort of tendentious interpretation of the kind of ambiguous spelling which marks the unvoweled writing of biblical Hebrew; but it occurred early on, and has been retained. It is almost as if Whitman were starting from the first reading and moving to the second one, but in his own way. For the rhetorical stance of the poem is to refuse the painter's vision—"Nay, do not dream, designer dark, / Thou hast portrayed or hit thy theme entire"—perhaps out of some of Whitman's kind of moral impatience with the image of a received and perhaps too easy piety. He does not want to be left with white-shrouded figures gazing out of the darkness at the light of the cross, but insists on "claiming" his right to make his own "symbol."

And he indeed does that, composing a characteristic series of vignettes of actual death scenes, then moving to a moment of apparent recollection of the sea's whisper of death at the end of his own earlier "Out of the Cradle Endlessly Rocking." The second strophe again categorically denies the adequacy of the painter's scene of "gloom's ravines . . . bleak . . . dark" and puts in its place "a scene, a song" of another kind. It is one of "broad blessed light and perfect air, with meadows, rippling tides, and trees and flowers and grass, / And the low hum of living breeze." The poet, in the words of the psalm, can feel no evil. And it is in this living landscape that death is seen as a sort of Hermes Psychopompos, "God's beautiful eternal right hand . . . holiest minister of heaven." And his valley is not a dark one, but the loveliest of places.

It seems plausible to think of the additional lines "On the Same Picture" as having been a first thought, more gently glossing the psalm text with his own historical view—as well as his sense of revisionary modernity—then put aside for the stronger rejection of the image in the two final stanzas we have. These constitute a conscious antiecphrasis, and the grim death that he allows, in "On the Same Picture," as having been rendered ("Grim, ready, the same to-day, for entrance, yours and mine / Here, here 'tis limned") he now rejects. The death he cares for is *not* limned in "this dark valley," and the painting becomes a mere instance of a rejected construction of what death is. It was not some kind of relation of desire for something *of* the image, the pattern of voice reaching out for the untouchable image that we have seen throughout these pages, which led to the poem. The fact of the commission seems to have led, ultimately, to the poet's averted gaze, which comprises the rhetorical action of the poem. It rejects the vision of the painting, its providential cross and its false hope of the transcendence of death at the price of the central Christian death on the cross that both was and was not one. For Whitman, the abolition of death would be the abolition of life.

Whitman frequently uses pictorial vignettes throughout his poetry. Sections 8, 9, 10, and 33 of "Song of Myself," for example, are typical. In fact, among the notional scenes of section 10 there is indeed one actual ecphrasis, although unacknowledged as such: it is the description beginning "I saw the marriage of the trapper in the open air in the far west," and derives from a painting by the Baltimore painter Alfred Jacob Miller (one of nine versions, not all of which are currently known—it is impossible to tell which one Whitman saw) called "The Trapper's Bride." It is not surprising to discover that among his unpublished poetry there is a remarkable, long series of notional ecphrases called "Pictures." It has interesting affinities with the mode of the gallery poem discussed in the Introduction. Whitman revised its opening lines into a late (1880) little poem called "My Picture Gallery":

> In a little house keep I pictures suspended, it is not a fix'd house,
> It is round, it is only a few inches from one side to the other;
> Yet behold, it has room for all the shows of the world, all memories!
> Here the tableaus of life, and here the groupings of death;
> Here, do you know this? this is cicerone himself,
> With finger rais'd he points to the prodigal pictures.

What seems an ad hoc trope here—the "prodigal pictures" of memory and of imagination being figured as paintings hanging in a gallery—is doubled with a metaphor connecting writing, painting, and thinking. In any event, the walls of the "little house" would seem to wall out glimpses of any actual works of art. This house—his head, his mental gallery—seems related to the chamber of Imagination or Memory (it is interestingly unclear to which of the two it belongs), lined with paintings, upstairs in the turret (or "head") of Spenser's House of Alma in book 2 of *The Faerie Queene*. It also evokes the collection of images lining the walls of the soul in the poem of Andrew Marvell discussed above. It is a gallery to which the poet is "cicerone himself," and it provides him with a store of fictions as a resource against visual and sentimental cliche. And perhaps against Inness's scene as well.

J. B. Millet, *L'Homme à la houe*

EDWIN MARKHAM

The Man with the Hoe
Written after Seeing the Painting by Millet

God made man in his own image, in the image of God made He him. —Genesis.

Bowed by the weight of centuries he leans
Upon his hoe and gazes on the ground,
The emptiness of ages in his face,
And on his back the burden of the world.
Who made him dead to rapture and despair,
A thing that grieves not and that never hopes,
Stolid and stunned, a brother to the ox?
Who loosened and let down this brutal jaw?
Whose was the hand that slanted back this brow?
Whose breath blew out the light within this brain?

Is this the Thing the Lord God made and gave
To have dominion over sea and land;
To trace the stars and search the heavens for power;
To feel the passion of Eternity?
Is this the Dream He dreamed who shaped the suns
And pillared the blue firmament with light?
Down all the stretch of Hell to its last gulf
There is no shape more terrible than this—
More tongued with censure of the world's blind greed—
More filled with signs and portents for the soul—
More fraught with menace to the universe.

What gulfs between him and the seraphim!
Slave of the wheel of labor, what to him
Are Plato and the swing of Pleiades?
What the long reaches of the peaks of song,
The rift of dawn, the reddening of the rose?
Through this dread shape the suffering ages look;
Time's tragedy is in that aching stoop;
Through this dread shape humanity betrayed,
Plundered, profaned, and disinherited,
Cries protest to the Judges of the World,
A protest that is also prophecy.

O masters, lords, and rulers in all lands,
Is this the handiwork you give to God,
This monstrous thing distorted and soul-quenched?
How will you ever straighten up this shape;
Touch it again with immortality;
Give back the upward looking and the light;
Rebuild it in the music and the dream;
Make right the immemorial infamies,
Perfidious wrongs, immedicable woes?

O masters, lords, and rulers in all lands,
How will the Future reckon with this Man?
How answer his brute question in that hour
When whirlwinds of rebellion shake the world?
How will it be with kingdoms and with kings—
With those who shaped him to the thing he is—
When this dumb Terror shall reply to God,
After the silence of the centuries?

For the first half of the twentieth century, the most widely known ecphrastic poem in the United States—and not only because of its use in the schools as a piece for memory and recitation—was the poem by Edwin Markham which appeared in the *San Francisco Examiner* in January of 1899 and as the title piece of a book later that year. Along with the author's equally famous verses on "Lincoln, the Man of the People" (he is known now for little else), it became sensationally popular. "The Man with the Hoe" was praised as a virtual manifesto by the labor movement, celebrated for what must have been taken to be the mutual authentication and reinforcement of its high rhetoric and higher radical moral sentiments. Interesting is the fact that of the poem's three—or, at most, four—lines of purported descriptive ecphrasis of the painting (indeed, the opening ones), the only line of precise observation is quite wrong: whether "Bowed by the weight of centuries" or only by the back-bending day's work, Millet's *bêcheur* most certainly does not gaze on the ground, but rather stares off into a middle distance. He is in that daze of exhaustion into which even the most intellectual of beings, pausing after heavy physical labor, easily sink, as was noted by an American commentator on the painting in the 1860s. ("The man leaned on his spade. In the moment of repose, every muscle in his frame had fallen . . . into relaxed, weary inactivity. It was not the classic repose of the *Genie du Repos Eternal;* it was not the grand strength in inaction of Michelangelo's *Slave.* No, it was the patient, hopeless weariness of the overtasked workman.")

Millet's painting of *L'homme à la houe,* completed in 1862, represents a farm laborer at momentary rest; that there is about him something of an embodiment of the famous Hobbesian characterization of the life of humanity in a state of nature—"solitary, poor, nasty, brutish and short"—seems to have been an object of discussion from the painting's first appearance. One critic remarked of the figure that "no glimmer of intelligence humanizes this brute in repose," and asks "Has he just been working or murdering?" [Aucune lueur d'intelligence n'humanise cette brute au repos. Vient-il de travailler ou d'assassiner?] One might say that Millet himself regarded the painting as neither pastoral nor georgic, neither a celebration of an ideal rurality nor a meditation, just this side of allegory, on rural work. Nor is there a conscious attempt to mock our intelligence by setting a trap for it, into which it falls in seeing the peasant as "brutish." There was considerable debate about whether the painting denied the possibility of hope for the redemption of this brutishness by any social progress, or implied that in the hopelessness itself lay a higher, more revolutionary hope that the very wretchedness of the figure might turn against its task, its masters—that here was a sort of Caliban. The briars in the lower left of the painting may perhaps allude to Genesis 3.18, "Thorns also and thistles shall it [the ground] bring forth to thee; and thou shalt eat the herb of the field." (Robert Herbert remarks that they [the briars] "evoke a crown of thorns for this *lamentable Christ du labour eternel.*")

In 1863 when Millet helped publish a photograph of the painting, he chose to accompany it a text from Montaigne (from his essay, in fact, "Of Physiognomy"):

> Let us look down upon the poor people that we see scattered upon the face of the earth, prone and intent upon their business, that neither know Aristotle nor Cato, example nor precept; from these nature every day extracts effects of constancy and patience, more pure and manly than those we do so inquisitively study in the schools: how many do I ordinarily see who slight poverty? How many who desire to die, or who die without alarm or regret? He who is now digging in my garden, has this morning buried his father or his son. The very names by which they call diseases sweeten and mollify the sharpness of them: the phthisic is with them no more than a cough, dysentery but a looseness, the pleurisy but a stitch; and, as they gently name them, so they patiently endure them; they are very great and grievous indeed, when they hinder their ordinary labour; they never keep their beds but to die.
>
> —tr. Charles Cotton

The epigraph to Markham's poem is not the biblical text we might expect (Genesis 3.18–19 [KJV]: "In the sweat of thy face shalt thou eat bread"), giving an etiology of the condition of rural labor. Rather, we are invited to regard the passage from scripture with an irony so crude as to border on sarcasm: something, it is implied, has gone wrong. Either human history has wrought this kind of damage ("Look at him!") on the representation of the divine in the human, or else the divinity that could be used by the institutions of human greed and power to maintain their hold was itself as brutal-looking as this, and the image is, ironically, a true one. The irony would be easily available to Markham's sort of western American radical thought. But it is interesting that, in revising the poem very slightly in 1920, the epigraph was removed. It was perhaps the very recent Russian revolution, too, which caused Markham to change two of the 1899 lines. "More fraught with menace to the universe" becomes "More packt with danger to the universe," but, far more significantly, the penultimate line is changed to read "When this dumb terror shall rise to judge the world." Although probably mostly Shelleyan, it seems to incorporate a strange assimilation of Trotskyan total revolution and Christian second coming.

The string of ecphrastic questions with which the first paragraph of blank verse concludes unquestionably echoes those put by Blake's Bard of Experience to his fearfully constructed Tyger. As they continue into the second paragraph, they make the ironies of the epigraph more clear. It is not nature, but society—the constraining garb of Hobbes's Leviathan itself, rather than the nakedness it is constructed to alleviate—that has bowed this creature over "the centuries" and which thus has much to fear. (Something seems interestingly puzzling about the poem's opening word, "bowed," by the way: one may perhaps discern here an overtone of a passive voice of a verb that rhymed with "load," meaning to be bent into a bow-shape, rather than the ordinary sense of to defer or genuflect as in W. E. Henley's "My head is bloody but unbowed," which rhymes with "aloud.")

The rhetorical questions originally generated by the muteness of the painting take over the poem in the third stanza (Hamlet's "What's Hecuba to him, or he to Hecuba" returns not inelegantly inverted in "what to him / Are Plato and the swing of Pleiades," perhaps the best lines in the poem. Had Markham read Montaigne's "ne sçavent ny Aristote ny Catone"?). These subsequent questions are directed to the putative lords of the world—in the manner of Swinburne's "Watchman, what of the Night?"—not to the painted image, and it is they which construe the painting as a piece of prophetic social realism. The speaker of "The Man with the Hoe" is not identified with what its author called "hoemanry"—as opposed to the yeomanry of landed farmers—and with which he associated himself. As he wrote, soon after the poem's publication,

> I was myself a working man, under hard and incorrigible conditions. The smack of the soil and the whir of the forge are in my blood . . . I came to see that Millet puts before us no chance peasant, no mere man of the fields. No, he bodies forth for us betrayed Humanity—the Toiler ground down through the ages of oppression, through ages of injustice. He shows us the man pushed away from the land by the monopoly of those who fail to use the land, till at last he had become a serf with no mind in his muscles and no heart in his handiwork.

So sensational was the matter of the poem and the painting that a competition was set in 1900 for a rejoinder to Markham's verses. It was won by a minor bard named John Vance Cheney, who would have none of this prophetic agenda, urging a reading of the figure as naturally noble, and starting out—perhaps unwittingly returning to an earlier association—with an epigraph from Montaigne. But what he ends up with oscillates between a "From each according to . . . to each . . ." and perhaps a latent social Darwinism. I quote from it only in part:

The Man with the Hoe
A Reply

Let us a little permit Nature to take her own way: she better understands
her own affairs than we. —Montaigne.

Nature reads not our labels, "great" and "small";
Accepts she one and all

Who, striving, win and hold the vacant place;
All are of royal race.

Him, there, rough-cast, with rigid arm and limb;
The Mother moulded him,

Of his rude realm ruler and demigod,
Lord of the rock and clod.

With Nature is not "better" and no "worse,"
On this bared head no curse.

Humbled it is and bowed; so is he crowned
Whose kingdom is the ground.

Diverse the burdens on the one stern road
Where bears each back its load;

Varied the toil, but neither high nor low
With pen or sword or hoe . . .

His changeless realm, he knows it, and commands;
Erect enough he stands,

Tall as his toil. Nor does he bow unblest:
Labor he has, and rest.

—And the hint of prayer here (as if the painted figure were from Millet's *L'Angelus*) is caught
up in the echo of the Prayer Book's formula in the next couplet:

Need was, need is, and need will ever be
For him and such as he;

Cast for the gap, with gnarled arm and limb,
The Mother moulded him . . .

"Bowed by the weight of centuries"? "Erect enough," goes the answer. Walt Whitman, in April 1881, saw in a private collection a group of Millet's paintings, and one could only wish that this one had been among them, and had elicited his comment. In general, he said of Millet's paintings that they possessed "that last impalpable ethic purpose from the artist (most likely unconscious to himself) which I am always looking for." And he continues (in the section from *Specimen Days* entitled "Millet's Last Pictures—Last Items"):

> To me all of them told the full story of what went before and necessitated the great French revolution—the long precedent crushing of the masses of a heroic people into the earth, in abject poverty, hunger—every right denied, humanity attempted to be put back for generations—yet Nature's force, titanic here, the stronger and hardier for that repression—waiting terribly to break forth, revengeful—the pressure on the dykes, and the bursting at last—the storming of the Bastile [*sic*]—the execution of the king and queen—the tempest of massacres and blood . . .

Would he have spoken differently of *L'homme à la houe*?

Neither Markham's verses nor those of the milder Cheney perform anything like a careful reading of the painting: the figure is treated as an icon, and the second response is to the first one, rather than directly even to the iconic reduction of the man with the hoe in the painting. The remarkable backlighting of the figure; the enigmas of the posture; the rigorous horizontal triangular form generated by the hoe and the figure's feet, shadowing the vertical one with the apex at its crotch, and, finally, the functional triangular structure of support, with the apex at the shoulder, in which the whole figure stands; the distant rises of mound, and the outcropping leading to the female figure tending the fires, in the left and right distances—it is as if they were not there. There is only the reading of the figure as too brutal or as adequately noble. A poem that engaged both of these notions, rather than propounding one half of a cloven fiction, would have been more proper to the painting, and to itself.

But perhaps the last word of comment here should be left to the particular wisdom of Gertrude Stein who (in "Pictures" from *Lectures in America,* 1935) is remembering seeing the painting when it was brought to San Francisco by its purchaser in her childhood:

> But I still know exactly how the Man with a Hoe looked. I know exactly how it looked although having now lived a great deal in the french country I see the farmers constantly hoeing with just that kind of a hoe. The hoeing with just that kind of a hoe as I see them all the time and meet them all the time have nothing to do with Millet's Man with a Hoe but that is natural because I know the men as men, the hoe as a hoe and the fields as fields. But I still know Millet's Man with a Hoe, because it was an oil painting. And my brother said it was a hell of a hoe but what it was was an oil painting. Millet's pictures did have something that made one say those things.

Mona Lisa

Yon strange blue city crowns a scarpèd steep
No mortal foot hath bloodlessly essayed:
Dreams and illusions beacon from its keep,
But at the gate an angel bares his blade;
And tales are told of those who thought to gain
At dawn its ramparts; but when evening fell
Far off they saw each fading pinnacle
Lit with wild lightnings from the heaven of pain;
Yet there two souls, whom life's perversities
Had mocked with want in plenty, tears in mirth,
Might meet in dreams, ungarmented of earth,
And drain Joy's awful chalice to the lees.

It is with more than perverse delight that one can turn to a poem about Mona Lisa that does not mention the sitter. Leonardo da Vinci's famous portrait of the wife of Francesco del Giocondo has become a kind of monument of its own. It "bids fair to be considered the best-known painting in the world," in John Pope-Hennessy's words, and has been the object of wonder ever since Vasari raved about the picture without actually having seen it:

> To look closely at her throat you might imagine that the pulse was beating. Indeed, we may say that this was painted in a manner to cause the boldest artists to despair. Mona Lisa was very beautiful, and while Lionardo was drawing her portrait he engaged people to play and sing, and jesters to keep her merry, and remove that melancholy which painting usually gives to portraits. This figure of Lionardo's has such a pleasant smile that it seemed rather divine than human, and was considered marvellous, an exact copy of Nature.

Since then, the picture has become the subject. Her famous smile, which may indeed be only the shadow of a smile—engendered by the *sfumato* of the painting rather than by a representation of any action of facial muscles—has helped color the painting's aura. The way in which the draped lower part of the seated figure expands to fill almost the whole width of the painted area; the invitations to speculation offered by the wide and deep landscape behind her (which Vasari totally ignores)—rather than a glimpsed portion framed by a window in an interior setting; and the relaxed but firm position of the hands—all these help frame Mona Lisa's

LEONARDO DA VINCI, *Mona Lisa*

own gaze straight out of the painting, as if regarding herself in a mirror. Or, perhaps, in the mirroring gaze of a viewer.

But then there is the landscape, whose allegorical character seems to inhere in its tonal palette, its formal complexity, and its continually puzzling relation to the sitter. As one astute observer has put it:

> Behind Mona Lisa looms another world. There is the winding road and a stone bridge spanning a stream, but these are forlorn signs of man's presence in a barren landscape. Beyond the valley earth color gives way to steel blue. A high plateau rises on the right, but plunges drastically downward on the left so that the land seems out of joint. The rocks are shrouded, and melt toward a horizonless distance. Glacial in its icy damp, this is a forbidden land where . . . one stares in wonder and dare not go on.

But it is just this matter that the poem in question confronts. Aside from her celebrated fiction, Edith Wharton wrote some very good verse, and published two volumes of poems. To grasp the point of this sonnet, one should know that it is one of a pair called "Two Backgrounds" which form in themselves a Browningesque sort of diptych of poems. In them, she tellingly interprets the landscapes behind the two figures—the Virgin in a Flemish painting ("La Vierge Au Donateur"—van Eyck's *Madonna of Chancellor Rolin?*), and Mona Lisa—as scenes of marriage and love, subtly reflective not only of the ignored dominant human image, but also of the nature of the landscape itself, in each case. Thus significant contrasts—realist-urban versus visionary country; closed versus widely open; deep-focused versus atmospheric; framed by an interior versus reaching across the panel—are implicitly invoked in the readings. The first of them describes the urban landscape showing through the window of the northern painting behind Mary and the donor:

> Here by the ample river's margent sweep,
> Bosomed in tilth and vintage to her walls,
> A tower-crowned Cybele in armoured sleep
> The city lies, fat plenty in her halls,
> With calm parochial spires that hold in fee
> The friendly gables clustered at their base,
> And, equipoised o'er tower and market-place,
> The Gothic minster's winged immensity;
> And, in that narrow burgh, with equal mood,
> Two placid hearts, to all life's good resigned,
> Might, from the altar to the lych-gate, find
> Long years of peace and dreamless plenitude.

This "narrow burgh" is the scene of bourgeois marriage, and the poem reads the Flemish city as mercantile built over feudal, with strong but delicate ambivalence—the benign, controlled structures produce lives of physical health and unimaginativeness, "dreamless plenitude."

Not so with Mona Lisa's prospects and distances. They lead the eye out toward a "strange blue city," metaphorical, heavenly seeming but fallen, the realm of passionate and desperate lovers: antithetical to the framed representation of the Stable City, the opened but more distant vision of the Dangerous one. And just as the erased encounter of the Virgin and a donor inheres in the values of the "narrow burgh" in the first poem, so the unmentioned Milanese bourgeoise transformed by art into an inscrutable erotic myth informs the scene of the second. Wharton very cleverly avoids all of the celebrated questions in which the portrait comes officially wrapped (the sitter's gaze, what it betokens, the nature of the smile—"a smile is the chosen token of all ambiguities," says Melville in *Pierre*) by looking only at the magnificent landscape behind her, extending almost two-thirds of the way down the panel, in a tone influenced partially by Rossetti, partially perhaps by George Meredith's sonnets in *Modern Love.*

She is, in fact, doing a fine literary end run around the canonical statement of that myth. Here it is, cast in an amusingly uncanonical form:

Mona Lisa

> She is older than the rocks among which she sits;
> Like the Vampire,
> She has been dead many times,
> And learned the secrets of the grave;
> And has been a diver in deep seas,
> And keeps their fallen day about her;
> And trafficked for strange webs with Eastern merchants;
> And, as Leda,
> Was the mother of Helen of Troy,
> And, as St. Anne,
> Was the mother of Mary;
> And all this has been to her but as the sound of lyres and flutes,
> And lives
> Only in the delicacy
> With which it has moulded the changing lineaments,
> And tinged the eyelids and the hands.

This is very bad free verse indeed, chopped out of Walter Pater's remarkable prose rhapsody on the work, of which he said that "of all ancient pictures time has chilled it least." The chopper and emender was W. B. Yeats, who had no ear for vers libre, but who responded to the passage's mode of mythmaking. Pater's whole long paragraph makes far better conceptual, and poetic, sense. He is in fact writing about the emergence of a mythological prototype from the particular occasion of commissioned portraiture. But this is not as if a painter like Sir Joshua Reynolds had rendered his subject, in appropriate dress, "as" some figure from classical mythology. Rather, as Pater insists, some romantic poem of Leonardo's own produces a particular aspect of an *Ewigweiblichen*—an eternal feminine presence that is no mere paradigmatic maternal *anima*, but instead, as Harold Bloom has pointed out, a figure of faintly smiling *Anangke* or Necessity. Pater implies that the mythical personage emerged during the four years of work on the painting:

> The presence that rose thus so strangely beside the waters, is expressive of what in the ways of a thousand years men had come to desire. Hers is the head upon which all "the ends of the world are come," and the eyelids are a little weary. It is a beauty wrought out from within upon the flesh, the deposit, little cell by cell, of strange thoughts and fantastic reveries and exquisite passions. Set it for a moment beside one of those white Greek goddesses or beautiful women of antiquity, and how they would be troubled by this beauty, into which the soul with all its maladies has passed!

The historically transcendent force of this presence is underscored by Pater's elliptical quotation from 1 Corinthians 10.11, suggesting that Mona Lisa's image—and, indeed, his own words truly identifying her—"are written for our admonition, on whom the ends of the world are come." And he continues:

> All the thoughts and experience of the world have etched and moulded there, in that which they have of power to refine and make expressive the outward form, the animalism of Greece, the lust of Rome, the mysticism of the middle age with its spiritual ambition and imaginative loves, the return of the Pagan world, the sins of the Borgias. She is older than the rocks among which she sits; like the vampire, she has been dead many times, and learned the secrets of the grave; and has been a diver in deep seas, and keeps their fallen day about her; and trafficked for strange webs with Eastern merchants: and, as Leda, was the mother of Helen of Troy, and, as Saint Anne, the mother of Mary; and all this has been to her but as the sound of lyres and flutes, and lives only in the delicacy with which it has moulded the changing lineaments, and tinged the eyelids and the hands. The fancy of a perpetual life, sweeping together ten thousand experiences, is an old one; and modern philosophy has conceived the idea of humanity as wrought upon by, and summing up in itself, all modes of thought and life. Certainly Lady Lisa might stand as the embodiment of that old fancy, the symbol of the modern idea.

The "modern idea" is both that of evolution and of recapitulation, but very strangely symbolized by the figure at whom Pater stopped looking long before the passage starts. Other Leonardesque figures—notably the Virgin and St. Anne—sit "among" rocks; La Gioconda's leap up far behind her, and surround her only in the picture plane. Pater's image is in itself a kind of conflation, like the very image upon which he broods. The painting is an occasion for his poetic meditation, which starts out by claiming that the sitter was an occasion for the poetic meditation of Leonardo.

Titian, *Sacred and Profane Love*

From The Testament of Beauty, *Book III*

       Art is the true and happy science of the soul,
exploring nature for spiritual influences,
as doth physical science for comforting powers,
advancing so to a sure knowledge with like progress:
but lovers who thereto look for expression of truth
hav great need to remember that no plastic Art,
tho' it create ideals noble as are the forms
that Pheidias wrought, can ever elude or wholly escape
its earthly medium; nor in its adumbrations
reach thatt detach'd suprasensuous vision, whereto
Poetry and Music soar, nor dive down in the mine
where cold philosophy diggeth her fiery jewels—
or only by rare magic may it sometimes escape.

And this was the intuition of our landscape painters,
whose venture seem'd humble in renouncing the prize
of the classic contest, when like truants from school
they made off to the fields with their satchels, and came
on nature's beauteous by-paths into a purer air:
For the Art of painting, by triumph of colouring
enticed to Realism, had confounded thereby
its own higher intention, and in portrayal of spirit
made way for Symbolism which, tho' it stand aloof,
is outfaced in the presence of direct feeling:
Sithence in the presence of feminin beauty
the highest Art lost mastery of its old ideal;
as in the great pictur of the two Women at a Well,
where Titian's young genius, devising a new thing,
employ'd the plastic power to exhibit at once
two diverse essences in their value and contrast;
for while by the æsthetic idealisation of form
his earthly love approacheth to celestial grace,
his draped Uranian figure is by symbols veil'd,
and in pictorial Beauty suffereth defeat:
Yea, despite all her impregnable confidence

in the truth of her wisdom, as there she sitteth
beside the fountain, dazzlingly apparel'd, enthroned,
with thoughtful face impassiv, averting her head
as 'twer for fuller attention so to incline an ear
to the impartial hearing of the importunat plea
of the other, who over-against her on the cornice-plinth
posturing her wonted nakedness in sensuous ease,
leaneth her body to'ards her, and with imploring grace
urgeth the vain deprecation of her mortal prayer.

Giorgione, his master, already had gone to death
plague-stricken at prime, when Titian painted thatt picture,
donning his rival's mantle, and strode to higher fame—
yet not by this canvas; he who had it, hid it;
nor won it public favour when it came to light,
untill some mystic named it in the Italian tongue
L'AMOR SACRO E PROFANO, and so rightly divined;
for tho' ther is no record save the work of the brush
to tell the intention, yet what the mind wrought is there;
and who looketh thereon may see in the two left arms
the symbolism apportioning the main design;
for while the naked figure with extended arm
and outspredd palm vauntingly balanceth aloft
a little lamp, whose flame lost in the bright daylight
wasteth in the air, thatt other hath the arm bent down
and oppositely nerved, and clencheth with gloved hand
closely the cover'd vessel of her secret fire.

Thus Titian hath pictured the main sense of my text,
and this truth: that as Beauty is all with Spirit twined,
so all obscenity is akin to the ugliness
which Art would outlaw; whence cometh thatt tinsel honour
and mimicry of beauty which is the attire of vice.

Allegory is a cloudland inviting fancy
to lend significance to chancey shapes; and here
I deem not that the child, who playeth between the Loves
at Titian's well, was pictured by him with purpose
to show the first contact of love with boyhood's mind;
and yet never was symbol more deftly devised:
Mark how the child looking down on the water see'th
only a reflection of the realities—as 'twas
with the mortals in Plato's cave—nor more of them

than Moses saw of God; he can see but their backs,
save for a shifty glimpse of the pleading profil
of earthly Love (which also is subtle truth); and most
how in his play his plunged hand stirreth to and fro
both images together in a confused dazzle
of the dancing ripples as he gazeth intent.

We may remember that Dante Gabriel Rossetti's strong misreading of the Leonardo *Virgin of the Rocks* commits no empirical mistakes, save for the crucial suppression of the figure of the angel. There are many instances of outright ad hoc mistakes in poems on or to works of art. Often, however, the received state of knowledge about an image from the past—a misattribution (like the Medusa to Leonardo), a mistitling (the *Torso Belvedere* construed as Hercules), an iconographic misreading—will have shaped the aura of the image itself, and becomes part of what is addressed in the poem. In book 3 of his strange, long, awkward *The Testament of Beauty*, Robert Bridges calls up the famous Titian in the Galleria Borghese usually called *Sacred and Profane Love* in apparent identification of the clothed (sacred) and nude (profane) female figures seated at the well, with a figure of Cupid behind them, absorbed in his playing with the water. Earlier in our century, Erwin Panofsky correctly identified the two figures: the nude one (not, as we might distinguish the terms, "naked") is that of a heavenly Venus, *Venere Celeste*, and the other, clothed in fashionable Venetian dress, *Venere Volgare*, her allegorical complement. (Panofsky indeed suggested that the painting should be retitled *The Twin Venuses*.)

As we see, Bridges gets this quite wrong—as well he might, given the received misinterpretation of the painting—and all the more so, since (1) he claims that the received title represents some revelation of the truth of the painting, and (2) his language so literally employs the interpretive modes of the iconographer. But it also uses poetry's own modes. Consider the over-reading of the figure's two left arms, for example: Could he have read Panofsky's remarks on the painting, Bridges might have seen the two right arms of the respective figures as *nude-straight* = *heavenly* and *clothed-bent* = *popularly erotic*. But seizing upon the reading of the nude as the profane, and the clothed as the sacred, condition, Bridges still contrives, in his final lines, to move metaphorically against his own conception: by speaking of the "mimicry of beauty which is the attire of vice" he allows an archaistic bit of personifying machinery ("the attire of" as a version of old chestnuts about nudity being clad in its innocence, etc.) to trip him up. For the profane love is indeed attired in the painting—and in fashionable contemporary Venetian clothing at that. (The heavenly love is not naked—bare or bereft of clothing, but nude—free of the visionary drapery which still hangs from, and frames, her body.)

It will be seen that in these lines Titian's landscape, and the relief carving on the well, might as well not exist. Nevertheless, Bridges is able to conclude his disquisition with a fecund poetic fable of his own that reads more deeply, and imagines more fully, than he does in the more literary, polemical, and—we now feel—erroneous account of the female figures. The last verse paragraph is of a different poetic order, and deploys the strong revisionary strategy of modern poetic ecphrasis. He propounds, only in order to reject, a perfectly good ad hoc allegory of the Cupid figure as Childhood encountering both *amor* and *caritas* during latency— "to show the first contact of love with boyhood's mind"—and instead yields to a vision that he seems almost to have been repressing earlier in these lines. Part of this vision involves stumbling on the poetic knowledge that erotic Bodily Beauty and Truth are both figured as female nudes—"of earthly love (which also is subtle truth)." And strangely enough, he seems to anticipate Panofsky, who, writing more prosaically, thirty-five years later, of how "Cupid, stirring, and, as it were, homogenizing the water, may be presumed to symbolize the principle of harmonization of virtue of which the two forms of love represented by the two Venuses, though different in rank, are one in essence."

Brueghel's Winter

Jagg'd mountain peaks and skies ice-green
Wall in the wild cold scene below.
Churches, farms, bare copse, the sea
In freezing quiet of winter show;
Where ink-black shapes on fields in flood
Curling, skating, and sliding go.
To left, a gabled tavern; a blaze;
Peasants; a watching child; and lo,
Muffled, mute—beneath naked trees
In sharp perspective set a-row—
Trudge huntsmen, sinister spears aslant,
Dogs snuffling behind them in the snow;
And arrowlike, lean, athwart the air
  Swoops into space a crow.

But flame, nor ice, nor piercing rock,
Nor silence, as of a frozen sea,
Nor that slant inward infinite line
Of signboard, bird, and hill, and tree,
Give more than subtle hint of him
Who squandered here life's mystery.

   That certain paintings of Pieter Bruegel the Elder should have become the targets of so much poetic opportunity since World War II invites some speculation. Certainly, literary realism could embrace him—whether aware of his frequently complex iconography or not—as a painter of everyday life. His paintings were reproduced widely and well in color. He was the northern Renaissance painter to be most ennobled by modernist art criticism (Roger Fry, for example). And whatever their iconographic program, the figures in his paintings, and the visions of space in his landscapes, invited narrative speculation. While we tend to think of Auden's "Musée des Beaux Arts" as initiating a fashion for the Brueghel poem among American writers of the forties, fifties, and thereafter, his was certainly not the first.
   A few years before Auden was in Brussels, Walter de la Mare addressed the well-known painting usually called *The Hunters in the Snow*, in the Kunsthistorisches Museum in Vienna, in a poem most of which is devoted to a strict ecphrasis of the painting. Sonnet-like in its divi-

PIETER BRUEGEL THE ELDER, *The Hunters in the Snow*

sion (the first fourteen lines of description, an added six introducing a "But . . ." qualifica-
tion), "Brueghel's Winter" starts reading the scene from the peaks in the upper right. Then it
moves down the remarkable diagonal generated from the axis of the forceful forward move-
ment of the hunters and their dogs, opposed by the contrary diagonal of the slope of the hill-
side before them, and echoed by parallel slopes in the distance (all these being cut by the
assertive verticals of the line of trees). These formal elements organize and map the planar
space of the painting, guiding the eye in its tour of the scene of winter life and activity. The
poem takes a rather rapid inventory of a scene which the viewer takes somewhat longer to
scan, given the shifts of scale, and the minuteness of some details: the tavern and its sign,
skaters and players of ice-games, people shooting birds and putting out a fire, a village and its
church, a mill on the stream on the lower right, a distant town, and so forth.

In de la Mare's inventory, order, relative length, detail, and qualification of description are
deployed along a simple principle of structure: odd-numbered lines unrhymed throughout;
seven even-numbered lines all rhyming with "below," followed by three rhyming with "sea" in
the final section. The retraction or qualification propounded there turns away from immedi-
ate ecphrasis to a matter of transcendence. This is itself, as the last word cannot help but
remind us, something of a "mystery" of another sort. Bruegel's painting is now thought to be
one of a series of twelve—only five of which are extant—of the months (not the seasons) of
the year, each one representing a month by characteristic human activities. This is the sort of
image perhaps most familiar today in the realistic vignettes framed in the zodiacal iconogra-
phy of the pictures of the months in the Chantilly Book of the Hours (*Les Très riches heures du
Duc de Berry*). The present painting is believed to be the "January" of such a series, although
de la Mare did not know this. In a sense, the end of his poem might seem to point beyond
the totally secular, realistic vision of the time of year with a thought something like "It might
as well be Christmas; but then where are the traces of this moment of transcendence?" Yet the
title of the poem is "Brueghel's Winter," and the "him / Who squandered here life's mystery"
is surely the painter, not Christ. This is less puzzling when we realize that "squander" is used
in an older sense to mean—with no connotations of profligacy—simply "scatter" or "dis-
perse." The painter is thus being characterized as having dispersed a great mystery, a general
spiritual substance, into wonderfully scattered, wonderfully vivid, instances of actuality in
human life. And whatever the painting's signs that seem to point beyond it, for this poet they
point not to spiritual mystery, but to artistic and imaginative mastery.

Another poem on this painting by John Berryman was written around 1939, in the poet's
own words, "against Yeats' gorgeous and seductive rhetoric, and, second, against the hysterical
political atmosphere of the period" following a return to New York from two years abroad.
Like Auden's "Musée des Beaux Arts," it also responds to an apparent injunction by the win-
ter painting to catalogue details. But the focus remains throughout on the three largest figures
in the foreground. It is through them that the poem takes its tour, in one, long, complex sen-
tence wandering across five-lined, unrhymed pentameter stanzas, through the landscape:

Winter Landscape

The three men coming down the winter hill
In brown, with tall poles and a pack of hounds
At heel, through the arrangement of the trees,
Past the five figures at the burning straw,
Returning cold and silent to their town,

Returning to the drifted snow, the rink
Lively with children, to the older men,
The long companions they can never reach,
The blue light, men with ladders, by the church
The sledge and shadow in the twilit street

Are not aware that in the sandy time
To come, the evil waste of history
Outstretched, they will be seen upon the brow
Of that same hill, when all their company
Will have been irrevocably lost,

These men, this particular three in brown
Witnessed by birds will keep the scene and say
By their configuration with the trees,
The small bridge, the red houses and the fire,
What place, what time, what morning occasion

Sent them into the wood, a pack of hounds
At heel and the tall poles upon their shoulders,
Thence to return as now we see them and
Ankle-deep in snow down the winter hill
Descend, while three birds watch and the fourth flies.

Like de la Mare, this poet seems intensely aware of the formal planar patterns and configurations that a modernist eye might bring to the painting. But unlike him, Berryman moves toward the Keatsian question of a moment of time frozen—"The long companions they [the returning hunters] can never reach" echoes what is said of the youth pursuing the maiden on the Grecian Urn: "Bold lover, never, never canst thou kiss, / Though winning near the goal." A version of the traditional poetic questions asked of figures in pictures—"What are they thinking of?"—returns in an interesting way here. The figures are of course unaware of their identity as figures in a painted landscape and as objects of poetic meditation, surviving the death and burial of their own world in "sandy time" (that which is marked by the lasting, but ever-shifting sand in hourglasses, rather than by the cyclically melting snow: François Villon's "les neiges d'antan"). The unknowingness of these painted figures about where they would end up in history is specifically pointed against the particular "evil waste" of Europe about to be, or already at, war. The hunters cannot imagine what sense of war about to descend again upon, say, Flemish villages might shadow them for a later viewer. Unlike Shakespeare's Cleopatra, who predicts that she and Antony will end up as characters in an English play, they are as unaware—for Berryman's poem—of history as they are of being in a painting. But in addition, it is made to parallel our own unknowingness, as viewers of the scene, of where, and from what conditions and motives ("What place, what time, what morning occasion"), they started out. Berryman's closing line very delicately and momentarily allegorizes the birds as embodying the functions of viewing eye and interpreting mind: "the fourth flies," takes off, from the scene it has entered in order to watch for a while.

Berryman himself, almost thirty years later, denying that his poem could legitimately be called "either a verbal *equivalent* to the picture or . . . an *interpretation* of it," remarked

> as far as I can make out, it is a war poem, of an unusual negative kind. The common title of the picture is "Hunters in the Snow" and of course the poet knows this. But he pretends not to, and calls their spears (twice) "poles," the governing resultant emotion being a certain stubborn incredulity—as the hunters are loosed while the peaceful nations plunge again into war.

Yet Berryman's cavil with narrowly conceived and limited characterizations of what poems say and do about pictures stops short of saying what other sort of relation—other than that of "equivalent" or "interpretation"—his poem has to the picture. It is clearly an interpretation, or implicit parable on the occasion of reading a memory (or reproduction) of the painting in a present, wintry light of a different sort.

A third poem directed to this picture, from the early 1950s, is one of a sequence on Bruegel paintings by William Carlos Williams. The poem is composed in tercets of the short, heavily but insignificantly enjambed free verse typical of the poet's later verse, each formed by three lines that are, typographically, short-shorter-short. The poem immediately abandons the hermeneutic question hinted at in its opening line's pun on "over-all picture." The details picked out in it ought to compose some "over-all" poetic picture of their own, but appear not to. Neither are they fully considered: the image on the signboard of the inn (which is named "Under the Stag"), for example, is in fact that of the vision of Saint Eustace, the patron saint of hunters (a Roman general, converted to Christianity after seeing a stag with a crucifix and subsequently martyred by being roasted). The catalogue is the driest, here, of those we have seen:

The Hunters in the Snow

The over-all picture
icy mountains
in the background the return

from the hunt it is toward evening
from the left
sturdy hunters lead in

their pack the inn-sign
hanging from a
broken hinge is a stag a crucifix

between his antlers the cold
inn yard is
deserted but for a huge bonfire

that flares wind-driven tended by
women who cluster
about it to the right beyond

the hill is a pattern of skaters
Brueghel the painter
concerned with it all has chosen

a winter-struck bush for his
foreground to
complete the picture . . .

The elements so flatly inventoried in the poem's unpunctuated, paratactic lines might possibly serve as a metaphor for the formal structures of the painting and their possible relation to narrative relations. But this does not occur; for instance, in the line "their pack the inn-sign" no structural relation in the painting can be traced in the run-on sentence. Systematically—and perhaps even grossly—abjuring such use of the linear structure in the poem, however, Williams allows a possibly fruitful poetic observation to enter only in the final tercet, which calls almost emblematic attention to the snow-covered bush in the painting, ignoring its formal function (it both lies right on the picture plane and points—with its longest branch—along a diagonal parallel to the principal one). Saying in a manifestly incomplete conclusion (the ellipsis marks replacing a full stop) that the role of the bush is to "complete the picture," returns us to the language of the opening line, where "picture" = interpretively constructed account or story.

Musée des Beaux Arts

About suffering they were never wrong,
The Old Masters: how well they understood
Its human position; how it takes place
While someone else is eating or opening a window or just walking dully along;
How, when the aged are reverently, passionately waiting
For the miraculous birth, there always must be
Children who did not specially want it to happen, skating
On a pond at the edge of the wood:
They never forgot
That even the dreadful martyrdom must run its course
Anyhow in a corner, some untidy spot
Where the dogs go on with their doggy life and the torturer's horse
Scratches its innocent behind on a tree.

In Brueghel's *Icarus*, for instance: how everything turns away
Quite leisurely from the disaster; the ploughman may
Have heard the splash, the forsaken cry,
But for him it was not an important failure; the sun shone
As it had to on the white legs disappearing into the green
Water; and the expensive delicate ship that must have seen
Something amazing, a boy falling out of the sky,
Had somewhere to get to and sailed calmly on.

This may be the most widely known—and certainly the most influential—ecphrastic poem of late modernity, and yet it is itself often misremembered as a gloss only on the Bruegel painting usually called *The Fall of Icarus*. It is in fact a poem which maintains a trace of the old, notional gallery poem of the seventeenth and eighteenth centuries in implying a walk among paintings (although all by Bruegel), a noting of a detail here and there significant for the particular matter of what the museum visitor may have on his mind to begin with, and a final pause before one central canvas. (William Butler Yeats's "The Municipal Gallery Revisited," published in book form in the same year as Auden's poem, is of the same type.) The poet had been visiting Brussels during the war-impending winter of 1938; the matter of human suffering seems as atmospheric for the poem as the pointedness of detail in northern painting. What Auden is observing here is a consequence of the context of humanized, naturalistic detail in which Flemish painting conceived of its transcendent biblical events.

PIETER BRUEGEL THE ELDER, *Landscape with the Fall of Icarus*

Walking through the Brussels Musées Royaux des Beaux Arts, the speaker encounters first Bruegel's *The Numbering of Bethlehem* and then a *Massacre of the Innocents* (in fact, a copy on canvas by his son, Pieter Brueghel the Younger, of panels by the Elder which are in Vienna and Hampton Court). He observes how peripheral, even heroic, acts of violent suffering, however central for the mythological systems in which they occur, are to the ordinary life always going on. (In a later poem, and in a Christian context of thought, Auden would describe this condition as "the Time Being," itself peripheral now to "the actual Vision"—a meantime in which "There are bills to be paid, machines to keep in repair, / Irregular verbs to learn.") The poem's own structure, sonnet-like in its proportions of longer first section to shorter, more pointed final one, keeps up a meandering metrical pace, muting its complex, interlocking rhyme scheme by varying so widely the length of the different lines. It also recapitulates the way in which the speaker's gallery walk homes in on the Icarus painting; even as the tiny images of business-as-usual in the previous two paintings give way to the strikingly prominent figure of the ploughman in his georgic indifference, so perhaps may the poet suddenly see himself mirrored there, about to turn away from some of the most important of failures.

While there has been some scholarly attempt at an interpretation of elements in this painting as alchemical symbolism, the truly knotty problems—neither of which comes up in these poets' ecphrases—are the missing figure of Daedalus (who in fact appears in another version of this painting in a private collection in New York), and, more important, the figure of the man lying under the tree on the left (is he dead?—no one has explained what the figure is doing in that attitude). But the foregrounding of the ploughman and the distant, kicking fragmentary feet of the over-reaching Icarus propound an immediately grasped parable in which—as one scholar has put it—"the realist with both feet planted firmly on the ground fails to recognize the dreamer."

Whatever private allegory may be at work in Bruegel's painting, Auden's concentration on the figure of the ploughman ironically reminds us of the original text in Ovid (*Metamorphoses* 8.182–235), from which the Renaissance derived its knowledge of the story of Daedalus and Icarus, and against which Bruegel's design was consciously working. For there, as Icarus flies recklessly behind his father (and I quote from Rolfe Humphries's fine translation),

> Far off, far down, some fisherman is watching
> As the rod dips and trembles over the water,
> Some shepherd rests his weight upon his crook
> Some ploughman on the handles of the ploughshare,
> And all look up, in absolute amazement
> At those air-borne above. They must be gods!
>
> [Hos aliquis tremula dum captat harundine pisces,
> aut pastor baculo stivave innixus arator
> vidit et obstipuit, quique aethera carpere possent,
> credidit esse deos.]

For Brueghel's ploughman, fisherman, and shepherd there are neither gods nor heroes. And Auden displaces their Ovidian stupefaction onto the "expensive delicate ship that must have seen / Something amazing."

William Carlos Williams almost inevitably includes some lines on this same painting in his 1954 ecphrastic collection, *Pictures from Brueghel.* As poetic interpretation, they seem particularly vapid, and do less for either a viewer or reader than the prose of a good art-historical writer could. (I think, for example, of Edward Snow's remarkable writing on some of the more complex Bruegel paintings like the *Children's Games.*) Perhaps because Williams was, at this point in his work, imaginatively tired with his old project of denying that there were valid allegorical or mythopoetic agendas for poetry, these poems are characteristically flat, rather than strong, in their interpretive reticence. At the end of the brief "Landscape with the fall of Icarus" Williams gets no further than Auden's "not an important failure":

> unsignificantly
> off the coast
> there was
>
> a splash quite unnoticed
> this was
> Icarus drowning

Randall Jarrell, a fine American poet not uninfluenced by Auden and author of several impressive ecphrastic poems of his own, took off from Auden's first line in his "The Old and the New Masters":

> About suffering, about adoration, the old masters
> Disagree. When someone suffers, no one else eats
> Or walks or opens the window—no one breathes
> As the sufferers watch the sufferer.

He then proceeds to give close ecphrases of two paintings, a *St. Sebastian Mourned by St. Irene* and, at greater length, Hugo Van der Goes's great *Portinari Altarpiece.* In the course of scanning this celebrated painting, the poem starts out with one notion of centrality, then becomes concerned with matters of hierarchical scale. The issue of centrality in the poem's own selective reading of the picture is itself implicitly touched upon: the poem's first glance is at the central panel of the triptych, but then takes in the side panels with out-of-time-scale later donors and earlier journey to Bethlehem. The problem of different time-frames occurring in one static image then allows the central issue of time to emerge, not so much in the paradoxes of the Christian meaning of a privileged incident occurring in time but with vast consequences for the matter of eternity, as in a frighteningly modern sense.

The following verse paragraph concludes the poem with a frightening vision of the ultimate decay of older notions of centrality (the consequences of Kepler and Galileo and Newton and Einstein's conceptual displacements). There is also a parable of the history of art, with a concluding abstraction crowning the successive displacements of image:

HUGO VAN DER GOES, *Portinari Altarpiece*

After a while the masters show the crucifixion
In one corner of the canvas: the men who come to see
What is important, see that it is not important.
The new masters paint a subject as they please,
And Veronese is prosecuted by the Inquisition
For the dogs playing at the feet of Christ,
The earth is a planet among galaxies.
Later Christ disappears, the dogs disappear: in abstract
Understanding, without adoration, the last master puts
Colors on canvas, a picture of the universe
In which a bright spot somewhere in the corner
Is the small radioactive planet men call earth.

ALBRECHT DÜRER, *The Knight, Death, and the Devil*

RANDALL JARRELL

The Knight, Death, and the Devil

Cowhorn-crowned, shockheaded, cornshuck-bearded,
Death is a scarecrow—his death's-head a teetotum
That tilts up toward man confidentially
But trimmed with adders; ringlet-maned, rope-bridled,
The mare he rides crops herbs beside a skull.
He holds up, warning, the crossed cones of time:
Here, narrowing into now, the Past and Future
Are quicksand.
                      A hoofed pikeman trots behind.
His pike's claw-hammer mocks—in duplicate, inverted—
The pocked, ribbed, soaring crescent of his horn.
A scapegoat aged into a steer; boar-snouted;
His great limp ears stuck sidelong out in air;
A dewlap bunched at his breast; a ram's-horn wound

Beneath each ear; a spur licked up and out
From the hide of his forehead; bat-winged, but in bone;
His eye a ring inside a ring inside a ring
That leers up, joyless, vile, in meek obscenity—
This is the devil. Flesh to flesh, he bleats
The herd back to the pit of being.

In fluted mail; upon his lance the bush
Of that old fox; a sheep-dog bounding at his stirrup,
In its eyes the cast of faithfulness (our help,
Our foolish help); his dun war-horse pacing
Beneath in strength, in ceremonious magnificence;
His castle—some man's castle—set on every crag:
So, companioned so, the knight moves through this world.
The fiend moos in amity, Death mouths, reminding:

He listens in assurance, has no glance
To spare for them, but looks past steadily
At—at—
                      a man's look completes itself.

The death of his own flesh, set up outside him;
The flesh of his own soul, set up outside him—
Death and the devil, what are these to him?
His being accuses him—and yet his face is firm
In resolution, in absolute persistence;
The folds of smiling do for steadiness;
The face is its own fate—*a man does what he must*—
And the body underneath it says: *I am.*

Albrecht Dürer's celebrated engraving usually known as *The Knight, Death, and the Devil* figures the devout Christian as a mounted knight in "the armor of God," of faith and righteousness (as in several New Testament texts). He moves through a world of phantoms—Death with an hourglass, the Devil with a pike, behind him—accompanied by his dog, emblematic of zeal, learning, and the keen scent of true reason. The knight's eye is fixed on the path ahead, that winding road which will eventually reach the distant fortress of Virtue set high on a hill at the top of the scene. Erwin Panofsky wrote eloquently of the rider here, that: "the very inarticulateness and plastic tangibility of this moving monument suggests an existence more solid and real than that of Death or the Devil who appear as little more than shadows of the wilderness."

Randall Jarrell wrote what he called a "description" of this engraving. His group of figures is arranged, in order of appearance, as "Death, the devil, and the knight," rearranging their relative prominences in the picture. The first two of them are characterized in great, and hardly shadowy detail: Death enters in a crowd of epithets whose interplay of sound-patterns suggests a sharply linear, rather than a more painterly-like texture ("*Cowhorn-crowned*, **shock**-headed, *corn***shuck**-bearded / Death is a scare*crow*"). The emblematic hourglass, traditionally borne by both Time and Death, becomes in Jarrell's poem a singularly modern symbol, redolent of Yeats's interpenetrating cones. And there is a terrifying pun on "quick-sand" (as engulfing "living" ground and as the all-too-quickly pouring sand of the hourglass, rushing past the pinched point of the present moment). The poem's reading of the devil's weapon (not a pickax or a spear as elsewhere described) is most significant, as it reflects a response to formal structures in the design—with a desire to see these as semiological in their own way—that could come only from a viewer trained in the visual agendas of modern art: "His pike's claw-hammer mocks—in duplicate, inverted—The pocked, ribbed, soaring crescent of his horn." And here again, the phonological structures themselves correspond to visual forms; even as art historians today will speak of "rhyming" forms to designate similar or parallel or analogous curves or contours, for example, the derisive, inverted imitation of "mocking" (instead of, say, "rhyming") moves the formal symmetries and relations into the devil's domain. Again, in the sounds in the sequence of "pike's—mocks—pocked," "pock" mocks "pike" both in word and object. And, finally, the concentricity of rings in the devil's eye may perhaps suggest the hellish siege of contraries in the mind of Milton's Satan and "The hell within him, for within him hell / He brings."

But the poem moves into a deeper mode of meditation when it becomes helpless in the face of the knight's own gaze out of the picture. The man, his horse, and his dog are all in profile, which seems to represent their equanimity, their "resolution." What is the knight seeing, then, out beyond our view? Not his professed goal, the castle—"some man's castle"—on the crag. But Jarrell, knowing the convention all too well, bypasses the necessary ecphrastic questioning of the image and instead allows the problem to cut away his statement. In his anacoluthon—the rhetorical figure of interruption—the eternal problem of word and image surfaces again. And the substitute completion of the sentence is only in a figurative way a completion of the reading: "a man's look completes itself" (a poetic fiction—even about a given image—completes itself; a man's life completes itself in telling its own story of itself). Jarrell's knight is in some ways more like a successful analysand than a soldier of the faith.

John Ruskin, whom Jarrell may well have read on this engraving, saw it as an image of Fortitude, representing

> a knight riding through a dark valley overhung by leafless trees, and with a great castle on a hill beyond. Beside him, but a little in advance, rides Death on a pale horse. Death is gray-haired and crowned;—separate serpents wreathed about his crown; (the sting of death involved in the kingly power). He holds up the hourglass, and looks earnestly into the knight's face. Behind him follows Sin; but Sin Powerless; he has been conquered and passed by, but follows yet, watching if any way of assault remains. On his forehead are two horns—I think, of sea-shell—to indicate his insatiableness and instability. He has also the twisted horns of the ram, for stubbornness, the ears of an ass, the snout of a swine, the hoofs of a goat. Torn wings hang useless from his shoulders, and he carries a spear with two hooks, for catching as well as wounding. The knight . . . rides quietly, his bridle firm in his hand, and his lips set close in a slight sorrowful smile, for he hears what Death is saying . . . His horse trots proudly and straight; its head high and with a cluster of oak on the brow where on the fiend's brow is the sea-shell horn. But the horse of Death stoops its head; and its rein catches the little bell which hangs from the knight's horse-bridle, making it toll, as a passing-bell.

It is hard not to quote this entire, as it is to refrain from citing Panofsky at greater length on this engraving:

> [the Horseman] is set out against a background of forbidding rocks and bare trees with a fortified hill town visible in the distance. From the gloom of this "rough and dreary" scenery there emerge the figures of Death and the Devil . . . Death wears a regal crown and is mounted on a meager, listless jade with a cowbell; but he is even ghastlier in that he is not depicted as an actual skeleton but as a decaying corpse with sad eyes, no lips and no nose, his head and shoulders encircled by snakes. He sidles up to the Rider and tries in vain to frighten him by holding up an hourglass while the swine-snouted Devil sneaks up behind him with a pickaxe. The Rider, on the other hand, is accompanied by a handsome, long-haired retriever whose presence completes the allegory. As the armored man personifies Christian

faith, so the eager and quick-scented dog denotes three less fundamental but no less necessary virtues: untiring zeal, learning and truthful reasoning . . .

Jarrell's story of the knight is not without learning, and is thoroughly without antilearned bluster. Indeed, it is not impossible that Panofsky's phrase "completes the allegory" is transumptively echoed in "a man's look completes itself." But instead of showing, as the learned art historian does, how Dürer was thinking of texts by his contemporary Erasmus as well as of technical problems in the execution of a perfect figure of a horseman, the poet somehow implicitly assumes that the realms of craft and moral imagination symbolize and model each other. And thereby he makes the picture into an illustration, as it were, of his own moral tale.

ANTHONY HECHT

At the Frick

Before a grotto of blue-tinted rock
Master Bellini has set down St. Francis.
A light split through the Apennines to lock,
Counter, and splice man's painful doubleness,
Else he could weakly couple at the belt
His kite-mind to his cloven nether parts
That seek to dance their independent dances.
The sudden light descending came to bless
His hands and feet with blisters, and to melt
With loving that most malleable of hearts.

Birds in the trees his chronicles recite:
How that God made of him a living net
To catch all graces, yet to let through light.
Fisher of birds and lepers, lost in thought,
Darkly emblazoned, where the oblivious mule
Champs at the grasses and the sunset rusts
The hilltop fortress, where the painter set
Heron and rabbit, it was here he caught
Holiness that came swimming like a school
Of silver fishes to outflash his lusts.

Now I have seen those mountains, and have seen
The fawn go frozen on the road with fear
Of the careening autobus, the sheen
Of its dilated eyes flash in its head
Like glass reflectors, and have seen the trees
As green as ever where their branches thresh
The warm Italian winds of one more year
Since that great instant. The painter's dead
Who brought the Doge and nobles to the knees
Of the wind's Brother Francis in the flesh.

GIOVANNI BELLINI, *St. Francis in Ecstasy*

Anthony Hecht's poem to Bellini's marvelous scene of St. Francis in a very natural land-scape calls attention by its title to the museum in which the painting is encountered. Secondarily, perhaps, it may faintly allude to W. H. Auden's title ("Musée des Beaux Arts") for his famous and influential meditation on Bruegel. But Hecht's poem moves through a sequence of objects for meditation that is framed by an implicit confrontation of the paint-ing in the museum (as the opening included an understood "Before [this astonishing painting I pause and . . .]"). There are prominent qualities of space and light in the picture: the rays of the sun which do not transmit—as in Bellini's Pesaro altarpiece—the stigmata to the saint; the phases of light and darkness as one moves from cavern interior, to bluish exterior rocks, to shadowed exterior landscape, and finally to sun-brightened one. These are addressed imme-diately in the poem's opening lines. But the remainder of the stanza leaps beyond the presence of the painting in its own allegorizing, returning to the stigmatization of St. Francis only at its end. In the second stanza, the poem's gaze returns to Bellini's painted scene again, through the agenda of the stories of the *Fioretti*, the "Little Flowers" of St. Francis. The saint's famous, legendary simple communion with animals—summoned up in the painting by the donkey, the heron, the rabbit peering out of his burrow—returns in the poem through the complex metaphor of the net, itself perhaps implicitly occasioned by the phenomenon of light filtered through tree leaves.

The poem remains true to its initial reading of the painting—"Before a grotto . . . Master Bellini has *set down* St. Francis" (my italics)—which places the saint in a scene, even as the poem's speaker will, in meditative response, place himself in that same scene (or approxi-mately—somewhere in the Veneto? not directly in La Verna, the literal locus of the stigmati-zation). But it does not read the scene in the way that another poem might—for the areas of light and shadowed darkness, the planes of spatial recession, and amid the forest of verticals, the repeated parallel diagonals (moving from right to left) of the edge of the lectern, the sloping rock outlined by foliage to the saint's left and, finally, the line of hillside behind the nearest, largest tower. Nor does it consider the laurel tree on the left, which almost seems to genuflect toward St. Francis. Rather, the matter of being "At the Frick," before the painting, returns; in the third stanza, the speaker, here at the Frick, recalls being there in the Veneto. But the remembered vignettes are of two sorts: the aggressive modernity of the threatened fawn and the antithetically transcendent quality of the wind blowing through the trees. The con-trast between Bellini's scene and the contemporary one is not that easily moralized.

In the last line, St. Francis is invoked as "the wind's brother," a quotation from the saint's own trope, his "Cantico delle creature," or "Song of Created Things," in which he praises God with all his creatures, starting out with

>   master brother sun who brings day, and you give us light
>   through him. And he is beautiful and radiant with great brightness
>   —from you, most high, he gets significance.

>   [messor lo frate sole
>   lo qual jorna et allumini noi per loi.

Et ellu è bellu et radiante con grande splendore
de te, altissimo, porta significatione.]

and moving through "sora luna e le stelle" [sister moon and the stars] to

brother wind and for air, cloudy and fair in every weather,
by which you give sustenance to your creatures.

[frate vento
et per aere er nubilo et sereno et onne tempo,
per lo quale a le tue creature dai sustentamento.]

For Hecht's poem, it is almost as if Bellini had painted St. Francis receiving the stigmata (at the end of the first stanza) and, by the end of the poem, in the act of singing his unpremeditated song, the "Cantico delle creature" itself (and indeed, art historian A. Richard Turner two decades later suggested that, if not the painting's proper title, it describes "its essential spirit"). Whether the poet was aware of the contending art-historical views (Millard Meiss opted for a scene of stigmatization) of the painting, his own meditation works through versions of both of them. More poetically than doctrinally directed, it is almost inevitable that the stigmata should come up in a passing figural moment, and the "great instant" celebrated here is—by means of, rather than in spite of, the poem's seeming disclaimers—as much a Bellinian as a Franciscan one.

The Rokeby Venus

Life pours out images, the accidental
At once deleted when the purging mind
Detects their resonance as inessential:
Yet these may leave some fruitful trace behind.

Thus on this painted mirror is projected
The shield that rendered safe the Gorgon's head.
A travesty. —Yet even as reflected
The young face seems to strike us, if not dead,

At least into an instantaneous winter
Which life and reason can do nothing with,
Freezing the watcher and the painting into
A single immobility of myth.

But underneath the pigments' changeless weather
The artist only wanted to devise
A posture that could show him, all together,
Face, shoulders, waist, delectable smooth thighs.

So with the faulty image as a start
We come at length to analyse and name
The luminous darkness in the depths of art:
The timelessness that holds us is the same

As that of the transcendent sexual glance
And art grows brilliant in the light it sheds,
Direct or not, on the inhabitants
Of our imaginations and our beds.

Velázquez's magnificent painting of Venus (1651?) seen from behind, her face shown only problematically in her mirror "in a glass, darkly," might be thought of as reinterpreting or revising images such as that of Titian's *Venus of Urbino,* or another mirrored Venus of Rubens, by rotating the figure. In general, it was during the later seventeenth century that a vogue for presentation of the female rump in painting manifested itself, as one writer has described it,

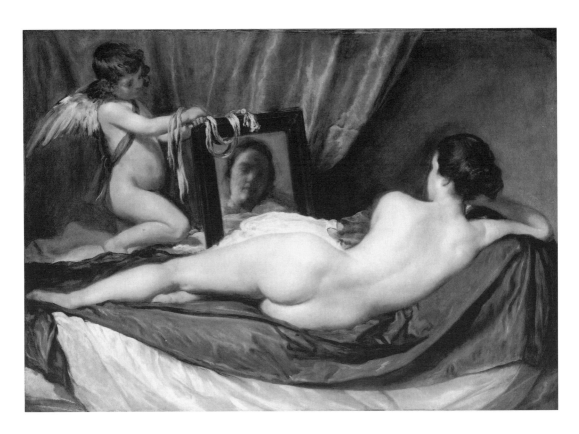

Velázquez, *The Rokeby Venus*

in "bursting into prominence below a slender waist and a narrow rib cage," so that the reversal may have been a response to a patron's fashionable request. But it is certainly more than that. Similarly, mirrors in sixteenth- and seventeenth-century art are mostly emblematic, but when held in the hand of a female figure, frequently nude, they can accompany and identify variously images of Truth, Beauty, Prudence, Vanity, Pride (the observation of Keats's Grecian Urn to the effect that "Beauty is Truth, Truth Beauty" might be said unwittingly to comment on the identity of images in iconographic conventions two thousand years later).

Venus's face is visible only in its slightly blurred, hazy representation in the mirror that is held, with a somewhat enigmatic look (slightly sad? pleased? adoring?), by her son, Cupid. Aside from the suggestion that this whole pictorial apparatus was constructed in order to hide his perhaps well-known model from easy identification, at least two allegories, by no means mutually exclusive, can seem to emerge. The first implies that the goddess's power is such that we may only perceive her visage through a glass, darkly; the second, that, were her gaze in fact directed at her own image here, that image might itself be brighter, perhaps as a function of the goddess's ocular power.

Robert Conquest's poem, from the early 1950s, assumed the meditative, interpretive tone, framed in the easy and well-articulated rhymed quatrains of some of the best verse of its time in England. It methodically diverts its gaze from some of the painting's more prominent features: the rump and the view from behind generally; the mirror itself, the quality of the face reflected there, the fact, already noted, that Venus does not appear to be viewing her own visage; the matter of the pink ribbon falling over the mirror frame in such a way as to adorn both the glass and the image in it; the way in which this ribbon is formally associated with the smaller vertical sinuosity of Cupid's body even as the major drapery—"transmuted," as the writer quoted above has suggested, "by the utter lack of swagger in its folds"—is with the horizontal curves of his mother's body; the rhyming curves of Cupid's right, and Venus's left, calf. Instead, he is concerned with the goddess's own mirrored gaze, reminding us in the second stanza of a very different mirror—the one given Perseus by Athena, in which to view safely the head of the gorgon Medusa, so that he might kill her without being turned to stone by her gaze. Perhaps there is an association here with the fact that subsequent to Medusa's death, Athena placed a representation of her head on the boss of her shield. Here, Venus's dimmed face—in a front view severed by the art of painting from the rear-viewed body—looks out at viewers of the picture, astonishing them, as it does the total surrounding painting within which it is another picture, "into / A single immobility of myth."

Conquest's poem exhibits a kind of cool, English counterpart to the French theoretical frenzy over the erotic epistemology of *le regard*, and the generalized matter of desire, which has become so influential among academic writers. But his moralization of the Rokeby Venus as a parable not only of sexuality, but of art, regarding itself that we may regard it, is brought home in the final quatrain. With its tactfully turned acknowledgment of the mediation—the indirectness—of the goddess's gaze for us, and its conjunction of wonder and desire, the poem concludes with "the transcendent sexual glance," adding that "art grows brilliant in the light it sheds, / Direct or not, on the inhabitants, / Of our imaginations and our beds."

The issue of the back view, together with the problematics of the forward-looking but reflected face as opposed to the directly viewed rearward body, is taken up in the present author's little epigram "To the Rokeby Venus." It plays on a little turn of wit about the famous Cnidian Venus, in several epigrams of the Greek anthology (to the effect that Paris, Anchises, and Adonis saw the goddess naked: how did Praxiteles get to?) with regard to the matter of reversals. Thus, the last two stanzas:

> Unseen by yours, our eyes are open to
> Unclouded, perfect grace;
> Your meditative son holds up to view
> The true, the mirrored face.

> Mars, Vulcan and Anchises in their kind
> Each had you in his day;
> Velazquez gazing at you from behind
> Saw more of you than they.

In regard to the question of the Gaze, it might finally be added that Robert Browning has a little couplet on the subject of a child "Viewing a Naked Venus in a Painting of 'The Judgement of Paris'"; but the scene has been repeated enough times before the Velázquez in the National Gallery to adduce the lines here:

> He gazed and gazed and gazed and gazed,
> Amazed, amazed, amazed, amazed.

RICHARD WILBUR

A Baroque Wall-Fountain in the Villa Sciarra
for Dore and Adja

Under the bronze crown
Too big for the head of the stone cherub whose feet
    A serpent has begun to eat,
Sweet water brims a cockle and braids down

Past spattered mosses, breaks
On the tipped edge of a second shell, and fills
    The massive third below. It spills
In threads then from the scalloped rim, and makes

A scrim or summery tent
For a faun-ménage and their familiar goose.
    Happy in all that ragged, loose
Collapse of water, its effortless descent

And flatteries of spray,
The stocky god upholds the shell with ease,
    Watching, about his shaggy knees,
The goatish innocence of his babes at play;

His fauness all the while
Leans forward, slightly, into a clambering mesh
    Of water-lights, her sparkling flesh
In a saecular ecstasy, her blinded smile

Bent on the sand floor
Of the trefoil pool, where ripple-shadows come
    And go in swift reticulum,
More addling to the eye than wine, and more

Interminable to thought
Than pleasure's calculus. Yet since this all
    Is pleasure, flash, and waterfall,
Must it not be too simple? Are we not

ANON., *Fountain*

More intricately expressed
In the plain fountains that Maderna set
    Before St. Peter's—the main jet
Struggling aloft until it seems at rest

    In the act of rising, until
The very wish of water is reversed,
    That heaviness borne up to burst
In a clear, high, cavorting head, to fill

    With blaze, and then in gauze
Delays, in a gnatlike shimmering, in a fine
    Illumined version of itself, decline,
And patter on the stones its own applause?

    If that is what men are
Or should be, if those water-saints display
    The pattern of our areté,
What of those showered fauns in their bizarre,

    Spangled, and plunging house?
They are at rest in fulness of desire
    For what is given, they do not tire
Of the smart of the sun, the pleasant water-douse

    And riddled pool below,
Reproving our disgust and our ennui
    With humble insatiety.
Francis, perhaps, who lay in sister snow

    Before the wealthy gate
Freezing and praising, might have seen in this
    No trifle, but a shade of bliss—
That land of tolerable flowers, that state

    As near and far as grass
Where eyes become the sunlight, and the hand
    Is worthy of water: the dreamt land
Toward which all hungers leap, all pleasures pass.

Given the elaborate systems of aqueducts dating from ancient times, it is not surprising that the fountains of Renaissance and baroque Rome should be so numerous and so celebrated. Varying widely in size, scale, fame, or anonymity of the designer and complexities of structure as well as of iconographic program, Roman fountains, from the *Fontana di Trevi* to the spigot by a carved relief pig on a wall in the Via della Scrofa, have provided easily accessible mental souvenirs for tourists. But they have also served as meditative loci for poets, as if in some spectral memory of Greek mythological fountains like the actual Pierian spring or the fabled Hippocrene, created when Pegasus struck the rock with his hoof. The contemporary tourist will frequently encounter them, elaborately illuminated, at night. As Alfred Corn observes of the stone figures in his "Parable at a Roman Fountain" (a capriccio of several), we may fancy that they return our gaze:

> We stand at the rim in rapt attitudes,
> Admiring the secular prisoners
> From the vantage point assigned to lovers;
> And think we detect old glimmers of grief
> And envy in a marble eye—the cold nudes
> Tempted, for love, to dress themselves in life.

In antiquity, natural springs and constructed fountains constituted and commemorated sacred spots: water breaking out of the ground in some divine manifestation, or as a mythological representation of eloquence. There remains even in our ordinary language an association of firstness, origination, and authority with natural springs (consider the use to which English puts its adaptation of the French word *la source*, for example). Large-basined fountains in towns and cities were contrived for communal access to water for drinking and washing. But other architectural, decorative fountains, seducing natural or conducted emissions of water into elaborate and joyful play before subsiding, in a final basin, into a solemn, working pool have remained figurative of poetry in ways that long outlast Apollonian mythologies. It is as if the water, playing in the air and falling back along intricate carved surfaces—sometimes in gross mimesis as it is spewed from human and animal orifices, sometimes more metaphorically caressing, and leading sunlight to caress, bodies and other voluptuous forms—were fictional, instead of literal, useful, workaday, water: water at play, like language at play in poetry. Modern poets thinking of the ways in which long, periodic sentences flow down—in many of Horace's odes, for example—through a sequence of fixed, short strophic basins, overflowing each only to proceed down to the next, have felt such poems to be fountain-like.

A masterpiece of such poetic meditation is Richard Wilbur's "A Baroque Wall-Fountain in the Villa Sciarra," directed, interestingly enough, at a little-known and hitherto uncelebrated fountain, in the park of Villa Sciarra on the Janiculum. Its elaborately ecphrastic opening scans the structure of the fountain from the top down: "sweet water" (rather than salt—there is nothing marine save perhaps the shells about this grotto scene and its appropriate group of figures) is the subject of the first sentence, the woodland god Faunus at the bottom, bearing up the basin, the subject of the second.

Wilbur's long, periodic sentences flow down through successive stanzas. This flow is matched by an interior movement through the lines in their zigzag, somewhat "baroque" pattern of length—3, 5, 4, 5 feet in each case, rhymed *abba* across this variation of length—and the implicit trope of word-order/water operates throughout this poem even more elaborately than as implied by Rilke in his fountain-poem quoted below. But there are additional complications: halfway through the seventh stanza, the ecphrasis proper comes to an end, with a contemplation of the "ripple-shadows" moving on the sandy floor of the bottommost basin. The rest of the stanza immediately takes up one of the traditional problems of poetic readings of visual images (one that can be observed as far back as Virgil, and in Rossetti and Jarrell) in pausing to take stock of its own ability to interpret. Starting with what seems to be an easy formulation (yet is not—consider the reverse sequence of cause and effect in the three nouns) "Yet since this all / Is pleasure, flash and waterfall, / Must it not be too simple?" the poem moves into a larger meditation.

First there is the matter of pure fountainhood, the question of water rising and falling without the complex distractions of sculptural form and phases of momentary containment. These are the "plain fountains" where water and light build their own structures of animation, and even—in the sounds of splashing—their own appreciative audience, with the primary jet of water finally coming down to "in a fine / illumined version of itself, decline, / And patter on the stones its own applause." The poem considers the possibility of moralizing on the human condition—"if those water-saints display / The pattern of our areté," if aspiration to height and triumphant, uncatastrophic return to depth is indeed a picture of our virtue. Then it returns abruptly to the matter of those other presences, more concrete than "water-saints," the "showered fauns." We are brought back to the earth of a "lower" mode of representation, more palpably iconic. It is significant that the humility of St. Francis of Assisi is here adduced—although there is no *sora neve* ("sister snow") in that saint's "Cantico delle creature" (see above), and Wilbur has delightedly and reverently made her up. "Are we not," the poem had previously asked, "More intricately expressed" in the higher form of rising and falling water in the "plain fountains"? "Expressed" is a central word here, doubling a more recent use ("represented") with an older, more etymologically original, one ("pushed out or up")—in the poem, we are expressed in the expressed water. Ultimately, there is the implication that our virtue, our particular kind of *areté*, retains, like that of water, the ability to be figurative. What the water, the poem, we ourselves all come down to is a mode below the sublimity of plainness and water-saintliness after all.

We might look at a few prior poems on more celebrated Roman fountains. The nineteenth-century Swiss novelist Conrad Ferdinand Meyer wrote a lyrical observation on the three tiered basins of a fountain in the Borghese gardens; although it does not use stanzaic equivalents for the separate tiers, it does allow the syntax, the narrative, and the characterization of the water's flow all to come to rest in a final shorter line, closing off the motion by rhyming *Flut,* "flood," with *ruht,* "rests." Here it is, as translated by Walter Arndt:

> The jet ascends and, falling, goes
> to fill the marble basin's round,
> which shrouds itself and overflows
> into a second basin's ground;
> the second gives—abounding soon—

its surging billow to the next,
and each both takes and spends its boon
and flows and rests.

[Der Römische Brunnen
Aufstieg der Strahl, und fallend giesst
er voll der Marmorschale Rund,
die, sich verschleirnd, überfliesst
in einer zweiten Schale Grund;
die zweite gibt—sie wird so reich—
der dritten wallend ihre Flut,
und jede nimmt und gibt zugleich
und strömt und ruht.]

But a beautifully intricate sonnet by Rainer Maria Rilke, from his *Neue Gedichte* of 1907, tropes the picturesque descriptiveness of Meyer's little poem. It plays allegorically with the fall and momentary haltings of the flow of the water to connect it both with the movement of the verse itself, filling the sonnet in one long sentence (and without a verb—almost as if the poem had started "Two basins: . . ."), and with the motions of a gazing and recollecting consciousness.

Roman Fountain
Borghese

Two basins, one rising from the other
in the circle of an old marble pool,
and from the one above, water gently bending
down to water, which stands waiting below,

meeting the gentle whisper with its silence,
and secretly, as in the hollow of a hand,
showing its sky behind darkness and green
like some unfamiliar object; while it

spreads out peacefully in its lovely shell
without homesickness, circle after circle,
just sometimes dreamily letting itself down

in trickles on the mossy hangings
to the last mirror, which makes its basin
gently smile from underneath with nuances.

—tr. Edward Snow

[*Römische Fontäne*
Borghese

Zei Becken, eins das andere übersteigend
aus einem alten runden Marmorrand,
und aus dem oberen Wasser leis sich niegend
zum Wasser, welches unten wartend stand,

dem leise redenden entgegenschweigend
und heimlich, gleichsam in der hohlen Hand,
ihm Himmel hinter Grün und Dunkel zeigend
wei einen unbekannten Gegenstand;

sich selber ruhig in der schönen Schale
verbreitend ohne Heimweh, Kreis aus Kreis,
nur manchmal träumerisch und tropfenweis

sich niederlassend an den Moosbehängen
zum letzten Spiegel, der sein Becken leis
von unten lächeln macht mit übergängen.]

The poem evolves its own analogy between the triad composed of the second quatrain and the two tercets of the sestet. Even the differing rhyme pattern of these last two is made momentarily significant, the *ede* of the final one betokening more of mirroring than the *xdd* (with its resonantly unrhymed-upon "shell") of the penultimate, and the nuanced rhyme of *übergängen* ("transitions," "passages," but, literally, "overgoings"). The texture of sound pattern—of internal rhyming and assonance—calls up momentary transitional patterns of light and sound in the continuing flow of water through the stages of a constructed fountain like this.

Neither of these poems on the Borghese gardens fountain considers the figures bearing up the highest basin, or their sexes and postures, nor any element of iconography. For the poems, the fountain might almost be abstract, save for the shell motif in the basins' form. But not so another poem on a celebrated Roman fountain by the Russian symbolist Vyacheslav Ivanov. The marble *Fontana delle Tartarughe*—the Tortoise Fountain—in Piazza Mattei has four bronze life-size figures above the middle basin, four young men gracefully and insouciantly poised each with one foot against a dolphin's head, and each with one hand pushing a scrambling turtle over the edge of the uppermost basin. The fountain is also graced by suppositions such as that Raphael had designed it (totally wrong: although indeed designed by a Florentine, Taddeo di Leonardo Landini under the direction of Jacopo della Porta, it was constructed in 1581–84), or that Bernini had added the tortoises during a restoration done in 1659 (quite possible, although not established). The upward thrust of all the sculptural activity—the bodily form and posture of the four youths, the evidently avid struggle of the turtles to achieve immersion in the water above them—contrasts energetically and playfully with the slighter, unhurried downward splashing of the thin streams of water, which will nevertheless continue indefinitely, long after the moment of activity frozen in the bronze might pass, and the motion of boys and water-seeking creatures would subside. Eleanor Clark, in her wonderful discussion of fountains in *Rome and a Villa*, observes that "The water moves up in two or three ways and down in three or four, through marble cockleshells and over the gleaming bodies of the boys, whose lifted arms and raised knees make opposing circular patterns through the water. The problematic part is their smiles; they are almost exactly like that of the Mona Lisa; it is very striking."

Ivanov's poem, the sixth of his group of "Roman Sonnets" (from the 1940s), here brilliantly translated by Lowry Nelson, Jr., directs its delighted, caressing gaze first to the dolphins, then to the boys themselves, almost as if they were live young Romans shoving live turtles into a nondescript fountain somewhere—as if only bronze living creatures, and neither marble structures nor the motions of water and light among them, had any agency:

> Over their backs they let the turtles slip,
> Those humped captives at basin's edge aground,
> Within they dive and freely splash and dip
> Forget their fear, crawl torpidly around;
>
> The adolescent boys dance on each head
> Of snub-nosed monster. Wondrous pranksters they,
> Those goggle-eyed gargoyles beneath their tread
> From rounded jaws are spouting powdery spray.
>
> The four of them, on dolphins romping, play.
> Now on their shins of bronze, on their bronze backs,
> Sparkles the greenly rippling laugh of day,
> And in this languor, indolently lax,
>
> I catch an echo of your cheering folly,
> Echo, Lorenzo, of your melancholy.

The startling intrusion of the presumed poetic melancholy of Lorenzo the Magnificent—perhaps suggested by a vaguely Florentine air to the whole fountain—is modulated by the matter of the indolence, almost the *otium* of pastoral tradition, that may have evoked Lorenzo de' Medici's own poetry. In general, Ivanov's poem, unlike Rilke's, has no interest in exploring the relation of its own sonnet structure to that of the fountain, and only in such phrases as "the greenly rippling laugh of day" touches on the matter of light reflected from water moving over bronze.

Giacomo della Porta, *Fountain of the Tortoises*

ALFRED WALLIS, *Voyage to Labrador*

W. S. MERWIN

Voyage to Labrador

Tonight when the sea runs like a sore,
Swollen as hay and with the same sound,
Where under the hat-dark the iron
Ship slides seething, hull crammed
With clamours the fluttering hues of a fever,
Clang-battened in, the stunned bells done
From the rung-down quartans, and only
The dotty lights still trimmed
Abroad like teeth, there dog-hunched will the high
Street of hugging bergs have come
To lean huge and hidden as women,
Untouched as smoke and, at our passing, pleased
Down to the private sinks of their cold.
Then we will be white, all white, as cloths sheening,
Stiff as teeth, white as the sticks
And the eyes of the blind. But morning, mindless
And uncaring as Jesus, will find nothing
In that same place but an empty sea
Colourless, see, as a glass of water.

The primitive painter from Cornwall, Alfred Wallis (1855–1942), was a fisherman and sailor whose work was discovered and celebrated by modern English artists. A pair of early poems by W. S. Merwin deals with two of his paintings in the Tate Gallery, one of which had been the subject of a remarkable disquisition by Adrian Stokes. Wallis, he starts out,

> often paints his seas with earth colours, white and black, colours of which, gath-
> ered up, will equal in hue or tone by some sort of affinity, the colour of his boats.
> But then he has been a fisherman all his life, accustomed to conceive the sea in rela-
> tion to what lies beneath it, sand or rock and the living forms of fish. For him the
> colour of the sea is less determined by its glassy surface that reflects the sky . . .
> Wallis in one picture has painted a red-brown boat upon a dirty white-brown sea
> with white icebergs at the back of the picture. The subject is a voyage to Labrador.
> A warm coloration is used successfully to convey the dead-cold sea of melted ice-
> slush. Were the hue of the sea without adjacence to the darker colour of the boat,

its disintegration of ice-slush would not have been suggested. One's sense of a coloured area added up to and "going into" another, allows the impression of augmentation and of disintegration. Boat and sea are in reality bound by interaction. Without any direct suggestion of weight or movement or buoyancy, this general, as well as particular, relationship is thus fixed. At the same time the significance of the slightest difference in colour and tone is dramatized. Great meaning of coldness belongs to the dirty white tinges in the sea, and equally to the slight reddening of the boat, haven of comparative warmth upon the waste.

Without reference to Stokes's particularly unique concerns about color, Merwin's poem starts out nonetheless with an affinity with the great critic's interest in what he later calls "this earth-coloured sea," through his metaphor of that sea as "Swollen as hay and with the same sound." Likewise, he concludes with what for the poem's structure of fictions is a return to a morning literalism after a night tossed by trope, but which also accords with what some critics have since written about Wallis's sea colors. The remarkable build of the long, clotted sentence that occupies this poem's first thirteen lines only clarifies itself as the verb ("will . . . have come") finally homes in on the looming icebergs, with which Stokes's account is not particularly concerned. And in general, the poem responds to some of the painting's formal naivete with occasional strangeness in its own diction—the "hat-dark" to characterize the night sky's mode of covering the painted world, for example. Similar, too, is the syntactic impasse of "hull crammed / With clamours the fluttering hues of a fever." "Sheening," meaning gleaming or glistening, suggests a regional archaism from the southwest of Britain (Thomas Hardy uses "sheening sea" in *The Return of the Native*, for example). But "quartans" for nautical quarter-watches—here rung down, below decks, by the bells—is (in the poet's own words) "a deliberate distortion of the nautical use . . . an attempt to convey or suggest with the twisted use of language the actual fevers and deliriums of his [Wallis's] physical and psychological state . . . 'quarters' are the obvious nautical reference, 'quartans' the feverish hallucinatory one, the 'stunned bells' echo both."

In such a world as Wallis's, Merwin implies, language can speak either for some consciousness *on* the boat (but not *of* it) or else, possibly, the icebergs; the poem opts for the first, but claims knowledge of the latter, and of their being "pleased, / Down to the private sinks of their cold." "Pleased"—neither wrathful nor frighteningly aloof in an imminent collision with so modest and weird a little vessel; but it seems nonetheless impossible to evade the matter of death here. It is not exactly that the voyage itself is headed there, and the ship part of Charon's fleet. And yet, past the icebergs, the voyagers will be whitened to the color of skeletons and winding-sheets. But the loss of darkness when morning comes, and when the ship of imaginative consciousness has passed, will entail a general loss of color; there will come a loss of the sea surface's reflective—and somehow thereby metaphorical—capacity to appear dirty-brown, earth-colored (as Stokes suggests it does here) or, at other moments blue, or green, or whatever. Even the flatly egregious pun on *sea*/*see* at the very end of the poem serves to underline the newly dawned literalism.

Merwin follows this poem with four lines on another Wallis painting, *Schooner under the Moon*, a more problematic picture than the first in that the ship, headed to the left, seems to be sailing uphill at an angle of forty-five degrees. (One critic has convincingly suggested that the square painting is actually lozenge-shaped, and should be hung rotated through the proper angle.) But Merwin seems concerned to append to the emptiness of the conclusion of the first poem a glimpse of something contingently other, some older entity beyond our knowing. The ship itself, rather than the journey perhaps upward, screens them ever from our sight:

Schooner under the Moon

Waits where we would almost be. Part
Pink as a tongue; floats high on the olive
Rumpled night-flood, foresails and clouds hiding
Such threat and beauty as we may never see.

ANON., *Charioteer*

JAMES MERRILL

The Charioteer of Delphi

Where are the horses of the sun?

Their master's green hand, empty of all
But a tangle of reins, seems less to call
His horses back than to wait out their run.

To cool that havoc and restore
The temperance we had loved them for
I have implored him, child, at your behest.

Watch now, the flutings of his dress hang down
From the brave patina of breast.
His gentle eyes glass brown

Neither attend us nor the latest one
Blistered and stammering who comes to cry
Village in flames and river dry,

None to control the chariot
And to call back the killing horses none
Now that their master, eyes ashine, will not.

For watch, his eyes in the still air alone
Look shining and nowhere
Unless indeed into our own

Who are reflected there
Littler than dolls wound up by a child's fear
How tight, their postures only know.

And loosely, watch now, the reins overflow
His fist, as if once more the unsubdued
Beasts shivering and docile stood

Like us before him. Do you remember how
A small brown pony would
Nuzzle the cube of sugar from your hand?

Broken from his mild reprimand
In fire and fury hard upon the taste
Of a sweet license, even these have raced

Uncurbed in us, where fires are fanned.

Sometimes historical knowledge about the ecphrastic object—its original condition, the larger entity or context from which it was fragmented—can become part of the matter of the object itself. The bronze charioteer found in the Delphic sanctuary of Apollo in 1896, and now in the museum at Delphi, is preserved as a single figure, although it originally held the reins of a four-horse chariot, or *quadriga:* the group was a votive offering, erected on the temple terrace, for victory in a chariot race. Merrill's poem starts out by asking the question we all might want to put first to any beautiful and evocative ruin or residue—*What happened to all the rest?*—by inquiring of the figure where the remainder of its group is. Only the horses are invoked, but they are immediately identified as those of the sun god, and the youthful figure momentarily become a version of Apollo himself, or perhaps his doomed son, Phaeton. This deliberate mis-taking of the human figure for a divine one leads the poem to meditate on the matter of travelers in antiquity coming with one kind of innocence to the god's sanctuary at Delphi. The reader is lead thence to the poet's own journey to Delphi, childlike in another way, but aware of the deep psychic consequences for a human viewer who looks into the god's mirroring gaze.

Confronting a piece of figure sculpture, a carved or cast human image, can place the viewer under a particularly strong meditative injunction. One gazes not only at an image, but at a *thing* as well. Rainer Maria Rilke, gazing at a torso of a *kouros,* possibly from Miletus, in the Louvre, saw no answering gaze from the headless trunk. Instead, his famous poem sensed a metaphoric version of that absent answering, half-mirroring look in the entire form itself. "Yet his torso still glows like a candelabrum" [Aber / sein Torso glüht noch wie ein Kandelaber]. It is this light, says Rilke's sonnet, which sees *you:* without it, this stone could not have burst, like a star, from its own margins, until "there is no place which doesn't see you" [da ist keine Stelle / die dich nicht sieht]. Rilke's poem reads the *kouros* as an "Archaic Torso of Apollo"; and, perhaps sensible of that particular god's energies, it ends with a famous injunction (but spoken by the torso? the poet? the reader? The ambiguity here echoes some of the indeterminacy of exactly what is said by whom at the end of Keats's great notional ecphrasis of the "Ode on a Grecian Urn"). "You must alter your life" [Du musst dein Leben ändern]: this is one of the things all true art says to the serious observer. Merrill's charioteer, speaking in our Proustian, Freudian twilight, tells him "you must remember your childhood."

After the opening question, the poem begins its own replacement for an answer by evoking details of the image (note, for example, the reference to "the flutings of his dress," a phrase bred in the elementary but joyfully acquired knowledge of the visual punning of the flutings of columns and the hanging folds of drapery in, say, the caryatid figures of the Erechtheum on the Athenian acropolis). It also avows the problematic character of the figure's gaze, with which the remainder of the poem is absorbed. Merrill's fictive charioteer is made to hold the reins on the horses of our own human sun—our erotic passions, which the poem itself, like innocent youth, gradually comes upon as a central matter. Merrill's exquisite poetic art allows this story to unfold in the versification of these lines: the tercets are composed of varying lines of three, four, and five beats, through which rhymes occur, wander away, and then return again. They themselves compose a kind of picture of forward motion, backward reflection, and, ultimately, reined-in control.

EDVARD MUNCH, *The Scream*

DONALD HALL

The Scream

1.   Observe. Ridged, raised, tactile, the horror
of the skinned head is there. It is skinned
which had a covering-up before,
and now is nude, and is determined

by what it perceives. The blood not Christ's,
blood of death without resurrection,
winds flatly in the air. Habit foists
conventional surrender to one

response in vision, but it fails here,
where the partaking viewer is freed
into the under-skin of his fear.
Existence is laid bare, and married

to a movement of caught perception
where the unknown will become the known
as one piece of the rolling mountain
becomes another beneath the stone

which shifts now toward the happy valley
which is not prepared, as it could not
be, for the achieved catastrophe
which produces no moral upshot,

no curtain, epilogue, nor applause,
no Dame to return purged to the Manse
(the Manse is wrecked)—not even the pause,
the repose of art that has distance.

2.   We, unlike Munch, observe his The Scream
making words, since perhaps we too know
the head's "experience of extreme
disorder." We have made our bravo,

but such, of course, will never equal
the painting. What is the relation?
A word, which is at once richly full
of attributes: thinginess, reason,

reference, time, noise, among others;
bounces off the firm brightness of paint
as if it had no substance, and errs
toward verbalism, naturally. Mayn't

we say that time cannot represent
space in art? "The fascination of
what's impossible" may be present,
motivating the artist to move.

So the poet, the talker, aims his
words at the object, and his words go
faster and faster, and now he is
like a cyclotron, breaking into

the structure of things by repeated
speed and force in order to lay bare
in words, naturally, unworded
insides of things, the things that are there.

Edvard Munch's celebrated image—it exists in drawn, painted, and lithographic versions done from 1891 to 1895—called in English *The Scream* (*Skrig,* in Norwegian), shows a figure on a bridge against a background view across the Oslo fjord to the Akershus headland. An 1895 lithograph of it, entitled *Geschrei,* includes the additional German inscription, "Ich fühlte das Grosse Geschrei durch die Natur" [I felt the great scream through Nature]. In an earlier painting related to it (*Despair,* 1892), instead of the agonized central figure, a man wearing a sort of bowler hat fills up the foreground in profile, leaning against the bridge railing; above him, the sky is blood-red. From what Munch wrote of the drawing, it seems to memorialize a particular visionary moment, and the two other smaller figures moving out of the picture further along the bridge on the left, present here as in the later woodcut, are clearly walking companions of the artist, who has put himself, brooding, into the foreground. Munch wrote several accounts of this moment:

> I walked with two friends. Then the sun went down. Suddenly the sky turned as red as blood, and I felt a touch of sadness. I stood still, and leant against the railings. Above the bluish-black fjord and above the city the sky was like blood and flames. My friends walked on, and I was left alone, trembling with fear. I felt as if all nature were filled with one mighty unending scream.

The marvelous power of the image in the later lithograph—having, as it must, to abandon the literal blood-red of the sky—derives from the major ambiguity with regard to the central figure, hairless, its body dissolved into a twisted patch of draped, ungendered shadow, its mouth compressed, rounded elliptically and elongated so as to seem to be producing, not an *eeeeeeee* or *aiiiiiiii,* but an *oooooooooo* sound. It hears the universal scream, but seems to be echoing it. At once the screamed-at and the screamer, totally dissociated in representational mode from the ordinary walkers on the bridge ahead (no longer to be considered its companions), the figure itself becomes a kind of expressionist allegory of screaming. It is as if to say that all human screams were somehow echoes of screams of pain or agitation or despair felt by their utterers. Much of the effect of the relation of person to nature in this image results from the graphic agitation of, and between, the two systems of form (such as the expressively skull-like shape of the hearer-screamer's pained head and elongated, cupping hands) and of the marks used to generate those forms (the parallel systems of straight and curved lines). Central figure, fjord, headland, and sky partake of the same agitated curvature; the inexorable vertical and diagonal parallels of bridge and immediate, indeterminate background (and this is quite different from the ground behind the figure in the heavily red 1893 tempera and pastel version) are of a contrasting order.

Donald Hall's poem, written around 1957, is the longest of a group, "Three Poems from Edvard Munch" (and the "from," rather than "to" or "for" is to be taken advisedly). It is particularly interesting in that it seems to have been done "from" the lithograph as well as from the tempera and the oil of 1892 (he had seen them in a large traveling exhibition). The blood-red is being addressed (it "winds flatly through the air"), while the head—or at least its represented horror—is "Ridged, raised, tactile," suggesting the paint surface but also the strong suggestion of woodcut ridges in the lines of the lithographic version. It is as a painting, however, that the image is ultimately considered. Hall's poem is framed in quatrains of nine-syllabled lines, unmarked by regular stresses, and with its rhymes necessarily thereby muted or suppressed. (Terminal rhymes in English verse must occur on stressed syllables. Marianne Moore used this muting device throughout her work.)

The poem is in two parts. The first speaks for and of the painting; the second speaks of, and for, and in, poetry about painting, and about the matter of intense feeling that is too easily invoked in discourse about lyric poetry. The two sections stand in a relation both of image/text, and text/interpretation. The poet starts out by avowing the power of the obvious: the horror, that horror located in the figure (the head "determined // by what it perceives"), but then modulating the viewer's response to a contemplative realm beneath that, in "the under-skin of his fear." By the middle of the first section, the poet has already gone down deeply into the ground of his own experience of the painting, and the fine parable of the landscape in the fourth and fifth stanzas no longer refers to any scene of Munch's, but to an epistemological metaphor, culminating in a bottom line, as it were, to the effect that there is no easily inscribed bottom line. This is a subtle version of the conventional ecphrastic anacoluthon, or breaking-off, the acknowledgment of a representational gap, which, as has been noticed, begins with Virgil.

The second part takes what has gone before as an occasion to discourse both of *ut pictura poesis* and of the question of thought and feeling. "We have made our bravo, / but such, of course, will never equal / the painting" uses "equal" in the sense of "be identical to," thereby affirming the domain of metaphor, as well as in the less interesting sense of "can equal, be as good as," thereby underlining the rhetorical modesty of calling the poem a "bravo."

(How seriously responsible must praise be in order to contemplate the possibility that its cry of "bravo!" might be sheer bravado?) The poem's quoted phrase, "experience of extreme disorder" is purely notional—it sounds like the language of a curatorial catalogue note, and perhaps additionally echoes Wallace Stevens's phrase, in a puzzlingly quasi-ecphrastic moment in "The Man with the Blue Guitar." The words "hoard of destructions" (Stevens later wrote that he couldn't remember whether they were Picasso's or a critic's) may have unconsciously provided both an allusive format and, obviously, a relevant thematic parallel. On the other hand, "The fascination of / what's impossible" directly takes Yeats's line, "The fascination of what's difficult," from a poem so entitled ("The fascination of what's difficult / Has dried the sap out of my veins, and rent / Spontaneous joy and natural content / Out of my heart," it begins). Again, a parallel poetic agenda is invoked: Yeats's "colt," Pegasus—and thus his poetry generally—suffers from being a dray horse, must still "strain, sweat and jolt / As though it dragged road-metal." By poetic extension, Hall's "what's impossible" here is a linguistic task related to ecphrasis itself, and, allegorically perhaps, to all poetic endeavors. But if his poem concludes, seemingly helplessly, in a self-descriptive passage, it nevertheless seems just at the end to associate its own lines, in their increasingly rapid activity, with the linear strokes of Munch's brush and crayon.

IRVING FELDMAN

"Se Aprovechan"

"They take advantage"—the soldiers need clothes,
while corpses don't, who have their repose
And nakedness like a second birth,
And nose-down sniff new science from the earth.
So what if nakedness admits the crows!

Such handsome athletic figures,
Twenty centuries of nudes! which now the soldiers
Like bungling apprentices of the muse
Or drunken helpers in a museum cellar,
Yank and tug at to uncover.

And doing so, give that hopeless bric-a-brac
A little of the rhetoric of passion back.
A giant tree with haunches of a mother,
In her anguish torn and flowering and black,
Rears up!—but the head is out of the picture.

Goya's *Desastres de la guerra*, as they are usually called (his title was, in part, "Fatales consequencias de la sangrienta guerra en España con Buonaparte"), are a striking and justly celebrated series of eighty-two aquatints depicting the terrible fighting of the years 1808–14 during the Napoleonic occupation. Fierce, unrelenting in what they depict, they frequently exhibit remarkable delicacy in their design and in the articulation of their media—a mixture of etching, aquatint, drypoint, engraving. One of the most remarkable of them, in this regard, is number 16, the one entitled "Se aprovechan" [They avail themselves]. This is not a scene of ordinary pillage or looting. It shows corpses being stripped of clothing by their former companions, Spanish troops ill-equipped and in need of anything they can lay their hands on. The three denuded figures and the fourth one in the foreground, still clothed, compose a compelling cruciform pattern, highlighted by the partly raised form of the central corpse, seeming animated only by the tug of the left sleeve of the garment off his arm. There is a reciprocating X pattern formed by the alignment of the tugging soldier and the garment crossing with the soldier's strongly elongated left leg; it is carried through in the great inverted lozenges of the widening tree trunk.

289

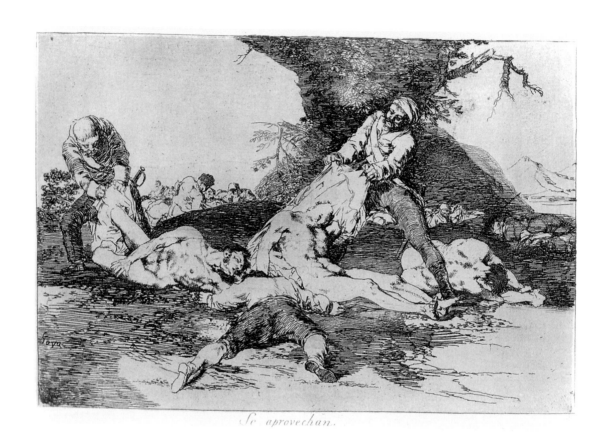

Se aprovechan.

Francisco José Goya y Lucientes, *Caprichos*, no. 16

It is allowing the huge trunk of this tree to suggest a female body—spreading base and roots for thighs, widening above to deploring, outstretched arms—that provides the conclusion to Irving Feldman's sonnet-like (fifteen lines in three stanzas) gloss on this print, one of a group of six similar ones called "Goya." The stripped figures start out as in their natural condition, with the text from Job 1.21 ("Naked came I out of my mother's womb, and naked shall I return thither") in the poetic background. But by the second stanza, the nakedness is read in another light, and the far from classically posed figures nonetheless become nude ones, and partake of a tradition of the nude figure as celebrated in Western art. It is as if "now the soldiers / Like bungling apprentices of the muse" reveal an underlying pictorial concern—artists like Goya did not learn to draw figures like these by working from corpses, but from the traditions of the studio, the drawn living model, the classical casts. Beneath the immediate *verismo* there lies the eternal artifice. In his final stanza, Feldman returns to the nakedness of the corpses, to the "second birth" of the third line of the poem. Allegorizing the tree's formal pattern ad hoc to this trope of birth, the tree is seen not only as a figure for the motherhood of all the dead and the living, but also as giving a kind of gestural birth to the structural patterns formed by living and dead bodies in the rest of the print. Only in the very last line does the reading—and somewhat characteristically, as has been seen—give up its claim to knowledge: the upper part of the tree, the metaphoric head and face, and thus the character, of the mother, is not to be seen. As if, like the face of Nature in Spenser's *Mutabilitie* cantos, not to be known.

ANDER GUNN, *untitled photograph*

THOM GUNN

Something approaches, about
which she has heard a good deal.
Her deaf ears have caught it, like
a silence in the wainscot
by her head. Her flesh has felt
a chill in her feet, a draught
in her groin. She has watched it
like moonlight on the frayed wood
stealing toward her
floorboard by floorboard. Will it hurt?

Let it come, it is
the terror of full repose,
and so no terror.

Poking around the rubbish,
she can't find what she wants.

Near Maidstone once, hop-picking
with the four babies and Tom,
she worked all day along the green
alleys, among the bins,
in the dim leafy light of
the overhanging vines.

In the village, shopkeepers
put cages on their counters
to prevent snatching. But Tom
took something! What was it?

All in the rubbish heap now,
some rotting, most clean vanished.

Among the special problems attendant upon the ecphrastic reading of photographs are those of a certain kind of *facticity* (as opposed to the *factitiousness*—the fictionality) of the drawn or painted image. When a poet asks of a human image in a photograph, "Who are you?" or "What are you doing (with that [whatever it is])?" there is always, at one level, a

ANDER GUNN, *untitled photograph (detail)*

totally authoritative answer, and though the human model of the printed shadow may not be around to answer, Professor Doktor Wasderfallist, the voice of What Is in Fact the Case, will always be available to say, e.g., "In *fact*, this is Mrs. Joe Bloggs, vital statistics as per request, 'caught' [and thereby "unawares"—a notion that merits more attention] by a 35mm. camera, lens, exposure, light conditions, and film data as per request, in such a way that a distant sign reading [whatever it is], which *in fact* she is unaware of, reads as a rubric for her image." This sort of fact helps frame one of the paradigmatic ironies of a certain sort of twentieth-century urban photographic image, but it is a fact about the "subject" of the photograph who, unless sitting or otherwise posed for the picture, we do not think of as a "model" for it. (On the other hand, even in the case of a painted portrait, where we might refer to the sitter as we do in photography as "the subject," there is often an additional—topical, thematic, icono-graphic, or mythological—"subject" in a different sense.)

Poetic ecphrasis, though, will cheerfully ask those questions, not of the human presence casting the shadow, but of the shadow itself, information about which can be the matter of interpretive invention, as that about the subject can never legitimately remain (e.g., Mrs. Bloggs is widowed, and so she is not on her way home to make Bloggs his tea, no matter what you claim the image implies). It is almost as if a poem will have it that the photograph is a lithograph, or an etched or engraved image—something envisioned by an artist, rather than recorded by a lens. The poem may implicitly be asking not "What—or who—is this, actual-ly?" but "What is this really?" Not "Here are the facts, à la Dr. Wasderfallist, about this image," but rather "Here is the truth of it."

Thom Gunn wrote a sequence of short poems (composing his book called *Positives*) in connection with a series of photographs taken by his brother, Ander Gunn. Starting with an image of a newborn infant, the sequence follows a human chronology, an ad hoc array of ages of mankind. In them, some general aspect of all of our natures usually emerges from an exem-plary glimpse at a particular person of a particular sex, age, or other condition of life. The last three images of a wretched, old, and (either as the poems would have it, or indeed in fact) homeless woman make up the book's only sub-sequence. The final two of these are uniquely paired in that the second is an enlarged detail of the first, zooming in on the old woman's face, hands, and upper body as if to pick up a previously unnoticed detail, and/or to remove by cropping what a deeper perception would want to rule out as inessential distraction, or even falsification of something.

In the second poem, the "rubbish" is quickly made figurative as the detritus both of the woman's past and her recollections of it—as if, at a certain point of wretchedness, all recol-lection were "poking around the rubbish," as if all attempts to cope with one's history were not a vigorous Shakespearean summoning up of memories of things past, but a mode of rag picking. To that degree, the old woman is not the object of sentimental gazing, but the figure of what we will all become. Her remembered green moment—albeit not one of leisured regard for the picturesque, but of a scene of labor—has now become the black-and-white rep-resentation of a scene of urban gleaning, dimly lit in unpicturesque and mordant ways.

But beyond the rubbish of souvenirs in the miserable present is only the immediate future. The close-up in the second picture focuses on the woman's gaze, removing the traceable line of sight through the fork of the tree in the first photograph and implicitly redirecting it into what now reads less as tree trunk than as bordering shadow. The first poem implicitly answered a question about what she was thinking; the second, one about what she was seeing, or at least looking toward. The two similes both point to consciousness in an interior space, perhaps inside "the abandoned house / where she slept on old papers" (from the poem on the first image, not shown here). The last three lines (composing, after what have been mostly seven-syllabled ones, a perfect *haiku*) speak not for the old woman, out of a narrator's construction of what she knows and feels, but from an ultimate distance.

There is another poignant irony, in that the second, enlarged image is additionally compelling in its prominent graininess. Such graininess is, of course, an eventual necessary consequence of the process of enlargement itself. The epistemological puzzle about the limits of photographic knowledge emerging from the fact that repeated enlargement, in its quest for finer detail, will only result in that very detail being obliterated by increasingly coarse grain was given sensational treatment in Antonioni's film *Blowup*, which was made during the same year that Gunn's *Positives* was published. In the last image here, it is not that the poem pretends that the texture is not present. Rather, it seems to use the viewer's sense of it metaphorically. The text, about approaching death, suppresses the true name of that "Something" even as it seems to repress the matter of the increasing, image-decaying, grain as itself a visual trope of the decomposition of body, of consciousness of life itself.

MARIANNE MOORE

Charity Overcoming Envy

Late-fifteenth-century tapestry, Flemish or French, in the Burrell Collection,
Glasgow Art Gallery and Museum

Have you time for a story
    (depicted in tapestry)?
    Charity riding an elephant,
on a "mosaic of flowers," faces Envy,
the flowers "bunched together, not rooted."
Envy, on a dog, is worn down by obsession,
his greed (since of things owned by others
he can only take *some*). Crouching uneasily
in the flowered filigree, among wide weeds
    indented by scallops that swirl,
little flattened-out sunflowers,
thin arched coral stems, and—ribbed horizontally—
slivers of green, Envy, on his dog,
    looks up at the elephant,
cowering away from her, his cheek scarcely scratched.
    He is saying, "O Charity, pity me, Deity!
    O pitiless Destiny,
    what will become of me,
maimed by Charity—*Caritas*—sword unsheathed
over me yet? Blood stains my cheek. I am hurt."
In chest armor over chain mail, a steel shirt
to the knee, he repeats, "I am hurt."
The elephant, at no time borne down by self-pity,
    convinces the victim
that Destiny is not devising a plot.

The problem is mastered—insupportably
tiring when it was impending.

Deliverance accounts for what sounds like an axiom.

    The Gordian knot need not be cut.

Anon., *Tapestry*

Marianne Moore's poem on this emblematic tapestry propounds a moral riddle that lurks both about, and somehow within, its interpretive one. The late fifteenth-century representation, in a millefleurs setting, of "Charity Overcoming Envy" (which is also the title of Moore's poem), would elicit immediate questions in any viewer: Who is this Charity mounted on a triumphal elephant and armed with a sword, menacing an enemy she has already chopped at and is now, brightly and coolly, about to cut again? Is she about to remove his right hand? Where are Charity's iconographically familiar flame, candle, flaming heart, or cornucopia? Why is she not in the process, so often assigned her, of doing one of the six works of mercy (attending to the hungry, the thirsty, the stranger, the naked, the sick, the prisoner [Matthew 25.35–37])? And what sort of envy is manifest in the male figure here? *Invidia*, from Ovid on, is usually seen as a woman (as so often with moral abstractions, because of the gender of the noun designating it in Latin); she is nasty-looking, often feeding on snakes or, proverbially, "eating her heart out." Even Spenser's male and malicious "Envie [who] rode upon a rauenous wolfe, and still did chaw / Betweene his cankred teeth a venemous toad," his clothing "ypainted full of eyes," and "maturing in his bosome secretly" a snake, is not this personage. His dog, rejoicing in the evil befalling him even as the rider does, according to the Latin inscription, is familiar from other images. Even that somewhat problematic inscription is of little help. It appears to read INVIDI DOLOR ANIMI DE PROSPERIS EST PROXIMI GAUDENS EIUS DE MALIS [MALO?] UT CANIS SED HOC ELEPHAS NESCIT VINCIT ET HOC NEPHAS CARITAS FRACERI, perhaps to be rendered as "The envious soul's sorrow is at the prosperity of its neighbor; it rejoices at the evil befalling him, like the dog. But the elephant does not know this. And charity smashes that evil."

Moore's poem asks the mute Other of the image none of those questions, so conventional yet imaginatively forceful, that are more familiar in poems of this kind. Instead, she queries the reader in indirect rhetorical fashion: "Have you time for a story / (depicted in tapestry)?" she asks. And she does so in a seven-syllable rhyming couplet whose form will not recur in the poem, almost as if this prominently framed utterance were her version of the Latin *titulus* of the tapestry. She then proceeds to tell her own tale, starting out with an echo of the kind of workaday ecphrastic prose one finds in an exhibition catalogue, occasionally almost literally quoting from curatorial comment: "Charity, riding an elephant, / on 'a mosaic of flowers,' faces Envy, / the flowers 'bunched together, not rooted.'" But then her final storytelling takes over, with its radical moral analysis of envy coming at once.

The final Gordian "knot" punningly echoes the "not" of negation; as a knot, it seems to have been tied by, and with, the twisting forces of the poem itself, the latter half of which is purely Moore's story of what Envy cries out. It is marked by extravagant diction, and strange, sporadic, cumulative rhyming (in Moore's characteristic mode, often occurring on unstressed syllables). It is also marked by the invidious knight's invocation of Destiny—a goddess not shown in the tapestry because she may or may not have been among its weavers—and the ad hoc pattern of attributes, of Envy "worn down by obsession" and the elephant "at no time borne down by self-pity."

That elephant, with its own version of a gaze out of the picture, is at first anomalous in its iconography, and on second thought emblematic both of temperance and *douceur* (according to an important Renaissance source). And it has a charming unnaturalness for a modern viewer. Yet Moore's story has it "convincing the victim"—with her typical wordplay, she enacts a victory with the Latin etymon of conquest in the gentler English "convince"—a moral equivalent of the warlike. And yet elephants, startling and lovely to our gaze, had, for Moore, reflective weight and substance as well. In an early poem, her "Melancthon" (meaning "black earth") is hardly a white elephant, but rather a figure of power, and in another poem called "Elephants" she had read the positions of the elephant's trunk almost as a Renaissance *impresa* or emblem might have:

> With trunk tucked up compactly—the elephant's
> sign of defeat—he resisted, but is the child
> of reason now. His straight trunk seems to say: when
> what we hoped for came to nothing, we revived.
> As loss could not alter Socrates'
> tranquillity, equanimity's contrived
> by the elephant . . .

But the trunk of Charity's mount signals another condition entirely, and there is something at once winsome and sad-eyed about him.

But then the poem continues past the picture, to an allegory of its own. Mastering a steed, or a canonical enemy, is a matter *in* the tapestry. But mastering a conceptual problem is a matter *of* the tapestry and its image with its own clearly labeled parable. Interpretive puzzles such as the reading of the tapestry with its Latin and its profusion of flowers and tiny enigmas—like that of the sword's point being lost behind the inscription (just about at *hoc nephas*)—succumb to the engagement with a sword-like pen mounted on meditative reading. What sounds like an axiom—"charity overcomes envy"—is revealed as the product of an etiological story after all. Yet the picture is nonetheless timeless in that the action portrayed in it is continual, being wrought anew in every human instance. Each of Moore's last three tiny struggles (a couplet and then two single lines, isolated like strophes) glosses the text above it, in a sequence of moralizations allusive of the medieval *applicatio* tacked on to an exemplum or tale. The very last line proclaims the general triumph of poetry, not over image or picture, but over the sword of the conqueror—Alexander, or even Charity—a triumph of *over*coming at the hands of *be*coming, neither particularly charitable nor envious, but distanced nobly like Moore's own moral tone throughout her poetry. This mastery is achieved without agon; rather than poetry killing falsehood at some risk to its own truthfulness (and this is how mythographers interpreted the story of Bellerophon on Pegasus killing the Chimera) we have here a fable of the deliverances of language itself.

The poem's very structure of rhetorical orders—*titulus*, ecphrasis, reading of spoken language into the world of flowers, and layers of inscription at the very end—is itself a trope or figure for the tapestry's own orders—of woven lines, primary and ancillary images, and rubrics. Plucking out of the realm of the tapestry the internal rhymes in the line at the end of the ecphrasis proper—"Destiny is not devising a plot"—the whole poem's concluding rhyme, as was observed before, puns insouciantly on the name of the emblematic figure of the problem: "The Gordian knot need not be cut." And, by the final implication of a poet who had alluded so often to painting and sculpture and photography in her work, the soul of text need not struggle with the body of image in some perverse *psychomachia.* The deliverance has been one of protecting body from itself, and reducing the very personhood of allegory from captivity by the reductive language of its own inscriptions. The poem generates an ultimate parable about ecphrasis itself. And in answer to its opening question—have we time for a story?—a reader can return a strong "Yes." We have gotten several stories, and stories about stories, for the price of one.

Henri Matisse, *L'Atelier rouge*

W. D. SNODGRASS

Matisse: "The Red Studio"

There is no one here.
But the objects: they are real. It is not
As if he had stepped out or moved away;
There is no other room and no
Returning. Your foot or finger would pass
Through, as into unreflecting water
Red with clay, or into fire.
Still, the objects: they are real. It is
As if he had stood
Still in the bare center of this floor,
His mind turned in in concentrated fury,
Till he sank
Like a great beast sinking into sands
Slowly, and did not look up.
His own room drank him.
What else could generate this
Terra cotta raging through the floor and walls,
Through chests, chairs, the table and the clock,
Till all environments of living are
Transformed to energy—
Crude, definitive and gay.
And so gave birth to objects that are real.
How slowly they took shape, his children, here,
Grew solid and remain:
The crayons; these statues; the clear brandybowl;
The ashtray where a girl sleeps, curling among flowers;
This flask of tall glass, green, where a vine begins
Whose bines circle the other girl brown as a cypress knee.
Then, pictures, emerging on the walls:
Bathers; a landscape; a still life with a vase;
To the left, a golden blonde, lain in magentas with flowers scattering like stars;
Opposite, top right, these terra cotta women, living, in their world of living's colors;
Between, but yearning toward them, the sailor on his red café chair, dark blue,
    self-absorbed.

These stay, exact,
Within the belly of these walls that burn,
That must hum like the domed electric web
Within which, at the carnival, small cars bump and turn,
Toward which, for strength, they reach their iron hands:
Like the heavens' walls of flame that the old magi could see;
Or those ethereal clouds of energy
From which all constellations form,
Within whose love they turn.
They stand here real and ultimate.
But there is no one here.

In 1911, Matisse produced a remarkable body of work in which he was predominantly concerned with color. It is almost as if pictorial, generic, and formal problems provided the occasion for painted color to assume the roles of subject, object, and form. Certainly this seems the case in *L'Atelier rouge*, in which the painter's flattening of all interior space allows the universal red to show through what should ordinarily be solid structures. Physically, it is a kind of map more than a depicted space. But metaphorically, it seems a conceptual place which the artist occupies not by inserting his own image into a containing image he created, but through the signal traces of his presence. For when we see a studio in the artist's absence, we may wonder whether he or she is somehow present in the paintings placed—or housed, or stored, or even dwelling—there. When he or she paints that studio from within it, one might distinguish different modes of presence: the surrounding scene as present object, the seeing, knowing, and representing present consciousness of the painter, ultimately a human presence in an acutely defined sense of his or her room. But in this case, red "occupies" the studio, and preoccupies the painter, in a remarkable way: it is almost as if the studio had found a place—a contingent place—for itself in redness, rather than the trivial matter of red color having laid claim, however transiently, to its walls. It is almost as if this were not a "Red Studio," but a studio of red—made *of, by, for* Red itself. Lawrence Gowing wrote of Matisse's painting that

> the same colour was seen as a continuous medium flooding everything. In *L'Atelier rouge* the space and its furniture are submerged in it. It is the substance of their existence; there are only the traces of yellow edges to show the immaterial frontiers where separate objects once existed. The identity of things is soaked out of them—all except Matisse's own pictures. They remain themselves, simple and lovely, situated at last in their own appropriate world.

W. D. Snodgrass had seen the Matisse painting in the Museum of Modern Art in New York, and his poem on it is one of a remarkable suite published in a book in 1975 (it includes two quite long and elaborate poems, on the Van Gogh *Starry Night* and the Manet *Execution of the Emperor Maximilian,* and two other shorter ones, on a Vuillard and the Monet *Nymphéas*). Here, Snodgrass reads the Matisse painting in a strangely pictorial, almost anecdotal way. He pays great attention to the presences of defined objects in the space of the room, and to the other absences those presences invoke. He acknowledges the power and dominance of the red, "this / Terra cotta raging through the floor and walls . . . And so gave birth to objects that are real." The "one" of the poem's framing first and last line who is not "here" is the poet's own projection of himself as an implied persona of the painter. Matisse is as present—and as dominant—in the real space of the studio in which he is working as is Snodgrass at his writing surface, as is the red in the painting, and the painting in the poem. Acknowledging this "one" propounds the notion of a creative and imaginative presence of another order.

Roger van der Weyden, *Calvary*

Untitled

Here is another poem in a picture:

at the end of the gallery, so you will see them as
you enter, Christ Crucified, the Virgin and Saint
John, attributed to a famous Flemish master.

The attribution of guilt is universal.

There is something distinctly fishy about these figures.
Literally. Streamlined and coldblooded. As weightless
as a fish might feel in water. The man of sorrows not
nailed to his cross but pinned there. Almost as if he
had no body. Nobody to suffer and depend on. No body
to depend on wood and iron and to suffer. Which heresy
pretended he did not? Nonetheless he suffers obviously,
enthroned on his gibbet, naked and erect as if he held
it up.

His mother, fainting in the arms of the disciple Jesus
loved, will never in the conceivable future fall to
earth. And this in spite of the gingerly way he holds
her as he leans slightly forward on tiptoe, his fingers
parted and outstretched as if to seize the air. His
tentative, mimic gesture of support. He does not grasp
at anything. There is no strain or effort apparent
anywhere in the composition.

She sinks down as if onto a chair, stricken by grief,
sustained in theory by love. Her hands are clasped,
her eyes are almost closed. And beneath the smooth
expressive drapery one has to infer the insubstantial
flesh. Goodness! one exclaims, What painting, a
craft in the radical sense pretentious, to suggest
what is equivocally there.

Each wears the appropriate expression like an honorary
degree: he an anthropomorphic mask of pity, she
negligently the distinction of her tears. Only the
saviour of their world wears nothing except a difficult
crown of thorns which hurts.

The cause of their distress is unconcerned. They
do not look upon him as their redeemer as yet, but
as a son and dear friend whose eccentricities have
got him into trouble. One can forgive too many and
love too much.

The birth and banquet of love look equally far away
and insignificant from here; the resurrection is also
inconceivable. Only the ignominious and painful
moment of death has any meaning now, a meaning
without a future or a past.

The background is conventional, a wall too high to
see over, too smooth to climb, draped here and there
with a red linen cloth, its folds still visible.

Beyond the wall there is a gold leaf sky.

Remember that everything is possible,
The picture, the poem and ourselves,
The blood that we see shed, the tears that we
Shed, the wall, and the anonymous cross.

The two panels of the *Calvary* of Roger van der Weyden in the Philadelphia Museum of
Art are probably not the two wings of a folding triptych, and must be regarded as complete
in themselves. One shows the crucified Christ in an environment, as Erwin Panofsky put it,

> entirely imaginary . . . Instead of being permitted to roam over a landscape with
> the city of Jerusalem emerging in the distance, our glance is blocked by a grim
> stone wall surmounted by gold ground and surprisingly hung with two cloths of
> honor of flaming vermilion, their surfaces broken only by a square pattern of
> creases . . . this wall [rises] behind a barren strip of land with a horribly real skull
> and a bone at the foot of the Cross.

In the other, the figures of the Virgin and St. John are (again, in Panofsky's words)

> svelte, rather than attenuated. Their long-limbed, delicately modeled bodies move
> with a resilient grace which is a perfect blend of Gothic fluency and Italian equili-

bration; and the lineaments of their draperies, which seem to consist of a thinner, more pliable fabric than in the early works, are animated by a new feeling for sustained melody.

The ingenious Canadian poet Daryl Hine, among many other things an extremely accomplished master of rhyme and accentual-syllabic rhythm, directs to the panel a poem in twelve uncharacteristic prose "stanzas" (albeit decaying, at the very end, into five lines of unrhymed pentameter). It employs uncharacteristically breathy sentence fragments instead of his typical, superbly crafted, periodic sentences, and it moves from high diction to the most pointed slang. The matter-of-factness of the opening and the erasure of any thematic rubric in the title emphasizes the first line's apparent denial of poetic status to the poet's language, as if to say: "Here is yet one more poem, but this time not *on* or *about* a picture. This is rather to assert that the poem is *in* the picture, and all the poem will do is to point out what, and where, it is." It is one degree of metaphoric removal from the traditional matter of giving voice to the mute image—the equivalent of saying "It *does* speak: you only have to listen."

But Hine's more familiar kind of wordplay takes over with the first ironic twist on the art-historical language of "attribution," in a line which speaks for both the Christian and secular domains (who, what, attributes the guilt, and to whom?). The whole first part of the poem is a sort of ill-tempered reading of a masterpiece whose appeal—like that of Gothic art rather than Italian, generally—to the unsentimental can itself, by the later twentieth century, become a new kind of sentimentality of its own. Hine's poem starts out with an implicit refusal of the conventional terms of admiration. The "something fishy" about the figures (*pace* Panofsky) speaks to the matter of a kind of representational guilt. Skepticism about this painting dominates the first part of the poem, misreading—taking no sensuous or learned delight in—the celebrated conventions of fifteenth-century Flemish painting at its greatest. (It is hard to agree with the poet that the wonderfully articulated, "boxy" drapery of the Virgin's robe is "smooth," even as we must conclude from Panofsky and other scholars that the background is far from "conventional").

The second half of the poem moves away from the mock-curatorial diction ("There is no strain or effort apparent anywhere in the composition") and the fairly tight ecphrastic program—the glossing of gesture and of figural form—into a rather Audenesque kind of homily, and in an Audenesque tone. This follows the final iconoclastic skepticism of "Each wears the appropriate expression like an honorary degree: he an anthropomorphic mask of pity, she negligently the distinction of her tears." Then the eighth stanza continues to consider the figures of St. John and the Virgin. But it associates their inner states with the condition of, and the local space inhabited by, the viewer, focusing on an absent middle image between the two wing panels as a conceptual abyss across which the two grieving figures contemplate "The cause of their distress." This gap suggests an equivocal state of suspended mythopoetic significance and existential pressure (Auden, as a Christian, speaks of it as a phase or time period in *A Christmas Oratorio*—"The time is noon"—the condition of ordinariness). For Hine, reading the paintings without faith but with a memory of it,

The birth and banquet of love look equally far away
and insignificant from here; the resurrection is also
inconceivable. Only the ignominious and painful
moment of death has any meaning now, a meaning
without a future or a past.

After this, the poem returns to pointed, implicitly allegorizing ecphrasis: the wall "too high
to see over," with an impenetrable "gold leaf sky" (suggesting an inability even of the poem
in the poem to get beyond a present moment of initially skeptical, finally penetrating, gaze).
But it is also as if the gold in the sky could buy—imaginatively—anything. Turning on that
line, taking up its pentameter cadence, the poem closes on a note of total generosity for
representation, for image-making and response to it, in the delicately placed reciprocating
tears and blood, and the intransigent iconicity of the cross, which—like the wall—there is no
getting past.

RICHARD HOWARD

Giovanni da Fiesole on the Sublime, or Fra Angelico's "Last Judgment"

How to behold what cannot be held?
Start from the center and from all that
lies or flies or merely rises left
of center. You may have noticed how
Hell, in these affairs, is on the right
invariably (though for an inside Judge,
of course, that would be the left. And we
are not inside). I have no doctrine
intricate enough for Hell, which I leave
in its own right, where it will be left.

Right down the center, then, in two rows,
run nineteen black holes, their square lids off;
also one sarcophagus, up front.
Out of these has come the world: out of
that coffin, I guess, the Judge above
the world. Nor is my doctrine liable
to smooth itself out for the blue ease
of Heaven outlining one low hill
against the sky at the graveyard's end
like a woman's body—a hill like Eve.

Some of us stand, still, at the margin
of this cemetery, marvelling
that no more than a mortared pavement can
separate us from the Other Side
which numbers as many nuns and priests
(even Popes and Empresses!) as ours.
The rest, though, stirring to a music
that our startled blood remembers now,
embrace each other or the Angels
of this green place: the dancing begins.

FRA ANGELICO, *Last Judgment*

We dance in a circle of bushes,
red and yellow roses, round a pool
of green water. There is one lily,
gold as a lantern in the dark grass,
and all the trees accompany us
with gestures of fruition. We stop!
The ring of bodies opens where a last
Angel, in scarlet, hands us on. Now
we go, we are leaving this garden
of colors and gowns. We walk into

A light falling upon us, falling
out of the great rose gate upon us,
light so thick we cannot trust our eyes
to walk into it so. We lift up
our hands then and walk into the light.
How to behold what cannot be held?
Make believe you hold it, no longer
lighting but light, and walk into that
gold success. The world must be its own
witness, we judge ourselves, raise your hands.

Fra Angelico's *Last Judgment* in the Museo di San Marco in Florence, probably painted around 1430, has a somewhat unusual shape. The top central lobe, in which Christ is shown giving judgment, contains a framing mandorla, itself again framed by an array of angels; on either side are the Virgin and St. John with other saints and apostles fanning out symmetrically behind them. Below the central lobe, starting just this side of an open sarcophagus and reaching back deeply into a perspectival space unopened above, stretches what seems almost a causeway of opened graves, from which the dead at either side have arisen in the Resurrection, reaching out back, and forming the gaze's road to a faint blue horizon. Paradise, on the Judge's right, and Hell to the left, compose the contents of the two rectangular sections on each side.

Richard Howard has written a dazzling array of ecphrastic poems, some of which have already been mentioned. His major mode as a poet is the dramatic monologue. In an elaborate long poem on Caspar David Friedrich's *The Chalk Cliffs of Rügen*, the speaker is one of the figures in the landscape. But this confrontation with Fra Angelico's painting occurs in the discourse of a notional speaker who seems to be standing facing the picture, like the viewer, or the reader-as-viewer, perhaps even standing next to him or her. "Giovanni da Fiesole" is a fictive version of the painter himself: Guido da Pietri entered the Dominican convent in Fiesole in 1407; on taking orders he became Giovanni Angelico da Fiesole. But, unlike Robert Browning's Andrea del Sarto or Fra Lippo Lippi, for example, he exists solely as creator, commentator, and, ultimately cicerone through his finished creation. Through the poem's five stanzas, constructed of ten unrhymed lines each of nine syllables, the painter/explainer seems to leave the reader/viewer's side. At the beginning he is clearly, like ourselves, an external viewer of the scene ("And we / are not inside"). By the third stanza the word "we" seems almost to include the persons in the painted scene. The "margin / of this cemetery," and the "mortared pavement" that separates "us from the Other Side" doubles the separation of viewer/painting and elect/damned in an uncanny way. By the fourth stanza, "we" seem now to have entered the painting's last world with Giovanni, to be dancing among the elected dancers themselves, and finally, doubling the two embracing figures vanishing into brightness, as Dantean visitors there, moving out, up, back to the left (the painting's heavenly right) "into the light." Certainly our reading eye has entered the picture in just that way: it is our vision which is the traveler, being handed on by the red-clad angel; the agent is our elected gaze, a suitable companion for the poem's Giovanni da Fiesole, who speaks for that gaze as it cannot—like the painting it scans—speak for itself.

Howard's intricate wordplay is cleverly functional, as well as almost palpably evident, in the last lines of the first stanza, where the speaker's disclaimer that he has "no doctrine / intricate enough for Hell" is considerably hedged by what follows: ". . . Hell, which I leave / to its own right, where it will be left." The previously considered matter of viewer's-right-to-stage-left aside, this rhetoric evokes the unwittingly dialectical wordplay of Milton's great Doctor of Hell, Satan. But this is balanced by the return of the opening pun of spatiality ("behold/be held"), now in an added new and gentler temporal dimension—in effect, "How to behold what cannot previously have been beheld, and to which everything is beholden?" We might call it a heavenly wit redeeming the hellish kind. The poem's own final answer to this question itself evades the compelling, dominant matter of Christ in the upper lobes of the panel, even as the narrative motion avoids more than a supposition about the "Judge above." And, just beyond that, the reader's own answer will ultimately resonate: ["How to behold what cannot be held?"] *By holding it in the hand of your eye.*

Howard has himself discussed this poem in its relation to a passage from Browning's "Fra Lippo Lippi" in which the protagonist conceives the program for his *Coronation of the Virgin*, painted for the convent of Sant'Ambrogio and now in the Uffizi. In Browning's poem, the poet's actual ecphrasis of an actual painting here masquerades—through the fiction of Lippo as dramatic monologist—as that particular type of notional one to be found in an artist's projection or plan (or, in one sense of the word, "design") for a piece. But it is the kind of notional ecphrasis which is in fact literally, *canonically*, "illustrated" by the completed painting. The irony of this visionary/empirical, anterior/posterior relation remains potently implicit in Browning, and surfaces in interesting forms in Howard's relation to his precursor. Browning's Lippo declares

> I shall paint
> God in the midst, Madonna and her babe,
> Ringed by a bowery-flowery angel-brood,
> Lilies and vestments and white faces, sweet

As puff on puff of grated orris-root
When ladies crowd to Church at midsummer.
And then i'the front, of course, a saint or two—
Saint John, because he saves the Florentines,
Saint Ambrose, who puts down in black and white
The convent's friends and gives them a long day,
And Job, I must have him there past mistake,
The man of Uz (and Us without the z,
Painters who need his patience).

The very modern wit of these last lines (anticipating Howard himself, or James Merrill, for example) leads to the more remarkable promise that follows:

Well, all these,
Secure in their devotion, up shall come
Out of a corner when you least expect,
As one by a dark stair into a great light,
Music and talking . . .

"They" are simultaneously the nuns, encountering the painting on the wall of their convent, and the figures previously catalogued in the ecphrasis. These themselves are treated in yet another mode of doubling: they come up "out of a corner when you least expect" (1) as they emerge for the scanning eye of the viewer, in the realms of darks and lights of the painting, and (2) as they emerge from the darkness of design and projection into the "great light, / Music and talking" of their realization on canvas. These lines at once embrace the work of execution, the finished work of art, and the particular work of encountering and apprehending it. Their epistemological range is rather complex, applying to a world "before" (temporally, prior to) the painting, a world inside it as viewed from "before" (spatially, in front of) it, and a world after its installation and completion as a commissioned object, inserted into an enclosed world of devotion. It is particularly the ways in which the antecedents of Fra Lippo's "these" are both in and out of the picture that constitute one sort of prototype for the location of Giovanni da Fiesole's shifting "we."

GIOVANNI PAOLO PANINI, *Capriccio of Roman Ruins and Sculpture with Figures*

A Capriccio of Roman Ruins and Sculpture with Figures

The light starts in a promising street,
Edges the stolen slabs of another art,
Up pitted columns, pediment by leaf,
And casts their shadows against the graying
Academy of clouds suspended above
An imagined forum as if in disbelief—
Airy element we too are in, until
Trappings catch the eye as they will . . .
A nude giant the world holds up,
Porphyry putti adorning death's home
Away from harm. The motto on these ruins
Reads *Restore.*

            And Time, ever the artist
In his studio, has hung this landscape
As a gallery of copies. How to take stock?
A stone lion wrings blood from a stone
Horse whose real counterparts—that is,
Those more at ease, brushed in extremes
Of the same chalk and bay as the dust
On their riders' faces—water near its pain,
Rendered so well it almost hurts to think
How telling such effects are. Echoes faint
Or feigned, realia in disregard. For instance
Take that river god, elbow propped forever
On a symbol of his source, how he seems to cut
The flesh-colored figure further on—a patron?
The painter? Like us at least in striking poses
To familiarize the world. So exactly does his
Duplicate the god one's first reaction is,
Divine.

         And soon enough, Is nothing sacred?
After all, these third-rate views are so lifelike.
Busy bromides we swallow whole to stomach ones
Of a kind, old masters or young turks. So
Busy, in fact, we never miss among the many

Objects of attention what is missing: a subject,
Like those a barely entitled woodcut allegory
Or palace ceiling owns. The question is raised,
The frame is apt reply.
                        You are the point
Of view, it says squarely, a single-minded
Perspective, with references, the clear scope
Of depths outlined until they vanish or you
Figure them out again. Our view precisely,
Though we are out of the picture . . . like him,
Alien in tunic and turban, who turns
The corner and sees all this and so creates
Pretended ruins of a city he does not know
Once was his. He may as well be lounging
In a stuffy museum roof, benched
Before overdrawn drafts of forms that call
To mind "the past," another of our handles
On what contains us. It takes time to tell
How much is owed to private slants of vision.
Askew with sense out of sight or mind,
The momentary lapse from commonplaces . . .

But he's gone. (And shouldn't we be on our way?)
Perhaps back to that street. Or in flight
From angles, uphill to a cypress grove,
Banking on the storm, late sun aloft,
Branching out in memories of itself.
Billowing shades ride out the sky's own
Threatening gestures. The eye becomes
The storm. A man becomes the sketch
He can erase to thunderheads of smudge.
The line between seems almost natural.

This view of the Forum complex in Rome, painted by G. P. Panini in 1741, is a typical *veduta ideata* of the kind more popularly associated with the prints of Piranesi. In such representations, actual architectural objects are combined into an "ideal" or "fanciful" scene whose composition accedes homage to the implorings of the picturesque, rather than to the sterner demands of topographical truth. Here, the relation of the Arch of Titus, the entrance to the Farnesian Gardens, and, on the far right, the Palatine Hill, are all correct, and even the Temple of Vesta has been shifted only a little; but the famous three columns of the temple of Castor and Pollux (almost emblematic, for the sightseer even in the eighteenth century, of the whole of the imperial forum), the porch of the Temple of Saturn, the angled view of the Arch of Septimius Severus, and other monuments have been considerably moved about. The allegorical figure of the river Tiber (in the Louvre, in fact) has been rotated so as to be seen from behind on the left of the painting. In the center, directly aligned with the central Castor and Pollux column, the figure "in tunic and turban" is being shown a bas-relief of three female figures. The effect of all this has been to create a sort of stage set for the figures in it, and all for the viewer's eye to fill, not with acts of a drama, but with a world of intermission.

An early poem by J. D. McClatchy addresses itself to this painting, which the poet would have visited frequently (it hangs in the Yale Art Gallery) while living nearby. It frames a complex, wide-ranging meditation on what to make of such a gathering, and piling-up, of pictorial fictions: real ruins with imaginary ruins in and among them ("stolen slabs"); distanced creatures juxtaposed with stone images of creatures like themselves, plausible people moving, working, idling, among familiar but impossible (given the topical rearrangements) spaces, and so forth. Even the first moralizing impulse, as reaction to the general condition of fragmented monuments ("The motto on these ruins / Reads *Restore*"), is resonantly intricate: what we see here is a picture-maker's "restoration" of a fragmented view. The topographical realities of placement and distance would not allow these arches and groups of columns—however each may be accurately rendered—to form such a perspectival system. The painting's own "restored" arrangement leads the scanning eye on a languid but well-directed walk, inventing "a promising street" like this. But the poem, full of knowledge of poetic ecphrasis and assuming the burden of its prior conventions, does not unfold a narrative along such a walk. Rather it pauses for a while to contemplate its own contemplation.

For of the landscape itself, Time's own "gallery of copies"—"How to take stock?" The juxtaposition of living beings and sculptured representations in this particular painting diminishes whatever epistemological or mythological contrasts might otherwise be suggested (as in some of the relations between Watteau's people and his statues, for instance). Here the distance, the light, the formal and tonal vocabulary, reconcile what could be interfering realms. In characterizing all this as "Echoes faint / Or feigned, realia in disregard," the poem makes its point by painting its own phonological shadows of these painted "echoes": the whole painted condition of this world of restoration is such that "faint" itself echoes "feigned" and the two concepts, as well as the words, are in assonance. Art's own "disregard" is more, indeed, of a "dys-regard," a weirdly angled look which puts things in what we more broadly and casually speak of as "its own perspective." And so, too, the ever self-conscious poem finds itself doing to Panini's scene what that very *veduta* does to topographical and biological realia.

But beyond this, how to take further stock? What is this painting *about?* It is only here, in the third verse paragraph, that poem and picture, painting and discourse about it, become more deeply identified; it is here that the viewer's voice, speaking in the Audenesque-cum-academic "we" that includes a notional adjacent viewer and an actual reader, chooses its own point of "perspective"—subjective now, not linear—from within the painting, identifying itself with the one central figure. But then the poem's scanning eye moves up—skyward—and thereby finally out of the picture. We have an almost pastoral closure, with the storm implicit in so much painterly cumulonimbus now becoming emblematic of external pressures acting on the viewer—of scene, of painted scene, of galleried painting—and on the poem itself. And metaphorically, the faintly threatening coming tempest allows a farewell acknowledgment to the "restoring," reordering, creating, power of the interpretive gaze: "The eye becomes / The storm." The subjective ocular instrument becomes one with the very heart—the oddly calm, oddly inactive heart—of the object of its gaze. And stock has been taken, indeed, even of this sort of stocktaking.

DAVID FERRY

Cythera

There they go, down to the fatal ship.
They know how beautiful they are.
The ship will sail very soon. The sea
Will cover them over very soon unknowingly.

Wave goodbye from the shore, children.
I can see how your faces change in the sight
Of their going away. Wave to them.

Their sails are of silk, they're very pretty.
The sunset is all smiles, radiance,
The hues of a first or last innocence.
You look hungry, children, tired, angry.

Very beautiful is the manner of their going.
Music is playing about the mast; their lovely faces
Look lovelier still compared to the angry children.

Watteau's *Le Pélerinage à l'isle de Cythère* in the Louvre, completed in 1717, has long been the object of lyrical meditation. Its subject is thought to have been suggested by a song in Florent Dancourt's comedy, *Les Trois cousines,* which Watteau saw in 1709. The contours of an ideal landscape, opening back and to the left, are traced by an extended group of sedate revelers in a procession that starts at the foot of an ancient image of Venus, half reclaimed by flowers and foliage, goes up a little hill, and descends, half-hidden, behind it. The serpentine array of people seems more choreographic than narrative; they seem to be performing quietly for themselves, rather than acting, doing, making, in the more usual sense. Indeed, we seem to see what is almost the same couple in varying positions of a sort of informal pas de deux. Time seems suspended; René Huyghe has said of the painting that it "moves from attentive immobility to yielding hesitation [which] it then abandons, with the departure of the enchanted boat for the island." Jean H. Hagstrum's reading of the picture as "an embarkation for ecstasy" points out that its "pictorial dynamics make of the embarkation a movement of real people in different states of real eagerness and real reluctance toward erotic experience." And Ronald Paulson remarks, first about Watteau's scenes generally, then about this one:

Jean-Antoine Watteau, *Le Pélerinage à l'isle de Cythère*

> The general movement of the serpentine lines connecting foreground and back-ground is back and to the left. While . . . all western paintings move from left to right, Watteau's almost always unfold in the opposite direction, back into the distance as if to represent an unwinding or regressing . . . [this painting] is a prime example, where the twilight sky, the pilgrims turning away from the shrine of Venus, moving back down the hill to the ship, follow exactly this retrogressive curve. Something is in process of change, coming to an end, people going home, the party over or about to be.

And indeed, it is now believed by some scholars that this painting, and another version of it in Berlin usually entitled *The Embarkation for Cythera,* may very well be departures *from,* rather than *for,* the island of love, thus legitimately occasioning observations like that in Paulson's last sentence. Somehow interiority, introspection, contingency, and awaiting sadness have seemed to emanate from this painted vision over the years. Derek Walcott, in "Watteau," one of the poems of his sequence *Midsummer,* observes that

> Nothing stays green
> in that prodigious urging toward twilight;
> in all of his journeys the pilgrims are in fever
> from the tremulous strokes of malaria's laureate.
> So where is Cythera? It, too, is far and feverish,
> it dilates on the horizon of his near-delirium, near
> and then further, it can break like the spidery rigging
> of his ribboned barquentines, it is as much nowhere
> as these broad-leafed islands, it is the disease
> of elephantine vegetation in Baudelaire . . .

Such a sense informs David Ferry's sad "Cythera," which imports a sobering aftermath into what is generally read as a shadowed festivity. The matter of children being abandoned is not merely literally that, but also evokes all the consequences both of an era whose preserved works of art and literature center on an aristocracy who would not survive the century, and of the era of our own modern lives which in retrospect seem to have been shrouded in pleasures. Rather than give an ecphrasis of Watteau's painting, it plunges immediately into its veiled interior.

Interestingly enough, another poem Ferry had written over thirty years earlier had also displaced its gaze from the precise scene of the painting in its opening play of anachronism. And it, too, seems concerned to interpret what is lurking in the painting's intermissions, acknowledging only implicitly the presence of the dance-like procession of figures, and the pattern they make in, and with, the landscape:

The Embarkation for Cythera

The picnic-goers beautified themselves,
And then set sail for Cythera, with jugs
To keep their coffee hot, martinis cold,
And hampers full of music. The water shone
For them that day, and like a street of jewels
Lay between their land and the island.

Their cockle hull was pretty, white and gold
As the Mozarteum, and their laughter picked
Its way, nicely as tunes of proper jump,
From port to starboard, gentlemen to ladies,
And return. They played their cards right, whiling
The days away by smiling and by thinking

Of the times to come, the banquets in the grove
Of the antless island of that ancient idol
Love, the girl who rose to be the pearl
To deck them out. Thinking of her, each lady
Fingered her necklace, and sweet music tattled
From the spinet of her desire; each lord

Touched at his sleeve for the ace he'd hidden there.

But here the modernity fades back into an earlier realm of lords and ladies, suffused in a delight of selfhood (the strict iambic pentameter of Ferry's lines enforces, at the end of the sixth line of the first stanza, an overtone of "I-*land*," stressed on the second syllable). Even a description of these people's playing falls into jingle—"whiling / The days away by smiling." Even their "thinking" is not philosophical meditation on the nature of their lives, for it is only "Of the times to come." And whether they cheat at cards or not hardly matters: they are unwittingly playing against History, whose deck is always stacked.

For the minor late-Victorian versifier Austin Dobson, the matter is slightly more trifling. He writes a rondeau, "After Watteau," in which one of the many figures in the painting doubles his voice with the somewhat condescending injunctions of the viewer:

> "*Embarquons-nous!*" I seem to go
> Against my will. 'Neath alleys low
> I bend, and hear across the air—
> Across the stream—faint music rare,—
> Whose "*cornemus*," whose "*chalumeau*"?

Hark! was not that a laugh I know?
Who was it, hurrying, turned to show
    The galley swinging by the stair?—
        "Embarquons-nous!"

The silk sail flaps, light breezes blow;
Frail laces flutter, satins flow;
    You, with the love-knot in your hair,
    "Allons, embarquons pour Cythère";
You will not? Press her then, Pierrot,—
        "Embarquons-nous!"

Paul Gauguin, *Le Cheval blanc*

VICKI HEARNE

Gauguin's White Horse

There he stood, quite suddenly,
Innocent nose to foreleg,
Bent against no betrayal,

As though all the gods had laps
And were not inflamed. Shadows
Bore fruit. Edible mosses

Exhaled an eternity
Of breath. Someone asks whether
Gauguin held his when this horse

Flowed out into the foreground
Like an ethics of texture.
Now, it matters. We, with our

Breath as heavy, as rapid
As paint, reach to pluck the horse,
Letting time back in, and take

Flesh for the trope of the horse,
The horse for a trope of grace,
Perception in place of the

Acts of the heart, for granted.
It was all actual. Here,
The emptied frame has become

What fills in for the prior
Question—not the one about
Wanting our innocence back,

Or how to send it forward,
A wisdom of matted manes,
Nor where the laps of the gods

Fall to when the sun rises.
The question is behind mouths
And won't come out of the frame

As long as we keep choking.
Ease in your throat is what lets
The head of the white horse swing

Downward through air, toward water.
Ours are the mouths Gauguin's brush
Bends to, compelled to answer.

Paul Gauguin's white horse in *Le Cheval blanc* of 1898 is not white in the painting: the greenish-grayish color is that of the light falling on it through foliage. The horse's form and posture are derived from those of a carved horse on the west frieze of the Parthenon, but the painting propounds no allusive meaning thereby. Indeed, its greatest interest seems to lie in the play of curves in the forms of vegetation, equine back and flanks, and the blending of horizontal and vertical planes which generate a perspective system and a prominent deployment of pattern suggestive of the Japanese prints that had influenced Gauguin's earlier canvases. And yet within all this context of structure, design, and flattened form, the contingent whiteness and the unequivocal riderlessness of the eponymous horse tease the viewer into moments of narrative and iconographic conjecture.

It might be thought that for Vicki Hearne, a trainer of horses and philosophical essayist on the relation of people to domestic animals, the matter of Gauguin's horse image could easily decay into an equestrian agenda, her ecphrastic comments reducing to objections about precise anatomical rendering, or matters of carriage and posture which reveal the results of training, and so forth. But when we hear her (fictional) "someone" characterizing the horse as having "Flowed out into the foreground / Like an ethics of texture," we know that the realm of form, of paint, and of imagination is her concern, rather than a particular corner of the animal kingdom where *Equus caballus* trots onto the terrain of human society. It is both poetically and philosophically sophisticated of this poet and philosophical writer about horses and dogs to distance her regard even from the screen of her own technically modulated sensibility, her own instinctive expertise. The question of this sort of equestrian lore becomes part of the problematics of interpretation: it is this kind of knowledge—of the cultural and intellectual history of such lore—the burden and the joy of which make the poet's breath come "as heavy, as rapid / As paint."

Through this poem's casually marked, lightly sounding seven-syllabled lines and unbounded tercets, a strangely oblique metaphoric concern gradually unfolds. First there is the consciousness that an actual, flesh-and-blood equine presence—one that we could "reach to pluck"—would itself be a metaphor for the painted object, even as that object would itself be allegorical. There is also the consequent, associated, allegory—the poet's own—of noticing, of *knowing,* for loving. As it moves toward a conclusion, the poem continues in pursuit of questions, about the very act of poetic questioning, about tropes and replacements and what can stand for what; at the end, it has returned to the ecphrastic scene and moment, briefly associating viewer, painter's brush, and horse in a strange figure of mirroring, seeing "The head of the white horse swing // Downward through air, toward water" and Gauguin's brush bending as if to drink of the gazing poet's language. It is not merely that the poet asks the painting to speak up: here, the painted figure demands it of the poet. The white horse that can make this demand with ultimate authority is often called Pegasus, and most often his wings, invisible in the picture of him, have become part of the texture of picturing itself.

PIERRE-AUGUSTE RENOIR, *Luncheon of the Boating Party*

Renoir

for Donald Davie

Under striped flutter of awnings, they have come
together this afternoon to glitter with
carafes and wine glasses, and the fluffy dog
perched on the table amid parings
of apples and peaches. They rehearse
a civilization here among
bright collaborations of sun. The two
gentlemen nearest us take their ease
bare-armed, in undershirts. At the next
table, brown jacket and bowler melt
into ingenious dapple and nonchalance,
and only the farthest gentlemen, vertical, sustain
in suits and top hats, a dark
decorum. And ladies, ladies—
bonnetted, buttoned at neck
and wrists, yet ripe
with sleep: their cheeks
and half-closed eyes give them away.
Flesh is fruit, whispers the brush, and sunlight
wine; all cloth
dissolves. And when these chroma
and characters have faded
into the single, sensual blur of an afternoon
lost, there will remain
ghostly vermilion, hieroglyphic lips,
awning stripes and anemones that once
so vulgarly blazed, now dimming to
the mystic map of sprawl, spatter, and glare:
not Jeanne, Marie-Thérèse, Alphonse, Auguste, but this—
this truest pattern, radiance revealed,
a constellation visible at dusk.

Renoir's gorgeous *Le Déjeuner des canotiers* in the Phillips Collection, painted 1880–81, shows a luncheon party on a covered terrace: the actual site was the upstairs terrace of a restaurant on an island in the Seine where oarsmen would indeed congregate. It is not in the least a narrative painting. In such a case, any interpretive program would have to deal not with (1) what people are revealed as being in what relation to others, or (2) what is precisely going on with respect to these relations at precisely the present moment, or (3) what pasts and futures are assumed and implied. Instead, the painting's story is of color, tone, light, clothes and bodies, pleasure, animation, and the energetic formal pictorial structures of energetic social informality. The diagonal compositional structures in the painting are very active. They move from the magnificent upper arm in the right foreground, back across through the intersection of the major diagonals (on the left shoulder of the man in the middle, and lying along the continuation of the farthest awning pole), out to the opening and the view down the river. There is an opposing perspective recessional heading back up to the right and into denser clusterings of people. It is not only these diagonals which recall Venetian painting; there is a specific relation to Veronese's *Wedding Feast at Cana* in the Louvre, which Renoir had long known and lovingly considered. But here the narrative details exist to be journalistically and formally plausible and sometimes, perhaps, in illumination of states of attention. Lawrence Gowing, in talking of Renoir as "an illustrator of human interaction," points to the girl at the bottom right, who

> lets the concentrated admiration of a bearded young man, who is oblivious of anyone else or of us, rest steadily upon her; the intentness is almost palpable. She receives it; it bathes her; she luxuriates in it, smiles a little to herself. Presently an inward look and something in her bearing admit complicity. The two are at one; their state is blessed.

Of course, a poem might invent its own more precise narrative for the painting by asking some ad hoc question (e.g., "What is that young woman at the upper right *doing?* Fiddling with her hat? Refusing—or pretending to refuse—to listen to something being said to her?") But it would somehow seem a reductive move, and perhaps even a comic one, to do so. One might also yield to a kind of photographic agenda. For the "identities" of the people in the party have been established with varying degrees of certainty: the woman Gowing considers is probably the actress Ellen André; the man leaning over her is an Italian journalist named Maggiolo; the man with the arm in the foreground is the engineer and painter Gustave Caillebotte. Charles Ephrussi, a banker and writer on art, is the top-hatted man at the back. At the lower left is Renoir's mistress, Aline Charigot, whom he later married and, behind her, Alphonse Fournaise, son of the restaurateur. Jeanne Samary, an actress, is the lady with her gloved hands at her ears, talking to two other friends of Renoir, Lhote and Lestringuez. The man with his back to us is Baron Barbier, and the woman drinking is a favorite model named Angèle. The party is neither a feast of the gods, nor a bourgeois genre-scene, nor a ritual repast. But in its own way it celebrates the marriage of Art and Friendship.

A younger American poet who had herself started out as a painter, and who has also written learnedly on French art and literature, reads this celebrated picture in a poem that itself exhibits, among other things, the "ingenious dapple and nonchalance" that it sees in the relation of pure color and muted significations of details of clothing—indeed, in the whole of the painting.

Warren holds back her own—and defers our—knowledge of the casual and professional models in the scene until the end of the poem. It is a familiar interpretive strategy to ask of a festive gathering "Well, what happens later?" Here, in the literal and figurative darkening of an oncoming evening, "when these chroma / and characters have faded" ("characters" meaning both persons and signifying marks), the banquet of sense will be over. The people will go sleepily home, but that is as nothing. For the "truest pattern" will emerge, even as the heart of the matter of this painting will emerge after the distractions of possible story, of psychologizing, even of the apparent underlying truth ("Flesh is fruit, whispers the brush, and sunlight / wine") have faded. Our knowledge of who these people are darkens as their names dim out; our apprehension loses its grasp of the fables whispered by the brush. But the ultimate structure, "the mystic map of sprawl, spatter, and glare" comes out like a premature star. The Evening Star—of oncoming love—is the one visible at dusk. At the end of the poem, the truth of the painting is revealed in that mystic map; the whole party that the painting *is*, rather than merely being *of*, has become translated, as in Ovidian mythography, stellified into an entire Evening Asterism. This is itself a splendid fable of how the truth of any particular painting remains ever visible to a knowing inner eye, and, perhaps, of how only in poetry may the fading necessary to that revelation occur.

SANDRO BOTTICELLI, *Mars and Venus*

RACHEL HADAS

Mars and Venus
(Botticelli, ca. 1475)

Gold tape gently billowing with her breathing,
triple V's at bosom and sleeve and ankle
point to partings, leading the eye to where her
                                        body emerges.

Wait: this painting is an enormous V-ness.
Look how unemphatically, almost absent-
ly her left hand seems to be plucking one more
                                        labial gilded

entry between her waist and her knee. Reclining,
she becomes a series of languid valleys
who herself creates an entire other
                                        landscape of V-ness

in her consort. Slumbering, numb, the war-god—
head thrown back; neck, shoulders, torso open—
seems oblivious equally to the lady
                                        and to the satyrs,

naughty toddlers, trying on Mars's helmet,
blowing conches into his ear, or crawling
gleefully through his corselet, their behavior
                                        an awful nuisance

all for nothing. Here in this vague green valley
lamb and lion, love and war are united
by indifference equally to these babies
                                        and to each other.

Do the little faunlets call Mars their Daddy?
Either way, his answer is not forthcoming.
Drained by amorous combat, the god is elsewhere.
                                        Vigilant Venus

gazes, not at him, nor at us, but rather
seems the merest eyeflick away from over-
seeing Sandro putting the final touches
                              onto this family

portrait: Mars and Venus, it's called. Or Father
sleeps while Mother's keeping a watchful eye out
not on the children (*are* these the couple's children?)
                              but beyond; elsewhere.

Violence sleeps. Desire is in need of further
sustenance: her V's are unfilled, her fingers
seem to press, to promise, half hiding, showing
                              translucent treasures

he has seen and savored to satiation.
Rhyming, secret, intimate, and familiar,
their two mysteries mingle in this: deferral
                              of ever after.

The adulterous love of Mars and Venus, wife of Vulcan, was violently and ludicrously exposed when her husband caught them in flagrante delicto and a net and brought them up to Olympus to general deific laughter. But the love of Venus and Mars is moralized early on as a fable of Love and War making love. (Indeed, by some accounts Cupid—Love with a small "l"—is the child born of this attachment, and "making love" has an additional sense; certainly this appropriately represents sexual love as being fathered by warfare, and conceptually accounts for his use of bow and arrow.) In such an account, it is Mars who is seen as being momentarily, at least, subdued. Lucretius, who allegorizes Venus and Mars as elemental forces of creation and destruction, has it that when Mars is with Venus, creative forces dominate the cosmos, but when he climbs out of her bed to go about in the world, her work is cyclically undone. The love of Mars and Venus was a popular *quattrocento* subject: Lorenzo de' Medici and Poliziano in his *Stanze* (now thought to have influenced Botticelli's mythological paintings) both treated of the matter. Renaissance Neoplatonic writers such as Ficino and Pico della Mirandola read Mars and Venus making love either as a more general pattern of the dialectical harmonizing of opposites (Strife and Concord), or as an outright victory of Humanitas over Discord and War. (The story, after all, is not one of Mars and Venus fighting, which, the outcome of such a battle aside, would by its very occurrence allegorically assert Mars's triumph.)

Botticelli's *Mars and Venus,* probably painted in 1483—there is no agreement about the patron or, save that it was made to decorate a marriage chamber, the occasion—is one of his mythological paintings whose literary sources and possible allegorical extensions have occupied scholars for decades. Formally, it may have been influenced by an antique relief of Bacchus and Ariadne. It is thought by many to have followed the suggestions of a Greek writer's ecphrasis of a Hellenistic painting. Lucian, in his dialogue called *Herodotus*, describes Aëtion's picture of *The Nuptials of Alexander and Roxana*, in which cupids play among the arms and armor of Alexander, two carrying his spear "like laborers bearing a heavy beam; two more hold the handles of his shield, dragging it along as another one of them—their king, doubt-less—lies on it" and in which one more "has got into the corselet, which lies hollow-side up." (The cupids here may have suggested the little satyrs in Botticelli's painting, which partake of the realms of Pan and Bacchus, and perhaps thereby of the woodland glade in which we find the two lovers.) The remarkable formal elements the painting presents include the larger pat-terns made by the two figures, embowered, in different modes of postcoital repose: parallel angles relating her right arm and his left one through the prominent angle of his right leg; his relaxed angularity opposed by her conscious sinuous curvatures, of posture, of braided and loose hair, of remarkably the handled folds in her drapery. Clothed—not *draped*—in visionary material, but clad in *quattrocento* dress, she is more in possession of her powers; nude, in what is usually her mode, he has abandoned his.

The satyr who blows the conch shell is unable to awaken Mars; neither is the swarm of wasps nesting in the tree on the right of the painting. (Their presence may in addition allude to the Vespucci family—wasps are *vespe* in Italian—the wedding of one of whose members might have occasioned Botticelli's painting. On the other hand, they might, as bees, promise the sweetness of the honey of eloquence, or Venus's persuasive powers, as well as erotic bliss.) The satyrs' playing with the instruments of warfare is an even more potent image of arms abandoned than the more traditional one of heroic poetry, hanging them up on a tree.

Rachel Hadas reads the painting in the early 1990s with an eye at once pictorially sophis-ticated, interpretively witty, and poetically masterful. That eye is a particular kind of educat-ed one characteristic of her generation, having been introduced by art-history courses to for-mal as well as iconographic pictorial questions. But as a poet, she would want to make her own kind of ad hoc iconographic sense out of any formal elements that present themselves for meditation. The big "W"-form that the paired bodies in the painting might be seen to compose (traced by Venus's head, down her left arm, up and down Mars's right leg, and up again along his body and head), she implicitly breaks down into its component, the repeated "V." Which is, given the inevitable program of the role of the two gods, another mark of the Victory of "Vigilant Venus" over the sleeping god of "Violence"; her emblematic form is her nature, and emblazoned in her name: "V-ness." It is the traces of her power in the very struc-tural and gestural patterns of the painting, all the "V"-forms seen perhaps as deriving from the hidden one, the "one more / labial gilded / entry between her waist and knee," that her poem celebrates. A trace of the true dialectic here is retained, toward the end, in the observa-tion that Mars is "drained by amorous combat," the traditional paradox of the strife that love indeed *is* being hereby acknowledged. Yet ultimately her formal triumph represents her moral one: in repose, Mars partakes in a more hard-edged way of her softer-angled pattern.

This poem is seriously and playfully concerned with the little satyrs, domesticating them momentarily to the level of low comedy in a kind of poetic mimesis of their mode of play. They use War's instruments as toys: she toys with their identity ("*are* these the couple's children?"—even as it asks this, the poem knows better). Venus's gaze is punningly associated (through the enjambed and thereby underlined "over- / seeing") with that of the painter completing the scene of her dominance: hers is transcendent, his, executive. Hadas's poem plays, too, with the originally passionate agenda (and certainly, ever so in the realm of Venus) of the sapphic meter whose stress-accented version it so elegantly employs. At the end, it asserts its own ecphrastic hegemony, reminding us that even the formal analysis of pictorial pattern will resort to terms like "rhyming" to describe similar patterns such as parallel curves or angles. And ultimately, it asserts its own modernity by implicitly claiming the painting as the vision of a Paterian sort of present moment, frozen in time—a sort of snapshot, with a "deferral / of ever after."

JOHN HOLLANDER

Effet de Neige

for Andrew Forge

SAYING:

Figures of light and dark, these two are walking
The winter road from the St. Simeon farm
Toward something that the world is pointing toward
At the white place of the road's vanishing
Between the vertex that the far-lit gray
Of tree-dividing sky finally comes down to
And the wide arrowhead the road itself
Comes up with as a means to its own end.
Père and Mère Chose could be in conversation
Or else, like us, sunk into some long gaze
Unreadable from behind—they are well down
The road, but not far enough ahead
For any part of them we can make out
To have been claimed by what we see of what
They move against, or through, or by, or toward.
Toward . . . that seems to be the whispered question
That images of roads, whether composed
By the design of our own silent eyes
Or by the loud hand of painting, always puts.
Where does this all end? What is the vanishing
Point, after all, when finally one reaches
The ordinary, wide scene which begins
To reach out into its own vanishing
From there. Toward . . .

SEEING:

:   :   :   :   :

SAYING:

Yes. You'd want that said, (if you
Want anything said at all, which I still doubt)
—The place the road ends, that patch of white paint
marked with a dark stroke from the left, encroached

339

CLAUDE MONET, *La Route de la ferme St.-Siméon*

Upon from the right by far trees, that white place
Sits at the limit of a kind of world
That only you and I can know. Les deux
Choses, Mère and Père, undreaming even of fields
Of meaning like these—the world created by
That square—Oh, 56 x 56
Centimeters—that the height of the canvas
Cuts out of its width (81). Unfair
To mark that square, perhaps: were Mère and Père
Chose to walk out of it, they'd have to pass
Out of the picture of life, as it were, out
Through the back of the picture at the patch of white
At the end of the road. Even if they are staring
Down the long course of the gray slush of things
How can they get the point of how a world
Like theirs ends? From what distant point of vision
Would their world not remain comfortably
Coextensive with everything? How could they know?
What can we know of whatever picture-plane
Against which we have been projected? What . . .

SEEING:

:   :   :   :   :

SAYING:
Oh, I know. The snow. The effective snow
Of observation lying on the ground
Given by nature will soak into it.
Wheel tracks entrench themselves in snow, yet painted
Traces of those deep cuts lie thickly upon
The high whites spread over the buried earth.
Shadows keep piling up as surfaces
Are muffled into silence that refuses
To pick up even the quickening of wind
In dense bare branches, or the ubiquitous
Snaps of ice cracking in the hidden air.
Silence. Your way of being. Your way of seeing
Still has to be intoned, as in a lonely
Place of absorbing snow, itself to be
Seen. What you know is only manifest
When I am heard, and what I say is solely
A matter of getting all that right . . .

SEEING:

:   :   :   :   :

SAYING:
I know,
I've drifted somewhat from the distant heart
Of the matter of snow here. Both of us have grasped
That patch of white at the very end of the road
As it sits there like an eventual
Sphinx of questioning substance, or a sort
Of Boyg of Normandy . . .

SEEING:

:   :   :   :   :

SAYING:
Yes. The obvious
Standing in the way of the truth. A white
Close at the end of distance the two Chose
People might see to be the opening
Out of the road into a way across
Wide, whited fields, a way unframed at last
By trees—or might see as the masonry
Of a far barn, just where the road curves sharply
Right, and appears from here to be overcome
By what it seems to have moved toward. In any
Event, the end of the painted road ends up
In white, in paint too representative
Of too much truth to do much more than lie
High on this surface, guarding the edge of Père
And Mère Chose's square of world, even as they
—Now that you notice it—have just moved past
The edge of that other square cut from the right
Side of the painting, the world of that wise, white,
Silent patch of ultimate paint. You are
Grateful, I know, for just such compensations,
That neither the motionless farm couple trudging
Toward the still dab of white that oscillates
From point to point of meaning—open? closed?—
Nor, indeed, the bit of paint itself can know of.

SEEING:

:   :   :   :   :

SAYING:

Mère and Père Chose are walking away from the
Two of us, Docteur and Madame Machin, who stand
Away from their profundity of surface.

SEEING:

:   :   :   :   :

SAYING:

The truth, blocking the path of the obvious.

Monet's painting of 1867 of a scene at the Saint-Siméon farm in his native Normandy engages a favorite motif of his at the time. Subtitled *Effet de neige* (or "snow effect"), the painting calls up the remarks of an unidentified contemporary commentator, translated by Andrew Forge in his remarkable book on Monet, who describes "an early encounter with Monet in the open air" by observing, "We perceive a foot stove, then an easel, then a gentleman swathed in three overcoats, his hands in gloves, his face half frozen: it was Monet studying a snow effect. Art has its brave soldiers." The author of the poem in question had been engaged, on several occasions while seeing the picture in the Fogg Museum at Harvard, by the small white brush stroke, angled at about forty-five degrees from right to left, at the very end of the road. In this meditation, not merely upon the painting but upon the possible rationale of poetic ecphrasis itself, the brush stroke—in high, almost gleaming white, lying palpably on the painted surface—became rather important. The poem is a strangely notional dialogue between the faculties of observation and discourse, standing in pretty much for painting and poetry. Certainly, images have to put up with a great deal: much is said of them, about them, and they suffer in silence. This poem acknowledges the problem of having to be spoken for.

The putative speaker of the poem, "Saying," is energetically ecphrastic and at the same time conscious of "Seeing's" implicit skepticism about the authenticity even of poetic language in the realm of the truly visual. His own response to this awareness helps to shape the ways in which the painting is scanned. A few glosses might be given: "Mère and Père Chose," the names given by the speaker to the two figures on the road, would be in vernacular English, "Mom and Pop Whatsisface"; similarly, Saying's name for himself and his mute consort Seeing—"Docteur and Madame Machin"—employs a slightly tonier idiom, also meaning "whatsisname." The great Boyg was the huge, black, occluding presence barring Peer Gynt's way in Ibsen's poetic drama. The word "obvious" occurs here in full consciousness of its earlier meaning (from its etymon, *ob + via*): "standing in the way of," "blocking the path of or toward." And since the poem otherwise discusses itself, and its genre, little more should be said save that it was in the poet's own effort to understand what he had done in the poem that the present book was conceived and written.

APPENDIX

I append here a selective list of actual ecphrastic poems in English not discussed or mentioned in this book. They are all directed toward extant and recoverable works of art, and the list does not include what I have called capriccios, or gallery poems, or those to or about an artist. Most of them have been important for me in one way or another, and only reasonable limitations of space prevented me from dealing with them. I have omitted a long list of additional poems on his own work, and on those of other artists, by Dante Gabriel Rossetti.

Aiken, Conrad, "Cirque d'Hiver"
Bishop, Elizabeth, "Large Bad Picture," "Poem"
Bishop, Morris, "Museum Thoughts"
Bolt, Thomas, "Thomas Eakins: Max Schmitt in a Single Scull"
Bowers, Edgar, "Of an Etching"
Browning, Robert, "Lines for a Painting by Leighton," from "Pauline" (lines on the *Andromeda* of
    Polidoro da Caravaggio)
Campbell, Thomas "Lines: On a Picture of a Girl in the Attitude of Prayer, by the Artist Grus,
    in the Possession of Lady Stepney"
Corn, Alfred, "On Looking at a Print by Fairfield Porter," from "Pages for a Voyage"
Cowper, William, "Sonnet to George Romney, Esq., on His Picture of Me in Crayons, etc.,"
    "On Flaxman's Penelope"
Dana, Richard Henry, "The Chanting Cherubs"
Davie, Donald, "Limited Achievement"
de la Mare, Walter, "Portrait of a Boy: Velazquez"
Dugan, Alan, "On Alexander and Aristotle, on a Black-and-Red Greek Plate"
Enright, D. J., "Henri Rousseau's 'Tropical Storm with Tiger,' or Home and Colonial"
Feldman, Irving, "Artist and Model," "All of Us Here"
Flecker, James Elroy, "On Turner's Polyphemus," "Resurrection"
Garrigue, Jean, "The Giralda," "An Improvisation on the Theme of the Lady and the Unicorn"
Gilder, Richard Watson, "Robert Gould Shaw (The Monument by Augustus Saint-Gaudens)"
Greger, Debora, "Two Rodin Torsos"
Hall, Donald, "Reclining Figure (after Henry Moore)"
Halleck, Fitz-Greene, "Red-Jacket"
Hearne, Vicki, "St. Luke Painting the Virgin"
Hecht, Anthony, "Apples for Paul Suttman"
Henley, William Ernest, "Ballade of a Toyokuni Colour-Print"
Hine, Daryl, "The Wreath"

Hollander, John, "Edward Hopper's Seven A.M. (1948)," "A Statue of Something," "Ave aut Vale," "An Old Engraving," "The Altarpiece Finished"

Hollander, Martha, "Ogata Kôrin on His Field of Irises"

Hope, A. D., "Massacre of the Innocents: After Cornelis van Haarlem," "Circe: After the Painting by Dosso Dossi," "Gauguin's Menhir, Tahiti"

Howard, Richard, "Thebais," "The Giant on Giant-Killing: Homage to the Bronze *David* of Donatello," "Personal Values," "Attic Red-Figure Calkyx, Revelling in Progress, Circa 510 B.C."

Jarrell, Randall, "The Bronze David of Donatello," "A Picture in the Paper"

Jennings, Elizabeth, "Mantegna's Agony in the Garden," "Michelangelo's First Pietà," "Caravaggio's 'Narcissus' in Rome," "The Nature of Prayer"

Justice, Donald, "Anonymous Drawing"

Keats, John, "On Seeing the Elgin Marbles," "On a Leander Gem Which Miss Reynolds, My Kind Friend Gave Me"

Kees, Weldon, "On a Painting by Rousseau"

Kennedy, X. J., "Nude Descending a Staircase (after Duchamp)"

Kirchwey, Karl, "Riace Bronze"

Lamb, Charles, "On the Same [*The Virgin of the Rocks*]," "Lines, Suggested by a Picture of Two Females by Leonardo da Vinci," "Lines, On the Same Picture Being Removed to Make Place for a Portrait of a Lady by Titian"

Lawrence, D. H., "Michelangelo"

Lowell, James Russell, "On a Portrait of Dante by Giotto"

Lowell, Robert, from *Day by Day,* "Marriage"; also many sonnets in *Notebook*

Merrill, James, "The Willoware Cup," "Hindu Illumination"

Monroe, Harriet, "Fra Angelico's Annunciation"

Moore, T. Sturge, "From Pallas and the Centaur by Sandro Botticelli," "From Pygmalion, by Edward Burne-Jones," "From Sappho's Death: Three Pictures by Gustave Moreau"

Moss, Howard, "A Lesson for Van Gogh," "Around the Fish"

Nemerov, Howard, "Brueghel: The Triumph of Time"

O'Hara, Frank, "On Seeing Larry Rivers' *Washington Crossing the Delaware* at the Museum of Modern Art," "Digression on 'Number 1, 1948'"

Prince, F. T., "Soldiers Bathing"

Prior, Matthew, "A Flower Painted by Simon Verelst," "Picture of Seneca Dying in a Bath, by Jordain. . . . etc.," "Seeing the Duke of Ormond's Picture at Sir Godfrey Kneller's"

Rich, Adrienne, "Pictures by Vuillard"

Rukeyser, Muriel, "Waterlily Fire"

Santayana, George, "Before a Statue of Achilles," "On an Unfinished Statue by Michael Angelo in the Bargello, Called an Apollo or a David"

Schwartz, Delmore, "Seurat's Sunday Afternoon along the Seine"

Scott, Winfield Townley, "Grant Wood's *American Landscape*"

Southey, Robert, "Stanzas, Addressed to W. R. [*sic*] Turner, Esq. R.A. on His View of the Lago Maggiore from the Town of Arona," "On a Picture by J. M. Wright, Esq."

Stickney, Trumbull, "On the Concert of Giorgione"

Swenson, May, "The Tall Figures of Giacometti," "De Chirico: Superimposed Interiors," "Merry Christmas. You're on the Right"

Symons, Arthur, "Studies in Strange Sins (After Beardsley's Designs)"

Turner, J. M. W., verses accompanying *Thomson's Aeolian Harp*

Van Duyn, Mona, "Goya's 'Two Old People Eating Soup'," "The Pietà, Rhenish, 14th c., The Cloisters"

Warren, Rosanna, "Wreckers: Coast of Northumberland," "Interior at Petworth: From Turner"

Wheelwright, John Brooks, "A Twin Toilet after Rowlandson"

Wilbur, Richard, "L'Etoile (Degas, 1876)" "Ceremony," "A Dutch Courtyard," "Museum Piece," "The Giaour and the Pasha"

Williams, William Carlos, "The Dance," from *Paterson* V [on Brueghel and on the Unicorn Tapestries]

Wordsworth, William, "To B. R. Haydon, On Seeing His Picture of Napoleon Buonaparte on the Island of St. Helena," "Before a Picture of the Baptist, by Raphael, in the Gallery at Florence," "The Pillar of Trajan"

Yeats, William Butler, "On a Picture of a Black Centaur by Edmund Dulac," "A Bronze Head," "Lapis Lazuli"

Notes to the Introduction

1. Jean H. Hagstrum, in his splendid and important *The Sister Arts* (Chicago, 1958), 18, first proposed using the term "iconic" for any poem which "contemplates a real or imaginary work of art." I have continued to use the older and more currently used term "ecphrasis" throughout (domesticating it, as I did not in my earlier writing on the subject, with the latinized spelling) and, particularly, to distinguish notional and actual modes, the particular concern of this book being the latter. Alastair Fowler, in his taxonomy of genres in *Kinds of Literature* (Cambridge, MA, 1982), 115–18, discusses the poem on a work of art as a subgenre. See also the excellent theoretical discussion of interpretations of the term, with a brief overview of recent critical constructions of it, in Grant F. Scott, "The Rhetoric of Dilation: Ekphrasis and Ideology," *Word & Image* 7 (1991): 301–10.

2. Murray Krieger, *Ekphrasis: The Illusion of the Natural Sign* (Baltimore, 1992), 67–114, has a long theoretical discussion of *enargeia*, distinguishing between a more Aristotelian and a more Longinian sense of the concept (what he calls *Enargeia I* and *Enargeia II*). For a good account of the use of *enargeia* in Renaissance rhetorical theory, see M. Hazard, "The Anatomy of 'Liveliness' as a Concept in the Renaissance," *Journal of Aesthetics and Art Criticism* 33 (1975): 407–18. See David Cast, *The Calumny of Apelles* (New Haven, 1981), for a detailed investigation of this. There is an excellent general discussion of this question by David Rosand in "Ekphrasis and the Generation of Images," *Arion* 1.1 (1990): 61–105.

3. *Leon Battista Alberti on Painting*, tr. John R. Spencer (New Haven, 1966), 90–91.

4. A fine discussion of these poems in relation to Rubens's painting can be found in Amy Golahny, "Rubens' *Hero and Leander* and Its Poetic Progeny," *Yale University Art Gallery Bulletin* (1990): 21–38, although I must disagree with her suggestion that Vos's alternating long and short lines are emblematic of waves. There is a great amount of seventeenth-century Dutch ecphrastic poetry by Vondel, Vos, and others, and this material deserves a systematic study of its own.

5. Horace, *Ars Poetica* (The art of poetry), ll. 361–65. Text from Loeb Classical Library (1929). For a splendid discussion of the history of some of the consequences of Horace's phrase up through the eighteenth century, see Hagstrum, 3–15; also, Renssalaer W. Lee, *Ut Pictura Poesis: The Humanistic Theory of Painting* (New York, 1967).

6. There is a very helpful edition of the *Paragone,* with an English translation, introduction, and detailed commentary by Irma A. Richter (Oxford, 1949). The remark above is on p. 59; see also another version of this, likewise privileging the visual, on p. 58: "Painting is poetry which is seen and not heard, and poetry is a painting which is heard and not seen."

7. David Scott in *Pictorialist Poetics* (Cambridge, 1988), chapters 5 and 6, writes with great imagination and perception about the rhetoric of what, following Théophile Gautier, he calls "transposition" in French poetry of the nineteenth century. Transposition and, in particular, formal analogy become a more complex matter in twentieth-century poetry and art. Kinds of contingent

quasi-ecphrastic relations do so as well; for example, Guillaume Apollinaire's "Les Fenêtres" alludes to Robert Delaunay's series of paintings of that name, but is much more of an extended "capriccio" on Delaunay's work generally, the contents of his studio, and his theories of color and simultaneity. There is a penetrating discussion of this in Albert Cook's *Figural Choice in Poetry and Art* (Hanover, 1985), 64–85. Analogous are the relations of William Carlos Williams's "the rose is obsolete" (from *Spring and All*) to a Juan Gris painting, and that poem's development of verbal tropes of cubist reorganizations of aspects of objects and propounding of a higher order of pictorial unity.

8. Murray Krieger, in his original article of 1967, "*Ekphrasis* and the Still Movement of Poetry, or *Laokoön* Revisited" (reprinted as the appendix to his *Ekphrasis*), is most concerned to correct what he feels are false analogies of spatialization in modernist literary theory. He also expands the concept of an ecphrastic "dimension of literature [which] reveals itself whenever the poem takes on the 'still' elements of plastic form which we normally attribute to the spatial arts" (266). He is in a sense concerned with a general rhetorical matter here (he might refer to it as a "theoretical" one), much as classicists are concerned with the branch of ecphrastic theory which concerns literary description in its role in oratory as well as in its vividness. But there, too, the matter of pause, if not that of a more modern conception of stillness, is important. Svetlana Alpers in "*Ekphrasis* and Aesthetic Attitudes in Vasari's Lives," *Journal of the Warburg and Courtauld Institutes* 23 (1960): 190–215, did an important and pioneering study of the role of ecphrases in the rhetoric of Vasari's biographical and critical accounts. Also see Hagstrum, 22–27, for an excellent brief summary of some of these issues.

For larger theoretical considerations than the scope of this book allows, I refer the reader to the growing number of fruitful studies that have been appearing in recent years. These include— aside from those by Hagstrum, Cook, Scott, and Krieger already mentioned—W. J. T. Mitchell, *Iconology: Image, Text, Ideology* (Chicago, 1986); James A. W. Heffernan's "Ekphrasis and Representation," *New Literary History* 22.2 (1991): 297–316; Bryan Wolf's "Confessions of a Closet Ekphrastic," *Yale Journal of Criticism* 3.3 (1990): 181–200; and particularly Paul Fry (whose approach to this matter is closely allied to mine and with whom I have had much fruitful discussion), in "The Torturer's Horse: What Poems See in Pictures," to appear in his *A Defense of Poetry* (Stanford, forthcoming). Most instructive are the discussions in Emilie L. Bergman, *Art Inscribed: Essays on Ekphrasis in Spanish Golden Age Poetry*, Harvard Studies in Romance Languages, no. 35 (Cambridge, MA, 1978). I admire particularly Françoise Meltzer's *Salomé and the Dance of Writing* (Chicago, 1987). For matters peculiar to the relations of painting and literature in modernity, see Wendy Steiner, *The Colors of Rhetoric* (Chicago, 1982). Richard L. Stein's *The Ritual of Interpretation* (Cambridge, MA, 1975) is a valuable and important study of Ruskin, Rossetti, and Pater with interesting theoretical implications. An extremely helpful survey and bibliography of work in one historical field can be found in Clark Hulse's "Recent Studies of Literature and Painting in the English Renaissance," *ELH* 15 (1985): 122–40. Although it is not concerned with ecphrastic writing as such, David Freedberg's powerful and comprehensive *The Power of Images: Studies in the History and Theory of Response* (Chicago, 1989) maps out an extensive background to all such discussions.

9. W. J. T. Mitchell, "Ekphrasis and the Other," *South Atlantic Quarterly* 91.3 (1992): 695–720, explores this matter with great energy and wit. It might be added that the introduction to Philostratus's gallery of *Imagines* could be thought of as literature's version of the primal scene of ecphrasis: a traveler, visiting a celebrated collection of paintings, encounters the son of the mas-

ter of the house. On hearing the guest praise the paintings, one by one, the boy asks that the visiting viewer should interpret them (*hermaneuein tas graphas*)—as if ecphrasis were the truest expression of admiration. I think here of Virginia Woolf's remark about Walter Sickert's paintings: "I'd like to possess them for the purpose of describing them." (Quoted by Ronald Paulson, *Literary Landscape: Turner and Constable* [New Haven, 1982], 3.) A central and still important discussion of Philostratus is Karl Lehmann Hartleben, "The *Imagines* of the Elder Philostratus," *Art Bulletin* 23 (1941): 16–44; and there is a lively critical one by Michel Conan, "The *Imagines* of Philostratus," *Word & Image* 3.2 (1987): 162–71.

10. The fashionable use of "gaze" in critical studies of film and photography, as well as of the painting of the eighteenth and nineteenth centuries, seems to have come, perhaps via Georges Bataille and Jacques Lacan, from Sartre's pages on *le regard* in *L'Etre et le Néant*, but was originally Englished by Hazel Barnes in her 1956 version as "the look."

11. Plato, *Republic*, book 10, 602. There is some disagreement about the interpretation of the degrees of removal in this passage.

12. See Thorleif Borman, *Hebrew Thought Compared with Greek*, tr. Jules L. Moreau (New York, 1970), 74–90.

13. There is a fine brief discussion of the ecphrasis of the shield and the work which contains it in Robert Lamberton, *Hesiod* (New Haven, 1988), 138–43.

14. See *Laocoön*, chapter 18, which interestingly compares Homer's lines with the ecphrasis of the shield of Aeneas in *Aeneid*, book 8, whose owner can delight in the images on it, not knowing what they will come to mean for him [*reumque ignarus imagine gaudet*]. It is at this point, too, that Lessing scorns what would become neoclassical ecphrastic tics: "By its eternal 'here is' and 'there is,' 'close by stands' and 'not far off we see,' the description becomes so cold and tedious that all the poetic beauty which a Virgil could give it was required to keep it from becoming intolerable" (*Laocoön*, tr. Edward Allen McCormick [Baltimore, 1984], 96). Also see K. J. Atchity, *Homer's Iliad: The Shield of Memory* (Carbondale, IL, 1978).

15. Theocritus, *Idylls and Epigrams*, tr. Daryl Hine (New York, 1982), 3–4.

16. Thomas G. Rosenmeyer, *The Green Cabinet* (Berkeley, 1969), 91. See also his pointed remarks on ecphrasis in antiquity generally, 192–93.

17. The various images appearing on post-Virgilian cups in subsequent pastoral tradition can be traced up through Milton's elaborate images in his Latin *Epitaphium Damonis*; Rosenmeyer, 305–6, has a useful consideration of these. For a good discussion of an early ecphrastic poem, see J. J. Pollitt, *Art in the Hellenistic Age* (Cambridge, 1986), 20. There is, incidentally, an ecphrasis of an embroidered coverlet with the story of Ariadne in Catullus's poem for the marriage of Peleus and Thetis (64, ll. 50–267).

18. For a lively discussion of this passage see Meltzer, 48–55. There is also the ecphrasis of Aeneas's shield (*Aeneid*, book 8, ll. 630–728; and see note 14, above). It mirrors, albeit prophetically and proleptically, the world of the *Aeneid*, as opposed to that of Achilles, which represents a world beyond that of the *Iliad*. These matters are discussed in great detail and with acute perception in chapters 3, 4, and 8 of Philip R. Hardie, *Virgil's* Aeneid: Cosmos *and* Imperium (Oxford, 1986).

19. Luca Signorelli actually "illustrates" these *intaglie* in a lunette in his *Last Judgment* in the Cathedral of Orvieto. Like Flaxman's shield of Achilles, it is quite anachronistic in the way it real-

izes the notional image, both in form and structure. For a sense of the reliefs in Dante—the scale of the figures in relation to the panel, the degree of depth, the expressiveness not only of gesture but of formal activity of light and dark, etc.—one might well think of Giovanni Pisano. Creighton Gilbert has suggested such an association in his *Poets Seeing Artist's Work: Instances in the Italian Renaissance* (Florence, 1991), 17–32. The reader may fruitfully compare Signorelli's depiction of this scene to Botticelli's and to one in a *quattrocento* miniature in Federigo da Montafeltro's Dante ms., which represents the *intaglie* as a classical relief. See J. J. C. Alexander, *Italian Renaissance Illuminations* (New York, 1977), 90–91. See also Marianne Shapiro, "Ecphrasis in Virgil and Dante," *Comparative Literature* 42 (1990): 97–115. Gilbert's "Boccaccio Looking at Actual Frescoes," in *Poets Seeing Artist's Work*, 167–96, is also of great interest.

20. Sandys also comments here, in full mythographic fig, that the olive may also be "expressing her [Pallas's] virginity, since oil will neither corrupt nor mingle with any other liquor." George Sandys, *Ovid's Metamorphosis*, ed. Karl K. Hulley and Stanley T. Vandersall (Lincoln, NE, 1971), 268. See also Leonard Barkan's superb discussion of the Ovidian passage in his *The Gods Made Flesh* (New Haven, 1986), 1–7.

21. Clark Hulse, *The Rule of Art* (Chicago, 1990), discusses some of these problems with great breadth and with splendid attention to detail, and is highly to be recommended. Stephen Orgel, in "'Counterfeit Presentments': Shakespeare's *Ekphrasis*," in *England and the Continental Renaissance*, ed. Edward Chaney and Peter Mack (Rochester, NY, 1990), 177–84, raises some fascinating theoretical questions about the ways in which verbal descriptions of images in the English Renaissance can seem to validate them. Also see Lucy Gent, *Picture and Poetry, 1560–1620* (Leamington Spa, Warwickshire, 1981). Norman K. Farmer, Jr., *Poets and the Visual Arts in Renaissance England* (Austin, TX, 1984), addresses a variety of aspects of the interrelations. Also see Louis L. Martz, *From Renaissance to Baroque: Essays in Literature and Art* (Columbia, MO, 1991); and Ernest B. Gilman, *The Curious Perspective* (New Haven, 1981), 1–15.

22. The text used here is that of the Arden edition of the *Poems*, ed. F. T. Prince (London, 1960). There is an excellent analysis of these passages by Clark Hulse in *Metamorphic Verse: The Elizabethan Minor Epic* (Princeton, 1981), 175–94. The underlying question of pictorial narrativity generally, and how it is construed by artists and viewers, is usefully considered by Wendy Steiner in *Pictures of Romance* (Chicago, 1988), 1–42.

23. Gent, 54–55, makes a similar, and very acute, observation about this passage.

24. The final outcome for the image of Sinon, by the way, is violent iconoclasm. Lucrece harps further on her identification of Sinon with her rapist Tarquin ("as Priam did him cherish, / So did I Tarquin, so my Troy did perish"); then, brooding on how "Priam's trust false Sinon's tears doth flatter, / That he finds means to burn his Troy with water," she loses all patience and "tears the senseless Sinon with her nails, / Comparing him to that unhappy guest / Whose deed hath made herself herself detest," giving this up only when she realizes that the painted image of a long-dead villain will indeed feel no wounds.

25. The way in which these images variously "mirror" Pierre and Isabel, the principal and incestuous spectators who are also, prophetically and allusively, versions of the subjects of the portraits, is most remarkable. The whole issue of ecphrasis in prose fiction is a fascinating one, particularly with respect to narratology. For example, does narrative pause for ecphrasis as for any description (of, say, natural scene rather than a landscape painting)? In nineteenth-century novels

about artists and their lives (e.g., from Balzac's *Le Chef-d'oeuvre inconnu* on through Hawthorne, James, Zola, Wilde, George Moore, and Kipling's *The Light That Failed*) ecphrases are hardly digressions, but almost as central as descriptions of persons and analyses of character. Interesting, too, is that sometimes whole fictions can be generated by ecphrastic questions: a famous case of a notional one is Longus's *Daphnis and Chloe,* which begins with the description of "an icon, or varied picture, reporting a history of love" in a grove on Lesbos. "There were figured in it young women in the posture of teeming their babes; there were others swaddling children that were exposed, children which by the destiny of draught did then tend their flocks of sheep and goats; there were many shepherds slain; young men banded together; incursions of thieves; impressions of enemies; inroads of armed men." (I quote from George Thornley's translation of 1657.) The author then declares that the story which follows is an interpretation of that picture. This might be compared with Heinrich von Kleist's *The Broken Jug;* in the preface to it, he gives an actual ecphrasis of an engraving (it has been identified as one by J. J. Le Veau after a painting by P. Debucourt) as the source, the starting point of his drama.

26. Ralph Waldo Emerson, "Experience" (Library of America edition, 1983), 490.

27. I quote from J. M. Edmonds's edition of the Anacreontea, in *Elegy and Iambus,* Loeb Classical Library (1931), vol. 2.

28. In act 3 of Kyd's *The Spanish Tragedy,* there is a grim prose scene in which Hieronimo instructs a painter to render what is in effect his own half-maddened vision of the scene of the murder of his son, shadowed with internal projections. It is interesting as a precursor of the later, more particularly satirical, tradition. Also see Mary Tom Osborne, *Advice-to-a-Painter Poems, 1633–1856* (Austin, TX, 1949).

29. See *The Poems of Edmund Waller,* ed. G. Thorn Drury (London, 1893), 335.

30. See also Whitman's early draft "Pictures," and the shorter version of it discussed below, in connection with Whitman's poem directed to a painting by George Inness. There are complex overtones to the notion of "confrontation" of a picture for Whitman, particularly—and unsurprisingly—in the case of a portrait of him. For this, see the strange "Out from Behind This Mask (To Confront a Portrait)," printed in 1876 with a wood engraving by W. J. Linton (after an 1871 photograph by G. C. Potter).

31. Wallace Stevens, *The Letters of Wallace Stevens,* ed. Holly Stevens (New York, 1966), 652–53.

32. Stevens, *Letters,* 649.

33. Alexander Pope, *Moral Essays,* Epistle 2.5–16.

34. "To a Lady," 17–20. An exemplary notional gallery in prose can be found in no. 83 of *The Spectator.* The notional gallery with a sequence of notional ecphrases in Tennyson's "The Palace of Art" (ll. 61–126) derives more from Spenser, and perhaps through Thomson's *The Castle of Indolence.* What may be an actual gallery poem from the seventeenth century, depending upon identification of the paintings by Titian in question, is "Upon Some Pieces of Work in York House" by William Lewis, Provost of Oriel College, Oxford, and published in *Parnassus Biceps* (London, 1656).

35. Robert Penn Warren's comments are in his edition of *Selected Poems of Herman Melville* (New York, 1970), 373–74, from which Vedder is also quoted.

36. See the *Greek Anthology* 9.713–42, 793–98. Julian's is no. 738. See Loeb Classical Library, tr. W. R. Paton (London, 1917), 3.392–403. Freedberg touches interestingly on these poems in *The*

Power of Images (Chicago, 1989), 291–94. See also Marino's poems derived from these in *La Galeria*, ed. Mario Pieri, 2 vols. (Padova, 1979), 1.286–87.

37. See also an interesting discussion of this poem by Adrienne Munich in *Andromeda's Chains: Gender and Interpretation in Victorian Literature and Art* (New York, 1989), 97–98.

38. [J. B. L. Warren] Lord de Tabley, *Collected Poems* (1903), 302–3.

39. Many other similarly unidentifiable images include the one invoked by Thomas Carew's "For a Picture Where a Queen Laments over the Tombe of a Slaine Knight": this may indeed have been addressed, as Rhodes Dunlap suggests in his edition of Carew's *Poems* (Oxford, 1948), 254, to a painting by Bresciano known to have been in the king's gallery at Whitehall. Another example is Hart Crane's "Interludium" addressed to Gaston Lachaise's *La Montagne*, a bulky, maternal female nude, a self "that heavens climb to measure": since a good many different versions of the piece exist, it is a matter of acute art-historical and biographical detective work to determine exactly which one Crane had seen before writing the poem. Swinburne's various rondels on "A Night-Piece by Millet" (I have not identified this yet), "A Flower by Fantin" (there are so many Fantin-Latour flower pieces), "A Landscape by Courbet," could presumably be tracked down or at least guessed at. (On the other hand, Swinburne's "Hermaphroditus," addressed to the Hellenistic piece in the Louvre, is one of those evanescent ecphrases that gives no visual reading of the image at all, but chants only of the mythical personage it represents.) Similarly, Arthur Symons's "For a Picture of Rossetti" and "For a Picture of Watteau," as well as his poem on a Dieppe painting of Walter Sickert, could each invoke one of many paintings.

40. Erwin Panofsky, "Titian's *Allegory of Prudence*," in *Meaning in the Visual Arts* (New York, 1955), 148. Also see the discussion of emblems and *imprese* by Michael Leslie, "The Dialogue between Bodies and Souls: Pictures and Poesy in the English Renaissance," *Word & Image* 1.1 (1985): 16–30.

41. Dick Higgins, *Pattern Poetry* (Albany, NY, 1987), explores an immense range of examples of shaped poems in many languages. There is some theoretical discussion of the mode in my own "The Poem in the Eye," in *Vision and Resonance*, 2nd ed. (New Haven, 1985), 245–68; and in the introduction to the reissue of my *Types of Shape* (New Haven, 1991), ix-xvii, which concludes with a selected bibliography.

42. *Poetics* 1454b.10–11; and see the discussion in Hagstrum, 6–8. An interesting case of addresses to a portrait which link it to a precursor image—that of poems by Lope de Vega and Francisco Lopez de Zarate—is treated by Larry L. Ligo, in "Two Seventeenth-Century Poems Which Link Rubens' Equestrian Portrait of Philip IV to Titian's Equestrian Portrait of Charles V," *Gazette des Beaux-Arts*, ser. 6, vol. 75 (May-June 1970): 244–54. Harold Goddard, in *The Meaning of Shakespeare* (Chicago, 1951), 1.4, quotes Samuel Butler to the effect that "A great portrait is always more a portrait of the painter than of the painted." The praise of portraiture, groping with the apparently unsayable, frequently has recourse to wit, as in Bassanio's ecphrasis of the image in the leaden casket in *The Merchant of Venice*, 3.2 (115–29 in Riverside Shakespeare Text):

> Fair Portia's counterfeit! What demigod
> Hath come so near creation? Move these eyes?
> Or whether, riding on the balls of mine,
> Seem they in motion? Here are sever'd lips,
> Parted with sugar breath; so sweet a bar
> Should sunder such sweet friends. Here in her hairs

> The painter plays the spider, and hath woven
> A golden mesh t'entrap the hearts of men
> Faster than gnats in cobwebs. But her eyes—
> How could he see to do them? Having made one,
> Methinks it should have power to steal both his
> And leave itself unfurnish'd, Yet look how far
> The substance of my praise doth wrong this shadow
> In underprizing it, so far this shadow
> Doth limp behind the substance . . .

43. William Butler Yeats, *The Trembling of the Veil*, in *Autobiographies* (London, 1956), 292. In this passage Yeats contrasts the animation of pose and drapery with the deadness in a Sargent portrait of Woodrow Wilson.

44. Michael Baxandall, *Giotto and the Orators* (Oxford, 1971), 93.

45. Baxandall, 94.

46. Roman Jakobson discusses the matter with respect to Blake, Paul Klee, and the Douanier Rousseau, and raises important theoretical questions, in "On the Verbal Art of William Blake and Other Poet-Painters," in *Language and Literature* (Cambridge, MA, 1987), 479–503.

47. Kenneth Gross, in *The Dream of the Moving Statue* (Ithaca, NY, 1993), 92–99, considers Michelangelo's quatrain in great detail. See also James M. Saslow's note on his translation of these lines in *The Poetry of Michelangelo* (New Haven, 1991), 419.

48. The text is from *Poems*, ed. John O. Hayden (New Haven, 1981), 1.666–67. The alternative version—acknowledging *grato* instead of *caro* in one version of the original text—goes: "Grateful is Sleep, my life in stone bound fast / More grateful still; while wrong and shame shall last, / On me can time no happier state bestow / Than to be left unconscious of the woe. / Ah, then, lest you awaken me, speak low."

49. An echo of Thomas Campbell's *The Pleasures of Hope* ("Degenerate Trade!" "Where is thy market now?") is pointed out in the excellent discussion of these lines in relation to the painting in the collection edited by Jack Lindsay, *The Sunset Ship* (London, 1966), 22–25, 50–53. This book offers a useful consideration of the literary backgrounds of Turner's verses generally. Also see Martin Butlin and Evelyn Joll, *The Paintings of J. M. W. Turner*, 2 vols., rev. ed. (London, 1984), 236–37. Andrew Wilton, *Painting and Poetry: Turner's 'Verse Book' and His Work of 1804–1812* (London, 1990), is generally useful.

50. See the remarks on these lines in Wilton, 135; the painting is Butlin and Joll, no. 97.

51. Edmund Waller, *Poems*, ed. G. Thorn Drury (New York, 1893), 203.

52. Iain Fletcher, in his edition of *The Collected Poems of Lionel Johnson*, 2nd ed. (New York, 1982), lxiv.

53. Roman Jakobson, "The Statue in Pus[h]kin's Poetic Mythology," in *Language and Literature* (Cambridge, MA, 1988), 318–67. Kenneth Gross's remarkable and imaginative *The Dream of the Moving Statue* is of great interest in this regard. Also of great interest is Michael North's *The Final Sculpture: Public Monuments and Modern Poets* (Ithaca, 1985).

54. Leo Steinberg informs me that there were a number of poems, for example, addressed to pieces of Donatello, raising the issue of homosexuality.

55. Filippo Baldinucci, *Vita di Gian Lorenzo Bernini* (1682), ed. Sergio Samek Ludovici (Milan, 1948), 18.

56. Herman Melville, *Collected Poems,* ed. Howard P. Vincent (Chicago, 1947), 254. In Melville's *Journal up the Straits* for January 3, 1857, a remarkable long entry anticipates much of what is in the poem, including anecdotal material about entering the pyramid. He remarks that it "looks larger midway than from top or bottom. Precipice on precipice, cliff on cliff." This, by the way, echoes a poetic device (see Byron's use of it below, p. 57) which the poem eschews. Most interesting—in view of the possibility that Jaweh's "I AM THAT I AM" lurks behind the Pyramid's utterance in the poem—are these observations: "It was in these pyramids that was conceived the idea of Jehovah. Terrible mixture of the cunning and awful. Moses learned in all the lore of the Egyptians. The idea of Jehovah born here." See *Journal up the Straits, October 11, 1856–May 5, 1857,* ed. Raymond M. Weaver (New York, 1935), 57–58.

57. The facade is favored in Renaissance and baroque poetry. Sometimes it can be interestingly moralized, as in Thomas Carew's "country-house" poem, "To My Friend G. N., from Wrest," where he privileges life and breath—in a mode following Ben Jonson's "To Penshurst"—over stone, however imposing: thus (and I modernize spelling here) even in an interior

> No sumptuous chimney-piece of shining stone
> Invites the stranger's eye to gaze upon,
> And coldly entertains his sight, but clear
> And cheerful flames cherish and warm him here;
> No Doric or Corinthian pillars grace
> With imagery this structure's naked face;
> The lord and lady of this place delight
> Rather to be in act, than seem in sight.

The lord and lady of the house are almost seen to stand in place of the vertical columns, in welcome. On this kind of poem generally, see William Alexander McClung's *The Country House in English Renaissance Poetry* (Berkeley, 1977), 46–118; and the same author's *The Architecture of Paradise* (Berkeley, 1983), 47–100. Giambattista Marino's long *Il Tempio* contains in its first part an elaborate architectural ecphrasis of a notional temple for an enthroned Marie de' Medici (stanzas 20–39); see James V. Mirollo, *The Poet of the Marvelous* (New York, 1963), 37–38, for an account of it.

58. Melville, *Collected Poems,* 248.

59. *Childe Harold's Pilgrimage,* 4.128.

60. 4.155.

61. 4.156–58.

62. Melville, *Collected Poems,* 240. Melville's poems on "Milan Cathedral," the Basilica del Santo in Padua ("In a Church at Padua")—indeed, all of those in the section of *Timoleon* called "Fruit of Travel Long Ago" (*Collected Poems,* 238–54)—are of great interest, and should be considered with these others. Some of them are discussed, mostly with respect to their relation to prose ecphrases in Melville's journals, in several essays in *Savage Eye: Melville and the Visual Arts,* ed. Christopher Sten (Kent, OH, 1992).

63. William Wordsworth, *Ecclesiastical Sonnets,* part 3, nos. 43–45. These poems bear interesting comparison with the octave of the second sonnet of Gerard Manley Hopkins's group "To

Oxford," in which matters of perspective and optical illusion are dominant:

> Thus, I come underneath this chapel-side,
> So that the mason's levels, courses, all
> The vigorous horizontals, each way fall
> In bows about my head, as falsified
> By visual compulsion, till I hide
> The steep-up roof at last behind the small
> Eclipsing parapet; yet above the wall
> The sumptuous ridge-crest leave to poise and ride.

Gerard Manley Hopkins, *Poetical Works*, ed. Norman H. Mackenzie (Oxford, 1990), 72; the editor notes (269) a scholarly suggestion that Oriel Chapel may be the one invoked here. Ellen Eve Frank, *Literary Architecture* (Berkeley, 1979), makes a claim for the chapel at Balliol.

64. Elizabeth Jennings, *Collected Poems* (London, 1986), 44. The poem itself is from the late 1950s.

65. Baldinucci, 18. The translation of the prose is from *The Life of Bernini*, tr. Catherine Enggass (University Park, PA, 1966). Of some interest for baroque fountain poetry is William Strode's "On the Picture of Two Dolphins in a Fountayne"; with a deft but mechanical skill it moralizes upon a fairly obvious paradox:

> These dolphins twisting each on either side
> For joy leapt upp, and gazing there abide;
> And whereas other waters fish do bring,
> Here from the fishes doe the waters spring,
> Who think it is more glorious to give
> Than to receive the juice whereby they live . . .

William Strode, *Poetical Works*, ed. B. Dobell (London, 1907), 46.

66. Alexander Pope, "On the Statue of Cleopatra, Made into a Fountain by Leo the Tenth" (1717), in *Poems*, ed. John Butt (New Haven, 1963), 111.

67. Thomas Warton, *Verses on Sir Joshua Reynolds's Painted Window at New College Oxford*, 2nd ed. (London, 1783). Also, see the discussion of the window in Nicholas Penny, ed., *Reynolds* (New York, 1986), 31.

68. Strode's poem (text from above), together with a consideration of George Herbert on stained-glass windows, is discussed in Gabriel Hammond's wonderful book on seventeenth-century English poetry, *Fleeting Things* (Cambridge, MA, 1990), 271–77. There is also the remarkable, long, anonymous "A Poem, in Defence of the Decent Ornaments of Christ-Church, Oxon., etc." in *Parnassus Biceps*.

69. Alan Trachtenberg in *Reading American Photographs* (New York, 1989), 12–16, discusses the particular aura of the daguerreotype—with its highly reflective surface and somewhat fleeting image—as a special instance.

70. David Ferry, *Strangers* (Chicago, 1983), 45. Ferry's reading totally obliterates one prominent presence in the photograph, as if the poem had decided to let sleeping dogs lie.

71. Scott, *Pictorialist Poetics*, 60–68, discusses this matter with great insight.

72. There are many instances of such verses added by the engraver, frequently Lépicié, of Chardin's paintings; those appended to *The House of Cards* and *Little Girl with Shuttlecock* are very revealing. See Pierre Rosenberg, *Chardin* (Cleveland, 1979), 231–43.

73. I give the text, with a stanza break before the last nine lines, and the italicization of "feel," from later editions.

74. *Greek Anthology*, 16.159–63. Loeb Classical Library (rev. ed., 1971), 5.252–54.

75. Théophile Gautier, *Poésies Complètes*, ed. René Jasinski (Paris, 1932). This is a remarkably interesting precursor of poems like Auden's celebrated "Musée des Beaux Arts" (see below), and I regret that I have no room here for a full discussion of it, and its relation to Gautier's poem on Dürer's *Melencolia I* (also below). See also the attempt to urge pictorial connections with these poems or moments in them in *Émaux et Camées, avec une iconographie rassemblé et commenté par* Madeleine Cottin (Paris, 1968).

76. Herman Melville, *Selected Poems*, ed. Robert Penn Warren (New York, 1968), 141, 372–73. Also see the discussion in Hennig Cohen, *The Battle Pieces of Herman Melville* (New York, 1963), 139, 274–76.

77. Baldinucci, 106–7.

78. Marino, *La Galeria*, 1.71–74. Also see Mirollo, *The Poet of the Marvelous, pace* his claim (47) that "the poet devotes the bulk of the poem to the painting itself, describing it minutely." Jessica Green, in an as yet unpublished paper, has argued that Marino was in fact addressing not the version of the painting in the Pitti Palace, but rather the one in the Hermitage (ca. 1560).

79. Trumbull Stickney, *Poems*, ed. Amberys R. Whittle (New York, 1972), 74. There is a valuable discussion of the appropriateness of sonnet form for ecphrastic poetry—including observations about the sonnet's rectangular appearance, in Stein, *The Ritual of Interpretation*, 159–67. See also Jennifer Wagner's Yale University dissertation (1990) on the sonnet in the nineteenth century, "Jealous of Dead Leaves."

80. Douglas Crase, "Blue Poles," in *The Revisionist* (New York, 1971), 17.

81. Donald Davie, *Collected Poems, 1950–1970* (London, 1972), 61.

82. Richard Howard, "The Chalk Cliffs of Rügen," in *Findings* (New York, 1971), 17.

83. Robert Duncan, *The Opening of the Field* (New York, 1960), 62.

84. John Ashbery, *Selected Poems* (New York, 1985), 188–204. An instructive comparison might be made with James Merrill's digression on Giorgione's *La Tempesta* in the "X" section of *The Book of Ephraim*, which itself is part 1 of *The Changing Light at Sandover* (New York, 1992), 83.

85. From *The Keepsake* (London 1928), 234–41. Edmund Blunden, in *Leigh Hunt: A Biography* (London, 1930), 229, remarks, "These are aphorisms and something more." They are, I think, true prose poems (unlike, say, the Ossianic texts, full of accentual-syllabic, often anapestic, cadences—*vers cachés*—as it were). The publication of Hunt's prose poems antedates that of Aloysius Bertrand's *Gaspard de la Nuit* by two years.

86. See John Sparrow, *Line upon Line* (Cambridge, 1967), for a detailed consideration of this format.

87. Samuel Taylor Coleridge, *Complete Poetical Works*, ed. E. H. Coleridge (Oxford, 1912), 2.842.

Notes to the Gallery

Sadoleto / *Laocoon*

H. H. Brummer, *The Statue Court in the Vatican Belvedere* (Stockholm, 1970), 118–19, quotes some of the Latin verse written about the piece. Also see P. P. Bober and R. O. Rubinstein, *Renaissance Artists and Antique Sculpture* (Oxford, 1986), 152–55; and J. J. Pollitt, *Art in the Hellenistic Age* (Cambridge, 1986), 120ff. My basic texts are Gotthold Ephraim Lessing, *Laocoön*, tr. Edward Allen McCormick (Baltimore, 1984); and J. G. Holland, *The Marble Prophecy and Other Poems* (New York, 1872).

Aretino / Titian et al.

On Titian and Aretino, see the fine article by Mary Rogers, "Sonnets on Female Portraits from Renaissance North Italy," *Word & Image* 2.4 (1986): 291–305; also, Erwin Panofsky, *Studies in Titian* (New York, 1969), 88–90. Hart Crane had the Lescaze drawing—now in the possession of Prof. Langdon Hammer—mounted and hung on the wall; the former owner, Crane's friend Slater Brown, reported this, and quoted Crane's letter about the drawing, in *The Visionary Company: A Magazine of the Twenties* 1–2 (Spring 1982): 68. For Crane's letter to Tate, July 19, 1922, see *The Letters of Hart Crane*, ed. Brom Weber (Berkeley, 1965), 93. Also see Langdon Hammer's superb discussion of Crane's poem in his *Hart Crane and Allen Tate: Janus-Faced Modernism* (Princeton, 1993), 56–62. Richard Howard's poem is from *Misgivings* (New York, 1979); see also Nigel Gosling, *Nadar* (New York, 1976).

Jonson / Elstrack

Jonson apparently had some afterthoughts about the frontispiece poem when he reprinted it in his 1640 folio edition. Most interestingly, line 5, "High" Providence—here alluding to the picture's spatial format—became "Wise"; and line 8, "And the reward, and punishment assured," became a more moralized "When Vice alike in time with Virtue dured." A fine study of such emblematic title pages as this one is by Margery Corbett and Ronald Lightbown, *The Comely Frontispiece* (London, 1979). Also see Walter J. Ong, "From Diagram to Allegory in the Renaissance Mind," *Journal of Aesthetics and Art Criticism* 17.4 (1959): 428.

Lovelace / Lely

There is an elegant and compelling reading of Lovelace's poem by Gerald Hammond in his remarkable *Fleeting Things* (Cambridge, MA, 1990), 91–95. Lely's painting is also discussed, and Lovelace's poem considered as encomium but without regard to the ecphrastic issues dealt with here, by Norman K. Farmer, Jr., *Poets and the Visual Arts in Renaissance England* (Austin, TX, 1984), 53–65. An interesting contrast is provided by Matthew Arnold's labored and uninspired misreading, in "A Picture at Newstead," of a Vandyck portrait in Newstead Abbey, similar in format to the Lely, of the Earl of Arundel and his grandson. Caring mostly to dissociate himself from concern for Lord Byron (born and brought up at Newstead) and romantic poetry in general; mistaking the grandson for a son; and taking as a truth an apocryphal tale of the father having unintentionally killed his son with a blow of rage, Arnold contrives to give this kind of poem a bad name.

ROGERS / *TORSO BELVEDERE*

The quotation from Winckelmann is from *Writings on Art,* ed. David Irwin (London, 1972), 136–37. A note in the 1892 edition of Rogers's *Poetical Works* alludes to a false tradition that the piece was discovered in the Campo di Fiore during the time of Julius II. It was in fact probably discovered in the early fifteenth century on property of the Colonna family in Rome and acquired by the Vatican in the 1530s. And see the discussion in Bober and Rubinstein, 166–68.

WORDSWORTH / BEAUMONT

Wordsworth's ecphrastic sonnet of 1811, "Upon the Sight of a Beautiful Picture, Painted by Sir G. H. Beaumont," had addressed a painting which the poet owned, but is now lost. The relation of this poem to the "Elegiac Stanzas" is discussed, among other interesting questions, by James A. W. Heffernan in "Wordsworth, Constable, and the Poetics of Chiaroscuro" in *Word & Image* 5.3 (1989): 260–77. Also see Geoffrey Hartman, *Wordsworth's Poetry* (New Haven, 1964), 284.

ALLSTON / RAPHAEL

Allston's poem was published in *The Sylphs of the Seasons, and Other Poems* (London, 1813); the text quoted here is from his *Lectures on Art* (New York, 1850). On Allston generally, see Bryan Wolfe, *Romantic Re-Vision* (Chicago, 1982), 3–24. The passage from Coleridge is quoted from a reprint in *Criticism: The Major Texts,* ed. W. J. Bate (New York, 1970), 364–75; and I am grateful to Paul Fry for pointing it out to me. Of interest, too, is Carl Woodring, "What Coleridge Thought of Pictures," in *Images of Romanticism,* ed. Karl Kroeber and William Walling (New Haven, 1978), 91–106.

BYRON / *APOLLO BELVEDERE*

The quotation is from J. J. Winckelmann, *Writings on Art,* ed. David Irwin (London, 1972), 140. Thomson, in this same passage in *Liberty,* invokes *The Dying Gladiator, Laocoön,* and the *Medici Venus.* There is a penetrating discussion of contemporary views of the concatenation of Byron's ecphrases by Bruce Haley, "The Sculptural Aesthetics of *Childe Harold IV,*" *MLQ* 44.3 (1983): 251–66. The anecdote about West is quoted from Van Wyck Brooks, *The Dream of Arcadia: American Writers and Artists in Italy 1760–1915* (New York, 1958), 1–2.

SHELLEY / *MEDUSA*

The text of the Shelley poem is imperfect; I have filled in obvious lacunae with bracketed suggestions. See Neville Rogers, "Shelley and the Visual Arts," *Keats-Shelley Memorial Bulletin* 10 (1959): 9–17. To Mario Praz's celebrated view that the poem "amounts almost to a manifesto of the conception of Beauty peculiar to the Romantics" might be compared that of Hazlitt, in his review of Shelley's *Posthumous Poems* (Edinburgh Review, 1824): "A dull, waterish vapour clouds the aspect of his philosophical poetry, like that which he himself described as hanging over the Medusa's Head of Leonardo da Vinci." Vasari's detailed description of Leonardo's painting of a head of Medusa on a round panel, in a room in which he had assembled "lizards, newts, maggots, snakes, butterflies, locusts, bats and other animals of the kind" (and then, being so absorbed in his painting that he did not notice how the dead animals had begun to stink), does not refer to the painting in question, although there is briefer mention of a subsequent one which may indeed be its prototype. This poem has been discussed in detail by Jerome McGann, "The Beauty of the Medusa," in *Studies in Romanticism* 11 (1972): 3–25; and by Carol Jacobs, "On Looking at Shelley's Medusa," *Yale French Studies* 69 (1985): 163–79.

Drake / Trumbull

The text of Drake's poem is from *The Culprit Fay and Other Poems* (New York, 1835). The critic quoted is Ronald Paulson, in "John Trumbull and the Representation of American Revolution," *SiR* 21 (Fall 1982): 353.

Rossetti / Leonardo

The quotation is from A. Richard Turner, *The Vision of Landscape in Renaissance Italy* (Princeton, 1966), 21. Turner also invokes a notebook entry of Leonardo's about exploring a "great cavern" on the slopes of Etna: "two contrary emotions arose in me, fear and desire—fear of the threatening dark cavern, desire to see whether there were any marvellous things in it."

Rossetti / Titian

See Philipp Fehl, "The Hidden Genre: A Study of the *Concert Champêtre* in the Louvre," *Journal of Aesthetics and Art Criticism* 16.2 (1957): 153–60. Richard Wollheim, *Painting as an Art* (Princeton, 1987), 312. There are fine discussions of the poem by Richard L. Stein in *The Ritual of Interpretation* (Cambridge, MA, 1975), 19–23; and by Jonathan Freedman in *Professions of Taste: British Aestheticism and Commodity Culture* (Stanford, 1990), 20–24. In regard to the last two lines, Stein (133) reminds us that "Rossetti's sonnets for pictures have no independent titles apart from the initial reference to the names of the paintings 'for' which they are written." Also see Maryan Wynn Ainsworth, *Dante Gabriel Rossetti and the Double Work of Art* (New Haven, 1976), 5; and Michael Kenneth Baquette, "Dante Gabriel Rossetti: The Synthesis of Picture and Poem," *Hartford Studies in Literature* 4 (November 3, 1972): 216–18. Rossetti's and his brother's comments on the poem are in the *Works*, ed. W. M. Rossetti (London, 1911), 665.

E. B. Browning / Powers

Donald Martin Reynolds, *Hiram Powers and His Ideal Sculpture* (New York, 1977), is the most detailed and learned study of the sculptor. Also see Sylvia F. Crane, *White Silence: Greenough, Powers, and Crawford, American Sculptors in Nineteenth-Century Italy* (Coral Gables, FL, 1972). Most useful for me—and from which I quote bits of newspaper material and a few words from a letter of Powers to E. W. Stoughton—was Samuel A. Robertson and William H. Gerdts, "The Greek Slave" in *Museum*, n.s. 17, nos. 1, 2 (1965). It reprints a good deal of bad American verse in praise of the statue. See also an interesting discussion of this poem by Adrienne Munich in *Andromeda's Chains: Gender and Interpretation in Victorian Literature and Art* (New York, 1989), 138–39. The Richard Henry Wilde poem is in Edward L. Tucker, *Richard Henry Wilde: His Life and Selected Poems* (Athens, GA, 1966).

Browning / Michelangelo

The Freud essay, "The Moses of Michelangelo," is in *Collected Papers* (London, 1925), 4.257–87. There is a fine discussion of it in Kenneth Gross, *The Dream of the Moving Statue* (Ithaca, 1993), 184–97.

BROWN / BROWN

Brown in 1854: "This work representing an out-door scene without sunlight, I painted it chiefly out of doors when the snow was lying on the ground. The madder ribbons of the bonnet took me four weeks to paint." *Pre-Raphaelite Diaries and Letters*, ed. W. M. Rossetti (London, 1900), 112. Most important, see Ford M. Ford, *Ford Madox Brown: A Record of His Life and Work* (London, 1896), 100–101; also, Raymond Lister, *Victorian Narrative Paintings* (New York, 1966), 27.

LECONTE DE LISLE / *VENUS DE MILO*

See Martin Robinson, *A History of Greek Art* (Cambridge, 1975), 1.553–55; the Heine passage is quoted from Hal Draper's translation of *The Complete Poems* (Boston, 1982), 696. The Lazarus sonnet is from *The Poems of Emma Lazarus* (Boston, 1888). For a theoretically oriented discussion of Vallejo's poem, with some reflections on the matter of *ut pictura poesis* in his poetry, see Christiane von Buelow, "Vallejo's *Venus de Milo* and the Ruins of Language," *PMLA* 104.1 (January 1989): 41–52; she points out the importance of the punning sense of *lacear* (= to adorn, beribbon). Also, Jean Franco, *César Vallejo* (Cambridge, 1976), 87–92, was very helpful on this poem. And I have learned much over the years from the brilliant discussion of the concept of fragmentation in Thomas McFarland, *Romanticism and the Forms of Ruin* (Princeton, 1981), 3–55, 382–418.

BAUDELAIRE / CALLOT

The best treatment of Baudelairean ecphrasis is by David Scott, *Pictorialist Poetics: Poetry and the Visual Arts in Nineteenth-Century France* (Cambridge, 1988), 67–68; the whole discussion of poems and pictures on pp. 38–70 is most instructive. Also see the commentary on the poem discussed here in the *Pléiade* edition of Baudelaire, 864–66. Of related interest is Pierre-George Castex, *Baudelaire Critique d'Art* (Paris, 1969). Paul de Man made some acute observations about Baudelaire and Callot that are included in the second edition of his *Blindness and Insight* (Minneapolis, 1983), 281–82.

LAZARUS / BARTHOLDI

Some useful information about the statue can be found in Willadene Price, *Bartholdi and the Statue of Liberty* (Chicago, 1959); and about Emma Lazarus, in Dan Vogel, *Emma Lazarus* (Boston, 1980). The passage from Kafka is quoted from Edwin Muir's translation (Norfolk, CT, 1940). May Swenson's poem first appeared in *A Cage of Spines* (New York, 1958). And, for a parting glimpse of the statue, here are the concluding lines of Thom Gunn's "Iron Landscapes (and the Statue of Liberty)," from *Jack Straw's Castle* (New York, 1976):

> From here you can glimpse her downstream, her far charm,
> Liberty, tiny woman in the mist
> —You cannot see the torch—raising her arm
> Lorn, bold, as if saluting with her fist.

SWINBURNE / WHISTLER

Stanley Weintraub, in *Whistler* (New York, 1974), 98, reports that "Whistler actually had Swinburne's poem printed on gold paper and pasted to the frame" and had two stanzas printed in the exhibition catalogue. Also, a letter from Swinburne to Whistler, April 2, 1865, says of the lines that "Gabriel praises them highly." See Swinburne's *Letters,* ed. Cecil Lang (New Haven, 1959), 1.119.

MELVILLE / TURNER

On the Turner painting, see Martin Butlin and Evelyn Joll, *The Paintings of J. M. W. Turner,* 2 vols., rev. ed. (New Haven, 1984), 1.229–31. The quotation from Ruskin can be found in the Cook and Wedderburn edition of his *Literary Works* (London, 1912), 13.171–72. A fine commentary on Melville's *Battle-Pieces* is to be found in the selected edition of his poems edited by Robert Penn Warren (New York, 1970); and all readers of Melville's poetry must be grateful to Hennig Cohen for his edition of *The Battle-Pieces of Herman Melville* (New York, 1963).

PIATT / CRAWFORD

George Cochrane Hazelton, *The American Capitol* (New York, 1902), 64–65, quotes the letters from Crawford and Jefferson Davis. Also see Sylvia F. Crane, *White Silence* (Coral Gables, FL, 1972), 381–85. Whitman's poems are "Washington's Monument, February, 1885," and "Red Jacket (from Aloft)."

THOMSON ("B. V.") / DÜRER

John Ruskin, *Modern Painters* (New York, [1871]), vol. 5, pt. 9, chap. 4. Erwin Panofsky, *Albrecht Dürer* (Princeton, 1943), 1.158–71. John Landseer, *Lectures on the Art of Engraving* (London, 1807), 215.; the French text of Gautier's poem is given in the appendix.

ROSSETTI / BOTTICELLI

The Ovid is from the *Fasti* 5.195–220. I quote here from *Leon Battista Alberti on Painting,* tr. John R. Spencer, rev. ed. (New Haven, 1966), 91. I have drawn most usefully from R. W. Lightbown, *Botticelli,* 2nd ed. (New York, 1989). The iconography of the Graces and the differing moralizations of them are discussed by Edgar Wind in *Pagan Mysteries in the Renaissance* (rev. ed., New York, 1968), 26–52. About Rossetti's sonnet two things might be remarked: according to his brother, it was the last of the sonnets for pictures by other artists (written in 1880); and apparently, he was working from a sepia photograph of the painting, which may have contributed to the poem's perplexed and autumnal tone.

WHITMAN / INNESS

Useful information about the unpublished "Pictures" can be found in the notes to the Comprehensive Reader's Edition of *Leaves of Grass,* ed. Harold W. Blodgett and Sculley Bradley (New York, 1965), 642–49.

MARKHAM / MILLET

Robert L. Herbert's exhibition catalogue, *Millet* (Paris, 1990), provides a wise and learned commentary on the painting and the milieu of its reception in France. The earlier commentator on the painting was Ednah Dow Cheney (no relation to John Vance Cheney), as quoted by Laura Meixner in her most useful "Criticism of Millet in Nineteenth-century America," *Art Bulletin* 65 (1983): 96. John Vance Cheney's poem is quoted from E. C. Stedman's *American Anthology* (1900). The passage quoted is from Gertrude Stein, *Lectures in America* (Boston, 1957), 55–56.

Wharton / Leonardo

The astute observer of the landscape behind Mona Lisa is A. Richard Turner, in his valuable *The Vision of Landscape in Renaissance Italy* (Princeton, 1966), 28. The landscape "appears to show the curvature of the surface of the earth" to John White, *The Birth and Rebirth of Pictorial Space* (New York, 1972). Yeats cut up Pater's prose to make the first poem in his unfortunate *The Oxford Book of Modern Verse* (Oxford, 1936). The best edition of Pater's *The Renaissance* is the fine one edited by Donald L. Hill (Berkeley, 1980), which shrewdly assesses the influence on this passage of Gautier and Swinburne. On the whole passage, see Richard L. Stein, *The Ritual of Interpretation* (Cambridge, MA, 1975), 133. Harold Bloom's remarkable essay on Pater is reprinted in his *Figures of Capable Imagination* (New York, 1976).

Bridges / Titian

See Erwin Panofsky, *Studies in Iconology* (New York, 1939), 150–60; and *Problems in Titian* (New York, 1969), 110–19; the quotation is on pp. 116–17. Also see Anne Hollander, *Seeing through Clothes* (New York, 1978), 157–59, 448.

De la Mare / Bruegel

Berryman discusses his poem in "One Answer to a Question," *Shenandoah* 7.1 (Autumn 1965): 68–70. At one point he compares it to "Auden's fine poem, 'Musée des Beaux Arts,' written later," but Auden's poem, written in December 1938, predates Berryman's. See also Arthur Evans and Catherine Evans, "Pieter Brueghel and John Berryman: Two Winter Landscapes," *Texas Studies in Literature and Language* 5.3 (1963): 310–18. Wendy Steiner, in *The Colors of Rhetoric* (Chicago, 1982), 80–90, discusses the Williams poem at considerable length. I'm afraid that Henry M. Sayre's good try—in *The Visual Text of William Carlos Williams* (Urbana, 1983), 128—at redeeming its run-on syntax from insignificance by arguing that the phrase "to the right" can apply equally to the sentence before or after it must fail: the women in the painting "cluster about" the fire, but to the left of it.

Auden / Bruegel

Edward Mendelson, *Early Auden* (New York, 1981), 362–64, was most useful to me. The scholar quoted was R. H. Marijnissen, *Bruegel* (New York, 1971), 37. Mary Ann Caws in "A Double Reading by Design: Brueghel, Auden, and Williams," *Journal of Aesthetics and Art Criticism* 51.3 (1983): 323–30, is clearly of another mind about the Williams poem, but her own imaginative exuberance does not convince me of Williams's. Nor does Wendy Steiner in *Colors of Rhetoric* (Chicago, 1982), 73. On the other hand, Cristina Giorcelli makes an ingenious and sophisticated case for another Williams poem in "William Carlos Williams' Painterly Poems: Two Pictures from a Bruegel" in *Word & Image* 4.1 (1988): 200–208.

Jarrell / Dürer

The extended quotations are from Erwin Panofsky, *Albrecht Dürer* (Princeton, 1943), 1.151–54; and John Ruskin, *Modern Painters*, vol. 5, pt. 9, chap. 4. It might be observed that Ruskin pairs this print with the *Melancholia* as the twin hopes of Fortitude and Labor—both presumably to get you through the early stages of the Reformation—while Panofsky groups them with the 1514 *St. Jerome in His Study,* as embracing the practical realm of action, the saint's world of sacred contemplation, and the life of the secular genius of the imaginative worlds of science and art.

HECHT / BELLINI

I am indebted to discussions in Rona Goffen, *Giovanni Bellini* (New Haven, 1989), 106–11; and A. Richard Turner, *The Vision of Landscape in Renaissance Italy* (Princeton, 1974), 57–65.

CONQUEST / VELÁZQUEZ

The writer briefly quoted is Anne Hollander, *Seeing through Clothes*, 231; also (on p. 54): "When Velásquez bunches drapery around the so-called Rokeby Venus, it has the distilled ideal quality conveyed by its conventional presence; but it is transmuted by the utter lack of swagger in its folds." "To the Rokeby Venus" appeared in John Hollander, *Harp Lake* (New York, 1988). An account of the attack by the young woman known as "Slasher Mary" upon the painting in 1914, with a picture of the dreadful consequences of her deed, is to be found in David Freedberg's *The Power of Images* (Chicago, 1989), 409–10. See also Martin S. Soria, "Sources and Interpretation of the Rokeby Venus," *Art Quarterly* 20 (1957): 30–38.

WILBUR / *FOUNTAIN*

I am grateful to Walter Arndt, in *The Best of Rilke* (Hanover, 1989), 92–93, for calling my attention to the relation between Meyer's poem and Rilke's. The quotation from Eleanor Clark's *Rome and a Villa* is from the expanded edition (New York, 1974), 74. The sixth of Vyacheslav Ivanov's "Roman Sonnets" is translated by Lowry Nelson, Jr.; Alfred Corn's poem is from his *All Roads at Once* (New York, 1976). Donald Davie's "The Fountain," in his *Collected Poems* (New York, 1972), recalls the rise and fall of water in a fountain of Bishop Berkeley's trope:

> For Berkeley this was human thought, that mounts
> From bland assumptions to inquiring skies,
> There glints with wit, fumes into fancies, plays
> With its negations, and at last descends,
> As if by law of nature, to its bowl
> Of thus enlightened but still common sense.

I might also commend here Jean Garrigue's "For the Fountains and Fountaineers of Villa d'Este," in her *Selected Poems* (Urbana, 1992). And, as a general afterthought, it is hard to resist quoting W. S. Merwin's brilliant translation of François de Malherbe's early seventeenth-century "Inscription for a Fountain" (from his *Selected Translations* [New York, 1968], 122):

> Passer-by see how this water
> Wells up and away is whirled:
> Thus flows the glory of the world.
> Only God remains forever.

MERWIN / WALLIS

Adrian Stokes, *Colour and Form* (1937) in *Critical Writings* (London, 1978), 2.32. The critic mentioned is Edward Mullins, in his *Alfred Wallis: Cornish Primitive Painter* (London, 1967), 93–94. W. S. Merwin's comments on "quartans" are from a letter to the present author.

MERRILL / *CHARIOTEER*

Merrill's poem first appeared in *The Country of a Thousand Years of Peace* (New York, 1959). Rilke's celebrated sonnet, from the second part of the *Neue Gedichte* (1908), addresses one of a number of archaic *kouroi* in the Louvre.

HALL / MUNCH

Reinhold Heller, *Edvard Munch: The Scream* (New York, 1972), was extremely useful, as were Arne Eggum's remarks in *Edvard Munch: Symbols and Images* (Washington, 1978), 162–63; and the comment by Thomas M. Messer in *Edvard Munch* (New York, 1985), 2.

FELDMAN / GOYA

Feldman's "Goya" appeared in his early *Works and Days* (New York, 1961). On the prints generally, see Pierre Gassier and Juliet Wilson, *Goya: Life and Complete Works* (New York, 1971), 217–22; on the "Disasters of War," Fred Licht, *Goya* (New York, 1979), 128–58. Nigel Glendinning, *Goya and His Critics* (New Haven, 1977), 242–54, discusses allusions to Goya and his work by many poets.

MOORE / *TAPESTRY*

Patricia Willis, who has provided so much interesting information about Moore's many allusions to pictures, has suggested that the death of e. e. cummings in 1962, while Moore was abroad working on the tapestry poem, may have reminded her of the elephant as cummings's personal totem; in this case, the victim to be convinced that destiny is not plotting could seem to be the mourning friend, the poet herself, who immediately submits, like Wordsworth in the "Elegiac Stanzas" [pp. 129–31], to "a new control." In her catalogue for an exhibition at the Rosenbach Museum and Library, *Vision into Verse* (Philadelphia, 1987), Willis illustrates a range of allusive—if not all actually ecphrastic—moments in Moore's poetry, including poems that engage Leonardo's St. Jerome, a Giorgione self-portrait, a Bewick wood engraving, an Isaac Oliver miniature, A. B. Durand's *Kindred Spirits,* and many anonymous images from photography and advertising. Willis comments on the tapestry poem on p. 87. Moore had worked from a copy of the *Scottish Art Review,* no. 6 (1957). Moore's poem, as it originally appeared in the *New Yorker,* reads at one point: "daisies, harebells, little flattened-out / sunflowers thin arched coral stems, and / ribbed horizontally—." The Renaissance iconographic source for the elephant is the French translation of Valeriano's *Hieroglyphica* (Lyon, 1615), B6v.

SNODGRASS / MATISSE

The comments on this painting are in Lawrence Gowing's wonderful *Henri Matisse* (New York, 1979), 114. Also see the excellent discussions of the picture in Pierre Schneider, *Matisse* (Paris 1984), chap. 13, passim.

HINE / VAN DER WEYDEN

Erwin Panofsky, *Early Netherlandish Painting* (Princeton, 1953), 249, alludes to the panels' "polyphony of warm lilac-rose, pale gray-blue, flaming vermilion, drab gray, and gold." The observations are quoted from pp. 235–36.

HOWARD / FRA ANGELICO

Howard's discussion of his own poem in relation to the Browning passage from "Fra Lippo Lippi" is to be found in his *Preferences* (New York, 1974), 119. That Browning's speaker's lines are a prima facie projection, and Howard's a reading of an image, Howard himself elegantly observes: "The phenomenon suggests, in the Victorian, a certain pre-emptive force, an eagerness to perform, while in the contemporary there is a corresponding passivity, an assumption that the picture, as it stands now, already, will disclose its significance."

McClatchy / Panini

The poem in question appeared in McClatchy's *Scenes from Another Life* (New York, 1981).

Ferry / Watteau

The quotations are from René Huyghe, *Watteau*, tr. Barbara Bray (New York, 1970), 84; Jean H. Hagstrum's *Sex and Sensibility* (Chicago, 1980), 301–2; Ronald Paulson, *English Art: Emblem and Expression* (Cambridge, MA, 1975), 97. The well-known ecphrastic exuberance of Edmond and Jules de Goncourt addresses this painting. See the translation by Robin Ironside of their *French Eighteenth-Century Painters* (London, 1948), 52–53; their general vision of Watteau's painted world can be found on pp. 5–8. Most useful, always, was the discussion by Donald Posner, *Watteau* (Ithaca, NY, 1984), 182–95.

Hearne / Gauguin

Hearne's poem was published in her second collection, *In the Absence of Horses* (Princeton, 1983).

Warren / Renoir

I am indebted to the discussion of this painting by John House in *Renoir* (London, 1985), 222–23. Lawrence Gowing is quoted from his "Renoir's Sentiment and Sense" in that same volume, p. 11. The Scottish poet Stewart Conn has written an elaborate poetic ecphrasis of this painting, consisting of a set of dramatic monologues, entitled respectively "Alphonse," "The Baron," "The Unknown Man," "Madame Renoir," and "Renoir"; they comprise the title poem of his *The Luncheon of the Boating Party* (Newcastle-upon-Tyne, 1992).

Hadas / Botticelli

Again, Lightbown (1969) has been most informative.

CREDITS

POETRY CREDITS

Index

Page numbers of works of art illustrated in the text are in boldface. Titles of works of art are in italics; titles of poems are in single quotation marks; titles of poetry collections and essays are in double quotation marks. Alternate titles are in square brackets.